T0184894

Communications
in Computer and Information Science   **1364**

More information about this series at http://www.springer.com/series/7899

Sabu M. Thampi · Guojun Wang ·
Danda B. Rawat · Ryan Ko ·
Chun-I Fan (Eds.)

Security in Computing and Communications

8th International Symposium, SSCC 2020
Chennai, India, October 14–17, 2020
Revised Selected Papers

 Springer

Editors
Sabu M. Thampi
Indian Institute of Information Technology
and Management - Kerala
Trivandrum, India

Guojun Wang ⓘ
Guangzhou University
Guangzhou, China

Danda B. Rawat
Howard University
Washington, DC, USA

Ryan Ko
University of Queensland
Brisbane, QLD, Australia

Chun-I Fan
National Sun Yat-sen University
Kaohsiung, Taiwan

ISSN 1865-0929   ISSN 1865-0937 (electronic)
Communications in Computer and Information Science
ISBN 978-981-16-0421-8   ISBN 978-981-16-0422-5 (eBook)
https://doi.org/10.1007/978-981-16-0422-5

This Springer imprint is published by the registered company Springer Nature Singapore Pte Ltd.
The registered company address is: 152 Beach Road, #21-01/04 Gateway East, Singapore 189721, Singapore

Preface

The 8th International Symposium on Security in Computing and Communications (SSCC'20) provided an opportunity to bring together researchers and practitioners from both academia and industry to exchange their knowledge and discuss their research findings in the area of computer security. The Symposium was organised by Vellore Institute of Technology (VIT), Chennai, India during October 14–17, 2020. Due to the recent pandemic situation, it was conducted as a virtual event. SSCC'20 was co-located with the International Conference on Applied Soft Computing and Communication Networks (ACN'20).

In response to the call for papers, 42 papers were submitted for presentation and inclusion in the proceedings of the conference. The papers were evaluated and ranked on the basis of their significance, novelty, and technical quality. A double-blind review process was conducted to ensure that the author names and affiliations were unknown to the Technical Program Committee (TPC). Each paper was reviewed by the members of the TPC and finally, 13 regular and 8 short papers were selected for presentation at the symposium.

We would like to thank the program chairs for their wise guidance and brilliant ideas in organizing the technical program. We would like to express our heartfelt gratitude to the members of the Advisory Committee. Thanks to all members of the TPC, and the external reviewers, for their hard work in evaluating and discussing papers. We wish to thank all the members of the Organizing Committee, whose work and commitment were invaluable. Our most sincere thanks go to all the keynote speakers who shared with us their experience and knowledge. We wish to thank all the authors who submitted papers and all participants and contributors to fruitful discussions. The EDAS conference system was very helpful during the submission, review, and editing phases.

We are very grateful to Vellore Institute of Technology (VIT), Chennai for organizing the Symposium. It could not have taken place without the commitment of the Local Organizing Committee. Finally, we would like to thank our publisher Springer for their cooperation.

October 2020

Sabu M. Thampi
Guojun Wang
Danda B. Rawat
Ryan Ko
Chun-I Fan

Organization

Chief Patron

G. Viswanathan (Chancellor)   Vellore Institute of Technology, India

Patrons

Sankar Viswanathan
(Vice-president)

Vellore Institute of Technology, India

Sekar Viswanathan
(Vice-president)

Vellore Institute of Technology, India

G. V. Selvam
(Vice-president)

Vellore Institute of Technology, India

Sandhya Pentareddy
(Executive Director)

Vellore Institute of Technology, India

Kadhambari S. Viswanathan
(Assistant Vice-president)

Vellore Institute of Technology, India

Rambabu Kodali
(Vice Chancellor)

Vellore Institute of Technology, India

S. Narayanan
(Pro-vice Chancellor)

Vellore Institute of Technology, Vellore, India

V. S. Kanchana Bhaaskaran
(Pro-vice Chancellor)

Vellore Institute of Technology, India

P. K. Manoharan
(Additional Registrar)

Vellore Institute of Technology, India

General Chairs

Selwyn Piramuthu   University of Florida, USA
Kuan-Ching Li   Providence University, Taiwan
Sabu M. Thampi   IIITM-Kerala, India

Program Chairs

Stefano Berretti   University of Florence, Italy
Michał Woźniak   Wrocław University, Warsaw, Poland
Dhananjay Singh   Hankuk University of Foreign Studies, South Korea

Organizing Chairs

Geetha S.   VIT, Chennai, India
Jagadeesh Kannan R.   VIT, Chennai, India

Organizing Co-chairs

Asha S.   VIT, Chennai, India
Pattabiraman V.   VIT, Chennai, India
Viswanathan V.   VIT, Chennai, India

Organizing Secretaries

Sweetlin Hemalatha C.   VIT, Chennai, India
Suganya G.   VIT, Chennai, India
Kumar R.   VIT, Chennai, India

TPC Members

http://www.acn-conference.org/2020/somma2020/committee.html

Organized by

Vellore Institute of Technology (VIT), Chennai, India

Contents

Pandora: A Cyber Range Environment for the Safe Testing and Deployment of Autonomous Cyber Attack Tools

Hetong Jiang[(✉)], Taejun Choi, and Ryan K. L. Ko

The University of Queensland, St. Lucia, Brisbane, QLD, Australia
{hetong.jiang,taejun.choi,ryan.ko}@uq.edu.au

Abstract. Cybersecurity tools are increasingly automated with artificial intelligent (AI) capabilities to match the exponential scale of attacks, compensate for the relatively slower rate of training new cybersecurity talents, and improve of the accuracy and performance of both tools and users. However, the safe and appropriate usage of autonomous cyber attack tools–especially at the development stages for these cyber attack tools – is still largely an unaddressed gap. Our survey of current literature and tools showed that most of the existing cyber range designs are mostly using manual tools and have not considered augmenting automated tools or the potential security issues caused by the tools. In other words, there is still room for a novel cyber range design which allow security researchers to safely deploy autonomous tools and perform automated tool testing if needed. In this paper, we introduce Pandora, a safe testing environment which allows security researchers and cyber range users to perform experiments on automated cyber attack tools that may have strong potential of usage and at the same time, a strong potential for risks. Unlike existing testbeds and cyber ranges which have direct compatibility with enterprise computer systems and the potential for risk propagation across the enterprise network, our test system is intentionally designed to be incompatible with enterprise real-world computing systems to reduce the risk of attack propagation into actual infrastructure. Our design also provides a tool to convert in-development automated cyber attack tools into to executable test binaries for validation and usage realistic enterprise system environments if required. Our experiments tested automated attack tools on our proposed system to validate the usability of our proposed environment. Our experiments also proved the safety of our environment by compatibility testing using simple malicious code.

Keywords: Cyber autonomy · Cybersecurity · Cyber range · Cyber tool automation · Binary exploitation

1 Introduction

The increasing rate and global nature [1] of cyber attacks and the recent trends towards cyber autonomy [2] have resulted in questions about the scalability of current cybersecurity approaches and the relatively-long time required to train cyber professionals in

© Springer Nature Singapore Pte Ltd. 2021
S. M. Thampi et al. (Eds.): SSCC 2020, CCIS 1364, pp. 1–20, 2021.
https://doi.org/10.1007/978-981-16-0422-5_1

comparison to the emergence of new cyber threats [3]. In an attempt to overcome this asymmetric attack and response rates, we are witnessing an increasing demand for cyber autonomy from the cyber-security industry. There is also an inability to train cybersecurity professionals quick enough to be able to address the increasing rate of cyber threats.

Donevski and Zia [4] stated that the current lack of cybersecurity professionals is one of the reasons the cybersecurity industry has struggled in addressing this scale problem. This is also widely termed as the 'cyber skills gap'. According to Smith [5], while it is a good effort, re-education may not a practical solution, as the rate of cyber threats is accelerating too fast for existing professionals to handle – overwhelming many cybersecurity professionals in the process. An augmentation of automation tools to automate most tasks while freeing up time and resources for cybersecurity professionals to make decisions aided by cyber automation promises to meet the exponentially-growing demands for cybersecurity, risk assessments and compliance [6]. Cyber autonomy also allows the cybersecurity industry address scale and new security issues introduced by cloud computing [7–9] and other emerging technologies.

Besides addressing the cyber skills gap and the accelerating rate of cyber threats, it is also important to be able to evaluate and test the usefulness of autonomous cyber attack tools often used in increasingly-automated red-teaming environments or security assessments. Having a technique or platform to test these cyber autonomy tools will facilitate more effective tool evaluation, especially before they are actually deployed into actual enterprise environment. Researchers have also found automated tools with AI algorithms to be cost effective solutions [10]. Furthermore, a diverse set of test areas for system hardening could be conducted by automated tools such as detecting SQL injection vulnerabilities [11], penetrating testing [12], man-in-the-middle attacks [13] and finding exploitable bugs in binaries [14].

Despite the usefulness of automated cyber attack tools, prototyped versions of the tools in their initial stages of development could cause unexpected results. Kaloudi and Li's survey paper [15] and the DARPA Cyber Grand Challenge (CGC) [16] described and demonstrated fully-automated AI-based automated attacks could evade detection measures respectively. The risks around deploying these tools before proper testing are evident. Without first testing within a proper testing environment, a prototyped automated attack tool may cause critical damage on real-world infrastructures. In fact, a prominent example is the Morris worm in 1988 [17], which was initially created to understand the size of the Internet at that time, but unintentionally rendered about 10% of the systems on the Internet unusable.

Despite possible threats caused by the unintended situations, the automation of exploitation tools is a popular topic for cybersecurity researchers. Web-based attack tools such as vulnerability scanning [1, 18], SQL Injection [11, 19] and Cross-Site Scripting [19] are the most commonly seen topics for network automation tools. Consequently, testing environments for network-based tools are commonly proposed.

In the case of binary exploitations, at the time of writing, there are few existing testing environments that are designed for automated binary exploit tools. Researchers usually utilize virtualization technologies to create test environments for binary experiments. However, this does not guarantee a safe environment. For example, vulnerabilities such as Venom [20] (CVE-2015-3456) and VMware Fusion's vulnerability (VMSA-2015-0004) (CVE-2015-2337) [21] allow malicious code to penetrate the barrier between VMs and Host, thereby causing damage to host systems.

Even with proper security measurements, some attack tools, especially automated tools with advanced technologies such as machine learning could be unpredictable [22]. Conversely, machine learning techniques could also help malware avoid detection. There is also no guarantee with regards to the outputs generated during the testing–putting the host system in increased risks. Therefore, a secure testing environment is required to prevent unpredictable propagation of risks into connected enterprise environments–achieving the true requirements of a 'sandboxed' environment.

To mitigate the above gaps and provide a solution for cyber ranges and test environments, we propose Pandora, a secure cyber range design for automated cybersecurity tools testing. The proposed design allows automated testing of any types of exploits without threatening the real-world infrastructures linked to the cyber range. Our approach also caters to the requirements of deployment fully-automated tools within the cyber range–preparing the users for an increasingly autonomous cyber environment.

In order to prove the functionality of the proposed cyber range, a vulnerable binary in our cyber range has been successfully and automatically exploited by a binary exploit tool. This was formed via combining a number of known cybersecurity tools, to represent an automated attack.

We carried out a comparison of simple malicious code in our suggested environment and a Linux Ubuntu 18.04 LTS Linux system to confirm the isolation of automated attack tools from real-world infrastructures connected to the cyber range. The code worked and achieved our goals within our isolated environment, but it does not work for any generic Linux system – proving the non-portability of the test from our environment to typical enterprise Linux environments.

The main contributions of our research are:

– We propose a cyber range design to mitigate potential risks of automated cybersecurity tools in their early-stage development. The design could be implemented using common off-the-shelf tools.
– We verified the proper working of our implementation by executing an automated tool in our system.
– We confirm the isolation of the designed cyber range from real-world infrastructures – achieving non-propagation of potential unknown risks.

Our paper is organized as follows. Section 2 discuss the background and related work. We provide the design of our proposed cyber range in Sect. 3 and in Sect. 4, we discuss case studies including an overview of hardware systems and software used. Result analyses of case studies including verification for incompatibility of the implementation are discussed in Sect. 5. We then conclude and propose future work in Sect. 6.

2 Related Work

2.1 Background

As described in [23], a cyber range is an environment that provides a realistic environment suitable for conducting 'live fire' type of exercises which train computer network operators for cyber defense, and support experimentation and testing via a combination of cybersecurity products. Typically, the architecture of a cyber range could be split into sub-components. For example, as shown in Fig. 1, Yamin *et al.* [24] suggested eight components comprising a cyber range. As long as the setup is correct and there are no misuse of tools, a cyber range environment allows anyone who wishes to have cybersecurity-related experiential training in cyber attack and defense to train within an environment with no direct risks on actual computer systems.

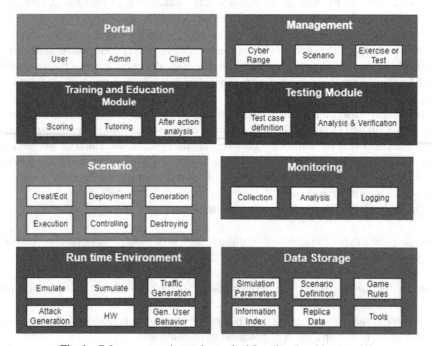

Fig. 1. Cyber range and security testbed functional architecture [1]

Considering the eight components of Fig. 1, our research focuses on the 'Runtime Environment' which provides a safe test environment for cybersecurity researchers. The 'Runtime Environment' component is composed of the 'Emulator', 'Simulator', 'Attack Generation', 'HW' (i.e. hardware), 'Traffic Generation', and 'Gen. User Behavior' subcomponents. However, the 'Traffic Generation' and 'Gen. User Behavior' are out of scope for this paper which focuses on demonstrating test environments for automated binary exploitation cyber attack tools.

In the case of the subcomponent 'HW', real physical hardware are required to provide computing power. Based on the 'HW', an 'Emulate' subcomponent could mimic an operating system to create a simulated test environment. To create a simulated victim system, vulnerable applications or disclosed common vulnerabilities and exposures (CVE [25]) could be set up on the emulated operating system. With the aforementioned subcomponents, an attack application automated will be tested as a subcomponent 'Attack Generation' as shown in Fig. 1.

Unlike many existing works that focusing on virtualization or containerization of test environments [24, 26–29], we concentrate on the security and simplicity of the testing environment. The reason for that many designs are focused on virtualization technologies is to increase the realism of the testing environment, thus, helping researchers to learn in an environment that may simulate a certain situation during a cybersecurity incident –making the testing as realistic as possible. However, as mentioned in Sect. 1, virtualization may not guarantee a threat free environment for its test infrastructure since vulnerabilities such as Venom [20] and VMware Fusion's vulnerability [21].

2.2 Related Research

While AI enhances the effectiveness of tools, it can also be used by malware. For example, Goosen [22] showed that, even with proper security measurements, some attack tools–especially automated tools with advanced technologies such as machine learning–could help malware avoid detection. On the other hand, we are seeing the emergence of other branches of AI, such as Amos-Binks' usage of automated planning (which is concerned with the realization of strategies or action sequence based on goals and constraints) for execution by intelligent agents [30].

In recent years, automated binary exploitation tools have emerged. One of the most prominent projects, Mayhem [14] by ForAllSecure has shown that it is possible to let a machine exploit binaries by itself using regular binary executables. While the current methods were not as good as human cybersecurity specialists with more creativity to invent new classes of attacks [2], the method has actually been realized into the computer, and computers generally spend less time examining binaries and are usually much more effective on a larger scale [2]. Some other automated approaches were able to search, discover, and patch vulnerabilities binaries. An example is the Cyber Reasoning System (CRS) Rubeus [31] by Raytheon during the DARPA CGC which uses machine learning and other AI technologies to help enhance its offensive abilities.

Over time, cyber ranges have been designed for different purposes. For example, the DETER Project [32] is one of the most prominent and earliest projects, and was designed for scientific and cybersecurity purposes. One of the essential stand-out characteristics of the DETER project was how realistic it was in terms of mimicking actual IT infrastructures.

Some other recent implementations are the cyber range for Cyber Defense Situation Awareness from Debatty and Mees [26], and the ones taking the approach for educational purposes such as the RC^{2}F framework [27] and the SEED Lab [28]. A few other cyber range designs focus on the increasing number of features and efficiency of challenge maintenance such as Yamin *et al.* [24], and the one by Frank *et al.* [29].

3 Proposed Framework

The related work above has revealed opportunities for new cyber range designs to accommodate cyber autonomy safely and securely, and retain the comprehensiveness and usability such that new researchers or students who would like to test or create new cyber autonomy tools can safely test the early-stage deployment without any risk of propagating unpredictable results to a connected enterprise network.

As such, one of the primary reasons for creating Pandora as a cyber range for automated tool testing is to contain the potential propagation of undesired outcomes of some automated tools. Therefore, our proposed framework should be able to help researchers test dangerous automated tools within a safe and secure environment, and also simple enough to work and analyze with. This means students and newcomers could also create their automated tools for small projects and experiments.

3.1 Threat Modelling

To encapsulate our framework's resilience against common threats faced by current approaches listed above, we developed a threat model for analysis. Our threat model is based on security vulnerabilities related to virtualization and communication.

3.1.1 Threat for Virtualization

As [20, 21] demonstrated that the barrier to segregate a virtual machine from its host machine is unsafe, we shall assume that an automated attack tool could affect its host machine beyond the test environment. In the case of a highly realistic virtual environment, the damages from tested tools could be severe depending on the level of emulation. Our threat model focuses on protecting realistically set-up infrastructures from unexpected attacks.

3.1.2 Threat for Communication

Vulnerabilities such as CVE-2018-10933 [33] demonstrated possibilities that might help the malicious clients get unauthorized access to other machines. In this vulnerability, the emulated network connection could be utilized as a path to allow a cybersecurity tool/weapon in development to access systems outside the testbed or cyber range. Other network security and communication vulnerabilities are already researched and hence, the protection of internal or external network for cyber range is out of scope for this paper.

3.2 Framework Design

With our attack models described, we now propose a design of a cyber range focused on the "run time environment" illustrated previously in Fig. 1, for testing automated cyber attack tools based on the modeled threats.

As shown in Fig. 2, our proposed design could be divided into two main parts: 'Virtualized Cyber Range' and 'Generic Operating System' and their subcomponents. A brief description about the design is described below and details such as code snippets of the specific implementation can be found later in Sect. 5.

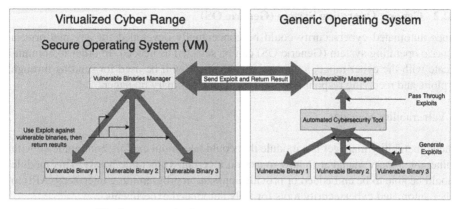

Fig. 2. Proposed cyber range design for cyber autonomy

3.2.1 Virtualized Cyber Range

Our proposed cyber range is designed to be installed within a virtual machine, which should have a secure operating system which has some level of incompatibility with any generic operating system. As discussed earlier, the intentional incompatibility is introduced to reduce risks of unpredicted propagation of damage caused by tools to environments outside the test operating system. A vulnerable binary manager will be running for managing all exploit and analysis work.

– Secure Operating System (Secure OS)

One of the ways that keep the cyber range secure at the operating system level is to ensure that any newly compiled binary or malicious code within the cyber range is incompatible with any other regular computer system. A secure operating system should be used for this purpose; also, tools for compiling binaries should be provided. Since the environment focused on tool testing rather than real-machine simulation, one should keep all functions simple for researchers and newcomers to use.

– Vulnerable Binary Manager

As shown in Fig. 2, the purpose of the Vulnerable Binary Manager is to execute vulnerable binaries within the secure environment, and use input exploits against the vulnerable binary and analyze the effect of exploitations. This will limit all exploit activities within the Secure OS – thus protecting the host machine.

– Vulnerable Binary

A vulnerable binary is a file that contains purposefully designed vulnerabilities for automated tools to exploit. The complexity of the vulnerabilities should be simple and meaningful, which should be able to demonstrate one or more functions of the automated cybersecurity tool. The vulnerable binary should be able to execute within the Secure OS, but not in any generic operating system for our intended incompatibility purpose.

3.2.2   Generic Operating System (Generic OS)

Since automated cybersecurity could be conceptually developed for any platform, a generic operating system (Generic OS) can be selected as needed. In order to communicate with the cyber range, a vulnerability manager will be used for sending through exploits and receiving responses from the vulnerable binary manager.

– Vulnerability Manager

The vulnerability manager is a module that could take input exploit, communicate with vulnerable binary manager to how to exploit a certain vulnerable binary. This module should be able to be embedded or provide application programming interfaces (API) to other automated cybersecurity tools for fully automated experiments.

– Automated Cybersecurity Tool

Secure OS is incompatible with any Generic OS for security purpose, and may lack some critical data due to simplification, which could cause difficulty for cybersecurity tool development and less powerful, therefore, cybersecurity tools should be deployed within a Generic OS. This also allows the cybersecurity tool targeting the Secure OS to easily port or make modifications for other purposes.

– Vulnerable Binary

Like the vulnerable binary in Secure OS, a vulnerable binary in the Generic OS is a file that contains purposefully designed vulnerabilities for automated tools to exploit.

3.2.3   Sequence Diagram

Figure 3 below describes how a user could interact with our proposed cyber range.

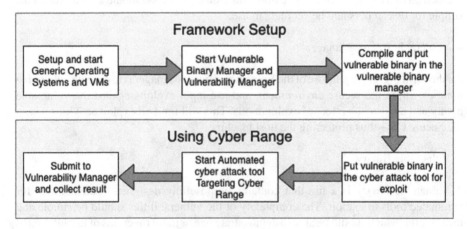

Fig. 3. Sequence diagram

Firstly, the users are required to setup up generic operating systems for both the virtualized cyber range and the environment for cyber attack tools. A virtual machine with a secure operating system should also be installed to the virtualized cyber range. Secondly, the user would start the vulnerable binary manager and vulnerability manager for the cyber attack tool to interact with the cyber range. The vulnerability manager could be embedded into cyber attack tool for easier managing. Thirdly, after the environmental setup, vulnerable binaries should be created, compiled and installed into the cyber range. Fourth, if a file-transfer function is not developed, vulnerable binaries should also be installed into the automated cyber attack tool for analyzing and exploiting. Finally, the user would use the automated cyber attack tool to exploit vulnerable binaries, generate exploits, then send exploits through the vulnerability manager to the cyber range for analyzing the effect of the exploit, and for collecting results.

4 Case Study and Experiments

In this section, we will describe our implementation and experiments based on the scope defined earlier.

4.1 Framework Implementation

We implemented the experiment using the following equipment:

4.1.1 Experiment Computer Hardware Specification

We intentionally implemented our experiments on a laptop to reduce the need for future researchers to procure specialized hardware. As such, we constrained our implementation around practical and commonly-accessible computing equipment to encourage reproducibility. As such, we implemented our experiment and recommend at least the following configuration:

- CPU: 4 processor cores
- Memory: 16 GB RAM
- Operating System: Windows 10/MacOS X 10.x or higher/Linux(kernel 4.0 or higher)

4.1.2 Virtual Machine Setting for Virtualized Cyber Range and Generic Operating System

Similarly, we implemented the virtualizes cyber ranged and Generic OS in the following environment:

- VMware Fusion 11.5.6
- CPU: 2 processor cores
- Memory: 8 GB RAM

4.1.3 Virtualized Cyber Range Implementation

– *DECREE – Secure Operating System*

To fulfil the requirement of our proposed design, we used DECREE [34] created by DARPA for the CGC [16] as the base of the cyber range structure in the case studies. DECREE is a modified i386 Debian Wheezy with Linux kernel 3.13.2, with only seven modified system-calls and minimum non-determinism in system level [34]. As such, this increases the replayability of the system, which is highly useful for our research purpose.

DECREE has a built-in custom-made compiler and correlated toolsets, which can be used to compile the C source code into a unique executable format called DECREE Binary, which makes the DECREE binaries incompatible with a generic operating system.

For the case studies, a virtual-machines cluster developed by DARPA called virtual-competition [35] will be used. It contains five pre-set virtual machines that represent each significant part of the competition but does not have any abilities to do analysis [36]. Software for the virtual-competition will not be used in this study.

– *cb-server – Vulnerable Binary Manager*

cb-server [37] will be used as the vulnerable binary manager, which is responsible to take exploit inputs from the vulnerability manager, analyze the exploit and use it against the vulnerable binary within the cyber range.

– *Vulnerable Binary*

legit_00003 [38] is a simple C program created by LegitBS during DEFCON 24 in 2016. It was originally designed for human to human attack and defense CTF with CGC infrastructure. It contains a simple menu with three options. The function of legit_00003 is simply let the user input their name, print their name or exit. It has a basic stack overflow vulnerability which can be found with fuzzing or symbolic execution techniques.

4.1.4 Generic Operating System (Generic OS) Implementation

– *Operating System*

The operating system of choice for both case studies is the Ubuntu 18.04 LTS with 4.15.0-76-generic kernel.

– *cb-replay-pov – Vulnerability Manager*

The program cb-replay-pov [37] will be used as the Vulnerability Manager, which is able to accept POV format file and communicate with the Vulnerable Binary Manager cb-server.

– *legit_00003 – Vulnerable Binary*

The same binary for Virtualized Cyber Range (see Sect. 4.1.3) has been used. In this implementation, the exploit process remains in a generic Linux OS that has an angr development environment [39] installed. The vulnerable binary needs to be copied into the host machine in order to generate exploit, which shows that the architecture design of the proposed testing environment is feasible.

4.2   Implementation of Automated Cybersecurity Tool

To simulate the automated attack tool, a combination of a fuzzing tool and an automated exploitation engine have used to represent an automated attack tool. To make the combination using two tools, we have programmed a script application.

4.2.1   Fuzzing Tool – Phuzzer

Phuzzer [40] is a Python wrapper for interacting with fuzzers created by the angr team; it has the American Fuzzy Lop (AFL) [41] as one of the core functions. Since the Cyber Grand Challenge considers a system crash as a vulnerability, this type of fuzzing methods for the simple program used in this case is an excellent choice. Therefore, in this case, Phuzzer is used to find the crash string from the vulnerable program.

4.2.2   Automated Exploit Engine – rex

rex [42] is an automated exploit engine created by the team Shellphish, from the University of California Santa Barbara. It is a tool designed to generate exploit for DECREE binary and simple Linux Binaries. In our case study, rex is used to exploit targeted vulnerable programs, using the relevant crash string from the fuzzing tool. Note that due to dependency issues, rex is recommended to executed within an angr development environment.

4.2.3   Script for Exploit

We wrote a script that combines phuzzer and rex to simulate the automated tool. The combined symbolic execution techniques and Phuzzer with AFL core are executed to find a string that could crash the legit_00003. After that, rex was executed to generate a Proof of Vulnerability (POV) (described in Sect. 4.3 later) format exploit. Figure 4 shows the core part of the code.

4.3   Case Study 1 – Automated Exploit

To confirm the functions of our implemented design with DECREE and correlated-infrastructure, we carried out an experiment for receiving and checking exploits input for both manual and automated methods.

```
// Use phuzzer to crash legit_00003
python -m phuzzer -d 6 -C ./legit_00003

// Use rex to exploit legit_00003
crashFile = open(glob.glob("/dev/shm/work/fuzzer-master/crashes/id*")[0], 'rb')
crashes.add(crashFile.read())
...
workBinary = archr.targets.LocalTarget("legit_00003", target_os='cgc')
crash = rex.Crash(workBinary, crashes.pop())
crash.explore()
...
arsenal = crash.exploit()
arsenal.best_type1.dump_binary("legit_00003_type1.pov")
...
```

Fig. 4. Script for automated exploit an POV generation

Since this case study builds on concepts from the DARPA CGC infrastructure, some information needs to be introduced in order to understand the procedures. For example, a Proof of Vulnerability (POV) is a type of XML or binary format file used to describe where is the vulnerabilities are and how to exploit the binary.

There is no binary execution within the host OS, nor any direct modification of the vulnerable binary. The POV data will be sent through Vulnerability Manager and received by Vulnerable Binary Manager inside of Virtualized Cyber Range. A faulty POV will result in Vulnerable Binary Manager return incorrect response, thus causing experiment failure.

4.3.1 Assumptions for Automated Exploit

For the purpose of our experiments and this research, we made a few assumptions:

- Since the goal of the study is to understand that if the designed framework works for automated attacks, we will not focus on the actual effects of the attacks.
- The focus of this study is to understand if the infrastructure functioned as intended. Hence, the actual contents of the POV will not be discussed.
- Manual attack processes will use pre-written C-format exploit created by the Legitbs which came along with the legit_00003 program.
- For our experiments, we assume that the vulnerability is known, so no vulnerability discovery processes will be made other than a simple fuzzing process.

4.3.2 Testing Procedures

- *Running Vulnerable Binary Manager*

The application cb-server will be running in Secure OS as the Vulnerable Binary Manager, waiting for input to exploit Vulnerable Binary.

- *Exploit Generation*

The provided exploit which came with legit_00003 will be used as a reference since it has been tested before and proved to be effective. In this study, this POV will be compiled and send to the Secure OS virtual machine with Vulnerable Binary Manager as a controlled group. The source code of legit_00003 and its C format POV can be found at [38]. The automated tool will generate a POV which represents an automated cybersecurity tool, subsequently uploaded to the Vulnerable Binary Manager, and the result will then be used for comparison.

– Exploit Vulnerable Binary

During the process, data will be sent by the Generic OS virtual machine, through the program Vulnerability Manager. The host machine has no direct connection to the VM that is executing the binary file with SSH. On the Secure Operating System side, Vulnerable Binary Manager will handle the exploit and analyze the input.

4.4 Case Study 2 – Incompatibility of the DECREE System

In our second experiment, we aim to demonstrate the advantage and usefulness of isolating the virtualized cyber range by making the Virtualized Cyber Range environment incompatible with Generic OS. A simple application with an indefinite loop to represent a simple 'malware' was executed in our Virtualized Cyber Range and a Linux machine for comparing the test results.

To program the simple malware for our experiment, we used an uncompiled version of legit_00003 as the template. In order to make sure that there is no influence from legit_00003, all unnecessary files and DECREE system calls were removed. Figure 5 shows the source code of the simple application tested. As shown in the source code, it the program will indefinitely print out an integer with an increment of 1. Note that the header file 'printf.h' is from the package that came with the legit_00003, and a minimum version of 'printf' statement.

5 Result and Analysis

5.1 Case Study 1 – Result

In Case Study 1, we carried out exploiting Vulnerable Binary using an implemented automated cybersecurity tool to validate our implementation. The result of 'pov_1.pov' is the given POV from the legit_00003 creator, and the other one is the output from the

```
#include "printf.h"

int main(void){
  int i = 0;
  while(1) {
    printf("%d\n", i);
    i++;
  }
  return 0;
}
```

Fig. 5. 'Malware' source code

automated attack tool. The provided POV from the legit_00003 creator was used as a reference to check the exploitation result of our attack tool.

There are two types of POVs [43]:

– Type 1 POV requires to demonstrate control of instructor pointer and one of the additional for the vulnerable binary within DECREE, which apply to this case.
– Type 2 POV requires to read the contents of arbitrary memory location.

Figure 6 shows the result of both POVs, which consists of the following values.

```
***********************          ***********************
POV Provided                     POV Automated Script
***********************          ***********************
# pov_1.pov                      # legit_00003_type1.pov
# negotiation type: 1            # negotiation type: 1
# type 1 masks: 7f7f7f7f 7f7f7f7f # type 1 masks: 7f7f7f7f 7f7f7f7f
# type 1 pov: 1e5d4c03 22392e5d 5 # type 1 pov: 00126a5e 4b6f5a78 5
```

Fig. 6. Result of both types of POVs

– *type 1 masks*

• According to the documentation of POV [43], the combination of the IP mask and Register Mask form the exploitation output to Type 1 mask. IP mask and Register Mask are required values for the Vulnerable Binary Manager to exploit a vulnerable binary in DECREE. Based on the delivered IP mask value and Register Mask value, the attack point of vulnerable binary will be pointed out.

– *type 1 pov:*

• type 1 pov shows the IP value and Register value that can be used to exploit the target vulnerable DECREE binary. The successful obtaining of the type 1 pov value will allow the POV to assert that it can control the instruction pointer and eight general-purpose registers [43]. The instruction pointer is a kind of memory pointer for an executable file and the eight general-purpose registers are designed registers for DECREE to exploit binary files compiled for DECREE system. However, since the CGC infrastructure was not fully open-sourced, we are unable to analyze the value. That said, checking the acceptability of the framework design can be done sufficiently by comparing the generated data from our attack and the provided data from vulnerable binary designer.

• The last digit of the *type 1 pov* value indicates which one out of eight valid general-purpose registers contains the required value [43]. Since the automated script received produced the same register as the provided one, it can be inferred and concluded that the value is correct.

5.2 Case Study 1 – Analysis

The functionality of our proposed design is our main focus for Experiment 1, which can be divided into two points: (1) communication and binary execution in two different environments with different executable formats, and (2) the performance of automated tool in such a special environment.

In this case study, the vulnerable binary manager cb-server is running within the secure operating system to handle the binary execution and exploit input. At the same time, the vulnerability manager is within a generic operating system that communicates with the vulnerable binary manager through the Transmission Control Protocol (TCP). This shows that, as long as a proper manager service is within each of the operating system, standard networking protocols could also make isolating the cyber range in the operating system level possible.

For the performance of automated tool, legit_00003, the vulnerable binary has a simple buffer overflow vulnerability leveraging the buffer size issue. The buffer overflow vulnerability enables attackers to take control of the computer system if they could control memory pointer to access some malicious code programmed by them. This type of buffer overflow attack is typical of many attacks experienced in the real-world today. The example POV contains a hard-coded input to fill out the buffer, and uses some techniques to exploit the target binary. Figure 7 shows the actual payload that exploits the legit_00003 from the POV provided.

```
...
senddata(1, "aaaaaaaaaaaaaaaaaaaaaaaaaaaaaaaa", 32);
senddata(1, "\xc4\xaa\xaa\xba", 4);
senddata(1, "junk", 4);
senddata(1, &regvalue, sizeof(value));   <-- "regvalue" and "ipvalue" was received
senddata(1, &ipvalue, sizeof(value));        from the server-side in previous part
...
```

Fig. 7. Payload from provided POV

Recalling Fig. 6, it was shown that generated POVs by the automated attack tool were similar and provided POV except the value of 'type 1 pov' since they are representing specific memory addresses of the vulnerable binary, which should be different every time. Also, considering the 'cb-replay-pov' and 'cb-server' acceptance mechanism that only accept right POV report, we can confirm that the exploit generated by automated script works very similar to manually exploit provided. Thus, the performance of automated tools in the proposed environment works as intended.

5.3 Case Study 2 – Result

Figure 8 shows the shell output of the programmed simple 'malware' in the Virtualized Cyber Range virtual machine. As it was intended, the malware prints infinitely numbers of integers start from 1 with an increment of 1.

```
$ ./sampleMalware
1
2
3
...
```

Fig. 8. Shell output of the sample malware

To compare its execution result, the 'malware' was copied to two different Linux distributions (Ubuntu 18.04 and Debian 4.19.132-1). As shown in Fig. 9, both operating systems failed to execute the sample malware with the same output.

```
bash: ./sampleMalware_00001: cannot execute binary file: Exec format error
```

Fig. 9. Shell output of the sample malware in a generic Linux System

5.4 Case Study 2 – Analysis

In Case Study 2, a sample 'malware' was successfully compiled into the DECREE binary format. As Fig. 8 has shown, the 'malware' can be successfully executed within DECREE but, as expected, cannot be executed within a generic Linux system as showed in Fig. 9.

The failure of executing the malware created for DECREE system in the generic operating system verified the program incompatibility between DECREE system and tested generic OS. This incompatibility confirms that automated cyber attack tools compiled for proposed cyber range are not able to propagate on to real-world computing systems linked to the cyber range in a corporate network (e.g. a Local Area Network (LAN)). The success of this case study also shows that the concept of using different operating systems in cyber range could provide a reasonable level of security while keeping the functionality of the cyber range. We acknowledge that there is also potential for further research to be conducted to verifying the security of our experiment through other techniques, such as formal verification.

Even though the process for creating the 'malware' was very simple with a vulnerable binary template, it was representative as the compile processes are very similar to the 'make' process of any generic C program. In order to create a DECREE binary without a template, a number of special modules are required as described in Fig. 10.

Although it is possible to extract all tools and related modules from DECREE to create an individual compiling script, the vulnerable binary template is still our preference because of its convenience. This also applies to other secure operating systems with the same type of incompatibility design. It is worth noting that a cybersecurity tool may be required to do multiple compilations or script generation over time, which may result in serious performance degradation due to the constant access of the secure operating system. In such a situation, the tool should be developed in a generic operating system with all the required packages integrated.

```
binutils-cgc-i386             Cross-binutils for CGC binaries
cgc-humint                    Human CGC Detector
cgc-network-appliance         CGC Network Appliance
cgc-pov-xml2c                 CGC XML to C conversion for PoVs
cgc-release-documentation     Cyber Grand Challenge CGCOS documentation
cgc-sample-challenges         CGC Sample Challenges
cgc-service-launcher          CGC Service Launcher
cgc-virtual-competition       Cyber Grand Challenge Virtual Competition
cgc2elf                       Convert ELF binaries to CGCOS binaries
cgcef-verify                  Verify executables are in the proper CGC Executable Format
clang-cgc                     LLVM/Clang for CGC
gdb-cgc                       The GNU Debugger with CGC CB support
libcgc                        CGC OS syscall library
libcgcdwarf                   CGC DWARF library
libcgcef0                     CGC Executable Format Library
libpov                        CGC POV library
linux-headers-3.13.2-cgc      Linux kernel headers for 3.13.2-cgc on i386
linux-image-3.13.2-cgc        Linux kernel, version 3.13.2-cgc
linux-source-3.13.2-cgc       Linux kernel source for version 3.13.2-cgc
magic-cgc                     CGC Magic
readcgcef                     CGC readelf equivalent
services-cgc                  CGC Services
strace-cgc                    A system call tracer
```

Fig. 10. Packages required for compiling the sample malware

6   Concluding Remarks and Future Work

We proposed Pandora, a simple and secure cyber range framework to allow cyberse-curity researchers to perform automated tool testing during the development process within a truly sandboxed environment. Our proposed design focus on the isolation of the test environments from real-world systems in order to address risk and malware prop-agation concerns for security testing of automated cyber attack tools. This addresses one of the developments and testing needs of cyber autonomy, an emerging and popular cybersecurity research topic.

Our approach leverages developed open sourced software packages used during the DARPA Cyber Grand Challenge to segregate the secure experiment system from host infrastructure and to provide a communication channel between the safe system and generic system.

We demonstrated successful test activities of an autonomous hacking application and compared malicious program execution results on our secure system against prevalent systems. Our two experiments demonstrated that our design achieved automated binary exploitations while making sure that a compiled program for the secure system in the range is not executable in generic system outside the range.

For future work, as our current version works only in the Intel i386 architecture, we aim to extend the secure operating system's hardware compatibility–a requirement for expanding feasible test infrastructures. The improvement of automation for the secure cyber range is another requirement to enable increased machine learning model training. The implementation of secure, real-time file transfer function for Vulnerable Binary Manager and Vulnerability Manager would be a critical step towards achieving fully automated cyber range.

Our work also has potential from an educational viewpoint. Since the cyber range works similar to a server that could take and evaluate exploit input, it might be possible to form a capture-the-flag (CTF) styled training or red-blue team training based on Pandora's design. The server for CTF training should be fully automated with a dynamic scoring system for tracking and analyzing the performance of the trainees. Finally, for students and newcomers with little experience working on security measures such as Address Space Layout Randomization and Structured Exception Handling Overwrite Protection [44], Pandora could enable trainees to train in a simple, security-oriented environments like DECREE, reducing configuration needs and freeing up time for actual training.

7 Access to Code and Artifacts

Our work builds on the work of many other open source projects and it continues beyond the time of publication. It is our intention to continue the open source nature of the project. All code created for this paper can be found in the following repository: https://cyber.uq.edu.au/repos/pandora-cyber-range

Other accompanying code and environments such as the angr development environment and legit_00003 can be found in the original authors' repositories.

Acknowledgements. Special thanks to DARPA who have created the DECREE system, virtual-competition and other infrastructure-related modules, which have been used during our experiments. Also, thanks to the team from Legitimate Business Syndicate who have created the vulnerable binary legit_00003, which was a critical part of the experiments. Finally, thanks to the angr team and Shellphish team, who have created and open-sourced their outstanding designs.

References

1. Delamore, B., Ko, R.K.L.: A global, empirical analysis of the shellshock vulnerability in web applications. In: 2015 IEEE Trustcom/BigDataSE/ISPA, pp. 1129–1135. (2015)
2. Brumley, D.: The cyber grand challenge and the future of cyber-autonomy. USENIX Login **43**, 6–9 (2018)
3. Ko, R.K.L.: Cyber autonomy: automating the hacker – self-healing, self-adaptive, automatic cyber defense systems and their impact on industry, society, and national security. In: Reuben Steff, J.B., Soare, S.R. Routledge, (ed.) Emerging Technologies and International Security – Machines, the State and War (in print). Routledge (2020)
4. Donevski, M., Zia, T.: A survey of anomaly and automation from a cybersecurity perspective. In: 2018 IEEE Globecom Workshops (GC Wkshps), pp. 1–6 (2018)
5. Smith, G.: The intelligent solution: automation, the skills shortage and cyber-security. Comput. Fraud Secur. **2018**, 6–9 (2018)
6. Papanikolaou, N., Pearson, S., Mont, M.C., Ko, R.K.: A toolkit for automating compliance in cloud computing services. Int. J. Cloud Comput. **2**(3), 45–68 (2014)
7. Ko, R., Choo, R.: The Cloud Security Ecosystem: Technical, Legal, Business and Management Issues. Syngress (2015)
8. Ko, R.K.L.: Data accountability in cloud systems. In: Nepal, S., Pathan, M. (eds.) Security, Privacy and Trust in Cloud Systems, pp. 211–238. Springer, Berlin Heidelberg, Berlin, Heidelberg (2014)
9. Ko, R.K., Lee, S.S., Rajan, V.: Understanding cloud failures. IEEE Spect. **49**, 84 (2012)
10. Yuen, J.: Automated cyber red teaming (2015)

11. Appelt, D., Nguyen, C.D., Briand, L.C., Alshahwan, N.: Automated testing for SQL injection vulnerabilities: an input mutation approach. In: Proceedings of the 2014 International Symposium on Software Testing and Analysis, pp. 259–269. ACM, San Jose, CA, USA (2014)
12. Tilemachos, V., Manifavas, C.: An automated network intrusion process and countermeasures. In: Proceedings of the 19th Panhellenic Conference on Informatics, pp. 156–160. Association for Computing Machinery, Athens, Greece (2015)
13. Stricot-Tarboton, S., Chaisiri, S., Ko, R.K.L.: Taxonomy of man-in-the-middle attacks on HTTPS. In: 2016 IEEE Trustcom/BigDataSE/ISPA, pp. 527–534 (2016)
14. Cha, S.K., Avgerinos, T., Rebert, A., Brumley, D.: Unleashing mayhem on binary code. In: 2012 IEEE Symposium on Security and Privacy, pp. 380–394 (2012)
15. Kaloudi, N., Li, J.: The AI-based cyber threat landscape: a survey. ACM Comput. Surv. **53**, Article 20 (2020)
16. Fraze, D.: Cyber Grand Challenge (CGC) (Archived). https://www.darpa.mil/program/cyber-grand-challenge
17. Furnell, S., Spafford, E.H.: The morris worm at 30. ITNOW **61**, 32–33 (2019)
18. Schagen, N., Koning, K., Bos, H., Giuffrida, C.: Towards automated vulnerability scanning of network servers. In: Proceedings of the 11th European Workshop on Systems Security, pp. Article 5. Association for Computing Machinery, Porto, Portugal (2018)
19. Zhang, X., et al.: An automated composite scanning tool with multiple vulnerabilities. In: 2019 IEEE 3rd Advanced Information Management, Communicates, Electronic and Automation Control Conference (IMCEC), pp. 1060–1064 (2019)
20. Geffner, J.: VENOM Vulnerability Details. https://www.crowdstrike.com/blog/venom-vulnerability-details
21. VMware: VMSA-2015–0004. https://www.vmware.com/security/advisories/VMSA-2015-0004.html
22. Goosen, R., Rontojannis, A., Deutscher, S., Rogg, J., Bohmayr, W., Mkrtchian, D.: Artificial Intelligence is a Threat to Cybersecurity. It's also a Solution. BCG Publication (2018)
23. Davis, J., Magrath, S.: A survey of cyber ranges and testbeds. Defence Science and Technology Organisation Edinburgh (Australia) Cyber and Electronic Warfare Div (2013)
24. Yamin, M.M., Katt, B., Gkioulos, V.: Cyber ranges and security testbeds: Scenarios, functions, tools and architecture. Comput. Secur. **88**, 101636 (2020)
25. MITRE: Common Vulnerabilities and Exposures. https://cve.mitre.org/
26. Debatty, T., Mees, W.: Building a cyber range for training cyberdefense situation awareness. In: 2019 International Conference on Military Communications and Information Systems (ICMCIS), pp. 1–6. (2019)
27. Wang, L., Tian, Z., Gu, Z., Lu, H.: Crowdsourcing approach for developing hands-on experiments in cybersecurity education. IEEE Access **7**, 169066–169072 (2019)
28. Du, W.: SEED: hands-on lab exercises for computer security education. IEEE Secur. Priv. **9**, 70–73 (2011)
29. Frank, M., Leitner, M., Pahi, T.: Design considerations for cyber security testbeds: a case study on a cyber security testbed for education. In: 2017 IEEE 15th Intl Conf on Dependable, Autonomic and Secure Computing, 15th Intl Conf on Pervasive Intelligence and Computing, 3rd Intl Conf on Big Data Intelligence and Computing and Cyber Science and Technology Congress(DASC/PiCom/DataCom/CyberSciTech), pp. 38–46 (2017)
30. Amos-Binks, A., Clark, J., Weston, K., Winters, M., Harfoush, K.: Efficient attack plan recognition using automated planning. In: 2017 IEEE Symposium on Computers and Communications (ISCC), pp. 1001–1006 (2017)
31. Raytheon Technologies: Cyber-Physical Systems and Autonomy. BHEF (2017)

32. Benzel, T.: The science of cyber security experimentation: the DETER project. In: Proceedings of the 27th Annual Computer Security Applications Conference, pp. 137–148. Association for Computing Machinery, Orlando, Florida, USA (2011)
33. Common Vulnerabilities and Exposures: CVE-2018–10933. https://cve.mitre.org/cgi-bin/cve name.cgi?name=CVE-2018-10933
34. Yan, L., et al.: DECREE: a platform for repeatable and reproducible security experiments. In: 2018 IEEE Cybersecurity Development (SecDev), pp. 11–20 (2018)
35. Defense Advanced Research Projects Agency: virtual-competition. https://github.com/CyberGrandChallenge/virtual-competition
36. Shoshitaishvili, Y., et al.: Mechanical Phish: resilient autonomous hacking. IEEE Secur. Priv. **16**, 12–22 (2018)
37. Defense Advanced Research Projects Agency: cb-testing. https://github.com/CyberGrandChallenge/cb-testing
38. Legitimate Business Syndicate: legit_00003. https://github.com/legitbs/quals-2016/tree/master/legit_00003
39. Shoshitaishvili, Y., et al.: SOK: (State of) the art of war: offensive techniques in binary analysis. In: 2016 IEEE Symposium on Security and Privacy (SP), pp. 138–157 (2016)
40. angr: Phuzzer. https://github.com/angr/phuzzer
41. Zalewski, M.: american fuzzy lop (2.52b). https://lcamtuf.coredump.cx/afl/
42. angr: rex, https://github.com/angr/rex
43. Defense Advanced Research Projects Agency: Proof of Vulnerability (POV) in CFE. https://github.com/CyberGrandChallenge/cgc-release-documentation/blob/master/walk-throughs/understanding-cfe-povs.md
44. Jiang, C., Wang, Y.: Survey on memory corruption mitigation. In: 2019 IEEE 3rd Information Technology, Networking, Electronic and Automation Control Conference (ITNEC), pp. 731–738 (2019)

A Communication-Induced Checkpointing Algorithm for Consistent-Transaction in Distributed Database Systems

Houssem Mansouri[1]([✉]) and Al-Sakib Khan Pathan[2]

[1] Laboratory of Networks and Distributed Systems, Computer Science Department,
Faculty of Sciences, Ferhat Abbas Setif University 1, Setif, Algeria
`mansouri_houssem@univ-setif.dz`
[2] Department of Computer Science and Engineering, Independent University,
Dhaka, Bangladesh
`sakib.pathan@gmail.com`

Abstract. For better protection of distributed systems, two well-known techniques are: *checkpointing* and *rollback recovery*. While failure protection is often considered a separate issue, it is crucial for establishing better secure distributed systems. This article is dedicated to the proposal of a new checkpointing algorithm for saving a consistent-transaction state in distributed databases ensuring that database management systems are able, after a failure, to recover the state of the database. The proposed communication-induced algorithm does not hamper the normal transaction processing and saves a global consistent-transaction state that records only the fully completed transactions. Analysis and experimental results of our proposal show that the proposed scheme saves a minimum number of forced checkpoints and has some performance gains compared to the alternative approaches.

Keywords: Checkpointing · Communication-induced technique ·
Consistent-transaction state · Distributed database systems · Rollback

1 Introduction

When a collection of related data is stored in some type of organized fashion, that is called a database. In case of a distributed database system, there is no common CPU (Central Processing Unit) that attaches all the various storage devices but rather the data could be stored in multiple computers that are physically separated by their locations. Sometimes, such a distributed database may span over a large network.

When a distributed database is used, the risk factors increase in a system significantly which also threatens the security of the total system. For instance, if a failure occurs in the system, that might leave the database with an inconsistent state because of abrupt termination of transactions. The term '*failure*' here refers to any event that affects the operation of the processor or main memory. This could be, for example, a power cut interrupting the data server, or a software failure. In such a setting, periodic saving of the

© Springer Nature Singapore Pte Ltd. 2021
S. M. Thampi et al. (Eds.): SSCC 2020, CCIS 1364, pp. 21–32, 2021.
https://doi.org/10.1007/978-981-16-0422-5_2

state of the database could help in case of failure. This is because, the entire system can be then restarted from a saved consistent state (i.e., last saved stable storage state). This helps curtail the amount of re-computation for lengthy and time critical transactions. Here, we address such an issue and use checkpointing method, which indirectly or directly also helps better-secure the system.

Compared to a centralized database setting, checkpointing (or, saving a snapshot of an application's state) in a distributed database is indeed much more difficult. This is because, different storages can be located at different locations which are far apart and there could be multiple access channels and thus, transactions can be running from multiple different sites at the same time. There are some classical checkpointing and recovery techniques designed for distributed systems in general [1]; however, given the practicality, these are not efficient enough to restore a distributed database to a correct state after failure(s). Special attention needs to be given to the *distributed* aspect of the database system. Hence, in this paper, we propose a communication-induced checkpointing algorithm especially designed for distributed database systems. A key feature of our algorithm is that it records a minimum number of forced checkpoints.

Different recovery techniques were developed in the literature as described in [2–5, 6]. While there are various failure recovery techniques, the most prevalent one is reconstructing the accurate state of the database with the aid of information about the operations occurred during the transactions, which would be usually recorded in some designated secondary storage space, which is commonly called a *log*. The information recorded in the log could be used for re-doing or un-doing operations or transactions for the database so that the best recorded consistent transaction state could be restored.

After this introduction, the structure of the paper is as follows: In Sect. 2, our system model is presented. Section 3 presents an overview of a global consistent-transaction checkpoint. Section 4 describes some related works that motivated us for this work. Section 5 presents our algorithm. Performance comparisons, simulation results, and some analyses are presented in two sections, Sect. 6 and Sect. 7. Finally, in Sect. 8, we conclude the paper with possible future research directions.

2 Our System Model

The distributed database model that we consider is shown in Fig. 1, similar to the model presented in [7, 8, 9] (can be considered a classical diagram). Here, a distributed database is considered which has a finite set of data items located at various sites. By the term "*data item*", we mean the smallest unit of data that is accessible to transactions. The transactions that occur through the network is considered reliable. The time for a transaction operation could be unpredictable but is finite. There is a Data Manager (DM) at each site that controls the data items. For simplicity, let us consider that the data manager, *DMx* controls access to each data item, *x*. This manager is also tasked with taking checkpoints of that data item in a periodic manner. The DM is the entity which reads and writes data items.

A transaction can be of type, either *read* or *write*. Reading of data item does not change the state of a data item but it would change when a transaction accesses the data to write something. There is a transaction manager, TM residing at each site, that controls the transactions. Similar to the previous assumption, *TMx* is the transaction manager for each data item, *x*.

Technically, we would consider the data item and its manager DM as a set of processes. Each of the processes is associated with a data item. Again, every transaction that the transaction manager controls is considered as a distinct process.

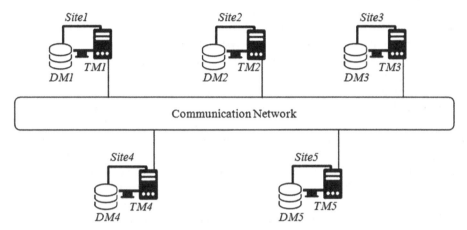

Fig. 1. Distributed database system scenario.

3   Overview of a Global Consistent-Transaction Checkpoint

We define the global transaction state of the distributed database as a collection of local checkpoints. One checkpoint is from each site. Mathematically, we can write it like this: $GCkpt(t) = (L1(t), L2(t), \ldots LN(t))$, where $GCkpt(t)$ is a global transaction having a unique identifier (t) and $Li(t)$ is a local checkpoint at data manager DMi [10, 11]. A global transaction state $GCkpt(t)$ is considered consistent *iff* (if and only if) some conditions are met like:

C1: If $Li(t)$ reflects the update of x for a data item, $x \in Di(a)$, then the update of y must also be reflected in $Li(t)$ for every data item, $y \in Di(a)$.

C2: For any data item $z \in Di(a)$, if $Li(t)$ reflects the update of z, then for every $y \in Di(a)$, the update of y must also be reflected in $GCkpt(t)$ at the designated sites.

C3: If $Li(t)$ reflects the updates of $Di(a)$, then for every $Ti(b)$, for which $Ti(b) \rightarrow Ti(a)$, the updates of $Di(b)$ must be reflected in $Li(t)$ as well.

Here, $D(a)$ is the set of data items updated by the set of transactions, $T(a)$ and $\rightarrow$ are the relations happened-before.

4   Related Work

In traditional distributed system, a consistent global state is defined as the state at which executions are failure-free (there should be no orphan message) [12–14]. When distributed database system is taken into consideration, checkpointing becomes more complex than that of the traditional distributed system because, there is the *atomicity* issue (i.e., the approach of either all occur, or nothing occurs) for global transaction which must be reflected during checkpointing. In this case, any partial transaction would not be counted but only fully completed/executed transactions during failure-free state should be recorded. Usually, in the research arena, fault tolerance like this and security issues are often considered separately. However, there is some link between these two issues in case of distributed database systems. If a partial transaction is recorded on one site while the other does not have a record of that, it can open up some unwanted security issues as an illegitimate third-party can claim a transaction taking advantage of the ignorance of one party (exploiting the partially done transaction's information). Overall, it can create a precarious situation that can be a real security risk for such setting.

Technically, if DMi records a checkpoint after a global transaction, $T(a)$ updates the database while at the same time, another site DMj records checkpoint before the transaction updates another database Sj, then there will be inconsistency in a global setting. In this case, a failure-recovery to the last checkpoint may produce an inconsistent state. Again, if the transaction $T(a)$ reads one or more data items that are modified by another transaction $T(b)$, in that case the changes for that must be also reflected in the checkpoint. To deal with such types of inconsistencies, the global state must adopt a consistent-transaction according to the definition stated in [4, 8, 15, 16].

Traditional consistency is defined as a global checkpoint which is consistent if all of its pairs of local checkpoints are consistent. The meaning of this is that there must not be any *orphan-message* in the scenario. An *orphan* message (m) is defined as a message for which the received event is recorded in the local checkpoint (Cj,y) of destination process (Pj) but its sent event is not recorded in the local checkpoint (Ci,x) of the sender process (Pi).

We call a checkpoint, *transitless global checkpoint* if all of its pairs of local checkpoints are '*transitless*'. This means that m message is in transit with respect to an ordered pair of local checkpoints (Ci,x, Cj,y) when *send*(m) belongs to Ci,x while *deliver*(m) does not belong to Cj,y. Again, we term a global checkpoint, strongly consistent-transaction (global consistent-transaction state) if all of its pairs of local checkpoints are '*consistent*' and '*transitless*'.

If we dig deep into this field, we would find that the issue of checkpointing for distributed database system has been extensively studied in some other works like [6, 17, 18, 19]. Several methods are already available, which could be generally classified into non-synchronized, synchronized, and communication-induced checkpointing approaches.

In [20, 21], the authors design some non-synchronized checkpointing algorithms. In these algorithms, each *DM* takes checkpoint autonomously without coordinating with the others. There is a condition that a checkpoint can be taken by a *DM* when a local timer expires or when the amount of data to be recorded would be small. The globally consistent-transaction state of distributed database is then constructed at the time of the recovery process by finding the consistent set of checkpoints among the recorded ones. On the other hand, [22, 23] talk about synchronized checkpointing algorithms, where checkpoints are taken by the *DM*s in a way to achieve global consistent-transaction state. For this, the *DM*s would need to coordinate among themselves. In this mechanism, implementation simplicity is the objective and it is expected that always a global consistent-transaction state would be available at the time of recovery operation.

The communication-induced checkpointing algorithms proposed in [19, 24, 25] allow the *DM*s to take checkpoints independently. These algorithms also force the *DM*s to take additional checkpoints with the goal that each of the checkpoints will be a part of a global consistent-transaction state of the database.

5   Proposed Checkpointing Algorithm

5.1   Motivation and Description of Our Algorithm

One vital issue about checkpointing is that it should be done when the system is running normally (without any problem). Hence, in this process of checkpointing, we need to keep the interference with transaction processing as minimum as possible. It implies that the regular transactions can be submitted when the process of checkpointing is ongoing or both the transaction execution and checkpointing should occur concurrently. Therefore, the communication-induced checkpointing technique is the most appropriate in such a situation.

DM can take either local checkpoint that it (i.e., *DM*) independently saves while forced checkpoints are those that must be saved by *DM* (kind of compulsion involved). Every *DM* can have a timer and after expiry of the timer, usually a local checkpoint is saved. Then, the timer is reset for next cycle. What communication-induced checkpointing does is that it piggybacks the information related to the algorithm on every transaction that happens. The receiver of each transaction then uses this information to determine whether a forced checkpoint is to be saved. This measure is applied to advance the global consistent-transaction state [26].

An initial local checkpoint is taken by each *DMi*. Then, it sets its checkpoint sequence number *Cknbri* to 0. Another integer variable *NCi* (set to 1) is initialized by *DMi*, which is then periodically incremented. This value basically holds the sequence number that would be assigned to the next local checkpoint. This is how the sequence numbers keep track of the latest checkpoints of the processes that are close to each other. This method is very useful in progression of the recovery line [27].

When a transaction manager *TMi* sends a transaction T to another *TMj*, the sequence number of current local checkpoint is piggybacked by *TMj*. After receiving the transaction, if *TMj* finds that the sequence number that is piggybacked with T is greater than the sequence number of the latest checkpoint, then, *DMj* is forced to take a checkpoint before processing T. For this, the *DMj* assigns the sequence number received in T as the sequence number of the newly saved checkpoint [26].

In addition to the integer variables, *Cknbri* and *NCi*, each *DMi* has two other integer variables: *Icnbi*, and *Lctni*. *Icnbi* is the incarnation number of *DMi* and *Lctni* contains the latest recovery consistent-transaction line number. With each transaction T, the current values of *NCi*, *Icnbi* and *Lctni* are piggybacked.

When a *TMi* receives a transaction, it sends a checkpointing request to *DMi* (in order to take a forced checkpoint) before processing the transaction if the value of *NCi* of the current checkpoint is less than the sequence number (of checkpoint) received with the transaction. Also, it sends an updating request to *DMi* (in order to update its data structures) if the local value *Icnbi* is less than the value received.

A *DMi* rolls back after a failure to its latest checkpoint, updates its data structures. Then, it informs other *DMj* about the failure and resumes its usual computation without waiting for any reply. On receiving the *rollback request*, each *DMj* would update its local data structure (compared to counterparts on the request) and would roll back to its earliest checkpoint whose sequence number is more or equal to *Lctnj*, if *Lctnj* is less than *NCj* (i.e., the local checkpoint sequence number). Otherwise, it takes a checkpoint with sequence number, *Lctnj*. In the next subsection, the pseudocodes of our algorithms are presented (shown as a single algorithm).

5.2   Algorithm Implementation – Pseudocode

Data structures at *DMi*
   Integer Cknbri := 0, NCi := 1, Lctni := 1;

Checkpointing Algorithm

Role of each *DMi*:
   When time for *DMi* to take a local checkpoint:
      If (NCi>Cknbri) then
         Take Local Checkpoint;
         Cknbri = NCi;
   When it is time for *DMi* to increment *NCi:*
      NCi := NCi+1;   // NCi incremented periodically
   When receiving *Updating Request:*
      Icnbi := T. Icnb;
      Lctni := T.Lctn;
   When receiving *Checkpointing Request:*
      Take Forced Checkpoint;
      Cknbri = T.NC;
Role of each *TMi*:
   When receiving transation *T*:
      If (T.Icnb>Icnbi) then
         Send Updating Request to DMi;
      If (T.NC>NCi) then
         Send Checkpointing Request to DMi;
         Process the message T;
   When sending transaction *T*:
      T.NC := NCi;
      T. Icnb := Icnbi;
      T.Lctn := Lctni;

Algorithm for failure recovery

Recovery process is initiated by a *DMi*:   // after failure
      Restore the latest local checkpoint;
      Icnbi := Icnbi + 1;
      Lctni := NCi;
      Send Rollback Request (Icnbi, Lctni) to all other DMj;
Role of all other *DMj*:
   When receiving *Rollback Request (Icnbi, Lctni)* from *DMi*:
      If (Icnbi>Icnbj) then
      Icnbj:= Icnbi;
      Lctnj:= Lctni;
      If (Lctnj>NCj) then
         Take Local Checkpoint;
         NCj:=Lctnj;
      Else
         Restore the earliest checkpoint with (NCj≥Lctnj);
         Delete all the checkpoints beyond;

6 Performance Comparison

We have compared the performance of our algorithm with two reference checkpoint algorithms [19, 24]. The rationale for choosing these algorithms is that irrespective of their publication years, till this time, these are considered as the two classic reference algorithms in this arena. Hence, showing comparative better performance than those algorithms suffices to prove the efficiency of our algorithm. It should be noted that we have considered similar settings fitting the communication-induced class proposed so far in the literature, using ten key criteria. The comparative chart is shown in Table 1.

Table 1. Comparative chart.

Criteria	Communication-Induced Checkpointing		
	[19]	[24]	Our Algorithm
1. Additional message	0	0	0
2. Piggybacked information's	high	high	Less
3. Rollback request number / failures	>1	>1	$=1$
4. Local checkpoint number	high	high	Less
5. Forced checkpoint number	high	high	Less
6. Useless checkpoint number	Less	Less	high
7. Rollback distance	$>R$	$>R$	$=R$
8. Concurrent failures processing	No	No	No
9. Checkpointing process period	Less	Less	high
10. Recovery process period	high	high	Less

The communication-induced checkpointing techniques used in the three algorithms do not require any extra message. On the other hand, additional or extra messages are required for coordinated checkpointing techniques for implementation of the checkpointing operation.

The techniques proposed in [19, 24] require piggybacking the extra information on the transaction. This is done to make sure that the receiving DM can take an extra forced checkpoint if and when required. But, in this way, greater overhead is incurred for checkpointing process because DMs do not skip taking local checkpoints if they are required to take forced checkpoints. The two other algorithms basically increase the number of forced checkpoints that are taken in order to reduce the generation of useless checkpoints, which is opposite in case of our algorithm.

Unlike the other two algorithms, for recovery, our algorithm needs only one *rollback request* to be sent to the other processes. For a particular failure, maximum number of rollback(s) of *DM*s is 1. If a *DM* has the latest checkpoint with maximum sequence number and it fails, all other *DM*s will be forced to rollback only one time. If a process has the latest checkpoint with the lowest sequence number, it would force other processes to roll back to a distance of at most R checkpoints. Here, R denotes the maximum of the ratios of checkpoint interval lengths of any two *DM*s.

As a common drawback, unfortunately all the three algorithms do not deal with concurrent failures. For this purpose, we hypothesize that no two failures will occur simultaneously in two different *DM*s. Also, all the three algorithms are not responsible for a second failure occurring during the rollback process from a first one.

On the other hand, the checkpoint phase of our algorithm is more complex than that of its counterparts in [19, 24] which take more execution times. But, it is the exact opposite for the recovery phase. Hence, our algorithm offers relatively faster recovery from failure.

7 Simulation Results and Comparisons

Let us now see the simulation results of the compared algorithms. Number of forced checkpoints versus number of transactions in the system with different data items are shown in Figs. 2(a–c).

The charts show the performance against the classical algorithm of Wu and Manivannan [19] and the algorithm of Baldoni et al. [24]. We consider three distributed database schemes: with 10, 30, and 50 data items. For this, we used a simulator named, *ChkSim* [28]. To have better understanding of the issue, during our experiments, we changed the number of data items and increased the number of random transactions$\times$ to see the corresponding changes for all the algorithms.

It is clear from the results that our algorithm shows relatively less number of forced checkpoints to determine a global consistent-transaction state. With the increase of the numbers of transactions and/or data items, the gains become more evident. Hence, our algorithm outperforms the compared two classic algorithms when the numbers of forced checkpoints are taken into consideration. This also implies that this algorithm is the best among these and other alternative approaches to take a global consistent transaction state. On the other hand, like many other algorithms, the number of not required or useless checkpoints also increases automatically.

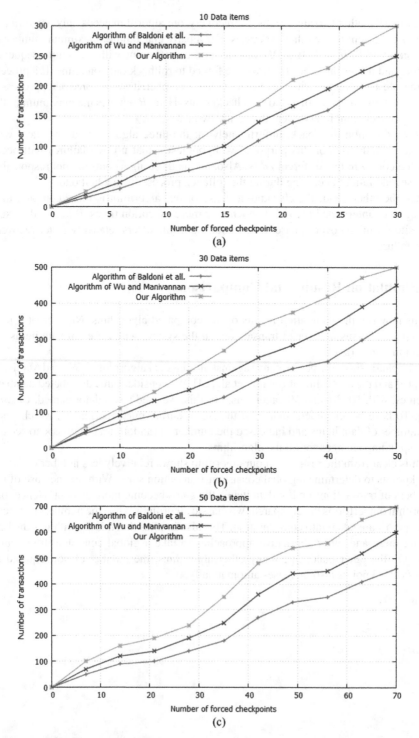

Fig. 2. Number of forced checkpoints vs. Number of transactions in the system when: (a) Data items = 10 (b) Data items = 30 (c) Data items = 50.

8 Conclusions and Future Work

Here, we presented a communication-induced checkpointing algorithm to provide a global consistent transaction state in distributed database systems, where no blocking of transactions takes place and no extra information needs to be piggybacked with the transactions unlike in the existing algorithms. Our algorithm allows *DMs* periodically to take local checkpoints asynchronously. It also gives guarantee that there will be always a recovery global consistent-transaction line at all time as it forces the *DMs* to record additional forced checkpoints at designated times. Hence, once a failure occurs, the distributed database system can quickly restore the last best recorded state. A failed *DM* can also roll back self-sufficiently to its latest local checkpoint and then can continue its computation. In this case, the *DM* does not need to wait for other *DMs* to roll back to a global consistent-transaction state.

The gain of our algorithm is that it reduces the number of forced checkpoints (as required), at the expense, unfortunately, with slight increase in the number of useless checkpoints. Hence, for a better secure and robust system, it can still perform better than other alternatives as the accurate best state can be restored when a failure occurs in such a system. A possible future work could be exerting more efforts to see whether the number of useless checkpoints can be minimized in this setting.

References

1. Mansouri, H., Pathan, A-S.K.: Review of checkpointing and rollback recovery protocols for mobile distributed computing systems. In: Ghosh, U., Rawat D.B., Datta, R., Pathan, A-S.K (eds.) Internet of Things and Secure Smart Environments: Successes and Pitfalls, CRC Press, Taylor & Francis Group (2020)
2. Pilarski, S., Kameda, T.: Checkpointing for distributed databases: starting from the basics. IEEE Trans. Parallel Distrib. Syst. **3**(5), 602–610 (1992)
3. Lin, J.L., Dunham, M.H.: A survey of distributed database checkpointing. J. Distrib. Parallel Databases **5**, 289–319 (1997)
4. Akanshika: Analysis of rollback recovery techniques in distributed database management system. Int. J. Modern Eng. Res. **3**(3), 1353–1356 (2013)
5. Sharma, S., Agiwal, P., Gaherwal, R., Mewada, S., Sharma, P.: Analysis of recovery techniques in data base management system. Res. J. Comput. Inf. Technol. Sci. **4**(3), 4–8 (2016)
6. Son, S.H., Choe, K.M.: Techniques for database recovery in distributed environments. Inf. Softw. Technol. **30**(5), 285–294 (1988)
7. Pilarski, S., Kameda, T.: A novel checkpointing scheme for distributed database systems. In: Proceedings of the 9th ACM SIGACT-SIGMOD-SIGART symposium on Principles of database systems, pp. 368–378 (1990)
8. Wu, J., Manivannan, D. Thuraisingham, B.: Transaction-consistent global checkpoints in a distributed database system. In: Proceedings of the International Conference on Data Mining and Knowledge Engineering, London (2008)
9. Lim, J.T., Moon, S.C.: Global checkpointing scheme for heterogeneous distributed database systems. Microprocessing Microprogramming **32**(1–5), 747–754 (1991)
10. Luo, C.: Interference-free checkpointing algorithm for distributed database system. In: Proceedings of International Conference on Industrial Control and Electronics Engineering, Xi'an (2012)

11. Mansouri, H., Badache, N., Aliouat, M., Pathan, A.-S.K.: Adaptive fault tolerant checkpointing protocol for cluster based mobile Ad Hoc networks. Procedia Comput. Sci. **73**, 40–47 (2015)
12. Mansouri, H., Pathan, A-S.K.: An efficient minimum-process non-intrusive snapshot protocol for vehicular Ad Hoc networks. In: Proceedings of the13th ACS/IEEE International Conference on Computer Systems and Applications, pp. 83–92. IEEE (2016)
13. Mansouri, H., Pathan, A.-S.K.: Checkpointing distributed application running on mobile Ad Hoc networks. Int. J. High Perform. Comput. Networking **11**(2), 95–107 (2018)
14. Mansouri, H., Pathan, A.-S.: A resilient hierarchical checkpointing algorithm for distributed systems running on cluster federation. In: Thampi, S.M., Martinez Perez, G., Ko, R., Rawat, D.B. (eds.) SSCC 2019. CCIS, vol. 1208, pp. 99–110. Springer, Singapore (2020). https://doi.org/10.1007/978-981-15-4825-3_8
15. Wu, J., Manivannan, D., Thuraisingham, B.: Necessary and sufficient conditions for transaction-consistent global checkpoints in a distributed database system. Inf. Sci. **179**(20), 3659–3672 (2009)
16. Son, S.H., Agrawala, A.K.: Distributed checkpointing for globally consistent states of databases. IEEE Trans. Softw. Eng. **15**(10), 1157–1167 (1989)
17. Son, S.H.: An adaptive checkpointing scheme for distributed databases with mixed types of transactions. IEEE Trans. Knowl. Data Eng. **1**(4), 450–458 (1989)
18. Kim, J.L., Park, T., Swarnam, P.I.: A protocol for consistent checkpointing recovery for time-critical distributed database systems. In: Proceedings of the 3rd International Conference on Database Systems for Advanced Applications, Daejeon (1993)
19. Wu, J., Manivannan, D.: An efficient non-intrusive checkpointing algorithm for distributed database systems. In: Chaudhuri, S., Das, S.R., Paul, H.S., Tirthapura, S. (eds.) ICDCN 2006. LNCS, vol. 4308, pp. 82–87. Springer, Heidelberg (2006). https://doi.org/10.1007/119479 50_9
20. Dadam, P., Schlageter, G.: Recovery in distributed databases based on non-synchronized local checkpoints. In: Proceedings of the Information Processing 80, Amsterdam, pp. 457–462 (1980)
21. Ren, k., Diamond, T., Abadi, D.J., Thomson, A.: Low-overhead asynchronous checkpointing in main-memory database systems. In: Proceedings of the International Conference on Management of Data, pp. 1539–1551 (2016)
22. Ferran, G.: Distributed checkpointing in a distributed data management system. In: Proceedings of the Real-Time Systems Symposium, pp. 43–49 (1981)
23. Kuss, H.: On totally ordering checkpoints in distributed databases. In: Proceedings of the ACM International Conference on Management of Data, pp. 293–302 (1982)
24. Baldoni, R., Quaglia, F., Raynal, M.: Consistent checkpointing for transaction systems. Comput. J. **44**(2), 92–100 (2001)
25. Son, S.H.: An algorithm for non-interfering checkpoints and its practicality in distributed database systems. Inf. Syst. **14**(5), 421–429 (1989)
26. Mansouri, H., Badache, N., Aliouat, M., Pathan, A.-S.K.: A new efficient checkpointing protocol for distributed mobile computing. J. Control Eng. Appl. Inform. **17**(2), 43–54 (2015)
27. Mansouri, H., Pathan, A.-S.K.: Checkpointing distributed computing systems: an optimization approach. Int. J. High Perform. Comput. Networking **15**(3–4), 202–209 (2019)
28. ChkSim: A Distributed Checkpointing Simulator. https://dcomp.sor.ufscar.br/gdvieira/chk sim/. Accessed 16 Sep. 2020

Evading Static and Dynamic Android Malware Detection Mechanisms

Teenu S. John$^{(\boxtimes)}$ and Tony Thomas$^{(\boxtimes)}$

Indian Institute of Information Technology and Management-Kerala,
Thiruvananthapuram, India
{teenu.john,tony.thomas}@iiitmk.ac.in

Abstract. With the widespread usage of Android mobile devices, malware developers are increasingly targeting Android applications for carrying out their malicious activities. Despite employing powerful malware detection mechanisms, an adversary can evade the threat detection model by launching intelligent malware with fine-grained feature perturbations. Since machine learning is widely adopted in malware detection owing to its automatic threat prediction and detection capabilities, attackers are nowadays targeting the vulnerability of machine learning models for malicious activities. In this work, we demonstrate how an adversary can evade various machine learning based static and dynamic Android malware detection mechanisms. To the best of our knowledge, this is the first work that discusses adversarial evasion in both static and dynamic machine learning based malware detection mechanisms.

Keywords: Android · Adversarial malware · Evasion techniques

1   Introduction

Nowadays Android malware are increasing rapidly. According to the McAfee mobile threat report issued in 2020, there is an increase in the malicious apps targeting Android operating system [3]. These malware can hide themselves after installation, mimic the legitimate applications icon and also use advanced evasion technique that downloads the malicious code after sometime. The conventional signature based detection mechanisms [1] cannot detect such obfuscated evasive malware. Hence many malware detection mechanisms are adopting machine learning to detect unknown malware. The advantage of machine learning is that it can automatically learn and predict the malware behaviour from raw data [34]. In Android, there are many works that show how machine learning can be used effectively for static, dynamic and hybrid malware detection mechanisms [42].

This work is done as a part of Centre for Research and Innovation in Cyber Threat Resilience project (CRICTR 2020-21), which is funded by Kerala State Planning Board.

In static Android malware detection, the Android application is examined without executing it [51]. The features used for static analysis are permissions, intents, static API calls, opcodes etc. The advantage of employing static analysis technique is that it has high code coverage. The drawback of static detection mechanism is that, it cannot detect obfuscated malware. Dynamic analysis on the other hand runs the application in an emulator and then captures the malicious behaviour of the application by examining the run time features such as system calls, dynamic API calls etc. [13,25,26,45]. The disadvantage of dynamic detection mechanism is that it has less code coverage. Moreover, malware developers can evade the dynamic analysis by examining the specific API's invoked by the application when it is made to run in a virtual machine. For example, if an application is executed in a virtual machine, then the *TelephonyManager.get-Device id()* API returns zero [47]. Petsas et al. [38] proposed an attack against virtual machines by examining the dynamic sensor information and VM-related intricacies of the Android emulator to evade detection. Wenrui et al. [24] proposed a mechanism to evade Android emulator runtime analysis using an evasive component that identifies whether the events are coming from a real user or from an automated tool. To solve the problems related to static and dynamic malware detection, several mechanisms have been proposed in the past that use hybrid analysis. The hybrid analysis uses a combination of both static and dynamic features for detection. The drawback of hybrid detection is that the resource consumption is more [12] when compared to static and dynamic malware detection mechanisms.

To detect malware, the static, dynamic or hybrid features of the application are fed into unsupervised or supervised machine learning classifiers. In supervised machine learning malware detection, the machine learning model is trained with thousands of benign and malware samples. However, adversaries can evade the most powerful machine learning models used for the malware detection by crafting malware that exploits the vulnerability of machine learning models. These malware are called adversarial malware. Adversarial malware pose a serious threat nowadays and is an emerging area of research [36].

There are some works that show how static detection mechanism using permissions and API calls can be easily evaded using adversarial attack. In [5], the authors evade the Drebin [11] detection method using some feature perturbation techniques. However, a research on how adversary evades the opcode based Android malware detection is yet to be explored and is an interesting area of study. This is because the opcodes contain valuable information to detect malware that employ code repackaging. The recent CoronaVirus application is one such ransomware [14] that uses code repackaging. The effectiveness of opcodes lies in the fact that despite obfuscation, the same family of Android malware share the same code parts and hence can be identified by examining the opcode patterns of the application [7,45].

Likewise in dynamic malware detection, system calls are very effective features for detecting obfuscated malware [16,33]. This is because, system call captures the interaction of the application with the operating system and hence reveal the actual behaviour of the application even if the application adopts dynamic loading, encryption and other techniques for evasion. Vinod et al. [49] showed label flipping attack against Android system call based malware detection where they poison the training data with adversarial samples. However, their attack injects individual system calls rather than sequences of system calls that is not effective.

In this paper, we show how static Android malware detection mechanism using opcodes and dynamic Android malware detection mechanism using system calls can be evaded by the adversary. We employ frequency based evasion in both static and dynamic malware detection mechanisms whereby the attacker injects the most frequent benign code sequences into the malware to subvert the detection. Our attack is realistic which shows that injecting a few sequences of benign code can evade the robust machine learning based malware detection mechanisms. Moreover, our attack is resilient against feature selection approaches [23] since we inject opcode sequences that replicate benign application behaviour.

The contributions in this paper are the following:-

1. We explore how an adversary injects benign opcode sequences to evade the static Android malware detection mechanism. For this we evade the mechanism employed in [16], which is a malware detection mechanism using opcode n- grams. This is the first work that shows adversarial attacks in the form of benign opcode injection.
2. We explore how the adversary injects benign system call sequences for evading dynamic Android malware detection mechanism. To show this, we evade the mechanism employed in [44] which is a malware detection mechanism using graph signal processing. We show that Android system call based malware detection mechanism using the powerful graph signal processing technique can be evaded by injecting a few benign system call sequences.

2   Related Works

The malware detection mechanism employed by the popular malware detection companies like Kaspersky [2] and Norton [4] use machine learning to detect polymorphic and obfuscated malware. However their detection capabilities can be deteriorated by an adversary that employs feature perturbations to evade detection. According to the recent threat report issued by Kaspersky [9], the adversarial attack against machine learning based malware detection can cause misidentified Trojans to infect millions of devices. There are many works in the past that discuss about adversarial attacks and defenses in Android malware detection. This section discusses about the attacks and defenses against Android malware detection classifiers that are implemented in the past.

There are two types of adversarial attacks. They are data poisoning and evasion attacks [32]. Data poisoning attacks are launched by contaminating the training instances of the classifier. Evasion attack on the other hand finely perturbs the applications features to evade detection. The evasion attack can be either problem space attacks or feature space attacks [39].

Chen al [19] proposed a data poisoning attack in Android malware detection where the adversary contaminates the training data with malicious samples. However, their attack required gradient information about the classifier. Abaid et al. [5] proposed an evasion attack in which evades the Drebin detection mechanism. They constructed attackers with different capabilities and showed that adversarial evasion is a feasible threat. Their attack reduced the detection accuracy of the classifier from 100% to 0%. However, their attack removed some features from the Android application, which may cause the application to lose its malware functionality.

The evasion attack can be either problem space attacks or feature space attacks [39].

In problem space attacks, the attacker transforms the malicious application to a new variant sample that is valid and realistic. Pierazzi et al. [39] proposed a problem space attack in android malware where the adversary employs opaque predicates by carefully constructing obfuscated conditions or program code that returns *False* but evades static detection. Their attack can be detected with the help of feature selection techniques mentioned in [31]. Yang et al. [53] proposed a problem space attack in which they craft adversarial malware samples. Their technique alters the semantics of the application, and the generated malware may loose its functionality. Rosenberg et al. [40] proposed an attack against the API call based malware detection mechanism. They added artifacts into the application which can be detected using dynamic analysis.

The feature space attack on the other hand makes fine grained feature perturbations on various static and dynamic features of the application for evasion. Gross et al. [27] proposed a feature space attack using Jacobian matrix perturbation to evade Drebin Android malware detection. However the generated malware can be detected using undeclared classes and unused permissions. Li et al. [35] crafted attack against Drebin android malware detection mechanism. Their attack employed multiple generative methods to craft malware that do not ruin the malware functionality. They also proposed an ensemble technique to defend against adversarial attack.

Demontis et al. [23] proposed a secure learning technique to detect adversarial attacks in Android malware detection. However, their technique cannot detect malware that replicated benign applications behaviour. Chen et al. [18] proposed an ensemble based defense against adversarial attacks in Android malware detection. They used a feature selection approach to detect adversarial malware. The disadvantage of all these defensive mechanisms is that they can only detect adversarial attacks that perturb syntactic features like permissions [19,23,28,53,53]. Moreover, perturbing syntactic features like Android permissions can be easily achieved unlike semantic features. Since many malware detection mechanisms are extensively using the information of the dex files for malware detection [20] the attack that manipulates the features of the dex file is critical.

In this work, we perturb the features in the classes.dex file by injecting Dalvik opcodes that occur in the benign Android applications. Chen et al. [21] proposed a similar attack that manipulates the API control flow graph to evade detection. However, their attack inserts *Nop* API calls that can be detected using white list filtering [21]. Moreover their attack requires sophisticated adversarial feature perturbation techniques to achieve high evasion rate. In this paper, we investigate evasion attack in the form of feature space attack in which the attacker subverts the malware detection mechanism by injecting the features of the benign application. Our attack is resilient against feature selection approaches as mentioned in [23]. In Android, malware developers can easily download evasive malware by launching an update attack [5] when compared to data poisoning attacks. This motivated us to explore evasion attacks in static and dynamic Android malware detection mechanisms. We believe that our work will help security researchers to develop suitable defensive mechanisms against adversarial attacks in Android malware detection classifiers.

3   Machine Learning for Android Malware Detection

There are many works that show the effectiveness of machine learning for malware detection. This section discusses about the various machine learning models implemented in the past for malware detection. In [54] the authors proposed a classifier fusion approach that combines several machine learning classifiers for detecting malware. They combined various classifiers like J48, Random Tree-100, and Voted Perceptron, REPTree and Random Tree-9. Among the various machine learning models used for malware detection, Support Vector Machines(SVM) are found to be extremely useful for detecting unknown malware. Justin et al. [41] proposed a malware detection mechanism using SVM to detect Android malware with control flow graphs(CFG). Shifu et al. [30] proposed Hindroid, a mechanism using standard multi-kernel learning with SVM to detect Android malware. Canfora et al. [17] proposed a malware detection mechanism using sequences of system calls with SVM for building a fingerprint of the Android malware applications. Wen et al. [52] proposed a malware detection approach based on big data analytics and SVM by extracting various static and dynamic features of Android malware. Besides SVM, decision trees and random forest also gave excellent results in detecting malware. Peiravain et al.[37] proposed a malware detection method with permissions and API calls to detect Android malware using decision trees. Alam et al. [6] proposed a malware detection mechanism using Random Forest. The features used were battery consumption, CPU usage, memory related features, permissions etc. Moutaz et al. [8] proposed a malware detection mechanism using API calls and permissions. Their detection mechanism gave 94.3% F-measure with random forest classifier. Among all other machine learning models, deep neural network gained popularity owing to its ability to detect malware without manual feature engineering [48].

Venkatraman et al.[46] proposed a malware detection with deep neural network and their detection mechanism gave 96% accuracy. However, all these malware detection mechanisms using machine learning can be evaded by an adversary that crafts intelligent malware using adversarial machine learning.

4   Method of Attack

In this work, we evade the state of the art malware detection mechanisms [44] and [16] that use system calls and opcode n- grams as features. To inject the features of benign application to the malware application, we use TF-IDF feature selection. We chose TF-IDF since both of these malware detection mechanisms [16,44] use the frequency counts of the opcode n- grams and system calls for constructing the features for malware detection.

5   Evading Opcode Based Android Malware Detection Mechanism

To evade the opcode based malware detection mechanism, an adversary may employ code injection attack to inject benign dalvik code parts to the malware application or may insert junk codes to evade the detection mechanism. Since a good feature selection approach can easily detect junk code insertion, we launch attacks in the form of benign opcode injection to test whether the classifier is able to detect malware. This section discusses about how an adversary can evade opcode n- gram based Android malware detection mechanism mentioned in [16]. In [16], the opcode n- grams obtained from benign and malware applications are given to SVM(Support Vector Machines) and Random Forest for malware detection. An accuracy of 95.67% accuracy was obtained using opcode 5- grams with SVM classifier while with Random Forest, an accuracy of 96.88% was obtained using opcode 2- grams.

5.1   Preprocessing

We replicated the experimental setup mentioned in [16] to explore how adversary evades the detection mechanism. For this, we took 5560 malware applications from the Drebin dataset [11] and collected 5560 benign applications. Table 1 shows the malware families that were taken for the experiments as mentioned in [16]. We took all the benign application categories as mentioned in the original work. The benign applications were downloaded from Google Playstore and were uploaded to VirusTotal to check for malicious behaviour. Using apktool [50], we first extracted the .dex files from the apk. Then by using smali tool [29], we extracted the smali files from the .dex files. These smali files contain the opcodes of an apk and can be used to construct opcode n- grams.

Table 1. Android malware familes

SI no	Android malware family	Obfuscation	Malware type
1	DroidKungFu	Repackaging, string encryption, native payload	Trojan
2	Fakeinstaller	Renaming	Trojan
3	Plankton	Dynamic loading	Trojan,botnet
4	Opfake	Renaming	Trojan
5	GinMaster	Renaming	Trojan
6	Basebridge	Renaming	Trojan
7	Kmin	–	Trojan
8	Geinimi	Renaming	Trojan
9	Adrd	Renaming	Trojan
10	DroidDream	Renaming	Botnet

5.2 Training the Classifier

We trained the classifier as mentioned in [16]. We took opcode n- grams with $n = 2$ and 5 since they gave the maximum accuracy when compared to $n = 1,3,4$. We took top 2000 number of opcode n- grams that distinguish benign from malware application by using the technique mentioned in the original paper. We trained the two classifiers Support Vector Machine(SVM) and Random Forest(RF) as mentioned in the original work. We obtained an accuracy 96.3% with 1000 number of opcode 2-grams and an accuracy of 95.3% on 2000 number of opcode 5-grams. The accuracy values were approximately equal to that of the original work. Table 2 shows this.

5.3 Testing the Classifier

To evaluate the performance of the classifier, we used metrics such as True Positive Rate(TPR), False positive(FPR), True negative Rate (TNR), False Negative Rate (TNR), Accuracy, Recall, F-measure. True Positives(TP) refers to the number of malware applications that are correctly classified as malware by the classifier. True Negatives(TN) refers to the number of goodware applications that are correctly classified as goodware. False Positives(FP) refers to the number of benign applications that are incorrectly classified as malware. False

Table 2. Performance of [16] before the attack

Number of opcodes	n-gram	Classifier	TPR	FPR	TNR	FNR	Accuracy	Precision	Recall	F-measure
1000	2- gram	Random forest	0.963	0.027	0.973	0.037	0.963	0.972	0.963	0.968
2000	5- gram	SVM	0.962	0.055	0.945	0.038	0.953	0.945	0.962	0.953

Table 3. Performance of [16] After the Attack

l	TPR	FPR	TNR	FNR	Accuracy	Precision	Recall	F-measure
50	0.751	0.027	0.973	0.249	0.862	0.965	0.751	0.844
100	0.489	0.039	0.961	0.511	0.725	0.926	0.489	0.640
150	0.305	0.033	0.967	0.695	0.636	0.902	0.305	0.455
200	0.191	0.027	0.973	0.809	0.582	0.876	0.191	0.313

Negatives(FN) represents the number of malware applications incorrectly classified as goodware applications. The accuracy, precision and F-measure are computed as follows:

$$Accuracy = \frac{TP + TN}{TP + FN + TN + FP} \tag{1}$$

$$Precision = \frac{TP}{TP + FP} \tag{2}$$

$$Recall = \frac{TP}{TP + FN} \tag{3}$$

$$F-measure = \frac{2 \times precision \times recall}{precision + recall} \tag{4}$$

5.4 Dalvik Opcode Injection

The aim of the Dalvik opcode injection attack is to evade the classifier by injecting benign opcode n- grams. We aim to use opcode injection attack rather than opcode elimination attack since the latter may destroy the malware functionality. The attack is achieved by using a JADX tool to find the java files corresponding to the smali files and injecting opcode sequences corresponding to the malicious class files.

We assume that the attacker has complete knowledge about the classifier and the features. To evade the detection mechanism the attacker injects benign opcode n- grams. We computed the most frequent benign opcode n- grams obtained using the TF-IDF method as mentioned before and injected them to evade the detection mechanism employed in [16]. Table 4 shows the top five opcode 5- grams obtained using TF-IDF method. In addition to the benign opcode n- grams obtained using TF-IDF, we also injected opcode n- grams for displaying text messages inside the malicious application to mimick the legitimate application behaviour. Figure 1 shows this. In this figure, the java code and its corresponding dalvik code to display a text message is shown. Here we aim to explore how injecting junk or random text messages can evade the opcode n-gram based detection mechanism.

We conducted the experiments on Random Forest classifier with opcode 2-grams, since it gave maximum accuracy in the original work. For testing the performance of the classifier, we took 500 benign application and 500 opcode injected malware applications. We took 50 samples from each of the Android malware families listed in Table 1. The performance of the classifier when we inject l benign opcode n- grams is shown in Table 3. When l increases, the FNR also increases which shows that the injected malware can evade the detection mechanism employed in [16]. Figure 2 shows how the detection accuracy of the classifier is reduced when we increase the value of l.

Table 4. Top five opcode 5- grams obtained from TF-IDF Method.

SI no	Opcode 5- grams	Category
1	array-length,const/1,const/,const-string,goto	Malware
2	const/1,const/,const/high1,const-string,const-wide/	Malware
3	aput-object,array-length,const/1,const/,const-string	Malware
4	aget-object,aput-char,aput-object,array-length,check-cast	Malware
5	iget-object,iput,iput-boolean,iput-object,move-exception	Malware
1	iget-object,iput-object,move-result-object,return-object,return-void	Benign
2	check-cast,const/,goto ,if-eqz,if-nez	Benign
3	mul-int/lit,new-instance,return,return-object,return-void	Benign
4	move-result-object,new-instance,nop,return-object,return-void	Benign
5	move-result,move-result-object,new-instance,nop,return-object	Benign

Fig. 1. Injecting benign opcodes for displaying text messages

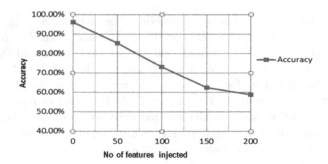

Fig. 2. Accuracy Values of [16] After Injecting l number of opcode $n-$ grams

6   Evading System Call Graph Based Android Malware Detection Mechanism

System call based Android malware detection mechanisms are found to be extremely powerful in detecting malware that evade static detection mechanisms [33]. Most of the system call based Android malware detection mechanisms are using frequency of occurrence of the system calls for detecting malware [17,25]. This is because certain system calls like *read()*, *write()* etc. are frequently invoked by the malware than goodware. This technique can be evaded by using a system call injection attack in which the malware injects some rare or benign system calls at runtime [15]. In this section, we show how an adversary can evade the system call based Android malware detection mechanism in [44]. The malware detection mechanism in [44] employs graph signal processing mechanism to detect Android malware. In this mechanism, the frequency of occurrence of the system calls are taken as the signals and then a graph shift operation is applied to the signals to obtain the processed graph signals. These graph signals are then fed into the machine learning classifiers to check whether the application is malicious or not.

6.1   Preprocessing and Signal Extraction

We took 2500 malware and goodware applications as mentioned in the original work [44] to replicate the experimental setup. The malware samples were taken from Drebin [11], AMD [10], and Contagio minidump [22]. We took 1,2,5,6,9,10 malware families mentioned in Table 1 and also the malware families in Table 5 as mentioned in [44] for conducting the experiments. The benign applications were downloaded from Google Playstore and checked with VirusTotal to check for malicious behaviour. We also eliminated semantically similar Android malware and took all the malware families mentioned in [44] and replicated the experimental set up. The Android applications were made to run in an emulator by injecting thousand pseudorandom events like key press event, touch event etc. to achieve high code coverage. We collected system calls using strace utility [43] and eliminated irrelevant system calls as mentioned in [44] and only selected relevant opcodes for malware detection to replicate the features for classification. After selecting the relevant opcodes, we constructed system call digraph and extracted the graph signals.

6.2   Training the Classifier

We trained the classifier as mentioned in the original paper. We took Random Forest Classifier, since it gave maximum accuracy. We took 80% samples for training and remaining 20% for training as mentioned in the original work [44].

6.3   Testing the Classifier

The accuracy, precision, recall and F-measure was computed as in Section 3.1. Table 6 shows the performance matrix of the classifier.

6.4   System Call Injection

The system call graph signal based detection mechanism takes the frequency of occurrence of the system call for constructing the graph signal. This mechanism can be evaded by injecting benign system call codes that mimick legitimate application behaviour. We model a perfect knowledge attack where the attacker has complete knowledge about the features and the classification model. The attacker can gather malware and benign system calls from public repositories and examine the most frequent system calls that are occurring in malware and benign applications. We inject a sequence of system calls rather than individual system calls since the application may not work properly if we do so. To inject a system call sequence, we first computed the most frequently occurring benign system calls from goodware applications using the TF-IDF method. We found that certain system calls like *unlink()*, *mkdir()*, *chmod()* are frequently invoked by the benign application. Our attack is similar to the attack as mentioned in [15]. We carefully selected the benign applications that are having the most frequent benign system call counts and then injected those system call sequences to evade the detection. We took 10 malware samples from each of the malware family and made a test set of 270 system call injected malware samples and 270 benign samples. Table 7 shows how the detection accuracy is reduced.

Table 5. Android malware familes

SI No	Android malware family	Obfuscation	Malware type
1	Andrup	String encryption, renaming	Adware
2	GoldDream	Repackaging, string encryption, native payload	Backdoor
3	Boxer	Renaming, string encryption	Trojan-SMS
4	FakeTimer	–	Trojan
5	Lotoor	Renaming, dynamic loading	HackerTool
6	Rumms	String encryption, renaming, dynamic loading	Trojan-SMS
7	NandroBox	Repackaging	Trojan
8	MMarketPay	Renaming	Trojan
9	Penetho	–	Exploit
10	Mercor	–	Trojan
11	FakeDoc	Renaming	Trojan
12	FakePlayer	Renaming	Trojan
13	Vidro	–	Trojan SMS
14	Tesbo	Repackaging, string encryption, renaming	Trojan
15	AndroRat	–	Backdoor
16	Mseg	Repackaging, renaming	Trojan
17	SpyBubble	–	Trojan
18	MobileTX	–	Trojan
19	Zitmo	Renaming	Trojan
20	Lnk	–	Trojan
21	FakeDoc	Renaming	Trojan

Table 6. Performance of [44] before the attack

TPR	FPR	TNR	FNR	Accuracy	Precision	Recall	F-measure
0.971	0.041	0.959	0.029	0.965	0.959	0.971	0.965

Table 7. Performance of [44] after the attack

TPR	FPR	TNR	FNR	Accuracy	Precision	Recall	F-measure
0.400	0.00	1.00	0.600	0.700	1.00	0.400	0.571

7 Conclusion and Future Work

In this paper, we showed that how an adversary can evade the static and dynamic Android malware detection mechanism employed by some of the state of the art machine learning models. We showed that by injecting only a few number of features, adversaries can induce misclassification. In future, we plan to model a limited knowledge attack and a blackbox attack to evade the system call and opcode based malware detection mechanisms. This is to explore how the adversary evades the detection model with less or no knowledge about the classifier. We also plan to develop suitable mechanisms to detect adversarial malware.

References

1. A guide to malware detection techniques and beyond. https://www.cynet.com/blog/a-guide-to-malware-detection-techniques-av-ngav-and-beyond/. Accessed 08 Sept 2020
2. Machine learning methods for malware detection. https://media.kaspersky.com/en/enterprise-security/Kaspersky-Lab-Whitepaper-Machine-Learning.pdf. Accessed 08 Oct 2020
3. Mcafee mobile threat report 2020. https://www.mcafee.com/content/dam/consumer/en-us/docs/2020-Mobile-Threat-Report.pdf. Accessed 08 Sept 2020
4. Securing against malware using artificial intelligence. https://www.nortonlifelock.com/blogs/feature-stories/securing-against-malware-using-artificial-intelligence. Accessed 08 Oct 2020
5. Abaid, Z., Kaafar, M.A., Jha, S.: Quantifying the impact of adversarial evasion attacks on machine learning based android malware classifiers. In: 2017 IEEE 16th International Symposium on Network Computing and Applications (NCA), pp. 1–10. IEEE (2017)
6. Alam, M.S., Vuong, S.T.: Random forest classification for detecting android malware. In: 2013 IEEE international conference on green computing and communications and IEEE Internet of Things and IEEE Cyber, Physical and Social Computing, pp. 663–669. IEEE (2013)
7. Alazab, M., et al.: A hybrid wrapper-filter approach for malware detection. J. Netw. **9**(11), 2878–2891 (2014)
8. Alazab, M., Alazab, M., Shalaginov, A., Mesleh, A., Awajan, A.: Intelligent mobile malware detection using permission requests and API calls. Future Gen. Comput. Syst. **107**, 509–521 (2020)
9. Alexander Chistyakov, A.A.: Ai under attack. https://media.kaspersky.com/en/business-security/enterprise/machine-learning-cybersecurity-whitepaper.pdf. Accessed 08 Oct 2020
10. Amd: http://amd.arguslab.org/ (2015)
11. Arp, D., Spreitzenbarth, M., Gascon, H., Rieck, K., Siemens, C.: Drebin: Effective and explainable detection of android malware in your pocket (2014)
12. Arshad, S., Shah, M.A., Wahid, A., Mehmood, A., Song, H., Yu, H.: Samadroid: a novel 3-level hybrid malware detection model for android operating system. IEEE Access **6**, 4321–4339 (2018)
13. Azab, A., Alazab, M., Aiash, M.: Machine learning based botnet identification traffic. In: 2016 IEEE Trustcom/BigDataSE/ISPA, pp. 1788–1794. IEEE (2016)

14. Barth, B.: Coronavirus app locks android screens with repackaged malware. https://www.scmagazine.com/home/security-news/cybercrime/about-corona-virus-app-locks-android-screens-with-repackaged-malware/, https://www.scmagazine.com/home/security-news/ cybercrime/about-coronavirus-app-locks-android-screens-with-repackaged-malware/. Accessed 08 Sept 2020
15. Bhandari, S., Panihar, R., Naval, S., Laxmi, V., Zemmari, A., Gaur, M.S.: Sword: semantic aware android malware detector. J. Inf. Secur. Appl. **42**, 46–56 (2018)
16. Canfora, G., De Lorenzo, A., Medvet, E., Mercaldo, F., Visaggio, C.A.: Effectiveness of opcode ngrams for detection of multi family android malware. In: 2015 10th International Conference on Availability, Reliability and Security, pp. 333–340. IEEE (2015)
17. Canfora, G., Medvet, E., Mercaldo, F., Visaggio, C.A.: Detecting android malware using sequences of system calls. In: Proceedings of the 3rd International Workshop on Software Development Lifecycle for Mobile, pp. 13–20 (2015)
18. Chen, L., Hou, S., Ye, Y.: Securedroid: enhancing security of machine learning-based detection against adversarial android malware attacks. In: Proceedings of the 33rd Annual Computer Security Applications Conference, pp. 362–372 (2017)
19. Chen, S., et al.: Automated poisoning attacks and defenses in malware detection systems: An adversarial machine learning approach. Comput. Secur. **73**, 326–344 (2018)
20. Chen, T., Mao, Q., Yang, Y., Lv, M., Zhu, J.: Tinydroid: a lightweight and efficient model for android malware detection and classification. Mob. Inf. Syst. **2018** (2018)
21. Chen, X., et al.: Android HIV: a study of repackaging malware for evading machine-learning detection. IEEE Trans. Inf. Forensics Secur. **15**, 987–1001 (2019)
22. Contagio: http://contagiodump.blogspot.com/ (2015)
23. Demontis, A., et al.: Yes, machine learning can be more secure! a case study on android malware detection. IEEE Trans. Depend. Secur. Comput. (2017)
24. Diao, W., Liu, X., Li, Z., Zhang, K.: Evading android runtime analysis through detecting programmed interactions. In: Proceedings of the 9th ACM Conference on Security & Privacy in Wireless and Mobile Networks, pp. 159–164 (2016)
25. Dimjašević, M., Atzeni, S., Ugrina, I., Rakamaric, Z.: Evaluation of android malware detection based on system calls. In: Proceedings of the 2016 ACM on International Workshop on Security And Privacy Analytics, pp. 1–8 (2016)
26. Du, Y., Wang, J., Li, Q.: An android malware detection approach using community structures of weighted function call graphs. IEEE Access **5**, 17478–17486 (2017)
27. Grosse, K., Papernot, N., Manoharan, P., Backes, M., McDaniel, P.: Adversarial perturbations against deep neural networks for malware classification. arXiv preprint arXiv:1606.04435 (2016)
28. Grosse, K., Papernot, N., Manoharan, P., Backes, M., McDaniel, P.: Adversarial examples for malware detection. In: Foley, S.N., Gollmann, D., Snekkenes, E. (eds.) ESORICS 2017. LNCS, vol. 10493, pp. 62–79. Springer, Cham (2017). https://doi.org/10.1007/978-3-319-66399-9_4
29. Gruver, B.: Smali/baksmali tool (2015)
30. Hou, S., Ye, Y., Song, Y., Abdulhayoglu, M.: Hindroid: an intelligent android malware detection system based on structured heterogeneous information network. In: Proceedings of the 23rd ACM SIGKDD International Conference on Knowledge Discovery and Data Mining, pp. 1507–1515 (2017)
31. Íncer Romeo, Í., Theodorides, M., Afroz, S., Wagner, D.: Adversarially robust malware detection using monotonic classification. In: Proceedings of the Fourth ACM International Workshop on Security and Privacy Analytics, pp. 54–63 (2018)

32. John, T.S., Thomas, T.: Adversarial attacks and defenses in malware detection classifiers. In: Handbook of Research on Cloud Computing and Big Data Applications in IoT, pp. 127–150. IGI global (2019)
33. John, T.S., Thomas, T., Emmanuel, S.: Graph convolutional networks for android malware detection with system call graphs. In: 2020 Third ISEA Conference on Security and Privacy (ISEA-ISAP), pp. 162–170. IEEE
34. Lee, J., Kim, J., Kim, I., Han, K.: Cyber threat detection based on artificial neural networks using event profiles. IEEE Access **7**, 165607–165626 (2019)
35. Li, D., Li, Q.: Adversarial deep ensemble: evasion attacks and defenses for malware detection. IEEE Trans. Inf. Forensics Secur. **15**, 3886–3900 (2020)
36. Li, D., Li, Q., Ye, Y., Xu, S.: Sok: Arms race in adversarial malware detection. arXiv preprint arXiv:2005.11671 (2020)
37. Peiravian, N., Zhu, X.: Machine learning for android malware detection using permission and API calls. In: 2013 IEEE 25th international conference on tools with artificial intelligence, pp. 300–305. IEEE (2013)
38. Petsas, T., Voyatzis, G., Athanasopoulos, E., Polychronakis, M., Ioannidis, S.: Rage against the virtual machine: hindering dynamic analysis of android malware. In: Proceedings of the Seventh European Workshop on System Security, pp. 1–6 (2014)
39. Pierazzi, F., Pendlebury, F., Cortellazzi, J., Cavallaro, L.: Intriguing properties of adversarial ml attacks in the problem space. In: 2020 IEEE Symposium on Security and Privacy (SP), pp. 1332–1349. IEEE (2020)
40. Rosenberg, I., Shabtai, A., Rokach, L., Elovici, Y.: Generic black-box end-to-end attack against state of the art API call based malware classifiers. In: Bailey, M., Holz, T., Stamatogiannakis, M., Ioannidis, S. (eds.) RAID 2018. LNCS, vol. 11050, pp. 490–510. Springer, Cham (2018). https://doi.org/10.1007/978-3-030-00470-5_23
41. Sahs, J., Khan, L.: A machine learning approach to android malware detection. In: 2012 European Intelligence and Security Informatics Conference, pp. 141–147. IEEE (2012)
42. Souri, A., Hosseini, R.: A state-of-the-art survey of malware detection approaches using data mining techniques. Hum.-centric Comput. Inf. Sci. **8**(1), 3 (2018)
43. strace: https://strace.io/ (2015)
44. Surendran, R., Thomas, T., Emmanuel, S.: Gsdroid: graph signal based compact feature representation for android malware detection. Expert Syst. Appl. 113581 (2020)
45. Venkatraman, S., Alazab, M.: Use of data visualisation for zero-day malware detection. Secur. Commun. Netw. **2018** (2018)
46. Venkatraman, S., Alazab, M., Vinayakumar, R.: A hybrid deep learning image-based analysis for effective malware detection. J. Inf. Secur. Appli. **47**, 377–389 (2019)
47. Vidas, T., Christin, N.: Evading android runtime analysis via sandbox detection. In: Proceedings of the 9th ACM Symposium on Information, Computer and Communications Security, pp. 447–458 (2014)
48. Vinayakumar, R., Alazab, M., Srinivasan, S., Pham, Q.V., Padannayil, S.K., Simran, K.: A visualized botnet detection system based deep learning for the internet of things networks of smart cities. IEEE Trans. Ind. Appl. (2020)
49. Vinod, P., Zemmari, A., Conti, M.: A machine learning based approach to detect malicious android apps using discriminant system calls. Future Gen. Comput. Syst. **94**, 333–350 (2019)

50. Winsniewski, R.: Android-apktool: A tool for reverse engineering android APK files. **10**, 2020 (2012)
51. Wu, D.J., Mao, C.H., Wei, T.E., Lee, H.M., Wu, K.P.: Droidmat: android malware detection through manifest and API calls tracing. In: 2012 Seventh Asia Joint Conference on Information Security, pp. 62–69. IEEE (2012)
52. Wu, W.C., Hung, S.H.: Droiddolphin: a dynamic android malware detection framework using big data and machine learning. In: Proceedings of the 2014 Conference on Research in Adaptive and Convergent Systems, pp. 247–252 (2014)
53. Yang, W., Kong, D., Xie, T., Gunter, C.A.: Malware detection in adversarial settings: Exploiting feature evolutions and confusions in android apps. In: Proceedings of the 33rd Annual Computer Security Applications Conference, pp. 288–302 (2017)
54. Yerima, S.Y., Sezer, S.: Droidfusion: a novel multilevel classifier fusion approach for android malware detection. IEEE Trans. Cybern. **49**(2), 453–466 (2018)

Multilevel Secure Container Deployment Framework in Edge Computing

Seema Nambiar, Nandakrishna, Chirag Tubakad, Adithya Kiran[✉],
and Subramaniam Kalambur

Computer Science and Engineering, PES University,
Bengaluru, Karnataka, India
adithyakiran1999@gmail.com

Abstract. Large scale distributed IOT applications like smart city, smart building etc. are becoming a reality. The microservice architectural pattern is now becoming common for its ease of development and is also used in edge systems. In order to secure containers, the gVisor container framework is emerging as an alternative to the standard Docker container, but has increased performance overheads in the network stack and file system processing. In this paper, we first characterize the performance of gVisor containers running real programs and demonstrate the loss in performance. Next, we propose a multi-level container deployment framework that chooses the right container framework trading off between performance and security based on the containers use in a microservice application. We demonstrate that using our framework, it is possible to ensure security with a relatively lower impact on performance.

1 Introduction

Various IOT applications like smart city, connected vehicles, smart manufacturing units produce a huge variety and volume of data. Data processing at edge is considered for various practical reasons including low latency requirements, privacy policies and data protection, network bandwidth constraints [1]. Edge devices are mostly resource constrained and heterogeneous in nature. Hence applications like smart city and connected vehicles are feasible only when there are scalable, light-weight architectures in place. Based on these requirements micro-services architecture [2] seems a good fit to build highly distributed applications in the IOT domain. Following this architecture, the IOT applications can consist of a series of micro-services performing specific tasks like data collection, data transformation and data analysis.

Containerization is a light-weight virtualization solution considered for these architectures. But regular containerization like Docker [3] introduces security challenges based on the fact that the containers share the services of the OS

© Springer Nature Singapore Pte Ltd. 2021
S. M. Thampi et al. (Eds.): SSCC 2020, CCIS 1364, pp. 49–61, 2021.
https://doi.org/10.1007/978-981-16-0422-5_4

kernel. Hence additional security mechanisms [4] using Linux security modules (LSM) like SELinux (https://www.redhat.com/en/topics/linux/what-is-selinux), Apparmor (https://apparmor.net/) are applied. A taxonomy for containers security is proposed in [5] which identifies three categories: configuration-based, code based and rules based. They also studied that most of the OS Level frameworks that currently exist to provide container level security is not suitable. These OS level frameworks have limitations since they require administrative access. Also, these frameworks apply to the whole OS and not to a single container and have non-negligible overhead on performance.

gVisor [6] is a container abstraction in which a userspace kernel intercepts and directs the system calls to an internal module called Sentry. File system accesses are performed through another module called Gofer. This improves the security at the expense of size and a performance overhead.

Previous work have demonstrated that gVisor does poorly on performance [7] when running specific micro benchmarks specifically related to file system and networking activity. However, the overall impact on an application's performance has not been studied. In our work we evaluate the suitability of running microservices on Edge systems. Microservices are network intensive and to study the challenges of using gVisor as a secure container in the Edge, we use system oriented benchmarks like Sysbench and Netperf to study overheads of containerization. We further extend the study by benchmarking an application benchmark suite - the DaCapo benchmark. Our studies demonstrate that gVisor based containers running applications are slower by approximately 70% over the standard Docker.

To alleviate this performance issue and ensure security on Edge systems, we propose a mechanism to use a mix of Docker and gVisor container technologies. We demonstrate the benefits of our proposed multilevel container deployment algorithm on the DeathStar microservice benchmark suite.

The rest of the paper is organized as follows. Section 2 discusses previous research on microservices architecture based on containers. We discuss the performance evaluation as well as security aspects that were previously researched using container technologies especially gVisor and Docker. In Sect. 3, we elaborate the proposed Multilevel Framework Algorithm that will be used in our experimental setup to check the right container framework as a trade-off between performance and security. Experimental analysis for both the performance of gVisor containers as well as multilevel container deployment is done in Sect. 4. Finally a summary is presented in Sect. 5.

2   Related Work

2.1   Performance Evaluation

The performance cost of using security oriented container platforms has been explored in [7]. The effect of gVisor's network stack on network throughput as well as the overheads of opening and closing file open, gVisor startup performance, memory efficiency, and system-call overheads has also been explored.

The paper concludes that while gVisor is more secure than Docker, the true cost of containing is high.

Anjali et al. [8] compare the performance of LXC, gVisor and Firecreacker based on how they use functionality in the host kernel. They study linux kernel code hotspots for different workloads on each of these platform. Further, they evaluated the run time cost of each platform using performance benchmarks. Performance results demonstrate that neither gVisor nor Firecracker are best for all workloads; Firecracker has high network latency while gVisor is slower for memory management and network streaming.

2.2 Microservices on IOT Edge Using Containers

IOT Edge is located at the edge of the network close to the IOT devices, as close as one hop to the devices. Edge computing is a computing paradigm which supports the integration of IOT devices with cloud based applications by filtering, aggregating and pre-processing of data using services deployed close to the IOT devices [9].

There have been various studies to use containers in an IOT context and deploying services on the edge as illustrated in the survey on security in microservices based fog applications [10]. They identify data, permission and network vulnerabilities as major challenges. Morabito et al. [11] evaluated the performance of Docker in the context of IOT. The performance has been evaluated using single board computers like Raspberry Pi 2 model B and Raspberry Pi 3 model B. They conclude that using containers does not incur a significant performance impact. However, they have not considered the security aspect in their study. Boudi et al. [12] examine the feasibility of using container-based security solutions in resource constrained edge devices. The performance of Docker container-based Intrusion detection system like Suricata in a real testbed of edge nodes is compared against its performance when running the IDS directly on bare metal. The results show that there is a low overhead of container based security functions with respect to native execution.

New CPU extensions like SGX [13] allow applications to keep their states in enclaves. This prevents privileged software such as the OS and the hypervisor from accessing the data. The state inside the enclave has to be kept small to ensure performance. Fetzer [14] propose a microservice based approach that keeps the state inside the enclaves small. To ensure confidentiality and integrity a secure container has been proposed which runs a single microservice instance in an SGX enclave. This work is based on the availability of SGX and might not work on edge devices with no provisions for SGX extensions.

Qu et al. [15] evaluate several microservice deployment policies. Considering the resource constraints on edge devices, running multiple micro-services in a single container is a possibility although there are operational challenges.

Previous work has demonstrated that some of the security challenges in deploying microservices at the edge can be solved using newer secure container technologies like gVisor and Firecracker however with a performance overhead. Our proposed mechanism, examines the entire microservice application and selectively deploys containers based on their vulnerability which differs from previous approaches to security at the edge.

3 Multilevel Framework Algorithm

In this study the allocation of microservices to gVisor and Docker containers is done as a graph model. This work proposes to use the Depth-first-search algorithm shown in Algorithm 1 to allocate microservices to either the gVisor or Docker container. The aim is to get a good performance measure based on request throughput and data transfer rate along with a feasible security model.

We use a simplified threat model, Fig. 1, where importance is given on securing the outer perimeter services of our application. This is based on the assumption that the services on the outer edge are the ones exposed to the users/clients and are the most vulnerable to attacks, while the inner layer containers are hidden and hence, less likely to be susceptible to attacks. Building up on this, we develop an algorithm to secure our microservice application.

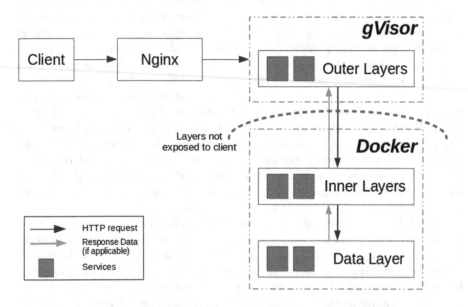

Fig. 1. Simple threat model, where the exposed outer layers are protected with gVisor.

A depth-first-search traversal is performed from the root of the graph model of the microservice application to determine all microservices that are at a depth of d from the *entry-root*. We define the *entry-root* of the graph as first microservice on which the clients request is received. All the microservices that fall within a distance d from the *entry-root* are more vulnerable to attacks from clients and hence, these microservices are allocated gVisor containers while the rest are allocated the standard Docker container. The load balancer/microservice dedicated to forward API calls is treated as the root of the graph from which the traversal is performed. The depth d is determined depending on the required robustness of the security model. Running any microservice in a gVisor container requires no changes to be made to the architecture or source code of the microservice application other than the addition of a runtime flag while building the container. In this study, we evaluated the performance using the social network and media microservice applications for two different depths d of values 1 and 2. Since the load balancer/request forwarding container does no processing we do not consider the case of $d = 0$.

Algorithm 1. Multilevel Framework Algorithm

1: G: Graph of the microservice application
2: *root*: nginx/Load balancer service in application
3: d: depth of service
4: **procedure** DEPTHDETECTION(G, s, d)
5:     $MarkedService[s] \leftarrow d$
6:     mark s as visited
7:     **for** each neighbour i of s in G **do**
8:         **if** i is not visited **then**
9:             DEPTHDETECTION(G, i, $d + 1$)
10:         **end if**
11:     **end for**
12: **end procedure**
13: **procedure** CREATECONTAINER($MarkedServices$, d)
14:     **for** each service s in $MarkedServices$ **do**
15:         **if** $MarkedServices[s] \leq d$ **then**
16:             deploy service s in gVisor
17:         **else**
18:             deploy service s in Docker
19:         **end if**
20:     **end for**
21: **end procedure**
22: DEPTHDETECTION(G, $entry - root$, 0)
23: CREATECONTAINER($MarkedServices$, 2) ▷ Set services in first two layer to gVisor

---

4   Experimental Analysis

4.1   Experimental Setup

The experiments were conducted on an AMD EPYC 7301 16-Core Processor with 64 GB RAM and OS as Ubuntu 18.04.4 LTS.

4.2   Performance of gVisor Containers

gVisor is an application kernel, written in Golang. It provides an additional layer of isolation between running applications and the host operating system essentially sandboxing containers. gVisor intercepts application system calls and acts as the guest kernel, without the need for translation through virtualized hardware. gVisor is more secure than standard Docker container, but the true cost of containing is high [7]. This cost may be a structural cost or an implementation cost. The performance model sections in [6] give us more details on gVisor.

gVisor incurs high latency especially when system and network activity is involved. To validate this we used two benchmarks sysbench (https://github.com/akopytov/sysbench) and netperf (https://hewlettpackard.github.io/netperf/). It was observed that gVisor container was 1.97 times and 2.81 times slower than the docker containers for the download and upload case using Netperf. For sequential and random reads using Sysbench, it was observed that Docker containers are 1.23x and 3.38x the speed of gVisor.

4.3 Security of gVisor Containers

gVisor offers a substantial improvement in security compared to standard Docker containers. This is because it tries to implement a majority of syscalls in its userspace kernel (Sentry) written in golang, it uses a Gofer process for accessing files and other resources and has its own network stack. It employs the principle of defense-in-depth and principle of least privilege [6] to maximise security. The main motivation is to minimise the attack surface of the host system by employing these methods.

gVisor was built to be able to withstand privilege escalation bugs like dirty cow to which Docker was susceptible. We tested gVisor and standard Docker containers for a few exploits like the dirty cow [16] (https://en.wikipedia.org/wiki/Dirty_COW) and privileged container escape using cgroup_release agent function[17] which are privilege escalation exploits to break out of the container. gVisor protects the host from these threats by effectively containing the malicious/vulnerable application whereas standard Docker container runtime has required patches and updates to fix these exploits, and leaves the host system vulnerable. Thus, gVisor is an effective container runtime to protect the host system especially when working with microservice applications.

4.4 Multilevel Container Deployment

Security is a crucial factor when running applications on edge systems that may not be trusted. gVisor offers higher security [6] compared to standard Docker containers. This security is offered at a small price in performance, as discussed earlier. Since Docker containers provide their own security, though not at the level that gVisor does, we try out a number of combinations of Docker and gVisor containers at different levels to test out the microservice applications performance.

We use an open source benchmark suite DeathStarBench [18] which is based on the microservices architecture pattern. It includes multiple applications of which the social network and media services applications will be used for our evaluation.

4.4.1   Microservice Workloads

Social Network. The social network application is a social network with uni-directional flow relationships, implemented with loosely-coupled microservices, communicating with each other via Thrift RPCs (Remote Procedure Calls). The social network application is provided with three different API that can be used to test the performance of the application. However upon closer inspection we see that for the user-timeline service and the home-timeline service the graph is not deep enough to make the mixed configuration that was stated earlier. Only the first layer configuration is supported whereas if we want to further modify it to check performance degradation or up-gradation it is not possible. Hence we choose only the compose post service as a benchmark API to measure the performance of the application. Figure 3 illustrates the compose post API call graph.

Media Microservice. The media microservice application allows users to browse movie information, write reviews and rate movies. The way this architecture works is that the client requests hit the load balancer which distributes the request among multiple nginx servers. Users can log into their account and insert reviews for a specific movie, watch videos and photos related to the movie and browse other information such as plot and cast. All movie reviews are stored as memcached and MongoDB instances. For the media microservices, we have five simple APIs available to us to add and register users and movies, and add plot and cast info for the movies. We also have a review composing service API, to compose reviews for the movies. The review-compose API is our main workload API that we use for performance testing. The architecture of the compose-review service API is shown in Fig. 2.

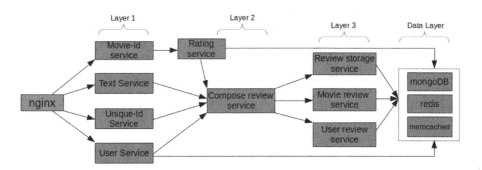

Fig. 2. Media Microservices Compose Movie Review Service Architecture [19]. Each of the services have their own mongoDB, memecached and redis containers.

4.4.2   Evaluation and Analysis

Workloads are generated using the wrk2 [20] library for our DeathStar applications. Wrk2 is a modern HTTP benchmarking tool capable of generating significant load when run on a single multi-core CPU. It combines a multithreaded design with scalable event notification systems such as epoll and kqueue. Wrk2 replaces individual request sample buffers with HdrHistograms. As a result of using HdrHistograms for full (lossless) recording, constant throughput load generation, and accurate tracking of response latency, wrk2's latency reporting is significantly more accurate. Latency refers to the time interval between the moment the request was made and the moment the response was received. This can be used to simulate the latency a visitor would experience on your site when visiting it using a browser or any other method that sends HTTP requests. wrk2 by default outputs two parameters i.e request throughput and data transfer rate. These two parameters are used as metrics for the performance analysis of our applications.

The API calls are all made to the open port on the nginx server which then redirects them to the required services and makes RPC calls to the required services. Various combinations of Docker containers and gVisor containers were used to evaluate the performance of the application. The combinations used were - a) all microservices of the application were the standard Docker container, b) the edge layer microservices were gVisor while the others were the standard Docker container (depth = 1), c) the microservices in the edge layer and its subsequent layer were gVisor while the remaining were the standard Docker container (depth = 2), d) only microservices that are in the data layer (innermost layer consisting of mongodb, redis and memcached containers) were gVisor with remaining being the standard Docker containers, e) all microservices were gVisor containers. The workload generator allows certain parameters like number of parallel connections, number of threads, duration for which requests are generated and the requests per second made to be varied.

Social Network. The social network application has a compose post API that is used for performance testing. As can be observed from the architecture in Fig. 3, it consists of 5 levels and a span of 12 unique nodes. As mentioned above, we tested different combinations of gVisor and Docker containers on the social network microservices application to understand their performance implications while trying to secure them.

All the references to the first layer and second layer has been explicitly mentioned in the graph and it explains the call from one service to another. This

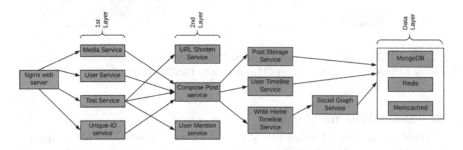

Fig. 3. Compose API call graph for the social media application

forms the basis for us to decide the various adaptive security configurations that we want to implement and test the performance metrics for the same, using our Algorithm 1.

The results were tabulated for only the compose-post API with the different modifications mentioned in the experimental setup section. The graphs were plotted using the same.

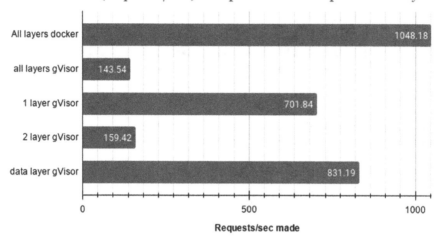

Fig. 4. Comparison of the actual request throughput for a requested throughput of 2000 requests/s for the social networking application

The standard deployment solution is to deploy all the containers with Docker; however, while this is high performance, it is not necessarily the most secure. Based on our approach, where we secure the containers at the frontier, in Fig. 4 and Fig. 5 we observe that we can get additional security without paying too much price in terms of performance.

With this configuration we see the maximum request throughput obtained and as a result has the highest data transfer rate for the social network application. When all the services are run in gVisor containers there is a performance degradation of about 86% which is a very substantial amount. Whereas if we just make the first layer as gVisor and the remaining Docker containers, it seems to perform better with a loss of just 21% compared to the case when all services are run in Docker containers whereas with the data layers services run in gVisor containers we see a loss of just 33%. These results directly translate to the data transfer rate and can be seen in Fig. 5.

Media Services. The media microservice application has a compose-review API that is used for performance testing. As can be observed from the architecture

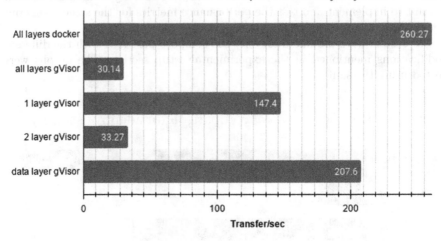

Fig. 5. Comparison of the data transfer rate when workloads are generated on various adaptive layers for the social networking application

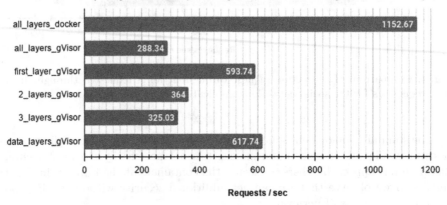

Fig. 6. Request Throughput Comparison of DeathStarBench Media Microservices, for the various combinations of gVisor and Docker Multi-level Container Architecture

in Fig. 2, it consists of 4 levels. As mentioned above, we tested different combinations of gVisor and Docker containers on the media microservices application to understand their performance implications while trying to secure them. The main metrics we obtained were request throughput (requests/sec completed) and data transfer rate (KB/s). The Fig. 6 illustrates the request throughput performance of our various microservice application setups, and Fig. 7 illustrates the data transfer rates comparisons.

Data Transfer Rate Variation With Adaptive Security Layers

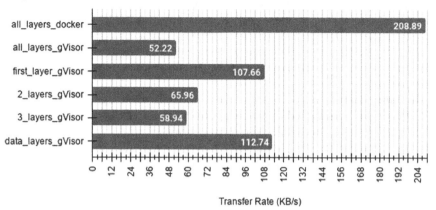

Fig. 7. Data Transfer Rate Comparison of DeathStarBench Media Microservices, for the various combinations of gVisor and Docker containers Multi-level Container Architecture

The initial setup involved running all the microservice application containers in standard Docker containers (using the default runc runtime). This provided us with a high performance microservice architecture application for composing reviews, but is lacking in security. For our security based setup we run all the layers of services in gVisor containers for maximum security. We observe a performance drop of about 75% of that of the initial low security, all Docker container setup, as we compromise performance for increased security.

However, we attempt to find a balance between performance and security by securing levels using our Algorithm 1 to secure only the frontier containers, that are exposed to the clients, based on depth. For depth parameter as one, only the first level of containers were run in gVisor and the rest of the levels were run in standard Docker containers. There was a performance improvement of about 105% of that of all gVisor containers. For depth as two, the first two levels were run in gVisor containers, followed by the remaining levels in standard Docker containers. We observed a performance improvement of 27% of that of all containers in gVisor. In case of media microservices, only the innermost layer, i.e., the data layer was used to store and process data. So finally we run only the data-layer containers in gVisor having all other levels run in Docker containers, with its performance being 115% of the performance when all layers are gVisor. These results are synonymous for both request throughput and data transfer rate as the metrics are directly related.

5 Conclusion and Future Work

Using benchmarks like Sysbench and Netperf it has been shown that gVisor's security enhancements come at a cost of performance. A multi-level microservice applications setup was created wherein a sandbox type gVisor container is used for security at different levels based on the security needs of the application. In this setup we see that security is achievable with a relatively lower impact on performance.

Multilevel containers can be run on edge devices like raspberry pi. The container types can be assigned dynamically based on a security model as well and will be taken up as future work. Also other container technologies like firecracker and kata containers can be used in implementing the multilevel framework algorithm for microservices. Finally we will also be comparing the security of the gVisor and docker containers by hosting untrusted vulnerable applications in the containers.

We are working on a more complex risk assessment procedure to determine the security level of the microservices. The risk assessment will take into account the likelihood and severity of an attack for a particular microservice configuration and make necessary container hosting changes.

References

1. Yousefpour, A., et al.: All one needs to know about fog computing and related edge computing paradigms: a complete survey. J. Syst. Archit. **98**, 289–330 (2019)
2. Fowler, M.: Microservices (2019). https://martinfowler.com/microservices/. Accessed 27 July 2020
3. Docker Documentation. https://docs.docker.com/. Accessed 27 July 2020
4. Combe, T., Martin, A., Di Pietro, R.: To docker or not to docker: a security perspective. IEEE Cloud Comput. **3**(5), 54–62 (2016). https://doi.org/10.1109/MCC.2016.100
5. Bélair, M., Laniepce, S., Menaud, J.M.: Leveraging kernel security mechanisms to improve container security: a survey. In: ACM International Conference Proceeding Series (2019). https://doi.org/10.1145/3339252.3340502
6. gVisor Documentation. https://gvisor.dev/docs/. Accessed 27 July 2020
7. Young, E.G., Zhu, P., Caraza-Harter, T., Arpaci-Dusseau, A.C., Arpaci-Dusseau, R.H.: The true cost of containing: a gvisor case study. In: 11th USENIX Workshop on Hot Topics in Cloud Computing (HotCloud 2019). USENIX Association, Renton, WA (2019). https://www.usenix.org/conference/hotcloud19/presentation/young
8. Anjali, T., Caraza-Harter, M.M.: Swift, blending containers and virtual machines: a study of firecracker and gVisor. In: VEE 2020 - Proceedings of the 16th ACM SIGPLAN/SIGOPS International Conference on Virtual Execution Environments (LXC), pp. 101–113 (2020). https://doi.org/10.1145/3381052.3381315
9. A.Reale, International Business Machines: A guide to edge IoT analytics. https://www.ibm.com/blogs/internet-of-things/edge-iot-analytics
10. Yu, D., Jin, Y., Zhang, Y., Zheng, X.: A survey on security issues in services communication of Microservices-enabled fog applications. Concur. Comput. **31**(22), 1–19 (2019). https://doi.org/10.1002/cpe.4436

11. Morabito, R.: Virtualization on internet of things edge devices with container technologies: a performance evaluation. IEEE Access **5**(c), 8835–8850 (2017). https://doi.org/10.1109/ACCESS.2017.2704444
12. Boudi, A., Farris, I., Bagaa, M., Taleb, T.: Assessing lightweight virtualization for security-as-a-service at the network edge. IEICE Trans. Commun. **E102B**(5), 970–977 (2019). https://doi.org/10.1587/transcom.2018EUI0001
13. Intel®Software Guard Extensions. Intel. Accessed 27 July 2020. https://software.intel.com/content/www/us/en/develop/topics/software-guard-extensions.html
14. Fetzer, C.: Building critical applications using microservices. IEEE Secur. Priv. **14**(6), 86–89 (2016). https://doi.org/10.1109/MSP.2016.129
15. Qu, Q., Xu, R., Nikouei, S.Y., Chen, Y.: An Experimental Study on Microservices based Edge Computing Platforms 1–6 arXiv:2004.02372v1
16. CVE-2016-5195 (2016). https://cve.mitre.org/cgi-bin/cvename.cgi?name=CVE-2016-5195. Accessed 29 Sept 2020
17. Understanding Docker container escapes (2019). https://blog.trailofbits.com/2019/07/19/understanding-docker-container-escapes. Accessed 29 Sept 2020
18. Gan, Y., et al.: An open-source benchmark suite for microservices and their hardware-software implications for cloud & edge systems. In: International Conference on Architectural Support for Programming Languages and Operating Systems - ASPLOS, pp. 3–18 (2019). https://doi.org/10.1145/3297858.3304013
19. Gan, Y., Delimitrou, C.: The architectural implications of cloud microservices. IEEE Comput. Archit. Lett. **17**(2), 155–158 (2018)
20. Tene, G.: Giltene/Wrk2. https://github.com/giltene/wrk2. Accessed 27 Jul 2020

Deep Hierarchical App Recommendation with Dynamic Behaviors

Taiguo Qu[1], Wenjun Jiang[1]([✉]), Dong Liu[1], and Guojun Wang[2]

[1] Hunan University, Changsha, China
{tgqu,jiangwenjun,ld815626}@hnu.edu.cn
[2] Guangzhou University, Guangzhou, China
csgjwang@gzhu.edu.cn

Abstract. Many app recommendation models have been proposed to provide mobile users with the apps that meet their individual needs. However, three main drawbacks limit their performance: (1) Neglect the dynamic change of user preferences in a short time; (2) Singly use either the machining learning or the deep learning method, which cannot learn discrete features or continuous features very well; (3) Directly deal with all apps without considering their hierarchical features. To overcome the above drawbacks, this paper proposes a Dynamic behavior-based age Hierarchy Model (DHM for short). To be specific, we integrate the Boosting Tree and Neural Network, combine the static data as basis and the dynamic behaviors as refinement, and update dynamic behaviors in time to improve the accuracy of personalized app recommendation. Then, this paper proposes a User Hierarchy based personalized App recommendation Model (UHAM for short), it exploits the user attribute layering method to make hierarchical recommendation for users in different age groups, which further enhance the efficiency. We conduct extensive experiments with a real app dataset, and the results validate the effectiveness of our model.

Keywords: App recommendation · Neural Network · Dynamic behaviors · Hierarchical recommendation

1 Introduction

Recommendation plays a pivotal role in providing users with apps that best meet their needs. It has been widely adopted by many online services and so on. Modeling users' preference on apps based on their past interactions (e.g., ratings and clicks [6,8]), known as collaborative filtering [19] is essential to app recommendation. However, users' preferences usually evolve with time, which hasn't been fully addressed, leading to poor performance. In this paper, we strive to propose a comprehensive and lightweight app recommendation model to deal with evolving dynamic user behaviors.

In recommendation system, user information and item information are usually represented as numerical data and category data. For which the model and

S. M. Thampi et al. (Eds.): SSCC 2020, CCIS 1364, pp. 62–76, 2021.
https://doi.org/10.1007/978-981-16-0422-5_5

the neural network are respectively suitable. Therefore, integrating the two models will help to treat the two types of data in recommendation. Although some app recommendation models have been proposed, three main challenges are still open. (1) Neglect the dynamic change of user preferences in a short time; (2) Singly use either the machining learning or the deep learning method, which cannot learn discrete features or continuous features very well; (3) Directly deal with all apps without considering their hierarchical features.

Our Motivation. Keeping the app recommendation task in mind, Our motivation is threefold corresponding to the above three challenges: (1) Deeply exploring the dynamic evolution of user preferences via behavior analysis. (2) Integrated deal with both discrete and continuous, static and dynamic information. (3) Enhance the recommendation efficiency by considering the hierarchical features of users found apps.

In this paper, we extract both dynamic and static information from users, apps, and device usage records. Combining the advantages of deep learning and machine learning models for treating different types of data, the integrated learning method is proposed. Moreover, use the static and dynamic information together, can help improve the accuracy of preference and recommendation.

The main contributions of this work are summarized as follows.

1. We propose the DHM model that combines static basic and dynamic behavioral information about the user to improve the accuracy of the personalized app recommendation system [1].
2. We propose the UHAM model, which recommends personalized apps for different users through correlation and hierarchical analysis of the user and application hierarchy.
3. Through experiments on real dataset, the experimental results verify that our model is more efficient than traditional personalized recommendation models.

2   Related Work

In this section, we briefly review the literature.

2.1   Challenges in Recommendation

Cold-Start [14,15]: (1) The recommendation system is a data greedy application. where the demand for data is not enough. (2) The cold start issues commonly exist in the Recommendation System. (3) When an app is released, there is not much usage data to be used for a personalized recommendation.

Data-Sparsity [7]: The recommendation accuracy has a high requirement for the quality of data. However, what we can get is a very large user-item matrix contains that many missing values or null values. So how to use these data to distill useful data is important for the recommendation system.

Preferences Evolution: Users' preferences usually evolve with time. Therefore, when considering the personalized recommendations, the time series information needs to be taken into account. When users are exposed to new information, friends, advertisements, and promotional information. Therefore, it is necessary to consider the evolution of user preferences. User behaviors can reflect user preference implicitly [9], while user-app ratings explicitly express their preference.

2.2 Personalized Recommendation System

The basis of personalized app recommendation is the personalized recommendation system. The purpose of the personalized recommendation is to accurately dig out the user's personalized preferences, gradually narrow the user's personalized preferences, and at the same time improve the accuracy of recommended items in the preferences.

With the continuous increase in the types and number of apps, we need a personalized recommendation system for the different preferences of different users. The main purpose of app store platform recommendations is to recommend more apps that users like and are likely to buy and to uncover users' real and hidden preferences from information about the platform's apps, users' information, and user behavior. After acquiring the user's information, the user information is processed using the common method of constructing a user profile. After constructing the user profile, the user profile is quantified and then processed using deep learning [12] or machine learning methods, and finally, the effect is measured by the evaluation index of the recommendation system to achieve the purpose of personalized recommendation.

There are three common methods of personalizing app recommendations. The first type is a content-based recommendation [18], the second type is a collaborative filtering-based recommendation [19], and the third type is a hybrid recommendation method that combines the above methods [2].

In the personalized recommendation system, we not only consider common recommendation system evaluation indicators such as accuracy, recall, coverage. But also consider the conversion rate from viewing the app to the final installation of the app after the user clicks on the app and the user's app Click-through rate.

This section introduces the three main problems in the recommendation system and the related work of the user personalized recommendation system. In the APP application platform and the information flow platform, when making recommendations, the selected user information, design models and methods are different, and there will be different degrees of differences according to their actual business. The information flow platform considers the real-time behavior changes of users and the push of real-time information. Therefore, capturing user behavior changes is particularly important in personalized recommendation systems.

3 Data Analysis

3.1 Dataset

The data used in this experiment is the data of Huawei Application Market, which comes from Huawei's algorithm competition[1]. It records the user's behavior, app, and user's basic information, as well as the user's operation information on the mobile phone and app within a month. The dataset contains five parts of data: user basic information, user behavior information, activity data of the app used by the users, and basic information of the app. The composition of the overall dataset is shown in Table 1.

Table 1. Details of the dataset used in experiments

Data	Data description
User_basic_info	User basic info
User_behavior_info	User use app behavior info
User_app_actived	Apps' activity info
User_app_usage	Log of user use app
App_info	App basic info

Through the statistics of the data set, the data set contains 2,500,000 users and 3,000,000 app data. The size of the data set is about 10G. Common methods cannot handle these data well, so we choose to block the data. Then count and process the missing data [16] and abnormal data in the user and app datasets, delete data with missing values greater than 25%, and perform average filling, weighted filling, and random forest filling for data with lower missing values. And perform LabelEncode processing on the categorical data, and convert the categorical data into better processed numerical data [5]. Finally, statistics on the distribution of the data, try to convert the distribution of the data into the form of the normal distribution, to facilitate the use of mathematical processing.

3.2 User Features

The user's information is the key data in the data set, and the basic information of the user and app is basically unchanged, and these data can be processed as static data. The use of apps by users and their behavior on smart mobile devices are constantly changing dynamic information [4], and these data can be treated as dynamic data.

---

[1] https://developer.huawei.com/consumer/cn/activity/digixActivity/Olddigixdetail/712.

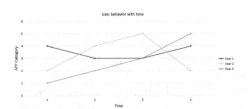
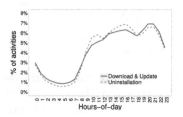

Fig. 1. User like APP category change.   **Fig. 2.** User activities during the day. (Color figure online)

Changes in User Preferences

From Fig. 1, we can see three users' prefer APP category always change with the time. We can get information from this picture. Users' preferences will change in a short time, which is consistent with our common sense of life. We need to grasp the short-term changes of users. On the one hand, we can accurately mine users' preferences, and on the other hand, we can expand users' preferences in the current category of app and increase users' stickiness. People in different time periods have different like APP category. Therefore, we can count the dynamic behavior [1] information of users in a period of time to mine the recent preferences of users, so that we can recommend users' favorite apps.

User's Actions on the App

We then look at how the users manage their apps throughout a day. Figure 2 plots the percentages of user activities over 24 h of a day. The common sense assumes that a download and an updating activity reflect a user's preference towards an app and an uninstallation indicates that the user is not in favor of the app. We thus aggregate downloading and updating activities (solid, blue line) in this plot and compare them with uninstallations (dashed, red line).

3.3 App Features

We start with the distributions of the popularity of apps. The popularity of an app can be measured using either the total number of downloads, the most recently downloads (e.g., in the past week or month), or the total number of users. When an app is rarely rated, a marketplace usually provide such a popularity measure as an indicator of the quality of the app. Figure 3 plots the distribution of the number of users per app (i.e., number of devices on which at least one activity of that app has been logged). The popularity of apps follows a typical Power Law distribution on this log-log plot. More than 95% apps are downloaded by less than 1,000 devices. A few apps are downloaded by millions of devices. This distribution is consistent with observations in many other behavior data at the population level, which usually indicate an effect of "rich get richer" . Indeed, the highly-ranked apps may attract even more users while barely-rated apps are buried in the long tail. Similarly, the number of ratings an app receives

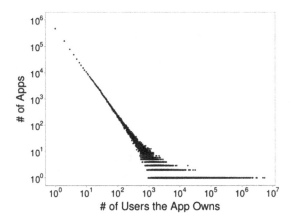

Fig. 3. The user use APPs distribution.

also presents a typical power law distribution, which we omit here for the sake of space.

In the experiment of verifying the model, we have a collection of users using the APP, but there is no text information. We treat these collections as textual information for the user, using methods that process textual data. By segmenting these data, the word vector is trained, and finally the set of APPs for each user is formed into a high-dimensional vector.

4   The Hierarchical App Recommendation Model

We design two models to realize user personalized app recommendation, one is an age group prediction model based on user's basic information and behavior information, and the other is a personalized app recommendation model based on user hierarchical results obtained from the first model.

4.1   Dynamic Hierarchy Model

In this section, we design the DHM to predict the age of users based on their dynamic behavior and basic information. Users of different ages have different preferences, and recommendations for users of different levels are beneficial to improve the performance of the model [17].

Data Processing
In the data analysis, it is found that the data in the data set is divided into numerical and categorical data. Since numerical data is suitable for processing using traditional machine learning methods, and categorical data is suitable for processing using neural network models, we consider using a fusion model for processing.

We use GBDT (Gradient Boosting Decision Tree) [11,13] to analyze the importance of features for static data so that we can select important features for the model.

We use the embedding method to deal with category data and dynamic user behavior data. Embedding is the low-dimensional dense representation of a high-dimensional sparse vector and can denote as follows:

$$E_{Vi}(x_i) = embedding\_select(V_i, x_i) \ . \tag{1}$$

Where x_i is the value of i-th feature, V_i stores all embeddings of the i-th feature and can be learned by back-propagation, and $E_{Vi}(x_i)$ will return the corresponding embedding vector for x_i.

Framework of the DHM Model

We use the age of the user as the predicted label value. Use different models to process different types of data, use GBDT and LightGBM [10] model to process numerical static data, and use Embedding and Neural Network to process category-based user dynamic behavior information data, the integrated learning method is used to weight the results of the two models to calculate the corresponding age group value. The structure of the model is shown in Fig. 4.

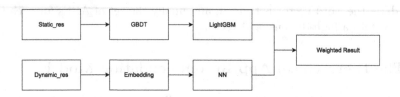

Fig. 4. The framework of the proposed DHM model.

The results of the two parts of the model are respectively predicted and output, and then the obtained age values are weighted and summed. The formula is as follows:

$$Result = \lambda * Static\_res + (1 - \lambda) * Dynamic\_res \ . \tag{2}$$

λ represents the output weight of the result, with a value between 0 and 1. $Static\_res$ represents the model processing result of static behavior, and $Dynamic\_res$ represents the model processing result of dynamic behavior. The two results are weighted and summed to finally get the user's age group prediction result.

4.2 User Hierarchy Based Personalized App Recommendation Model

Based on the dynamic behavior information and the age hierarchy prediction model in the previous section, we design the UHAM.

User-App Preference

When making personalized recommendations for apps based on user hierarchy, it is necessary to build a user's rating for the app. Because the rating data is sparse or missing, so it's necessary to construct corresponding tags as the evaluation criteria, so proposed the value of user preference for apps. As the label of the data, the user's preference for the app is constructed according to the user's app operating behavior and time, and finally achieves the purpose of the personalized hierarchical recommendation of the app. We selected 50 million users' preference data for the app to make personalized recommendations. The definition formula for preference is as follows:

$$Pref(user, app) = W_1 * duration\_value + W_2 * times\_value . \qquad (3)$$

$duration\_value$ represents the total time of user use the app. $times\_value$ represents the number of times the user operates the app. $Pref$ represents the value of user's preference for the app. W_i represents the weight value corresponding to feature i. The weight value is set from the data of the judgment of the importance of the corresponding feature in the dataset. GBDT is used as the model for feature importance selection. Finally, the value of W_1 is set to 0.3 and the value of W_2 is set to 0.7.

Framework of the UHAM Model

To extract the hierarchical matching features between users and apps, the corresponding features are extracted from the existing user data and app data. The static and dynamic feature data of users are extracted, and the feature data of the app is extracted at the same time. These features are extracted as the input features of the model. The feature introduction is shown in Table 2.

Table 2. Feature of user and app hierarchy matching

User static features	User dynamic features	App features
User age	Download and install of app	App category
User gender	Operation of equipment	App version
User equipment model	App usage time	App attribute

We propose a personalized app recommendation model based on user hierarchy. First, construct the input data information of the model. Second, preprocess the data. Third, combine user age hierarchy and app hierarchical information to construct the required dataset. Finally, combine users of each age group with corresponding apps and app types to achieve the role of the hierarchical association. The flow chart of the model is shown in Fig. 5.

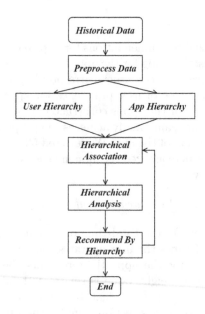

Fig. 5. The process of UHAM model.

The amount of data in the feature table is relatively large. After matching the app data, the magnitude of the data will be relatively large. Therefore, it is necessary to consider using a model that can be processed in parallel and has a faster computing speed to process these data. XGBoost optimizes based on the traditional decision tree model and adds regular terms for a penalty, which can realize parallel training and supports column sampling, which can reduce overfitting and reduce calculation. Therefore, XGBoost is selected as the core model of regression prediction in UHAM.

5 Experiments

In this section, we will perform experimental validation of each of the two models and compare them with several widely used baseline models. In particular, we will present the details of the experimental setup, including the models compared, and some specific experimental settings. Finally, we will analyze the performance of the models to demonstrate their validity and advantages over the baseline models. This experiment uses a dataset from the Huawei Application Market.

5.1 Experiments on DHM

Value of λ. This model obtains the final result by weighting and summing the two parts of the output. Because this model mainly considers the influence of dynamic behavior information, the weight of the model for dynamic data processing is higher. Through many experiments, it is found that the predicted value weight of the neural network model is set to 0.7, and the predicted value weight of the tree model for processing static data is 0.3, a better prediction result can be obtained.

Experiments Setup Baselines: we compare DHM with the following baseline models:

1. LR, which is Logistic Regression, a generalized linear model.
2. Wide&Deep [3], which combines a shallow linear model with a deep neural network.
3. LightGBM [10], which is a widely used tree-based learning algorithm for modeling tabular data.
4. DHM(ND), which only uses the NN model to deal with dynamic data.
5. DHM, which is the framework in this paper to deal with static data and dynamic user data.

Experiments Results
In this experiment, we choose two multi-category evaluation index Kappa and Hamming_distance. Because binary classification regulation not suitable for multi-classification. The coefficient of Kappa was based on confusion matrix calculation.

$$Kappa = \frac{P_o - P_e}{1 - P_e} \ . \tag{4}$$

P_o represents the total classification accuracy. P_e represents the sum(P_e was calculated by the number of samples * the number of samples)/sample total square. When the Kappa value was close to 1, it means the model result was correct.

$$Hamming\_distance(\hat{y}_i, y_i) = \frac{1}{L} p \sum_{j=1}^{L} l(\hat{y}_{ij} \neq y_{ij}) \ . \tag{5}$$

The value of $Hamming\_distance$ represents different meanings. Smaller distance values represent better classification accuracy. $\hat{y}_{ij}$ represents the y_{ij} label predict value. y_{ij} represents the true value of label i. L was the number of labels. $l(x)$ was indicator function. The distance is 0 when the prediction result is completely consistent with the actual result when the distance is close to 1, it means the prediction result is completely inconsistent with the actual value.

Table 3. Model in experiments

Model	Acc	Kappa	Hamming
LR	0.69	0.22823	0.57569
Wide& Deep	0.57	0.36567	0.48703
LightGBM	0.65	0.23620	0.57534
DHM(ND)	0.60	0.34521	0.45732
DHM	0.89	0.70585	0.20345

The overall comparison results could be found in Table 3. From the table, we know that the dynamic hierarchical model proposed in this paper is 29% more accurate than the DHM (ND) model lacking dynamic behavior information, and the Kappa index for multi-classification is 35% higher than that of deep learning. Wide&Deep model, the accuracy rate increased by 30%, Kappa, and Hamming increased by 34% and 28%. The addition of dynamic behavior information can greatly improve accuracy.

5.2   Experiments on UHAM

This model combines the prediction results of DHM to make personalized app recommendations for users of different ages. By processing users of six age groups, the effect of personalized app recommendation is realized. The data set contains one month's usage data of users in the app store. When dividing the data set, select the user's data for the first 21 days for training, and select the data for the next 10 days as the data for testing and prediction.

Experiments Setup

Baselines: we compare UHAM with the following baseline models:

1. UserCF, which is a user-based collaborative filtering method that recommends apps that may be of interest to users by calculating the similarity between their favorite apps.
2. UserCF-IIF, which counts the most popular apps among users according to their similarity of interest, and penalizes the similarity, which can reduce the influence of popular apps on the similarity among users.
3. ItemCF, which recommends to users the most similar apps to their favorite apps. It mainly calculates the similarity between apps through user behavior.
4. MostPopular, which calculates which apps users are most likely favorite based on popularity among apps.

In the UHAM model, the learning rate, tree depth, and leaf node weights are chosen to be tuned, and the step size of the parameter selection is set in the grid search. The accuracy eventually peaks at a learning rate of 0.6, a tree depth of 40, and a leaf node weight of 7, and the model parameters at this point are used as the optimal model parameters.

The algorithm uses the Top-K recommendation method to measure the effect of recommending the top K apps to users. Therefore, the best top K apps are selected from all the apps preferred by the user by setting different values of K and measuring the effect of the value of K on the effect of the model through experimentation. Through experimentation, it is finally determined that the model has the highest accuracy when K is 10.

Experimental Results

We use six common collaborative filtering methods for comparison. We choose precision, recall, coverage, popularity to measure the model result.

$$precision = \frac{|hits|}{|preset|} \; . \tag{6}$$

Accuracy correlates the number of recommended apps to users with the number of apps that users themselves like and measures whether the recommended apps are real apps that users like.

$$recall = \frac{|hits|}{|testset|} \; . \tag{7}$$

The recall is the proportion of all true positive classes that are predicted as positive classes.

$$coverage = \frac{|U_{u \in U} R(U)|}{|I|} \; . \tag{8}$$

In the formula of coverage ratio, the user collection is U, the recommended products $R(U)$ for user U, and I represents the total number of products. Coverage rate mainly reflects the recommending system's ability to recommend long-tail data, in simple terms, it is the ratio of recommended apps to all the apps that users like.

$$popularity = \frac{|U_{u \in U} R(U)|}{|P|} \; . \tag{9}$$

In the popularity formula, P represents all currently popular apps, U represents the set of users, $R(U)$ represents the apps recommended to users and finally calculates the popularity of apps recommended to users. The popularity is used to measure the percentage of the recommended apps among the popular app, the higher the value indicates the more popular the recommended app is, the better recommendation will be.

Based on the hierarchical recommendation result, we build a rating matrix between users and apps. From the experimental results in the table below, we can see that the overall indicators of the app-based collaborative filtering method are more stable and accurate than others.

Therefore, we can get the final conclusion. Based on the layered strategy and the model that takes into account changes in user behavior, we can more accurately obtain the results of personalized recommendations. After stratified processing based on user age, we obtain a list of apps that users of different age levels like and use collaborative filtering methods to measure the effect of our adoption of stratification, which proves that our stratification and changes in user dynamic behavior have improved personalized app recommendations effect.

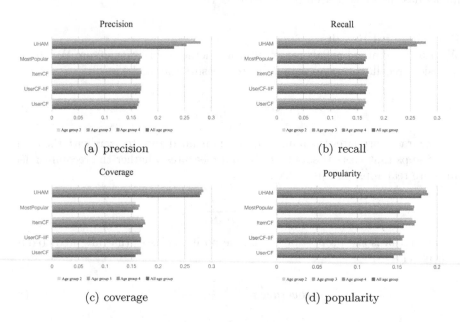

Fig. 6. Comparison of different models.

Based on the analysis of the experimental results, it is found that when making personalized app recommendations based on user hierarchy, the dynamic behavioral information of users and the user-app relationship are used. In the Fig. 6, the proposed UHAM model is compared with the closest method, UserCF-IIF, and the accuracy is improved by about 10%. Comparing the UHAM model proposed in this chapter with the closest method, UserCF-IIF, the accuracy increases by about 10%, the recall rate increases by about 10%, the coverage rate increases by about 12%, and the popularity increases by about 7%. If we compare it with UserCF-IIF, the accuracy rate increases by 10%, recall rate increases by 12%, coverage increases by 13%, and popularity increases by 7%. The comparison results between different models are shown in Fig. 3. Therefore, from the above experimental results, we can see that the personalized app recommendation model based on user hierarchy is more effective than the personalized recommendation method based on collaborative filtering. The performance of the personalized recommendation model can be greatly enhanced by capturing dynamic behavioral information about users and making hierarchical recommendations to them.

6   Conclusion and Future Work

This paper proposes a hierarchical recommendation method for personalized apps based on deep learning. In this paper, the DHM model is proposed to mine the dynamic behavior information of users to obtain the changing app preference information of users. The dynamic behavior information and static information are processed by different models in the way of model integration, and then the output results are given different weights to improve the accuracy of user age stratification. This paper also proposes a UHAM model based on the DHM model, which mines the hierarchical relationship between users and the app based on the hierarchical prediction results of the DHM model. By matching and associating the hierarchical relationship, the fine-grained preference information of users to the app can be more accurately mined. At the same time, this paper uses a neural network to process the changing user behavior information and uses batch processing operation to mine the changing user behavior information.

Compared with the traditional recommendation method based on the basic information of users and apps, the proposed method can capture users' personalized preferences and greatly improve the effect of personalized app recommendation.

Acknowledgment. This research was supported by NSFC grant 61632009, Guangdong Provincial NSF Grant 2017A030308006, the science and technology program of Changsha city kq2004017 and Open project of Zhejiang Lab 2019KE0AB02.

References

1. Agichtein, E., Brill, E., Dumais, S.: Improving web search ranking by incorporating user behavior information. In: Proceedings of the 29th Annual International ACM SIGIR Conference on Research and Development in Information Retrieval, pp. 19–26 (2006)
2. Burke, R.: Hybrid recommender systems: survey and experiments. User Model. User-Adapted Interact. **12**(4), 331–370 (2002)
3. Cheng, H.T., et al.: Wide & deep learning for recommender systems. In: Proceedings of the 1st Workshop on Deep Learning for Recommender Systems, pp. 7–10 (2016)
4. Church, K., Ferreira, D., Banovic, N., Lyons, K.: Understanding the challenges of mobile phone usage data. In: Proceedings of the 17th International Conference on Human-Computer Interaction with Mobile Devices and Services, pp. 504–514 (2015)
5. Dorogush, A.V., Ershov, V., Gulin, A.: Catboost: gradient boosting with categorical features support. arXiv preprint arXiv:1810.11363 (2018)
6. Graepel, T., Candela, J.Q., Borchert, T., Herbrich, R.: Web-scale bayesian clickthrough rate prediction for sponsored search advertising in microsoft's bing search engine. Omnipress (2010)
7. Grčar, M., Mladenič, D., Fortuna, B., Grobelnik, M.: Data sparsity issues in the collaborative filtering framework. In: Nasraoui, O., Zaïane, O., Spiliopoulou, M., Mobasher, B., Masand, B., Yu, P.S. (eds.) WebKDD 2005. LNCS (LNAI), vol. 4198, pp. 58–76. Springer, Heidelberg (2006). https://doi.org/10.1007/11891321_4

8. Guo, H., Tang, R., Ye, Y., Li, Z., He, X.: Deepfm: a factorization-machine based neural network for CTR prediction. arXiv preprint arXiv:1703.04247 (2017)

9. He, X., Zhang, H., Kan, M.Y., Chua, T.S.: Fast matrix factorization for online recommendation with implicit feedback. In: Proceedings of the 39th International ACM SIGIR Conference on Research and Development in Information Retrieval, pp. 549–558 (2016)

10. Ke, G., et al.: Lightgbm: a highly efficient gradient boosting decision tree. In: Advances in Neural Information Processing Systems, pp. 3146–3154 (2017)

11. Ke, G., Xu, Z., Zhang, J., Bian, J., Liu, T.Y.: Deepgbm: a deep learning framework distilled by gbdt for online prediction tasks. In: Proceedings of the 25th ACM SIGKDD International Conference on Knowledge Discovery & Data Mining, pp. 384–394 (2019)

12. LeCun, Y., Bengio, Y., Hinton, G.: Deep learning. Nature **521**(7553), 436–444 (2015)

13. Liao, Z., Huang, Y., Yue, X., Lu, H., Xuan, P., Ju, Y.: In silico prediction of gamma-aminobutyric acid type-A receptors using novel machine-learning-based SVM and GBDT approaches. BioMed. Res. Int. **2016** (2016)

14. Lika, B., Kolomvatsos, K., Hadjiefthymiades, S.: Facing the cold start problem in recommender systems. Expert Syst. Appl. **41**(4), 2065–2073 (2014)

15. Lin, J., Sugiyama, K., Kan, M.Y., Chua, T.S.: Addressing cold-start in app recommendation: latent user models constructed from twitter followers. In: Proceedings of the 36th International ACM SIGIR Conference on Research and Development in Information Retrieval, pp. 283–292. SIGIR '2013, Association for Computing Machinery, New York, NY, USA (2013). https://doi.org/10.1145/2484028.2484035

16. Little, R.J., Rubin, D.B.: Statistical Analysis with Missing Data, vol. 793. John Wiley & Sons, Hoboken (2019)

17. Liu, D., Jiang, W.: Personalized app recommendation based on hierarchical embedding. In: 2018 IEEE SmartWorld, Ubiquitous Intelligence & Computing, Advanced & Trusted Computing, Scalable Computing & Communications, Cloud & Big Data Computing, Internet of People and Smart City Innovation (SmartWorld/SCALCOM/UIC/ATC/CBDCom/IOP/SCI), pp. 1323–1328. IEEE (2018)

18. Pazzani, M.J., Billsus, D.: Content-based recommendation systems. The Adaptive Web, pp. 325–341. Springer, Berlin (2007)

19. Sarwar, B., Karypis, G., Konstan, J., Riedl, J.: Item-based collaborative filtering recommendation algorithms. In: Proceedings of the 10th International Conference on World Wide Web, pp. 285–295 (2001)

New Security Architecture of Access Control in 5G MEC

Zbigniew Kotulski$^{(\boxtimes)}$ ⓘ, Wojciech Niewolski ⓘ, Tomasz W. Nowak ⓘ,
and Mariusz Sepczuk ⓘ

Faculty of Electronics and Information Technology, Warsaw University
of Technology, Warsaw, Poland
{z.kotulski,w.niewolski,t.nowak,m.sepczuk}@tele.pw.edu.pl

Abstract. The currently developed 5G networks using MEC technology
(5G MEC) allow for the harmonious cooperation of many areas of the
economy (called the vertical industries) within an integrated information
network. Providing the necessary security in such a complex configuration of business partners requires the design of consistent and effective
security architecture. In this paper, we present a new concept of an access
control architecture for the 5G MEC network in line with the 5G network
model and MEC architecture proposed by international standardization
organizations. We give an overview of the high-level security architecture of 5G MEC networks, which provides security solutions for the
network's components and establishes secure access to all cooperating
entities. Next, we introduce the MEC Enabler, a new network's module,
which manages security credentials required to access resources of MEC-
hosted services. We consider a series of several use cases with increasing demands on network data resources and computing power. Finally,
we present a sample protocol diagram for gaining access to resources
(authentication in a service using MEC technology) in our access control
architecture.

Keywords: 5G mobile networks · MEC · Access control · Security
architecture · MEC Enabler

1 Introduction

5G mobile networks requirements assume very high-quality parameters of communication, including low latency, high data rate (area and peak), high efficiency
(spectral and energy), and network reliability and availability, see [1]. To achieve
high-quality network connections, new technological radio transmission solutions
and effective solid links are being expected. However, the software solutions used
to make the mobile network easy to configure and adapted to the needs of different users are equally important. Thus, the Software Defined Networks (SDN)

This paper has been supported by The National Center for Research and Development,
Poland, under Decision No. DWM/POLTAJ7/9/2020.

and Network Functions Virtualization (NFV) technologies, extensively used in modern communication networks, became the pillars of the contemporary mobile networks, see [2]. The third pillar of the fifth-generation mobile networks, with the greatest impact on the quality parameters of the network, is the Multi-access Edge Computing (MEC) technology [3]. Its present specification [4] enables the coexistence of edge computing platforms designed with different specifications. Using edge servers in 5G MEC networks intends to shift an IT (Information Technology) service environment and cloud-computing capabilities to the edge of the mobile network to reduce latency and improve network operation and service delivery. Such a MEC-supported mobile network makes it possible to serve 5G virtual industries (see [5]) with a unified technological platform. MEC servers support various applications offered by service providers for vertical industries of the 5G mobile network [6]. These applications can belong either, to owners of verticals, or external MEC-hosted services providers.

As it is seen, the fifth-generation mobile network integrated with the Multi-access Edge Computing technology (5G MEC) combines many subjects and objects implementing complex business ventures requiring high-quality communication. A dedicated security protection system is an indispensable condition of the proper functioning of such a complicated network structure, where coexist and cooperate many entities: network infrastructure providers, mobile network operators, service providers, and end-users [7]. In the literature, can find many security models and security recommendations for 5G networks. Some of them are extensions of the cellular networks' security solutions to modern mobile networks (5G), see e.g., [8], some other are security recommendations or specifications proposed by worldwide network operators or communication equipment manufacturers, see e.g., [9]. There are also research papers proposing new security solutions dedicated to 5G mobile networks with MEC technology and using the latest proposals increasing the flexibility of solutions and the possible achieved level of security (see e.g., paper [10], where contextual security approach to 5G MEC is considered).

Another aspect of the 5G MEC networks' security solutions is integrating tools and methods dedicated to modern networking technologies applied to constitute 5G networks. Thus, the secure links based on the SDN infrastructure (see e.g., [11]) or complete network authentication and traffic protection systems (see [12]) can be applied to protect the network's data plane. For specific network areas assigned to users or services, the secure slices (see e.g., [13]) with a high isolation level (see [14]) could be used. Finally, the cloud-dedicated security solutions help in access to external or service-assigned private resources (see e.g., [15,16]). These particular solutions can protect some areas of the network or increase the security of the network services. However, to obtain a network solution which can be called the network security architecture, one must realize a consistent sequence of steps, from a complete 5G network security architecture, defining all entities and relations among them (see, e.g., [17]), to detailed specifications of network security protocols, authenticating communication parties, and establishing secure links (see, e.g., [18]).

The purpose of this paper is to propose a new security architecture for access control in 5G MEC networks, which would be communication technology-independent, neutral due to the security policies applicable to all parties using the network and consistent with the applicable network standards. The architecture must be compatible with 5G proposed standards and integrated with MEC technology. It should also allow service providers to apply their own security policies for access control. Our approach extends the considerations of the work [19], which proposed a domain-based approach to online security and authentication. The authors of [19] proposed security areas related to network authentication protocols and secure access to services (six domains describing the security requirements between different components of the network) and security areas covering network areas (two domains covering network slices and UE-User Equipment). In our approach we have added two more network domains (the MEC server and a cloud) and have modified the other security domains, especially introducing a new module (MEC Enabler) responsible for security credentials management for the whole 5G MEC network. Our architecture is compatible with Attribute-Based Access Control (ABAC) or Policy-Based Access Control (PBAC), see [20], which solves many problems on the interface of all 5G-MEC network-involved partners. It is also suitable for modern IT technologies and 5G vertical industries [21].

The rest of the paper is organized as follows. Section 2 introduces the high-level security architecture of access control, network stakeholders involved in the 5G MEC network, and its domains of security. Section 3 lists five use cases of MEC-based services depending on the size of the network resources required by an end-user. Section 4 specifies the credentials management scheme and introduces the MEC Enabler module, which is the crucial component of our security solution. Section 5 gives several examples of security protocols realizing the use cases proposed in Sect. 3. Section 6 concludes the paper and gives an overview of possible extensions and more detailed specifications of the security solution proposed in this paper.

2 The High-Level Security Architecture of Access Control

In the 5G MEC framework, several stakeholders exist, which are interested in access control solutions. The main parties are:

- End-Users: all users that are using or will use the 5G MEC environment for consuming services.
- Service Providers: all organizations that are deploying solutions into MEC hosts. Most of them are delivering MEC applications that might run in multiple instances even on a single MEC host server. Additionally, there is a set of MEC services hosted within the MEC Platform which also might support multi-tenancy.

- Network Providers: physical (MNO - Mobile Network Operator) and virtual (MVNO - Mobile Virtual Network Operator) operators that provide the radio access layer and/or the connectivity with external networks.
- MEC Providers: organizations that enable the MEC environment for 5G networks hosted by Network Providers.

With those parties we have many access control relationships that were described in Table 1. Relationships marked with ⋆ might use the MEC Enabler component for executing the access control process.

Table 1. Relationship between stakeholders. The columns specify stakeholders, which are checked within the access control protocols, while the rows specify stakeholders that define security requirements.

	End-users	Service providers	Network providers	MEC providers
End-users	⋆ Actions performed on other End-User's data, objects	⋆ Actions performed on End-User's data, objects	⋆ Actions performed on End-User's data, objects	⋆ Actions performed on End-User's data, objects
Service providers	⋆ Ability to execute actions by End-User	⋆ Ability to use APIs (Application Programming Interfaces) delivered within other MEC applications and MEC services	Validating the communication process: endpoints checking in L2 - L4 (Layer 2 to Layer 4) of ISO OSI RM (ISO Open Systems Interconnection Reference Model) [22]	Mutual authentication during the deployment process. Authenticating and authorizing incoming requests and notifications from MEC Providers The last sentence includes external resources like clouds and on-premise solutions
Network providers	End-Users are using basic authentication and authorization typical for cellular (or wireless) networks	Validating the communication process: endpoints checking in L2 - L4 of ISO OSI RM [22].	Network Providers are using basic authentication and authorization typical for the backbone and the providers' networks	Validating the communication process: endpoints checking in L2 - L4 of ISO OSI RM [22]
MEC providers	⋆ Actions performed in the MEC environment - checking that messages are not harming MEC infrastructure by quotas, message size limits, or location Checking that the user has given access to the action on the MEC service or the MEC application instance	⋆ Validating the deployment process: checking the identity of Service Provider during deployment a new version of a MEC application or service.	Validating the communication process: endpoints checking in L2 - L4 of ISO OSI RM [22]	⋆ Processes between MEC Providers, e.g. support for mobility management and traffic or computation balancing

The paper [19] defines eight security domains for the 5G access control architecture: (1) network access security, (2) network domain security, (3) initial authentication and key management, (4) re-authentication and key management, (5) security capability openness, (6) applications security, (7) slices security, and

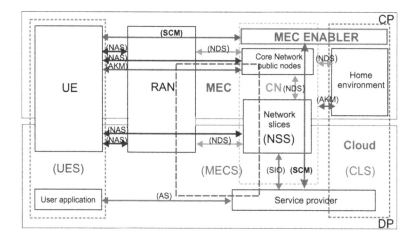

Fig. 1. The high-level access control security architecture in 5G MEC.

(8) security visualization and configurability. Similar approach can be found in [23] where security for 5G network was divided into horizontal and vertical domains. Each of them includes safety aspects dedicated for part of infrastructure.

In our model presented in Fig. 1 we decided to prepare some adoptions and extensions on the basis of block model from [19], because it is more focused on access control. Moreover, the created architecture determines the security domains between the individual blocks. The new model, designed for 5G MEC, consists of the following elements:

1. (NAS) Network Access Security: security of user data should be guaranteed, and this includes confidentiality and integrity of both signaling (i.e., signaling in, both, RAN - Radio Access Network, and CN - Core Network) and user data between the UE and the network in Control Plane (CP) or Data Plane (DP) [19]. It consists of initial authentication of UE, and secure communication of UE in CP and UP.

2. (NDS) Network Domain Security: the secure exchange of both signaling and user data between different network entities:
   – RAN and CN public nodes,
   – CN public nodes and Home environment,
   – CN public nodes and Network slices, and
   – Home environment and Network slices [19].
   It also covers the secure communication of MEC Enabler with the MEC server and required network resources.

3. (AKM) Initial Authentication and Key Management: various mechanisms for authentication and key management should be included that embody the unified authentication framework, including:
   – operator-security-credentials-based security credential authentication between UE and the mobile network; and

– the key management of user data protection after successful authentication [19].

This enables home operator certification of users to enhance their access to
the network and protection of communication.

4. (SCM) Security Credentials Management (re-authentication and key management in [19], providing access either to general service or to a MEC-
hosted service): service authentication and relevant key management
between UE and the external data network (i.e., Service Provider) governed
by MEC Enabler:
   – served for legitimate users of the network;
   – served for the secured communication (via slices or protected links);
   – main security service for access to the MEC-hosted services;
   – management of access rights by credentials;
   – gives credentials to the progression of services considered as use cases in
   Sect. 3; and
   – enables services in the external operator's domain or over the cloud.
5. (SIO) Security Interoperability (also via MEC): support of the openness
of security capability between the 5G network entity, and external Service
Provider. It might involve MEC Enabler in the process.
6. (AS) Applications Security: support for secure communications between UE
and the Service Provider [19]. Those security solutions:
   – can be inside a slice (partially, where a slice exists);
   – can be governed by Network Provider;
   – must be governed by Service Provider; and
   – can be governed by End-User.

It includes also the security of UE and Service Provider as a part of the
End-to-End (E2E) chain.

7. (NSS) Network Slices Security: it includes security of slices in terms like
access control, authorization, and isolation [19]. This domain contains Virtual Machines' (VM) and containers' security because VM or container is
often included in a slice as an endpoint. NSS domain should obey the following rules:
   – slice and virtual machine are managed by Network Providers on the order
   of the Service Provider: opened, decommissioned, or modified;
   – they are independent of End-User;
   – they are related to Service Provider; and
   – their security is synchronized with (MECS) MEC Security.
8. (UES) User Equipment Security: this domain contains software and hardware security at the user's side. Both the execution state of security characteristics and the capability of security characteristics to guarantee service
security should be perceived.
9. (MECS) MEC Security: affects Service Provider's software, virtualization
platform (VM), and hardware that hosts the edge server and MEC host.
Both the execution state of security characteristics and the capability of
security characteristics to guarantee service security should be perceived.

10. (CLS) Cloud Security: the aim is to secure resources and communication inside the cloud and the operator's home domain. In general, this domain is outside of the scope of this paper, however, should be addressed in real scenarios and solutions. CLS domain provides access to services' resources required in Cases 2–5 in Sect. 3 with the heritage of security areas from the basic service domain 5G MEC network.

The security topic in the MEC environment is multidimensional, affects various layers and levels of abstraction - from hardware, through the virtualization layer, finally, the MEC applications and services are also included in the security solutions. Near (hosting 5G network) and far (other MEC solutions, potentially hosted by another Network Operator) neighborhood is also increasing the complexity level of a whole solution.

3   Use Cases of MEC-Based Services

Access to 5G MEC services and resources can be considered in four aspects: End-User access, Service Provider access, MEC Provider access, and 5G Network Provider access. In this paper, we focus only on user access because we analyze how services can be delivered to End-Users. As it was mention in earlier Sections 5G MEC network might include: 5G RAN and CN control infrastructure that is used to register UE, MEC infrastructure in which can be created services close to the users, 5G CN data infrastructure that has much more resources to create services than MEC and external cloud computing environment that can have the resources necessary for proper communication with 5G infrastructure. Based on this division, we can distinguish the following cases of access control of the user to the service in the 5G MEC network:

1. A customer uses the service at MEC. MEC resources are sufficient.
2. A customer uses the service at MEC. MEC resources are sufficient but the service needs to communicate with another service at MEC.
3. A customer uses the service at MEC. The resources are sufficient but the service needs to communicate with an external cloud.
4. A customer uses the service at MEC. Resources are insufficient. A slice creation on CN resources is required.
5. A customer uses the service at MEC. Resources are insufficient. A slice creation on CN resources is required. Communication with an external computing cloud is required.

In Case 1, the user wants to use a MEC service. All resources of the MEC platform are sufficient for providing the service. Access control is checked only for a particular MEC platform with the service. The user can or not have access to this service.

In Case 2, the user wants to use a MEC service. All resources of the MEC platform are sufficient for providing the service but the service needs to communicate with another service at MEC. Access control is checked for the first service (main check) and the second service (additional access check between services). The user can or not have access to the first service.

In Case 3, the user wants to use a MEC service. All resources of the MEC platform are sufficient for providing the service but the service needs to communicate with another service at the external cloud. Access control is checked for the first service (main check) and the second service (additional access check between services at MEC and cloud). The user can or not have access to the first service.

In Case 4, the user wants to use a MEC service. The resources of the MEC platform are insufficient for providing the service and there is a need to create a slice in the CN. Access control is checked for the first service (main check) and the second service (additional access check between service and CN infrastructure responsible for creating slices). The user can or not have access to this service.

In the last case (Case 5), the user wants to use a MEC service. The resources of the MEC platform are insufficient for providing the service and there is a need to create a slice in the CN. Moreover, the service needs to communicate with another service at the external cloud. Access control is checked for the first service (main check) and additional access check between services at MEC and cloud and between service and CN infrastructure responsible for creating slices. The user can or not have access to this service.

Based on those cases, we can choose a proper access control solution that will address all needs. For this document, we will focus on Case 1, as the following only extend it.

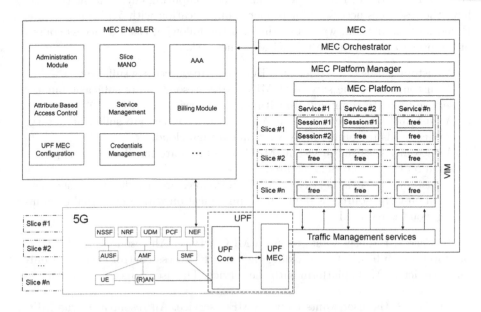

Fig. 2. The new network architecture with the MEC Enabler.

4   MEC Enabler: 5G MEC Access Control and Credentials Management System

The MEC paradigm needs specific methods of authentication and authorization that are compliant with the edge computing model, which allows improving the service quality but on the other hand, it has limited resources. Therefore, in order to not create a connection to the MEC infrastructure for each authorization request, the authors of this publication propose to delegate part of these functionalities into a new element - the MEC Enabler (see Fig. 2), which is planned to be implemented beyond the MEC architecture.

Presented in Fig. 2 architecture connects four environments: 5G CN, 5G RAN, MEC, and a new module MEC Enabler. The mentioned module should take over the role of the AAA (Authentication, Authorization, and Accounting) server for all requests before any connections are established with MEC. Then, if the request is authorized, the MEC Enabler will properly control the configuration process of access to the MEC infrastructure and will create an information token that will enable to use of selected MEC services. The procedure of token creation and its protection can be based on solution analyzed and provided by ETSI (European Telecommunications Standards Institute) [24] and relays on JSON (JavaScript Object Notation) Web Tokens with the appropriate digital signature. This solution will allow reducing the management process and network resources utilization for non-legitimate connections.

The role of the MEC Enabler forces the need for its integration with MEC Orchestrator and from the network configuration perspective with Network Exposure Function. Connection with MEC Orchestrator allows the MEC Enabler to check privileges to MEC applications and manage all internal communication access for service realization. What is important, this interface can be also used for the configuration of traffic rules in the UPF (User Plane Function), which partially belongs to MEC. The second part of UPF (UPF Core) can be controlled thanks to integration with 5G network modules, which according to 3GPP (3rd Generation Partnership Project) specification should support a new type of a Common API Framework (CAPIF) [25]. This interface allows also to establish End-to-End connection between devices and MEC applications by appointment and configuration of all elements in the chain. Having information from both sides (network and edge computing), the MEC Enabler has also the ability to match and bind proper slices from these areas and even in case of the MEC party, to send creation commands, if necessary. The interpretation of the mentioned slices can be simple or more complex. In a simple scenario, one slice will be dedicated to services belongs to the same group with common QoS (Quality of Service) needs, for example, application connected to the e-health. A more complex scenario presents a slice as a part of an operator's network and another slice represents some other part of the network which is also integrated with the same MEC or even another isolated operator's network.

The mentioned situations confirm the need for a central point for MEC, which stores information about policy access for clients which can belong to different slices. Moreover, the distribution of authorization knowledge can be easily done by the implementation of a token-based method in the MEC Enabler, which is aware of all MEC requests and can play the role of a trusted party for all operators which share network resources. As it was described in [26] token based solution for Edge environments can implicate additional delays which are undesirable for MEC services. Therefore to minimized latency and at the same time uses token based mechanism, its implementation can be based on solution similar to Cellular-Based OIDC Authentication [26]. This means that realization of some of MEC Enabler functionalities should be done in the 5G network. One of possible way to achieve it, is to use NFV resources for creation of new service chains like in the paper [27]. Of course, to be compliant with the 3GPPP standard, the MEC Enabler should support the M3GPP-1 interface (MEC Orchestrator-3GPP Core Network Interface) [4] which is common for ETSI MEC and 5G network.

As was described, the MEC Enabler needs to implement additional functionalities which allow fulfilling its main role. These functionalities are presented in form of blocks inside the MEC Enabler. Each of them plays a separate role for integration with the 5G network or to manage MEC resources or even both. In the description below there is a short presentation of internal modules.

- Administration Module: this module is dedicated to supporting all management operations and it can configure other modules.
- Slice MANO (Management And Network Orchestration): the role of this module is to manage the slice life cycle in the MEC area. This manager can also reserve resources for specific slices and mark them according to service type, network identification, or by any other rule.
- Attribute-Based Access Control - this module stores all policy data about services, slices, available connections, and some other MEC information.
- Service Management: functionalities included in this module allow checking available services, its utilization, and also the amount of resources dedicated to them. In the specific use cases, it can also manage the life cycle of services in the MEC using MEC orchestrator API but for that it is necessary to implemented also load balancing which analyzes service placement [28].
- Credentials Management: this module is delegated for the creation of tokens, which can be used for authorization to MEC resources. Created token is monitored by this module and refreshed or deleted according to service needs.
- Billing Module: this module is dedicated to billing and stores information about MEC usage, which can be used in the various business models.
- UPF MEC Configuration: the role of this module is to match and proper configure UPF MEC, to link proper network slices with dedicated for them MEC resources. In case when each slice represents some other operator, this module establishes a connection between the operator and the MEC computation part assigned to it.
- AAA: this module is responsible for authentication, authorization, and accounting of all requests to MEC services. After positive verification, UPF MEC Configuration Module prepares a network configuration that allows creating a connection with the chosen service, and Credentials Management generates a token for service authorization. Implementation of this module in the MEC Enabler will significantly improve the protection of Edge resources.

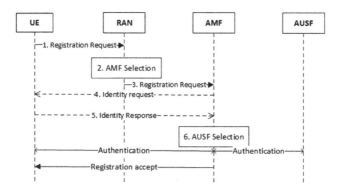

Fig. 3. The first phase of Access Control: the UE registration to the 5G network.

The MEC Enabler can contain more logical blocks but in this paper, the main focus is on the realization of AAA and its role in the ecosystem.

5   Examples of Exchange of Access Control Messages in the 5G MEC

The process of access control includes three phases: UE registration to the 5G network, the discovery of proper UPF Core, and access to a MEC service. In the registration part devices are verified whether they can be connected to the 5G network. In the discovery phase network must find proper UPF which can communicate with the MEC network. Moreover, at this phase is checked if it is possible to establish a connection between UPF Core to UPF MEC. Finally, when the UPF Core can communicate with UPF MEC authentication and authorization to selected MEC services are performed. To show how the created process of access control works, we focus on Case 1 in which the user wants to get access to the MEC service, and the resources are enough to provide it. Figure 3 shows the steps of UE registration to the 5G network in such a case.

The flow in the registration phase was created based on the registration procedure showed in [29], which allows the use of the network resources. First of all, UE sends a registration request to the gNB (generic NodeB; it is simplified as a RAN in this paper) with all necessary information about UE (UE context) such as SUCI (Subscription Concealed Identifier), last visited TAI (Tracking Area Identity), Requested NSSA (Network Slice Selection Assistance Information) and many more. Then, the RAN choose AMF (Access and Mobility Management Function). The AMF performs most of the functions that the MME performs in the 4G network. One of these is UE authentication. AMF sends an identity request to the UE (optional request for additional data) and when it gets a response, AUSF (Authentication Server Function) performs the selection procedure. Thereafter, authentication messages are exchanged between the AUSF, AMF, and the UE. Finally, if everything went correctly, the UE is registered as reported by the AMF.

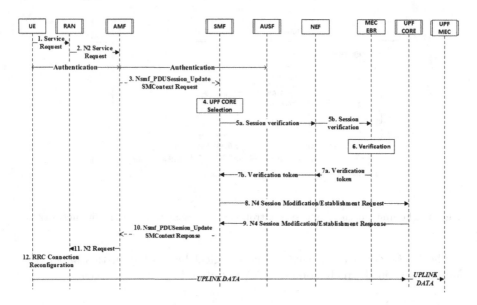

Fig. 4. The second phase of Access Control: the UPF Core and MEC discovery.

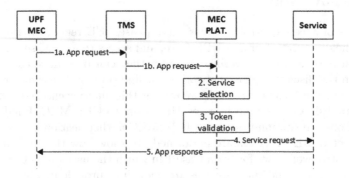

Fig. 5. The third phase of Access Control: the request to MEC service.

The next step is the discovery of UPF Core (see Fig. 4). This phase is needed to connect UE with the appropriate UPF Core, which will communicate directly with the service in MEC. Firstly, again authentication between UE and AUSF is performed. After that, the AMF module sends a request to SMF (Session Management Function) to start the UPF Core discovery and selection procedure.

In the classical approach to 5G MEC network SMF is responsible for UPF management (e.g. configure traffic steering rules), so it must communicate with a new authentication and authorization service to ensure proper access control to MEC. To check if UE can have access to a MEC service, SMF through NEF (Network Exposure Function) sends a verification request to the MEC Enabler (MEC EBR). The MEC EBR checks if UE via UPF Core can establish a session with UPF MEC and if UE can use a particular MEC service. As a result of verification, a token is created. The token contains the necessary information as a result of two previous checks. If everything is going well and SMF receives the token, it sends the request to UPF Core for an update session. Finally, after receiving a response about correct data update from UPF Core, a sequence of messages confirming the possibility of sending data from the UE to UPF Core and UPF MEC is sent.

The final phase of access control to the MEC service is internal access in MEC infrastructure (see Fig. 5). This applies to direct access to the service in which the authenticity of the token delivered by UPF MEC is checked. In [30] authors underlined that MEC operators can support different means of authentication and authorization and it is beyond the scope of MEC standard. In our solution, UPF MEC sends an application request to TMS (Traffic Management Service). The TMS is responsible for sending service access information to the MEC platforms. The MEC platform chooses proper service and verification of the received token. After that the MEC platform sends a request to the chosen service and data from the service are sent to the UPF MEC and finally to the UE. The proposed message flow in this phase is similar to the standard proposed in RFC 7519 for JWT (JSON Web Tokens) [31] which makes it easy to implement and use.

6 Conclusions and Future Work

5G MEC networks will become a fully-fledged alternative to 5G mobile networks, as long as the use of MEC technology to provide services will significantly improve network efficiency, data transmission quality and will improve its security level. The aim of this work was to create such a network security architecture, in particular a new access control management scheme in 5G, which would be fully integrated with the MEC technology and compliant with the current and planned standards of mobile networks. We expect that our solution will be a step to the maturity of the 5G MEC network solution.

The heart of the new architecture is the MEC Enabler module. The MEC Enabler architecture is a new approach that is independent of final MEC implementation, because its placement is outside the MEC. Therefore, each edge solution, which supports CAPIF or M3GPP-1 interface indicated by 3GPP, can be integrated with the MEC Enabler. This makes it very flexible and ready to use with different edge clouds' realizations provided for 5G. Moreover, the MEC Enabler can implemented as a virtual network function or a 5G Core element. The main role of the MEC Enabler is to secure edge services from non-authorized usage and to follow each connection to it. This model provides also a way of network and computation resources protection from the unnecessary allocation, which at the edge solutions are more limited than in the cloud. There are still some open research topics related to the MEC Enabler realization like slices, cooperation with MEC Platform, or other resources sharing between operators, but they are planned to be investigated by the authors in the future. The other way for further research is the scalable decomposition of the MEC Enabler into smaller components to archive high availability and resilience to failures.

The proposed security architecture scheme allows us to operate in a hierarchy of use cases, each of which requires increased network-based or network-located resources. This provides high flexibility and enables a wide range of business applications for the 5G MEC network, however, requires additional design and verification work to be practically applicable. In this paper, we have made the initial analysis of the proposed architecture. We have checked its consistency with the present standards of mobile networks (5G architecture) and MEC technology. We also have checked its formal correctness concerning proposing information exchange schemes for several use cases. In the next steps, an in-depth system analysis will be required, in particular checking how the new security solution affects the performance and quality parameters of the 5G MEC network.

References

1. Minimum requirements related to technical performance for IMT-2020 radio interface(s), Report ITU-R M.2410-0, ITU (2017)
2. Blanco, B., et al.: Technology pillars in the architecture of future 5G mobile networks: NFV MEC and SDN. Computer Standards and Interfaces **54**(4), 216–228 (2017). https://doi.org/10.1016/j.csi.2016.12.007
3. Hu, Y.Ch., Patel, M., Sabella, D., Sprecher N., Young, V.: Mobile edge computing. A key technology towards 5G, ETSI White Paper No. 11, September 2015
4. Harmonizing standards for edge computing - A synergized architecture leveraging ETSI ISG MEC and 3GPP specifications, ETSI White Paper No. 36, July 2020
5. 5G empowering vertical industries, The white paper on vertical sectors published by the 5G Public Private Partnership (2016)
6. Requirements definition and analysis from vertical industries and core applications, 5G EVE. Deliverable D1.2 (2019)
7. Kekki, S. et al.: MEC in 5G networks, ETSI White Paper No. 28, June 2018
8. Ferrag, M.A., Maglaras, L., Argyriou, A., Kosmanos, D., Janicke, H.: Security for 4G and 5G cellular networks: a survey of existing authentication and privacy-preserving schemes. J. Netw. Comput. Appl. **101**, 55–82 (2018). https://doi.org/10.1016/j.jnca.2017.10.017
9. A guide to 5G network security. Conceptualizing security in mobile communication networks - how does 5G fit in? Ericsson AB (2018)
10. Han, B., Wong, S., Mannweiler, C.H., Rates Crippa, M., Schotten, H.D.: Context-awareness enhances 5G Multi-access edge computing reliability. IEEE Access **7**, 21290–21299 (2019). https://doi.org/10.1109/ACCESS.2019.2898316
11. Nife, F., Kotulski, Z., Reyad, O.: New SDN-oriented distributed network security system. Appl. Math. Inf. Sci. **12**(4), 673–683 (2018). https://doi.org/10.18576/amis/120401
12. Nife, F., Kotulski, Z.: Application-aware firewall mechanism for software defined networks. J. Netw. Syst. Manage. **28**, 605–626 (2020). https://doi.org/10.1007/s10922-020-09518-z
13. Kotulski, Z., et al.: Towards constructive approach to End-to-End slice isolation in 5G networks. EURASIP J. Inf. Secur. **2018**(2), 1–23 (2018). https://doi.org/10.1186/s13635-018-0072-0

14. Kotulski, Z., Nowak, T., Sepczuk, M., Tunia, M.: 5G networks: types of isolation and their parameters in RAN and CN slices. Comput. Netw. **171**, 107135 (2020). https://doi.org/10.1016/j.comnet.2020.107135

15. Aikat, J., et al.: Rethinking security in the era of cloud computing. IEEE Secur. Priv. **15**(3), 60–69 (2017). https://doi.org/10.1109/MSP.2017.80

16. Kumar, R., Goyal, R.: On cloud security requirements, threats, vulnerabilities and countermeasures: a survey. Comput. Sci. Rev. **33**, 1–48 (2019). https://doi.org/10.1016/j.cosrev.2019.05.002

17. ENISA Threat Landscape for 5G Networks. Threat assessment for the fifth-generation of mobile telecommunications networks (5G), European Union Agency for Cybersecurity, November 2019

18. Gong, S., Azzaoui, E.L., A., Cha, J., Park, J.H.: Secure secondary authentication framework for efficient mutual authentication on a 5G data network. Appl. Sci. **10**(2), 727 (2020). https://doi.org/10.3390/app10020727

19. Ji, X., Huang, K., Jin, L., et al.: Overview of 5G security technology, SCIENCE CHINA. Inf. Sci. **61**, 081301:1–081301:25 (2018). https://doi.org/10.1007/s11432-017-9426-4

20. Silva, E.F., Muchaluat-Saade, D.C., Castro Fernandes, N.: ACROSS: a generic framework for attribute-based access control with distributed policies for virtual organizations. Future Gener. Comput. Syst. **78**(1), 1–17 (2018). https://doi.org/10.1016/j.future.2017.07.049

21. Baltaci Akhuseyinoglu, N., Joshi, J.: A constraint and risk-aware approach to attribute-based access control for cyber-physical systems. Comput. Secur. **96**, 101802 (2020). https://doi.org/10.1016/j.cose.2020.101802

22. ISO/IEC: ISO/IEC 7498–1:1994(E) Information technology - open systems interconnection - basic reference model: the basic model (1996)

23. Arfaoui, G., et al.: A security architecture for 5G networks. IEEE Access **6**, 22466–22479 (2018). https://doi.org/10.1109/ACCESS.2018.2827419

24. Security architecture and procedures for 5G System (3GPP TS 33.501 version 16.3.0 Release 16), ETSI TS 133 501 V16.3.0, August 2020

25. Functional architecture and information flows to support Common API Framework for 3GPP Northbound APIs, 3rd Generation Partnership Project, Technical Specification Group Services and System Aspects, 3GPP TS 23.222 V17.1.0, July 2020

26. Li, C., et al.: Transparent AAA security design for low-latency MEC-integrated cellular networks. IEEE Trans. Veh. Technol. **69**(3), 3231–3243 (2020). https://doi.org/10.1109/TVT.2020.2964596

27. Doan, T.V., et al.: Reusing sub-chains of network functions to support MEC services. In: IEEE Symposium on Computers and Communications (ISCC), Barcelona, Spain, pp. 1–8 (2019). https://doi.org/10.1109/ISCC47284.2019.8969699

28. Brik, B., Frangoudis, P.A., and Ksentini, A.: Service-oriented MEC applications placement in a federated edge cloud architecture. In: IEEE International Conference on Communications (ICC), Dublin, Ireland, pp. 1–6 (2020). https://doi.org/10.1109/ICC40277.2020.9148814

29. 5G; Procedures for the 5G System (5GS) (3GPP TS 23.502 version 16.5.0 Release 16), ETSI TS 123 502 V16.5.0, July 2020

30. Sabella, et al.: Developing software for multi-access edge computing, ETSI White Paper No. 20, February 2019

31. Jones, M., Bradley, J., Sakimura, N.: JSON Web Token (JWT), Internet Engineering Task Force, RFC 7519, May 2015. https://doi.org/10.17487/RFC7519

A Fast Authentication Scheme for Cross-Network-Slicing Based on Multiple Operators in 5G Environments

Jheng-Jia Huang[1], Chun-I Fan[2,3,4(✉)], Yu-Chen Hsu[2], and Arijit Karati[2]

[1] Department of Information Management,
National Taiwan University of Science and Technology, Taipei, Taiwan
[2] Department of Computer Science and Engineering,
National Sun Yat-sen University, Kaohsiung, Taiwan
`cifan@mail.cse.nsysu.edu.tw`
[3] Information Security Research Center,
National Sun Yat-sen University, Kaohsiung, Taiwan
[4] Intelligent Electronic Commerce Research Center,
National Sun Yat-sen University, Kaohsiung, Taiwan

Abstract. With 5G Network Slicing, the 5G telecommunication operators can achieve the goal of supporting users with a variety of different services and can also create a slice with certain unique characteristics. For example: Enhanced Mobile Broadband slicing, Ultra-reliable and Low Latency Communications slicing, etc. However, the traditional authentication mechanism does not address any concrete strategy for network slicing handover in 5G, so that the computational process must be still calculated by the core network. Hence, we propose a network slicing handover authentication scheme that not only satisfies the standards defined by 3rd Generation Partnership Project but also achieves low time latency through delegating computation overhead to the edge clouds. In addition, we incorporate the concepts of the proxy re-signature and certificateless signature in the scheme. As a result, when users need to use the network slicing services across the telecommunications operators, they can still meet the requirements of reducing the time latency in the process of the authentication flows.

Keywords: Authentication · 5G · Network slicing · Proxy re-signature · Low latency

1 Introduction

The 5G environment requires a high-speed data rate while providing many kinds of services to numerous devices and users. Therefore, the concept of network slicing has

This work was partially supported by Taiwan Information Security Center at National Sun Yat-sen University (TWISC@NSYSU) and the Ministry of Science and Technology of Taiwan under grants MOST 109-2221-E-110-044-MY2 and MOST 109-2222-E-011-007-MY2. It also was financially supported by the Information Security Research Center at National Sun Yat-sen University in Taiwan and the Intelligent Electronic Commerce Research Center from The Featured Areas Research Center Program within the framework of the Higher Education Sprout Project by the Ministry of Education (MOE) in Taiwan.

S. M. Thampi et al. (Eds.): SSCC 2020, CCIS 1364, pp. 92–106, 2021.
https://doi.org/10.1007/978-981-16-0422-5_7

been proposed lately so that each network function can correspond to different services. According to the white paper "View on 5G Architecture" [1] released by 5G Infrastructure Public Private Partnership (5G-PPP) Architecture Working Group in December 2017, network slicing is an end-to-end concept covering all network segments including radio access networks, core network, transport, and edge networks. This will enable network operators to provide networks on an as-a-service basis and meet the wide range of use cases. Consequently, 5G uses Network Function Virtualization (NFV) and Software-Defined Networking (SDN) for implementing the network slicing [2,3].

3GPP defines the slice architecture in TS23.501 [4] where the Network Slice Selection Assistance Information (NSSAI) is a collection of max eight Single-Network Slice Selection Assistance Informations (S-NSSAIs). Therefore, it indicates that each user can access at most eight services by one telecommunications operator. Because of the heterogeneous networks and network slicing, the security issues have become more complicated than the traditional network, which means that there must be some new mechanisms to support diverse network and user's requirements. Although 3GPP released its first 5G security specifications in March 2018 [5], it does not fully address the security challenges in 5G, especially the framework of fast and secure authentication mechanisms. Consequently, a fast, safe, and lightweight authentication scheme for the 5G is a goal of telecommunication operators continuous efforts.

However, the existing literature has not been sufficiently studied for network-slicing-based 5G networks. Chiu [6] proposed a fast authentication mechanism tailored for the 5G network environment, and it can also integrate the access authentication of heterogeneous networks. Unfortunately, Chiu's scheme is only applicable to the network slicing created by one telecommunications operator and does not match with the real situation of multiple operators in modern society. To solve the aforementioned problem, we apply the proxy re-signature and certificateless method to improve Chiu's scheme. In addition, the traditional single service provider has been gradually transformed into the cooperation of multiple service providers to provide user-oriented services [7]. As a result, we propose a secure and fast authentication handover technique which can be used in multiple operators case in the 5G environment.

We propose a novel authentication scheme tailored for the 5G network environment. Compared with prior related works discussed in Sect. 3, the scheme provides the following features:

1) The proposed scheme has low-latency and high-reliability in the 5G environment.
2) The proposed scheme supports the access authentication of 5G heterogeneous networks.
3) The proposed scheme supports the environment of multiple operators. The scheme allows the user to switch services to other network slices without registering other telecommunication operators, which reduces the user's time cost.
4) The proposed scheme satisfies the security standard TS33.501 [5] defined by 3GPP, therefore, we can avoid malicious attacks, for examples: replay attack, man-in-the middle attack, in 5G heterogeneous networks.

2 Preliminaries

2.1 5G Environments

In terms of the 5G security, the encryption and decryption between the operator and the users are under the Elliptic Curve Integrated Encryption Scheme (ECIES) which was first proposed by Victor Shoup [8] in 2001. Figure 1 and Fig. 2 show that the encryption and decryption process in 5G. There are two pairs of keys. One is the user device side *Eph.public key* and *Eph.private key*, where both of the keys are generated by *Eph.key* pair generation. The other pair is in the operator side. The user has the public key of home network (HN), which is stored in the **SIM** card. It may be noted that a private key can be used to derive a unique public key, but a private key cannot be derived from a public key. To generate an encryption key *Eph.shared key*, the user combines its self-generated private key with the operator's public key. The key point is to use the characteristics of elliptic curves: $(sk_1 \cdot pk_2) = (sk_2 \cdot pk_1)$.

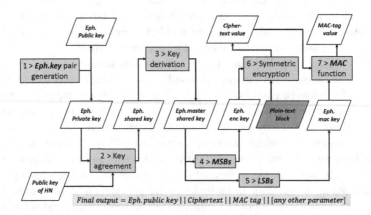

Fig. 1. Encryption based on an elliptic curve integrated encryption scheme at the user

2.2 Bilinear Pairings

We use pairing operations to set up the user signature and parameters in the scheme.

Definition 1. *Let G_1 be a cyclic additive group of prime order q, and G_2 be a cyclic multiplicative group of the same order q. There exists a bilinear mapping $e : G_1 \times G_1 \rightarrow G_2$ which satisfies the following properties:*

1. **Bilinearity:** $e(aP, bQ) = e(P,Q)^{ab}$, where $P, Q \in G_1, a, b \in \mathbb{Z}_q^*$ chosen at random.
2. **Non-degeneracy:** There exists $P, Q \in G_1$ such that $e(P,Q) \neq 1$ where 1 is the identity element of G_2.
3. **Computability:** There is an efficient algorithm to compute $e(P,Q)$ for all $P, Q \in G_1$.

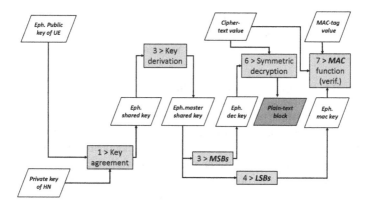

Fig. 2. Decryption based on an elliptic curve integrated encryption scheme at the operator

2.3 Boneh-Boyen Signature Scheme

The Boneh-Boyen short signature scheme [9] is briefly described as follows. Let $(G_1, *), (G_2, *)$, and $(G_T, *)$ be three cyclic multiplicative groups of prime order p, and $e : G_1 \times G_2 \longrightarrow G_T$ be an efficiently computable bilinear pairing. Suppose that $m \in \mathbb{Z}_p^*$ is a message which will be signed.

2.4 Proxy Re-signature Scheme

In the proposed scheme, not only the operators verify that the legality of the users who are associate with other operators, but also the computing cost is reduced. Therefore, the computing process does not need to be returned to the core network in 5G. Therefore, the concept of the proxy re-signature different from the proxy signature could be a possible solution. It may be noted that the proxy signature allows an original signer to delegate his/her signing right to another party so that the party can sign any messages by using the original signer's signing right [10]. However, the proxy re-signature allows a semi-trusted proxy acts as a translator between Alice and Bob to translate a signature from Alice into a signature from Bob on the same message. Consequently, we use the proxy re-signature in the proposed scheme and briefly review definitions of an ideal proxy re-signatures scheme [11, 12].

3 Related Works

Based on the framework of 3GPP TS 33.501 for the 5G System, we will review some suitable 5G network slicing authentication schemes suitable for 5G network slicing. For examples: In 2017, Yang *et al.*'s proposed a blockchain-based trusted authentication architecture [13] for 5G with blockchain-based anonymous access scheme in cloud radio network. And then in 2018, Ni *et al.*'s proposed an efficient service-oriented authentication scheme [14] which was compared with Chiu's work [6]. In 2019, Ying *et al.*'s proposed an efficient and anonymous 5G authentication protocol [15] that can provide better performance without using any pairing operation during registration, the mutual authentication process, and the password change phase. Finally, the proposed work will compare with Ni *et al.*'s work and Ying *et al.*'s work in Sect. 5.

3.1 Yang *et al.*'s Blockchain-Based Architecture

In 2017, Yang *et al.*'s first propose a novel blockchain-based trusted authentication (BTA) architecture for 5G, by introducing a blockchain-based anonymous access scheme. The scheme can address the network access authentication with tripartite agreement among the equipment manufacturer, uses and network operator in the access area, effectively reduce the network operating and connection costs and enhance the radio frequency, which enables the blockchain as a service.

3.2 Ni *et al.*'s Network Slicing Scheme

In 2018, Ni *et al.*'s proposed an efficient service-oriented authentication scheme [14]. Their scheme consists of the following six algorithms: **System Initialization**, **Network Slicing**, **5G Network Access**, **Service Delegation**, **Service Authentication**, **Key Negotiation**.

3.3 Ying *et al.*'s Authentication Protocol

In 2019, Ying *et al.*'s [15] proposed an efficient and anonymous mutual authentication for multi-server-based 5G networks, which could achieve the security level of 80 bits through Elliptic Curve Cryptography (ECC). They also provided the anonymity and untraceability of mutual authentications to ensure that these identities cannot be retrieved by adversaries.

4 The Construction

In this section, we design an efficient and secure authentication scheme useful for the multiple operators in 5G. Here, we enhanced the Chiu's [6] scheme by incorporating the concepts used in Fan *et al.*'s [16] certificateless short signature and Libert *et al.*'s [17] proxy re-signatures. The proposed scheme consists of four algorithms: *Setup, Registration, Authentication, Handover*. Further, the *Handover* phase involves two different procedures or algorithms: *Handover 1* is performed under a uni-operator similar to Chiu's handover phase, and *Handover 2* is performed for crossing operators.

4.1 Notations

The notations that we used in the scheme are defined in Table 1.

Table 1. The notations

Notation	Meaning
$\left\{(UPK,UPK'),USK\right\}$	A user's public/private key pair
$\{OPK_i,OSK_i\}$	An operator's public/private key pair
$\{SPK_j,SSK_j\}$	A slice base station's public/private key pair
$\left\{SID_j^{i'}s\right\}$	The set of the identities of the slices j's for each operator i
$\left\{SLK_j^{i'}s\right\}$	The set of the long-term secret keys of the slices j's for each operator i
$\left\{V_j^{i'}s\right\}$	The set of the count values of the slices j's for each operator i
UID	The identity of the user
ULK	The long-term secret key of the user
Q_{UID}	$Q_{UID} = H_1(UID)$
G_1	A cyclic additive group of prime order q
G_2	A cyclic multiplicative group of prime order q
q	A large prime
k	The system security parameter where $q > 2^k$
e	A bilinear mapping $e : G_1 \times G_1 \to G_2$
P	A generator of group G_1
Z	$Z = e(P,P)$
H	A hash function $H : \{0,1\}^* \to \{0,1\}^\lambda$
H_1	A hash function $H_1 : \{0,1\}^* \to Z_q^*$
H_2	A hash function $H_2 : \{0,1\}^* \to G_1$

4.2 Setup

In the Setup phase, we set the parameters similar to Chiu *et al.* [6]. However, we assume that the environment has m operators instead of one, and each operator can construct at most n network slices. The process is defined as below.

- The identities of the n slices: they are deployed by the operator i: $SID_i = \{SID_j^i \mid 0 < j \leq n\}$, for each operator i, $0 < i \leq m$.
- The long-term secret keys of the n slices: they are deployed by the operator: $SLK_i = \{SLK_j^i \mid 0 < j \leq n\}$, for each operator i, $0 < i \leq m$.
- The count values of the n slices: they are deployed by the operator: $V_i = \{V_j^i \mid 0 < j \leq n\}$, for each operator i, $0 < i \leq m$.

By Sect. 2, the encryption and decryption procedures are under the ECIES scheme. So, each operator uses the *keygen* algorithm to generate a pair of keys (OPK'',OSK'') which is stored and handled by the operator. Besides, the *keygen* can generate a different pair of public/private keys (UPK'',USK'') for the user in each session. The (E,D) is a pair of symmetric encryption and decryption functions, respectively. Besides, the public and private keys, some parameters, and re-signing keys are as follows:

- The operator's private key: $OSK_i = s_i \in Z_q^*$.
- The operator's public key: $OPK_i = P_i = s_i \cdot P, i \in m$.
- The user's private key: $USK = u \in Z_q^*$.
- The user's public key: $UPK = u \cdot P$ and $UPK' = u(OPK + Q_{UID}P)$.
- The slice base station's private key: SSK_j, and public key: SPK_j.
- The set of re-signing key: $RK_w^i = \frac{1}{s_i} \cdot (p_w) = \frac{s_w}{s_i} \cdot P$, where $0 < w \le m, 0 < i \le m, w \ne i$. The re-signing slice base station can get re-signing keys by the operator i: $RK_i = \{RK_w^i \mid 0 < w \le m, w \ne i\}$ for each operator i, $0 < i \le m$, and store it secretly.

Figure 3 shows the Setup phase in the scheme.

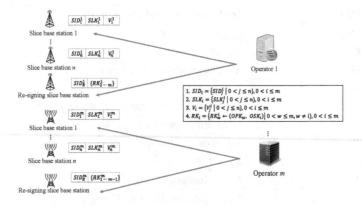

Fig. 3. The Setup Phase

4.3   Registration

In this phase, the user can apply for registration from a telecommunication operator, just like applying for a mobile phone number. When users apply for the operator's services, they need to provide some information as follows:

- The user's partial public information (Q_{UID}, UPK) with identity UID.
- The serial numbers of the slices which the user wants to access: $\Gamma_{UID} \subseteq [1, n]$.

While the operator receives the user's registration application, it will calculate the authentication information for the user, and the operator maintains a list to store the following contents.

- The long-term secret key between the operator and the user: ULK
- Key generator: $keygen$.
- Receiving the public key of the operator under the ECIES key generator: OPK''.

- Slice information from the operator i: $slice = \{E_{SLK_j^i}(V_j^i)||SID_j^i \mid j \in \Gamma_{UID}\}$.
- The operator helps user generate *Partial-Signing-Key*: $K_\sigma = \frac{1}{(s_i+Q_{UID})+H_1(UPK)}P$.

At last, the operator i gives user *SIM* card, where $SIM = \{ULK, keygen, OPK'', slice = \{E_{SLK_j^i}(V_j^i)||SID_j^i \mid j \in \Gamma_{UID}\}, K_\sigma\}$. Figure 4 shows a detailed process of the Registration phase.

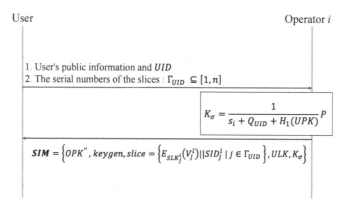

Fig. 4. The Registration phase

4.4 Authentication

In this phase, the user establishes a session key with the target slice base station and receives a signature from the operator which can be used in the Handover phase.

- **Step 1:** A user sends a service request and his/her *UID* to the slice base station SID_j^i.
  - The user randomly chooses $y \in Z_p$ as a session number.
  - The *keygen* generates (UPK'', USK'') for the user in this session.
  - The user uses OPK'' which is stored in the *SIM* card and USK'' to generate a share key $x = H(OPK'' \cdot USK'')$.
  - The user computes $SUCI = E_x(E_{ULK}(SUPI||UID||y)||UID)$ (where *SUPI* is the user device identification code).
  - The user computes $c_1 = slice \parallel SUCI \parallel UPK''$, and sends c_1 to the slice base station SID_j^i.
- **Step 2:** The slice base station SID_j^i checks the user 's access right.
  - The slice base station SID_j^i parses c_1, uses SLK_j^i to decrypt *slice*, and then verifies $V_j^{i'} \overset{?}{=} V_j^i$.
  - If that formula holds, then the slice base station accepts the user's request. Otherwise, the slice base station aborts the request.

- The slice base station computes $c_2 = E_{SLK_j^i}(c_1||V_j^i)||SID_j^i$, and sends c_2 to the operator.
- **Step 3:** The operator verifies the slice base station and the user. Finally, the operators signs a signature σ and sets parameters for the handover phase.
  - The operator uses the corresponding long-term secret key SLK_j^i to parse c_2. The operator verifies whether $V_j^{i'} \overset{?}{=} V_j^i$. If the formula does not hold, the operator aborts the request.
  - The operator uses its private key OSK'' and the user's public key UPK'' to generate the session key $x = H(OSK'' \cdot UPK'')$. Then the operator uses x to decrypt $SUCI$ to get $E_{ULK}(SUPI||UID||y)||UID$.
  - Then, the operator uses ULK to decrypt $E_{ULK}(SUPI||UID||y)$ and then checks if $UID' \overset{?}{=} UID$. If the formula holds, the operator keeps y. Meanwhile, it generates a random number T_1, an expiration date T_2, and computes $m_1 = H_1(T_1||y)$.
  - The operator decrypts $E_{SLK_j^i}(V_j^i)$ with the corresponding SLK_j^i in $slice$ by SID_j^i and computes the count value $V_j^i = V_j^i + 1$.
  - According to the $slice$, the operator computes
    * $slice' = \{E_{SLK_j^i}(V_j^i||E_{ULK}(y))||SID_j^i \mid j \in \Gamma_{UID}\}$.
    * the operator randomly chooses $t \leftarrow Z_p^*$, and the operator computes signature $\sigma = (\sigma^{(T_2)}, \sigma^{(1)}, \sigma^{(2)})$ where
      - $\sigma^{(T_2)} = s \cdot T_2$
      - $\sigma^{(1)} = s \cdot H_2(m_1) \in G_1$
      - $\sigma^{(2)} = (s \cdot t \cdot H_2(m_1), t \cdot p, t \cdot P) = (\sigma_0, \sigma_1, \sigma_2)$.
    * $c_3 = E_{SLK_j^i}(E_{ULK}(slice'||y||\sigma||T_1||T_2||m_1)||V_j^i \mid j \in \Gamma_{UID})$.

The operator sends c_3 to the slice base station.

- **Step 4:** The slice base station verifies the operator.
  - After receiving the ciphertext c_3, the slice base station uses SLK_j^i to decrypt c_3 and then verifies if $V_j^{i'} - 1 \overset{?}{=} V_j^i$.
  - If it passes the verification, the slice base station updates the count value.
  - Finally, the slice base station sends $c_4 = E_{ULK}(slice'||\sigma||y||T_1||T_2||m_1)$ to the user.
- **Step 5:** The user verifies the slice base station and the operator.

  - After receiving c_4, the user can use ULK to decrypt c_4 and verify $y' \overset{?}{=} y$.
  - If the formula holds, the service request is accepted and the user keeps y, σ, T_1, T_2 and updates the count value. Otherwise, the user aborts.

Figure 5 shows the Authentication phase.

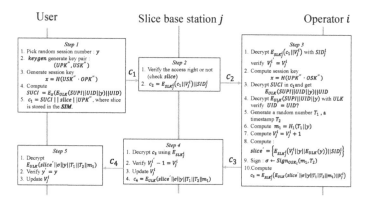

Fig. 5. The Authentication phase

4.5 Handover 1

In the scheme, we not only propose a new handover phase but also show that it can be applied to Chiu's handover phase [6]. Suppose that the user has already had the session number y in the authentication phase, which can be used as a session key between the user and the target slice base station in this phase. Consequently, we briefly describe this phase in the scheme.

- The user randomly chooses $r_1 \in Z_p$ as a session number and the timestamp T_{h_1}. Then, the user uses the target slice base station's public key to encrypt.

$$E_{SLK_j^i}\left(V_j^i||y||E_{ULK}(y)\right)||r_1||T_{h_1}$$ by using an already known public-key cryptosystem to compute the ciphertext $f_1 = e_{SPK_j}\{E_{SLK_j^i}(V_j^i||y||E_{ULK}(y))||r_1||T_{h_1}\}$. And then, the user sends it to the target slice base station.

- After receiving f_1, the slice base station firstly decrypts f_1 by using SSK_j. Then, the slice base station checks the timestamp T_{h_1} is less than the time fresh threshold $\triangle T'$ or not and verifies $V_j^{i'} \stackrel{?}{=} V_j^i$.

- If f_1 passes the verification, the target slice base station accepts this access and chooses $r_2 \in Z_p$ as the other session number. After that, the slice base station computes $H(r_1||r_2)$ as the session key in Handover 1 phase and uses it to encrypt $E_{ULK}(y)||r_2$ to compute the ciphertext f_2. And then, the target slice base station sends $f_2||r_2$ to the user. Otherwise, the slice base station outputs $\perp$ and aborts.

- After receiving $f_2||r_2$, the user computes the session key $H(r_1||r_2)$ to decrypt f_2, and then uses the long-term key to decrypt $E_{ULK}(y)$ and verifies $y' \stackrel{?}{=} y$. If the formula holds, this handover is authenticated successfully. Otherwise, the user outputs $\perp$ and aborts. Figure 6 shows the Handover 1 phase.

4.6 Handover 2

Suppose that the user wants to access the other network slicing services which are managed by different operators. In many situations, there are many unpredictable reasons

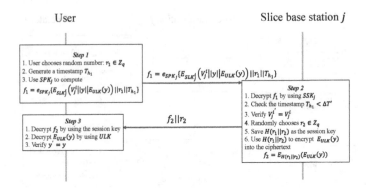

Fig. 6. The Handover 1 phase

leading to the situation that the user's main operator services can not be accessed, which may bring the user a great loss, especially in an emergency. Therefore, we let the scheme support handover among different operators. The detailed steps are shown as follows.

- **Step 1:** The user has already had the session signature σ, m_1, T_1, T_2 and y in the authentication phase. Then, the user generates a timestamp T_{h_2} and a user signature γ to send the handover 2 request to the target re-signing slice base station SID_R^w, $0 < w \leq m$, $w \neq i$ where
  - $m_2 = H_1\left(T_{h_2}||SID_R^w\right)$
  - $\gamma = \frac{1}{u+m_2} \cdot K_\sigma$

After that, the user computes $M = \{\sigma||m_1||UID||T_2||T_{h_2}||\gamma||r_3\}$, where $r_3 \in Z_q$ is a random number chosen by the user, and uses the target re-signing slice base station's public key SPK_R to encrypt M by using an already known public-key cryptosystem to compute the ciphertext d_1. Then, user sends d_1 to the slice base station.

- **Step 2:**
  - After receiving d_1, the target re-signing slice base station firstly decrypts d_1 by using SSK_R and checks if the expiration date T_2 is greater than the current date $\triangle T$ or not. Then, the station also checks the timestamp T_{h_2} is less than the time fresh threshold $\triangle T'$ or not. The re-signing slice base station parses and verifies the time signature by checking $e\left(\sigma^{(T_2)}, P\right) \overset{?}{=} e\left(T_2, p_i\right)$. If it is not true, the station aborts this handover 2 request.
  - Secondly, the station checks the validity by verifying σ and γ.
    * $e\left(\sigma^{(1)}, P\right) \overset{?}{=} e\left(H_2\left(m_1\right), p_i\right)$.
    * $e\left(\gamma, UPK' + H_1(UPK)UPK + m_2(OPK + Q_{UID}P + H_1(UPK)P)\right) \overset{?}{=} Z$.
  - Then, the target re-signing slice base station acting as a proxy entity chooses $t \in Z_q^*$ and computes the resignature $\beta = \left(\sigma^{(1)}, \sigma^{(2)'}\right)$ where

$$\sigma^{(2)'} = \left(\sigma_0', \sigma_1', \sigma_2'\right) = t \cdot \left(\sigma^{(1)}, p_i, RK\right) = \left(s_i t \cdot H_2\left(m_1\right), t \cdot p_i, t \cdot \frac{s_i}{s_i^*} \cdot P\right)$$

- If we set $\bar{t} = t \cdot \frac{s_i}{s_i^*}$, we have

$$\sigma^{(2)'} = \left(\sigma_0', \sigma_1', \sigma_2'\right) = \left(s_i^* \cdot \bar{t} \cdot H_2\left(m_1\right), \bar{t} \cdot p_i^*, \bar{t} \cdot P\right)$$

Finally, the re-signing slice base station uses r_3 to encrypt $\beta \| SID_R^w$, where r_3 is the session key in the Handover 2 phase, and then it computes the ciphertext $d_2 = E_{r_3}(\beta \| SID_R^w)$ and returns d_2 to the user.

- **Step 3:** After receiving d_2, the user decrypts d_2 by using the session key r_3. And then, the user gets β and checks $SID_R^{w'} \overset{?}{=} SID_R^w$. If the equation holds, it means that the user can access the target operator's services by using the signature β.
- If the following formulas are true, the signature β is valid.

$$e\left(\sigma_0, P\right) \overset{?}{=} e\left(\sigma_1, H_2(m_1)\right), e\left(\sigma_1, P\right) \overset{?}{=} e\left(p_i, \sigma_2\right)$$

- When the user finishes using the service, the re-signing slice base station generates the end using time T_e so that the station can send the user signature γ and T_e to its operator. At last, the target operator will confirm and charge with the user's main operator based on the user's signature γ and the using period $(T_e - T_{h_2})$. This procedure can be completed offline to reduce the computational and transmission costs of the user, which can improve the efficiency in the scheme. Figure 7 shows the Handover 2 phase.

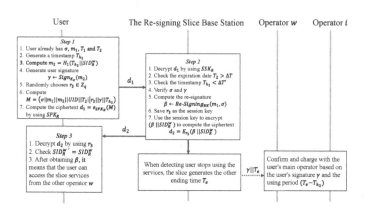

Fig. 7. The Handover 2 phase

5   Comparison

This section demonstrates the performance aspect of the proposed scheme. We evaluate the execution overhead of the scheme and compared with other related schemes [6, 14, 15].

5.1 Properties Comparison

We compare the properties of the 5G authentication schemes including the handover phase. The comparisons between the scheme and others in the following Table 2.

Table 2. Properties

	Ni *et al.* [14]	Chiu *et al.* [6]	Ying *et al.* [15]	Ours
The TS 33.501 standard	Yes	Yes	No	Yes
Time latency	High	Low	Low	Low
Multiple operators	No	No	Yes	Yes
Handover slices different operators	No	No	No	Yes

5.2 Performance Comparison

In order to compare the efficiency between the proposed scheme and the other three works, we define some notations in Table 3 and the underlying platform on a computer with Intel Core i7-8700 CPU @3.6 GHz and 16 GB memory based on the Java library [18–21], and the execution costs of these operations are listed in Table 4. Eventually, we can calculate the total computational overhead throughout the procedures including the authentication phase and the handover phase in each scheme, respectively, in Table 5.

Table 3. The Notations

Notation	Meaning
T_{mul}	The computational cost of a multiplication operation
T_h	The computational cost of a hash function
$T_{E/D}$	The computational cost of a symmetric key encryption/decryption
$T_{e/d}$	The computational cost of a asymmetric key encryption/decryption
T_p	The computational cost of a pairing operation
T_{exp}	The computational cost of an exponentiation computation
N_s	The number of slices where the user has the access right

Table 4. The cost of computational overhead

	T_{mul}	T_h	$T_{E/D}$	$T_{e/d}$	T_p	T_{exp}
Time (ms)	0.029	0.13	0.098	8.74	3.32	16.23

Table 5. Performance

	Ni et al. [14]				Chiu et al. [6]			
Computational overhead		User	Slice	Operator		User	Slice	Operator
	T_{mul}	48	10	42	T_{mul}	–	–	–
	T_h	16	8	34	T_h	1	–	1
	$T_{E/D}$	4	–	10	$T_{E/D}$	4	$3+N_s$	$5+N_s$
	$T_{e/d}$	–	–	–	$T_{e/d}$	–	–	–
	T_p	10	12	24	T_p	–	–	–
	T_{exp}	2	–	8	T_{exp}	–	–	–
	Totals (ms)	69.52	41.17	216.14	Totals (ms)	0.52	1.08	1.40
	Ying et al. [15]				Ours			
Computational overhead		User	Slice	Operator		User	Slice	Operator
	T_{mul}	–	–	–	T_{mul}	1	1	5
	T_h	7	–	3	T_h	5	2	2
	$T_{E/D}$	6	–	6	$T_{E/D}$	1	$5+N_s$	$8+N_s$
	$T_{e/d}$	–	–	–	$T_{e/d}$	2	2	2
	T_p	–	–	–	T_b	–	2	–
	T_{exp}	–	–	–	T_{exp}	–	–	–
	Totals (ms)	1.498	–	0.978	Totals (ms)	18.26	25.68	19.45

Note: $N_s = 8$

In the performance comparison, although the adopted pairing operation and the public-key cryptosystem might increase computational cost during the authentication and user handover, the proposed scheme supports legal user validation in the multi-operators setting. To the best of our knowledge, the proposed scheme is the first solution to achieve supporting network slice handover among different operators in the 5G authentication environments.

6   Conclusion

In this work, we proposed a fast and secure scheme for Cross-Network-Slicing based on multiple operators in 5G environments. It is expected that the idea can meet the characteristics of 5G environments to reduce the latency. We applied proxy re-signature and certificateless signature to improve Chiu's scheme that achieves the authentication requirements. Specifically, users are able to authenticate their identities among different network-slicing from different operators in an efficient way. Although there are still many problems in the safety development of 3GPP standards, we still are trying to fulfill the security issues that may be possible. In addition, we will implement the proposed scheme by using the open-source platform for 3GPP standards (e.g., OAI [22], Free5GC [23], etc.) in the future. Currently, the proposed scheme cannot be used in mixed services with multiple operators. Therefore, one can use the proposed scheme on multiple services from the different operators at the same time, and try to reduce the incurred computation cost which could be an interesting future work. Moreover, we expect that the proposed scheme can be used to design a secure and fast authentication handover method for 5G which satisfies the 3GPP standards.

References

1. Redana, S., et al.: View on 5G architecture. Technical report 7 (2016)
2. Kaloxylos, A.: A survey and an analysis of network slicing in 5G networks. IEEE Commun. Stand. Mag. **2**(1), 60–65 (2018)
3. Foukas, X., Patounas, G., Elmokashfi, A., Marina, M.K.: Network slicing in 5G: survey and challenges. IEEE Commun. Mag. **55**(5), 94–100 (2017)
4. 3GPP: Ts 23.501 system architecture for the 5G system, 3GPP. Technical report (2017)
5. 3GPP: Ts 33.501 security architecture and procedures for 5G system, 3GPP. Technical report (2018)
6. Chiu, W.-R.: Cross-network-slice authentication scheme for the 5th generation mobile communication system, Master thesis, National Sun Yet-sen University (2018)
7. Wahab, O.A., Bentahar, J., Otrok, H., Mourad, A.: Towards trustworthy multi-cloud services communities: a trust-based hedonic coalitional game. IEEE Trans. Serv. Comput. **11**(1), 184–201 (2018)
8. Shoup, V.: A proposal for an ISO standard for public key encryption (version 2.1), IACR e-Print Archive, vol. 112 (2001)
9. Boneh, D., Boyen, X.: Short signatures without random oracles. In: Cachin, C., Camenisch, J.L. (eds.) EUROCRYPT 2004. LNCS, vol. 3027, pp. 56–73. Springer, Heidelberg (2004). https://doi.org/10.1007/978-3-540-24676-3_4
10. Mambo, M., Usuda, K., Okamoto, E.: Proxy signatures: delegation of the power to sign messages. IEICE Trans. Fund. Electron. Commun. Comput. Sci. **79**(9), 1338–1354 (1996)
11. Blaze, M., Bleumer, G., Strauss, M.: Divertible protocols and atomic proxy cryptography. In: Nyberg, K. (ed.) EUROCRYPT 1998. LNCS, vol. 1403, pp. 127–144. Springer, Heidelberg (1998). https://doi.org/10.1007/BFb0054122
12. Ateniese, G., Hohenberger, S.: Proxy re-signatures: new definitions, algorithms, and applications. In: Proceedings of the 12th ACM Conference on Computer and Communications Security, pp. 310–319. ACM (2005)
13. Yang, H., Zheng, H., Zhang, J., Wu, Y., Lee, Y., Ji, Y.: Blockchain-based trusted authentication in cloud radio over fiber network for 5G. In: 2017 16th International Conference on Optical Communications and Networks (ICOCN), pp. 1–3. IEEE (2017)
14. Ni, J., Lin, X., Shen, X.S.: Efficient and secure service-oriented authentication supporting network slicing for 5G-enabled IoT. IEEE J. Sel. Areas Commun. **36**, 644–657 (2018)
15. Ying, B., Nayak, A.: Lightweight remote user authentication protocol for multi-server 5G networks using self-certified public key cryptography. J. Netw. Comput. Appl. **131**, 66–74 (2019)
16. Fan, C.-I., Hsu, R.-H., Ho, P.-H.: Truly non-repudiation certificateless short signature scheme from bilinear pairings. J. Inf. Sci. Eng **27**, 969–982 (2011)
17. Libert, B., Vergnaud, D.: Multi-use unidirectional proxy re-signatures. In: Proceedings of the 15th ACM Conference on Computer and Communications Security, pp. 511–520. ACM (2008)
18. Digital-Signature-using-RSA-and-SHA-256 (2018). https://github.com/henmja/Digital-Signature-using-RSA-and-SHA-256. Accessed Aug 2018
19. AES 256bit Encryption/Decryption and storing in the database using Java (2016). https://medium.com/@danojadias/aes-256bit-encryption-decryption-//and-storing-in-the-database-using-java-2ada3f2a0b14. Accessed Aug 2018
20. Class BigInteger. https://docs.oracle.com/javase/7/docs/api/java/math/BigInteger.html. Accessed Aug 2018
21. Class Cipher. https://docs.oracle.com/javase/7/docs/api/javax/crypto/Cipher.html. Accessed Aug 2018
22. OpenAirInterface. https://www.openairinterface.org/. Accessed Sept 2020
23. free5GC. https://www.free5gc.org/. Accessed Sept 2020

A Survey of Security Attacks on Silicon Based Weak PUF Architectures

Chintala Yehoshuva, R. Raja Adhithan, and N. Nalla Anandakumar$^{(\boxtimes)}$

Hardware Security Research Lab,
Society for Electronic Transactions and Security (SETS), Chennai, India
chintala.yehoshuva@gmail.com, raja@setsindia.net, nallananth@gmail.com

Abstract. Physically Unclonable Functions (PUFs) are popular hardware-based security primitives that can derive chip signatures from the inherent characteristics of ICs. Due to their assumed security and cost advantages, one important category of PUFs, so-called weak PUFs which is used in numerous security applications such as device ID generation, IP protection and secure key storage. Nevertheless, a number of recent works have been reported several attacks on weak PUFs architectures. This paper presents a brief survey of existing attacks on silicon-based weak PUF architectures with their detailed comparison and associated countermeasures.

Keywords: Physical Unclonable Functions (PUFs) · Weak PUFs · Invasive attacks · Side channel attacks

1 Introduction

PUFs are emerging as hardware cryptographic primitives. A lot of PUF structures have been reported in the literature since the first PUF structure was introduced in 2002 by Pappu et al. [31]. Among the different PUF structures, silicon-based PUFs are most interesting with regard to manufacturing cost and have been traditionally used for hardware security applications. Silicon PUFs use the intrinsic manufacturing variability of silicon-based digital ICs (i.e., which rely on transistor-level variations) to create a unique digital output for each device. The PUF response is used either via a random variable in a encryption operation or challenge-response pair (CRP) protocol for authentication.

Generally, silicon PUFs can be categorized into two major classes based on the their challenge-response space size [47], namely, Strong PUFs and Weak PUFs. Strong PUFs have an exponentially large CRP space and can be used directly for authentication. In that case, we assumed that the adversary might have access to the PUF CRPs. However, it is very difficult to attack the CRPs in a minimum amount of time such as few days/weeks. Arbiter PUF, XOR Arbiter PUF and Lightweight PUF [47] are perfect examples of the Strong PUFs. Alternatively, weak PUFs can offer only a limited a number of CRPs that grow only linearly. An adversary can't easily access the weak PUFs response because their

© Springer Nature Singapore Pte Ltd. 2021
S. M. Thampi et al. (Eds.): SSCC 2020, CCIS 1364, pp. 107–122, 2021.
https://doi.org/10.1007/978-981-16-0422-5_8

responses remain inside the PUF-carrying hardware [41]. The SRAM-PUF, Ring Oscillator PUF, Anderson PUF, Memristor PUF, Thyristor PUF and OTP PUF are good examples of weak PUF designs [47]. In the present scenario weak PUFs are more suitable than strong PUF because on strong PUF various modelling attacks had been implemented [25,32,35]. On the other hand, weak PUF structures are the least susceptible to machine learning (ML) based modeling attacks. This means that the majority of current weak PUF architectures are impossible to the modeling attacks. Furthermore, weak PUFs are more suitable for many real time applications such as unique identity (ID) generation, seeding a PRNG, IP (Intellectual Property) protection, key generation, secure data storage, making random permutations [8] and mitigate counterfeit ICs [5]. However, in recent years, some of the weak PUF architectures have been subjected to various classes of new attacks. In this paper, we give a brief survey and overview of several security attacks on the weak PUF architectures and associated countermeasures against these attacks.

The paper is structured as follows: Sect. 2 describes the classification of weak PUFs. Several types of attacks on weak PUFs with their comparison are given in Sect. 3. Some published associated countermeasures against these type of security attacks are analyzed in Sect. 4, while the conclusion is summarized in Sect. 5.

2   Classification of Weak PUFs

In this section we present different classifications of weak PUFs. Weak PUF architectures can be broadly classified into two main categories like delay based PUFs and memory based PUFs (see in Fig. 1).

2.1   Delay Based Weak PUFs

Delay based PUFs derive responses from inherent delay characteristics of transistors and wires in ICs. Delay-based weak PUFs mainly includes RO PUF, Loop PUF, Anderson PUF, Clock PUF, TERO PUF, Thyristor based PUF etc. Different types of delay-based weak PUFs are explained below:

RO PUF (Ring Oscillator PUF): A RO circuit consists of an odd number of NOT gates connected in a ring form whose output oscillates between two binary voltage levels specifically '0' and '1'. Due to random process variations, two identical ring oscillators can not produce the same frequency. The frequency differences of selected pairs of ROs is used to produce the PUF output [3,38].

Loop PUF: Cherif et al. [11] have proposed the Loop PUF and is composed of many number of controllable delay stages are connected in a loop. It has nearly the same concept of the RO PUF. When compared to the RO PUF design, the Loop PUF compares several elements sequentially instead of parallel comparisons to generate the PUF signature.

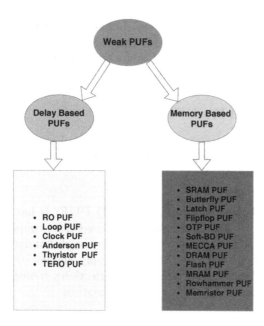

Fig. 1. Classification of weak PUFs

Clock PUF: The Clock PUF [45] has been proposed by Yao et al. in 2013 that derive bits from pairwise skews between sinks of an on-chip clock network. Due to manufacturing imperfections, sinks of a clock network can produce different clock signals transitions (small amount of clock skew different). In order to construct clock PUF, two sinks of the clock network will be selected with help of challenge (input) and fed them into the arbiter unit (SR-latch) to determine which of two given clock signals transitions first and this random transition is used to create a PUF response.

Anderson PUF: It was proposed by Anderson et al. in 2010 [4]. The PUF is composed of two shift registers, two carry chain multiplexers, and one D flip-flop. The two pairs of shift registers and multiplexers should be identical, but their delays are different due to manufacturing process variations. They exploit this property for the generation of the PUF signature.

Thyristor PUF: It was proposed by Bai et al. in 2016 [6] and is using thyristor components for the generation of the PUF output. In the Thyristor PUF, several identical thyristor sensors are manufactured on the same type of chip. Due to the due to intrinsic manufacturing imperfections, each sensor produces different delay values. Hence, this PUF generates a response by using the different delay values.

TERO PUF: The TERO PUF is very similar to RO PUF has been proposed by Bossuet et al. [9]. RO PUF uses a transient oscillating state only but the TERO PUF uses two states such as a stable state and a transient oscillating state in order to generate PUF response.

2.2 Memory Based Weak PUFs

A memory-based weak PUF uses the arbitrary initial state of many cells in the memory array during device power-up to extract a unique PUF response which is completely device-dependent.

Static Random Access Memory (SRAM) PUF: It has been proposed by Holcomb et al. [18] in 2007 and is formed by two cross coupled inverters. This PUF uses the randomness in the startup behavior of standard SRAM memory in digital chips. When switch on the power supply, the initial bit of SRAM may be either '1' or '0' due to manufacturing imperfections. Hence, the startup state values of SRAM memory is used as a PUF signature.

Butterfly PUF: It is similar to SRAM PUF. Two unstable cross-coupled latches are used instead of two cross-coupled inverters to build a Butterfly PUF [22]. For SRAM PUF, a power-up is normally required to generate a response but this mechanism is not necessary for the butterfly PUF.

Latch PUF: It is similar to SRAM PUF and Butterfly PUF. This PUF was designed in 2007 by Su et al. [37,44] using two cross-coupling NAND (or NOR) gates. Due to the unstable (meta-stable) cross-coupled nature of NAND or NOR gates, the output of the latch is unpredictable. Hence this PUF generates a response by using the meta-stable property.

Flip-Flop PUF: The flip-flop PUF is similar to SRAM PUF. It was proposed by Roel Maes et al. [24] in 2008 that use the startup values of FFs (flip-flops) instead of SRAM memory cells. The main security benefit of a FF PUF is the fact that FFs are easily spread over an IC chip when compared to the SRAM PUF. Hence to probe each individual start-up bit and also reverse engineering of the chip are very difficult.

OTP (One Time Programmable) PUF: This PUF [33] uses an breakdown of insulator in a MIM device to switch between '0' (insulating) and '1' (conducting state). The constant stress is applied to same kind of two transistors. The breakdown strength of the two devices is varied due to manufacturing process variation. The device which will break down is considered as response a 1 otherwise 0. This unpredictable nature of breakdown results in a random response of OTP PUF.

Soft-BD (Soft Gate Oxide Breakdown) PUF: It has recently been proposed by Chuang et al. in 2017 [12]. The PUF concept is one soft break down spot occur in any one of the two NMOS in an in-deterministic way. Hence this PUF generates a response by using the in-deterministic way of the soft breakdown.

MECCA PUF: It has been proposed by Krishna et al. in 2011 [21] and consists of an array of SRAM cells is similar as the standard SRAM PUF. This PUF produce a response by exploiting the intrinsic process variations in reading/writing reliability of cells in SRAM memories.

DRAM PUF: The DRAM PUF [43] is constructed with help of a transistor and a capacitor. This PUF mainly relies on the fact that the capacitor which is located in the DRAM initializes to random values during its startup. When compared to SRAM PUFs, DRAM PUF offer high uniqueness and a large number of challenges.

Flash PUF: In Flash memory, the threshold voltage of each memory cell varies due to manufacturing variations. Depending on the variations in the threshold level, 1's or 0's are extracted from the flash memory cells. Mainly, the unpredictable nature of threshold voltage in the transistor is used to generate the PUF signature [19].

MRAM (Magnetoresistive Random-Access Memory) PUF: The MRAM [14] is a nonvolatile magneto-resistive memory. Moreover, the MRAM offers low power options when compared to current flash memory because they rely on resistance.

Rowhammer PUF: The Rowhammer PUF was proposed in 2017 by Schaller et al. [36]. This PUF evaluates by rapidly accessing the DRAM memory cells, some of the neighbouring a cell is to induce a bit-flip in that cell. Moreover, the bit-flip value of each cell is determined by manufacture process variations of each cell. They exploit this property for the generation of the PUF signature.

Memristor PUF: This PUF design has been build based on thin-film memristor technology [20] which utilizes a weak write mechanism to obtain cell behaviour which is influenced by manufacturing process variation and hence used this property for the generation of the PUF signature.

2.3 Strength and Weaknesses

In general, every PUF will have its own strength and weakness. The following Table 1 describes the strengths and weaknesses of various weak PUF architectures.

3   Security Attacks on Weak PUFs

Several existing PUF architectures have been reported in the literature they are vulnerable to many security attacks such as modelling attacks, invasive attacks, side-channel attacks and fault injection attacks. We are going to discuss some major types of security attacks on weak PUFs in this section. Moreover, in this paper, we categorize the security attacks on weak PUFs as 1) machine learning-based modeling attacks; 2) non-invasive attacks; 3) semi-invasive attacks; 4) invasive attacks; 5) cloning attacks.

Table 1. PUF architecture summary

Types of week PUF	Strengths	Weaknesses
RO PUF	It is easy to implement	Suffers due to environmental sensitivity
TERO PUF	Environmental resiliency	Need further investigation
SRAM PUF	Response has good statistical properties	Provides low number of CRPs
OTP PUF	Response is highly random in nature	Need high supply voltage
DRAM PUF	It provides more CRPs than SRAM PUF	Refreshing is needed
Loop PUF	Response is random than RO PUF	Slow response
Clock PUF	It is simple in operation	The response is less random in nature
Anderson PUF	The response has good entropy	Occupies more area
Flip flop PUF	Simple in operation	The response has less entropy
Butterfly PUF	Good response than Flip flop PUF	Complex in structure
Flash PUF	Simple non-volatile PUF	More dependent on input
MRAM PUF	Low power than flash PUF	Occupies more area
Rowhammer PUF	Good response than DRAM PUF	Complex structure than DRAM
MECCA PUF	Good entropy and faster than SRAM PUF	Complex structure than SRAM

3.1 Modeling Attacks (ML) on Weak PUFs

The vast majority of existing PUF architectures are susceptible to ML using a machine learning algorithm (MLA). In this attack, an attacker has to develop a mathematical model of the PUF that have the same CRP behavior of the chip. In general, the modeling attacks are the most powerful attack for strong PUFs. In the weak PUFs, RO PUFs can be modelled by using an MLA such as quick sort [32] and linear regression [28], if sufficient number of CRPs is able to collect by an adversary. However, these attacks become infeasible by use the very few number of challenges to generating a PUF output for key generation scenarios [27].

3.2 Non-invasive Attacks on Weak PUFs

A PUF architecture may be attacked passively by using side-channel information such as execution time, power consumption or EM radiation emanating from a chip containing a PUF.

Power Analysis (PA) Attack: Power analysis attack is one type of non-invasive side-channel attack (SCA) where the power consumption of data is used as the side channel to attack the target ICs. An overview of power analysis based SCA as shown in Fig. 2. The computer (PC) inputs a set of known challenges to the PUF device which does the signature generation. While the device performs the PUF operation, the oscilloscope measures power consumption. First, samples power traces are obtained for several thousands of required challenges, and then they are analyzed on a computer by using methods of statistical analysis such as Correlation Power Analysis (CPA) or Differential Power Analysis (DPA) to derive the secret information of the target device [29]. Some of the prior works are focusing on attacking the strong PUF designs by using the power side channel information [7,25]. More recently, few works have analyzed the side-channel vulnerabilities of the Loop PUF [41] and Soft-BD PUF [13] against simple power analysis (SPA) attack. Apart from the widely used the CPA and DPA, the SPA does not require the knowledge of the input data.

Electro-Magnetic (EM) Analysis Attack: The EM analysis attack is one of the non-invasive side-channel attack where EM radiation is an exploitable side channel to attack the target device and it can be also performed without physical contact to the chip. The EM analysis based SCA overview is shown in Fig. 3. Initially, the waveforms of the emitted target device EM radiation are acquired by an EM probe, low-noise amplifier, an oscilloscope. Next, the collected EM traces are subjected to conduct simple EM analysis or differential EM analysis under the Hamming-distance model to predict the secret information of the target device.

There are few numbers of attacks on the weak PUFs have been reported in literature wherein EM radiation information is exploited to wage most effective

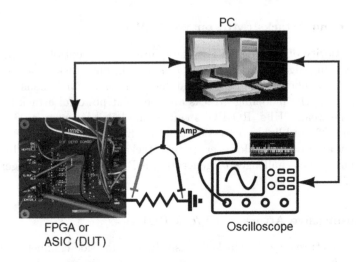

Fig. 2. Power Analysis based SCA overview

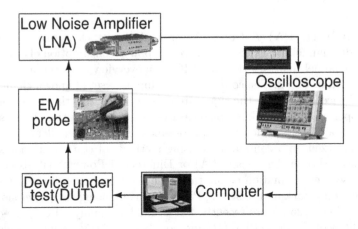

Fig. 3. EM Analysis based SCA overview

modeling attacks [26,42]. The RO PUFs are prone to localized EM attacks is showed in 2013 by Merli et al. [26]. They first demonstrated the feasibility of locating a single RO. Further, they also showed how to mount local EM attacks on RO PUFs by exploiting location dependent EM leakage. Recently, Tebelmann et al. successfully demonstrated that TERO PUFs [42] and Loop PUFs [41] are vulnerable to an EM-based SCA without depackaging the chip by using the above EM analysis based SCA experimental setup (see Fig. 3).

Data Remanence (DR) Attack: Data remanence attack is an active attack and also one type of fault injection attack. The attack typically aims at retrieving information by injecting faults into the target. In the literature, a few numbers of publications have practically demonstrated that data remanence effect can be also used to inject faults by disturbances the temperature into the SRAM PUF [2, 46]. In the work [46] is using temperature in conjunction with the power-off time to produce a range of responses partially matching the legitimate one and then tried to recreate the legitimate PUF response by applying differential fault analysis. Furthermore, the authors of [2] control the number of faults induced in the SRAM cells by controlling the temperature one can quite precisely and to the get responses by applying differential fault analysis.

Fault Injection Modeling (FIM) Attack: In [15], Delvaux et al. injecting faults into some of the specific components of the RO PUF architecture to attain the PUF response with the help of the PUF modeling technique. The PUF model is built based on the reliability of the PUF response as affected by environmental noise.

3.3 Semi-invasive Attack on Weak PUFs

A semi-invasive attack is to access to the chip surface only which means that it does not destroy layers of the chip.

Photon Emission Analysis (PEA) Attack: Photonic emission analysis is an emerging semi-invasive attack that exploits the switching transistors on the integrated circuits that emit photons (i.e., particles of light). The authors [39] physically characterize the basic components of RO PUF such as ROs, counters. First, emitted photons from the RO PUF are collected by using the microscope and are fed to a beam splitter (BS) which divided into two separate optical paths. The long-wave photons are reflected onto the Silicon Photo Avalanche diode (SPAD) while short-wave photons are transmitted to the Silicon Charge Coupled Devices (Si-CCD) camera [39]. Then, the reflected and transmitted photons with time tags (each occurring event) information allowing a direct calculation of PUF-internal delay components.

Semi-invasive EM Attack: Merli et al. [27] (in 2011) demonstrated that standard RO PUF architecture is vulnerable to global EM analysis. They discussed in that paper how to extract full list of RO frequencies from the EM measurement data on the depackaged chip.

Laser Fault Injection (LFI) Attack: In the laser fault injection attack, pulsed lasers are used to inject faults into running target devices for the purpose of retrieving intermediate/secret information. The pulsed laser can be used to induce faults in silicon devices. In 2015, Tajik et al. [40] can be done the experiment through the backside of IC after depackaging the chip and also showed that how this attack can dramatically reduce the RO PUF entropy.

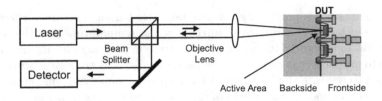

Fig. 4. Illustration of OCP attacks [23]

Optical Contactless Probing (OCP) Attack: The OCP attack is one of the semi-invasive attack which can enable an adversary to probe different volatile and on-chip secret data from the IC backside without making any physical contact. The authors of [23] have demonstrated that infrared Laser Voltage Probing (LVP) can be used to characterize ROs frequency which is used in RO PUFs. In this method, a laser beam is focused on the IC backside, traverses the active IC area, and reflected back based on the metal structures as shown in Fig. 4. Then, the returning beam is fed to the detector to measure of the beam intensity. Based on this information, ROs frequency was characterized.

3.4 Invasive Attacks on Weak PUFs

An attacker can depackage of the IC's backside and attempt to read out the secret when the chip is running or powered off. In 2013, Nedospasov et al. [30] have been shown that how SRAM PUFs are successfully attacked by using the invasive attack techniques, if not properly implemented PUF circuits. In this attack, authors stimulate the inverters of an SRAM PUF cell by using a near-infrared laser to reveal the SRAM cell data's.

3.5 Cloning Attacks on Weak PUFs

In this attack, an adversary makes the exact physical copy (or clone) of the original PUF with identical character. In 2013, Helfmeier et al. [17] have demonstrated that SRAM PUF outputs can be physically cloned by a FIB (Focused Ion Beam). Creating a physical clone of a PUF using the method requires laboratory equipment and environment, thus very expensive and difficult to achieve. However, other silicon-based weak PUFs have not been reported to date.

3.6 Comparative Analysis of Implementation Attacks on Variants of Weak PUFs

Table 2 shows a summary of the implementation attacks on weak PUFs that have been reported in this section, which includes the attack location, chip damage level, leakage sources, attack cost, etc. As seen from the table, PA and EM based attacks setup cost are low to moderate level when compared to other attack methodology Lab setups because they are require very expensive laboratory equipment and environment. However, power and EM based attack detection chances are low on weak PUF architectures when compared to attack methodologies such as OCP, PEA, DR, FIM, LFI and SIEM. Moreover, IC damage level is very high for LFI, SIEM and cloning type of attacks when compared to other attacks. Most of these attacks have been carried out on some main types of PUFs such as SRAM PUF, Soft-BD PUF, RO-PUF, TERO PUF and Loop PUF. However, many of these attack methods are suitable for other types of weak PUF designs as described in Section 2.

Table 2. Comparison between Implementation Attacks on variants of weak PUFs

Specifications	Attack location	Attack detection chances	IC damage level	Attack based on	Attack cost (Relative)	Observed in
PA attack [13,41]	External to the chip	Low	Low	Power leakage	Low	Soft-BD PUF [13] Loop PUF [41]
EM attack [26, 41,42]	On the chip	Low	Low	EM emission	Moderate	RO PUF [26], TERO PUF [42] Loop PUF [41]
PEA attack [39]	On the chip	Low to moderate	Low	Photon emission	High	RO PUF [39]
OCP attack [23]	Back side of the chip	Moderate	Low	Reflections of photons	High	RO PUF [23]
DR attack [2,46]	External to the chip	Moderate	Low	Remanance decay	High	SRAM PUF [2,46]
FIM attack [15]	External to the chip	High	Low	Injecting faults and modelling	Moderate	RO PUF [15]
LFI attack [40]	On the chip	High	High	Injecting laser	High	RO PUF [40]
SIEM attack [27]	On the chip	Moderate	High	Injecting EM	High	RO PUF [27]
Cloning attack [17]	On the chip	High	High	FIB	High	SRAM PUF [17]

4 Countermeasures

In this section, we are now going to discuss some published countermeasures against the above attacks on weak PUFs.

4.1 Countermeasures Against Modeling Attacks

In recent years, researchers proposed many different countermeasures in order to resist modeling attacks for strong PUFs. Authors of [48] have discussed various defense mechanisms against modeling attacks for strong PUFs. These mechanisms can broadly be divided into two categories: CRP obfuscation and structural non-linearization. The CRP obfuscation methods hides the mapping of challenge-response pairs to prevent adversary from collecting valid CRPs information to model the strong PUFs. On the other hand, structural non-linearization methods are to implement non-linear PUF structures in order to resist the machine learning based modeling attacks. For the weak PUFs, there are some defense mechanisms that have been reported in the literature to boost the RO PUF security against modeling attacks by improving CRP space [1] and challenge obfuscation [28].

4.2   Countermeasures Against Non-invasive Attacks

Countermeasures of Power and EM Attacks: In order to secure a crypto-system, numerous countermeasures have been proposed to minimize or stop the side-channel leakage from the weak PUF implementations [10,26,27,41]. More recently, Tebelmann et al. [41] introduced a temporal masking countermeasure to protect the Loop PUF which randomly alters the order of challenges retaining the security subject to the power and EM attacks. Furthermore, two countermeasures have been proposed in the work [26] to prevent localized EM attacks for RO PUF using randomization of RO measurement logic and interleaved placement. Another countermeasure is proposed to protect against EM attacks for RO PUF which uses asynchronous counters and reduced width of counters [27]. Recently, Yuan et al. [10] had shown that current starved inverters are used in the RO PUF design instead of normal inverters to minimize the EM emissions which are significantly enhanced immunity to the EM attack.

Countermeasures Against DR Attacks: A variety of countermeasures against DR attacks have been reported [2,46]. In TIFS 2015, Shaza et al. [46] proposed countermeasures use of remanence decay which is to improve the of SRAM PUF cloning-resistance. Recently, the authors of [2] discussed and assessed some potential countermeasures to make the DR attacks harder to perform against SRAM PUFs such as obfuscation of the memory, physically destructing the device.

4.3   Countermeasures Against Semi-invasive Attacks

There are several countermeasures against semi-invasive attacks that have been reported in the literature [23,40]. In [23], the author's proposed countermeasures against OCP attacks for RO PUF such as obfuscated key registers by randomizing their order and randomized reset states of the registers. Due to these randomizations, the measurement data distinction would be severely impeded. Tajik et al. [40] suggested that some of the countermeasures by using redundancy in arithmetic operations to protect the PUFs. Sahoo et al. [34] introduced two countermeasures such as rollback and random-sliding to protect the delay PUFs against laser fault attacks proposed in 2015 by Tajik et al. [40].

4.4   Countermeasures Against Invasive and Cloning Attacks

To protect against invasive attackers, the authors in [30] proposed two countermeasures techniques such as serialized PUF implementation that exposure of the PUF response is minimized and implementing an asynchronous reset for the SRAM which is possible to destroy digital values inside the SRAM. Additionally, they also suggested that tamper evidence applied must to all parts of the IC to withstand such attacks. Furthermore, the authors of [16] have proposed a defence mechanism for RO PUF by utilizing the inverters voltage sensitivity in order to enhance the resistance of the RO PUF against the cloning attack.

5   Conclusion

In the past two decades, there has been of in-depth examination on PUF since the introduction of its concept into the research community. Among the different PUF forms, silicon-based weak PUFs are most interesting in terms of manufacturing cost and more suitable for many practical hardware security applications. In this paper, we have surveyed the recent attacks on silicon-based weak PUF architectures and provided their detailed comparison. Finally, we have also discussed associated countermeasures to prevent these attacks.

References

1. Amsaad, F., Choudhury, M., Chaudhuri, C.R., Niamat, M.: An innovative delay based algorithm to boost PUF security against machine learning attacks. In: 2016 Annual Connecticut Conference on Industrial Electronics, Technology Automation (CT-IETA), pp. 1–6, October 2016
2. Anagnostopoulos, N.A., Arul, T., Rosenstihl, M., Schaller, A., Gabmeyer, S., Katzenbeisser, S.: Low-temperature data remanence attacks against intrinsic SRAM PUFs. In: 2018 21st Euromicro Conference on Digital System Design (DSD), pp. 581–585. IEEE (2018)
3. Anandakumar, N.N., Hashmi, M.S., Sanadhya, S.K.: Efficient and lightweight FPGA-based hybrid PUFs with improved performance. Microprocess. Microsyst. **77**, 103180 (2020)
4. Anderson, J.H.: A PUF design for secure FPGA-based embedded systems. In: 2010 15th Asia and South Pacific Design Automation Conference (ASP-DAC), pp. 1–6, January 2010
5. Aniello, L., Halak, B., Chai, P., Dhall, R., Mihalea, M., Wilczynski, A.: Anti-BlUFf: towards counterfeit mitigation in IC supply chains using blockchain and PUF. Int. J. Inf. Secur. (2020)
6. Bai, C., Zou, X., Dai, K.: A novel thyristor-based silicon physical unclonable function. IEEE Trans. Very Large Scale Integr. (VLSI) Syst. **24**(1), 290–300 (2016)
7. Becker, G.T., Kumar, R., et al.: Active and passive side-channel attacks on delay based PUF designs. IACR Cryptology ePrint Archive 2014, 287 (2014)
8. Bernardini, R., Rinaldo, R.: Making random permutations from physically unclonable constants. Int. J. Inf. Secur. **16**(3), 249–261 (2016). https://doi.org/10.1007/s10207-016-0324-2

9. Bossuet, L., Ngo, X.T., Cherif, Z., Fischer, V.: A PUF based on a transient effect ring oscillator and insensitive to locking phenomenon. IEEE Trans. Emerg. Topics Comput. **2**(1), 30–36 (2014)

10. Cao, Y., Zhao, X., Ye, W., Han, Q., Pan, X.: A compact and low power RO PUF with high resilience to the EM side-channel attack and the SVM modelling attack of wireless sensor networks. Sensors **18**, 322 (2018)

11. Cherif, Z., Danger, J., Guilley, S., Bossuet, L.: An easy-to-design PUF based on a single oscillator: the loop PUF. In: 15th Euromicro Conference on Digital System Design, pp. 156–162, September 2012

12. Chuang, K., et al.: Physically unclonable function using CMOS breakdown position. In: 2017 IEEE International Reliability Physics Symposium (IRPS), pp. 4C–1.1-4C-1.7, April 2017

13. Chuang, K.-H., Bury, E., Degraeve, R., Kaczer, B., Linten, D., Verbauwhede, I.: A physically unclonable function using soft oxide breakdown featuring 0% native BER and 51.8 fJ/bit in 40-nm CMOS. IEEE J. Solid-State Circ. **54**(10), 2765–2776 (2019)

14. Das, J., Scott, K., Rajaram, S., Burgett, D., Bhanja, S.: MRAM PUF: a novel geometry based magnetic PUF with integrated CMOS. IEEE Trans. Nanotechnol. **14**(3), 436–443 (2015)

15. Delvaux, J., Verbauwhede, I.: Fault injection modeling attacks on 65 nm arbiter and RO sum PUFs via environmental changes. IEEE Trans. Circuits Syst. I Regul. Pap. **61**(6), 1701–1713 (2014)

16. Gao, M., Lai, K., Zhang, J., Qu, G., Cui, A., Zhou, Q.: Reliable and anti-cloning PUFs based on configurable ring Oscillators. In: 2015 14th International Conference on Computer-Aided Design and Computer Graphics (CAD/Graphics), pp. 194–201, August 2015

17. Helfmeier, C., Boit, C., Nedospasov, D., Seifert, J.: Cloning physically unclonable functions. In: 2013 IEEE International Symposium on Hardware-Oriented Security and Trust (HOST), pp. 1–6, June 2013

18. Holcomb, D.E., Burleson, W.P., Fu, K.: Power-up SRAM state as an identifying fingerprint and source of true random numbers. IEEE Trans. Comput. **58**(9), 1198–1210 (2009)

19. Kim, M., Moon, D., Yoo, S., Lee, S., Choi, Y.: Investigation of physically unclonable functions using flash memory for integrated circuit authentication. IEEE Trans. Nanotechnol. **14**(2), 384–389 (2015)

20. Koeberl, P., Koçabas, Ü., Sadeghi, A.: Memristor PUFs: a new generation of memory-based physically unclonable functions. In: Macii, E. (ed.) Design, Automation and Test in Europe, DATE 13, Grenoble, France, March 18–22, 2013, pp. 428–431. EDA Consortium, San Jose/ACM DL (2013)

21. Krishna, A.R., Narasimhan, S., Wang, X., Bhunia, S.: MECCA: a robust low-overhead PUF using embedded memory array. In: Preneel, B., Takagi, T. (eds.) CHES 2011. LNCS, vol. 6917, pp. 407–420. Springer, Heidelberg (2011). https://doi.org/10.1007/978-3-642-23951-9_27

22. Kumar, S.S., Guajardo, J., Maes, R., Schrijen, G.-Ja., Tuyls, P.: The butterfly PUF protecting IP on every FPGA. In: 2008 IEEE International Workshop on Hardware-Oriented Security and Trust, pp. 67–70. IEEE (2008)

23. Lohrke, H., Tajik, S., Boit, C., Seifert, J.-P.: No place to hide: contactless probing of secret data on FPGAs. In: Gierlichs, B., Poschmann, A.Y. (eds.) CHES 2016. LNCS, vol. 9813, pp. 147–167. Springer, Heidelberg (2016). https://doi.org/10.1007/978-3-662-53140-2_8

24. Maes, R., Tuyls, P., Verbauwhede, I.: Intrinsic PUFs from flip-flops on reconfigurable devices. In: 3rd Benelux Workshop Information and System Security, p. 17 (2008)
25. Mahmoud, A., Rührmair, U., Majzoobi, M., Koushanfar, F.: Combined Modeling and Side Channel Attacks on Strong PUFs. IACR Cryptology ePrint Archive 2013, 632 (2013)
26. Merli, D., Heyszl, J., Heinz, B., Schuster, D., Stumpf, F., Sigl, G.: Localized electromagnetic analysis of RO PUFs. In: 2013 IEEE International Symposium on Hardware-Oriented Security and Trust (HOST), pp. 19–24. IEEE (2013)
27. Merli, D., Schuster, D., Stumpf, F., Sigl, G.: Semi-invasive EM attack on FPGA RO PUFs and countermeasures. In: Proceedings of the Workshop on Embedded Systems Security, p. 2. ACM (2011)
28. Miskelly, J., Gu, C., Ma, Q., Cui, Y., Liu, W., O'Neill, M.: Modelling attack analysis of configurable ring oscillator (CRO) PUF designs. In: 2018 IEEE 23rd International Conference on Digital Signal Processing (DSP), pp. 1–5, November 2018
29. Nalla Anandakumar, N.: SCA resistance analysis on FPGA implementations of sponge based MAC PHOTON. In: Bica, I., Naccache, D., Simion, E. (eds.) SECITC 2015. LNCS, vol. 9522, pp. 69–86. Springer, Cham (2015). https://doi.org/10.1007/978-3-319-27179-8_6
30. Nedospasov, D., Seifert, J., Helfmeier, C., Boit, C.: Invasive PUF analysis. In: 2013 Workshop on Fault Diagnosis and Tolerance in Cryptography, pp. 30–38, August 2013
31. Pappu, R., Recht, B., Taylor, J., Gershenfeld, N.: Physical one-way functions. Science **297**(5589), 2026–2030 (2002)
32. Rührmair, U., Sehnke, F., Sölter, J., Dror, G., Devadas, S., Schmidhuber, J.: Modeling attacks on physical unclonable functions. In: Proceedings of the 17th ACM Conference on Computer and Communications Security, CCS 2010, pp. 237–249. ACM (2010)
33. Sadana, S., Lele, A., Tsundus, S., Kumbhare, P., Ganguly, U.: A highly reliable and unbiased PUF based on differential OTP memory. IEEE Electron Device Lett. **39**(8), 1159–1162 (2018)
34. Sahoo, D.P., Bag, A., Patranabis, S., Mukhopadhyay, D., Chakraborty, R.S.: Fault-tolerant implementations of physically unclonable functions on FPGA. In: Chakraborty, R.S., Mathew, J., Vasilakos, A.V. (eds.) Security and Fault Tolerance in Internet of Things. IT, pp. 129–153. Springer, Cham (2019). https://doi.org/10.1007/978-3-030-02807-7_7
35. Santikellur, P., Bhattacharyay, A., Chakraborty, R.S.: Deep learning based model building attacks on arbiter PUF compositions. IACR Cryptology ePrint Archive 2019, 566 (2019)
36. Schaller, A., et al.: Intrinsic Rowhammer PUFs: leveraging the Rowhammer effect for improved security. In: 2017 IEEE International Symposium on Hardware Oriented Security and Trust (HOST), pp. 1–7, May 2017
37. Su, Y., Holleman, J., Otis, B.: A 1.6pJ/bit 96 % stable chip-ID generating circuit using process variations. In: 2007 IEEE International Solid-State Circuits Conference. Digest of Technical Papers (2007)
38. Suh, G.E., Devadas, S.: Physical unclonable functions for device authentication and secret key generation. In: 2007 44th ACM/IEEE Design Automation Conference, pp. 9–14. IEEE (2007)
39. Tajik, S., Nedospasov, D., Helfmeier, C., Seifert, J., Boit, C.: Emission analysis of hardware implementations. In: 2014 17th Euromicro Conference on Digital System Design, pp. 528–534, August 2014

40. Tajik, S., Lohrke, H., Ganji, F., Seifert, J.P., Boit, C.: Laser fault attack on physically unclonable functions. In: 2015 Workshop on Fault Diagnosis and Tolerance in Cryptography (FDTC), pp. 85–96 (2015)

41. Tebelmann, L., Danger, J.L., Pehl, M.: Self-secured PUF: protecting the loop PUF by masking. Cryptology ePrint Archive, Report 2020/145 (2020). https://eprint.iacr.org/2020/145

42. Tebelmann, L., Pehl, M., Immler, V.: Side-channel analysis of the TERO PUF. In: Polian, I., Stöttinger, M. (eds.) COSADE 2019. LNCS, vol. 11421, pp. 43–60. Springer, Cham (2019). https://doi.org/10.1007/978-3-030-16350-1_4

43. Tehranipoor, F., Karimian, N., Yan, W., Chandy, J.A.: DRAM-based intrinsic physically unclonable functions for system-level security and authentication. IEEE Trans. Very Large Scale Integr. (VLSI) Syst. 25(3), 1085–1097 (2017)

44. Yamamoto, D., Sakiyama, K., Iwamoto, M., Ohta, K., Takenaka, M., Itoh, K.: Variety enhancement of PUF responses using the locations of random outputting RS latches. J. Cryptogr. Eng. 3(4), 197–211 (2012). https://doi.org/10.1007/s13389-012-0044-0

45. Yao, Y., Kim, M., Li, J., Markov, I.L., Koushanfar, F.: ClockPUF: Physical Unclonable Functions based on clock networks. In: 2013 Design, Automation Test in Europe Conference Exhibition (DATE), pp. 422–427, March 2013

46. Zeitouni, S., Oren, Y., Wachsmann, C., Koeberl, P., Sadeghi, A.-R.: Remanence decay side-channel: the PUF case. IEEE Trans. Inf. Forensics Secur. 11(6), 1106–1116 (2015)

47. Zhang, J.-L., Qu, G., Lv, Y.-Q., Zhou, Q.: A survey on silicon PUFs and recent advances in ring oscillator PUFs. J. Comput. Sci. Technol. 29(4), 664–678 (2014). https://doi.org/10.1007/s11390-014-1458-1

48. Zhang, J., Wan, L.: CMOS: dynamic multi-key obfuscation structure for strong PUFs. CoRR abs/1806.02011 (2018)

On the Feasibility of DoS Attack on Smart Door Lock IoT Network

Belal Asad[1] and Neetesh Saxena[2(✉)]

[1] Department of Computing and Informatics, Bournemouth University, Poole, UK
belal_ea@hotmail.com
[2] School of Computer Science and Informatics, Cardiff University, Cardiff, UK
nsaxena@ieee.org

Abstract. The Internet of Things (IoT) is one of the most extensive technological evolution of the computing network. This technology can transform the physical world into a virtual world for testing and emulation to evaluate the key issues present in the physical devices. This work aims to explore the security in IoT devices and demonstrates the security gaps in the behavior of the smart door lock. In this paper, we conducted two surveys to gather consumers' requirements about the IoT devices as to whether they do understand the security risks involves with these devices. Further, we carried out a denial of service attack on a smart lock device to demonstrate that such devices are not secure. This work also highlights the security weakness and suggest guidelines to improve the overall system using cloud and edge computing and authentication and access control-based solutions.

1 Introduction

The Internet of Things (IoT) is a new revolution of the networking technologies that uses the advantages of the wireless sensors network. The IoT platform has several types of applications that diversified in all areas of every-day life and several types of communication technologies are required to allow the connection between the IoT devices. The communication technologies could be divided into four different fields: the technology used to connect the IoT devices to the network, technology used for data collection and changes detection, technology to make these devices take action, and technology used to make the small devices have the ability to interact and connect. The massive connectivity in one platform makes this platform risky in security aspects. IoT platform needs to be flexible, extendable, and acceptable to mobility that allows the network and different devices the ability to communicate. All previous requirements make the security of the IoT network more challenging. Nowadays, IoT devices are involved in our daily life and deal with sensitive data through smart homes, smart gates, cars, etc. Such data needs to be protected.

The IoT technologies' deployments have been increased in the last few years, so the associated challenges and issues have also increased. The connection between people and objects can be made through any path, network, and service, as shown in Fig. 1(a). Using different types of technologies on a single platform creates several threats. There are many ways to attack this vulnerable system, such as accessing personal information,

© Springer Nature Singapore Pte Ltd. 2021
S. M. Thampi et al. (Eds.): SSCC 2020, CCIS 1364, pp. 123–138, 2021.
https://doi.org/10.1007/978-981-16-0422-5_9

disabling the connection, and destroy the process of the device by loading massive fake data. One of the applications of the smart city is a smart home and its smart appliances and devices, such as an intelligent gate or door. The business layer is not a part of the original IoT architecture, but it is considered under a five-layer architecture, as shown in Fig. 1(b).

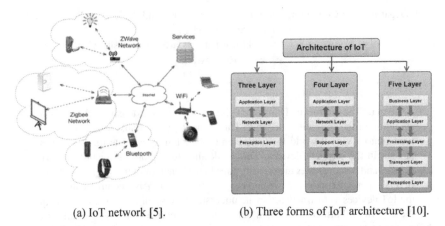

(a) IoT network [5].   (b) Three forms of IoT architecture [10].

Fig. 1. Internet of things network and three forms of architecture. (a). IoT network [5]. (b). Three forms of IoT architecture [10].

This work aims to identify the security issues challenges, as well as analyzing the most recent used security techniques. Secondly, it is to understand how the IoT devices' security work and behave through the network, and thirdly, it is to know how to develop a secure smart door and how the current technologies can be a benefit.

We summarize our contribution to this work as follows. (1) Investigated the currently used technologies and systems, also captured the reviews and opinions, (2) design and build a small emulation smart door system for Denial of Service (DoS) attack evaluation, (3) design the test cases on the emulation system, and (4) evaluate and analyze the results of the attacked system and suggest improvements.

The rest of the section of this paper is organized as follows. Section 2 starts with related work. This section helps to understand the current security issues in IoT platforms, as it presents the IoT architecture following it by the current security features and requirements. Furthermore, this section ends up with smart cities security, which illustrates the security risks and challenges for smart cities. Section 3 presents the results and evaluation of the work. Section 4 offers analysis and discussion around the findings and observations. Finally, Sect. 5 summarizes the conclusion.

2   Related Work

This section explores the identification of IoT technologies and illustrates the persistent inadequacies of currently available systems. The scope of the work starts with the modern IoT architecture, followed by the security issues and their requirement in each level of the architecture. Also, it shows the critical security challenges in the IoT system. Finally, it ends up with the authentication and authorization in the IoT followed that with the current security risks in smart cities.

2.1 Network Security in IoT and IoT Architecture

In recent days, the industrial companies propose several applications related to the IoT based on cyber-physical systems (CPS) and machine to machine communications (M2M). These fields also deal with their sensitive data [4]. The IoT platform faces more security issues challenges than the traditional Internet-based systems due to the reason that the IoT platform works and extends the Internet through sensor networks, traditional Internet, and mobile networks to provide flexibility and scalability [3]. Therefore, new algorithms and technologies need to be developed to achieve higher satisfaction for security requirements. The information security of the system in the traditional Internet must be compatible with several critical properties such as undeniability, confidentiality, integrality, and identification. The IoT platform is based on the conventional Internet, but it will be applied to critical and sensitive areas of the national economy, for example, smart transportation, and health care systems. Thus, the security of information and network in the IoT platform require higher availability and dependability [2]. In general, the IoT architecture consists of three different main layers and these layers simplify into four layers [7], as shown in Fig. 2. This addresses the IoT levels (perception, network, and application) and most modern architecture with four layers (perception, network, support or processing, and application); each of these layers has its security and management issues.

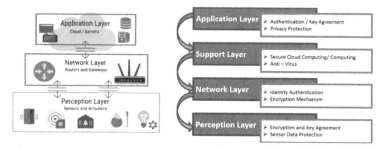

Fig. 2. Internet of things architecture [10].

2.2 Security Features

Network security issues can create troubles in building a secure preserved IoT system. This section explores the security problems in each layer of the IoT architecture as follows:

Perception Layer. This layer consists of simple nodes (sensors) with short of power and storage capacity; consequently, applying the traditional security algorithm is impossible

[3]. The most security issues in this layer are related to sensors, whereas this layer consists of sensors such as the global positioning system (GPS), wireless sensor networks (WSNs), and radio-frequency identification (RFID), etc., therefore, this layer is the main target of attackers [13]. Further, the key security issues in this layer are as follows:

i) *False sensor data:* The IoT systems depend on the sensors to collect information from the physical world to enhance the experiences of the IoT applications [9]. The attackers can control the demands of the IoT devices by altering the sensor data. The false sensor data or fake data can be injected through communication mediums, physical access, or the sensors of the IoT devices. The attackers can take advantage of the power analysis on IoT devices, as the power analysis using an encryption algorithm can detect details about the encryption process in the IoT system such as key size, block size, also the existent encryption key. The attacker can use the captured information to encrypt fake data and substitute the authentic data on the device [9]. Consequently, the false encrypted data can be injected in the communication medium to change the actual action of the system. The security issues of RFID technology are also related to false sensor data. RFID is contactless technology depends on identifying the target tag signal, the identifying process does not need manual involvement [3]. RFID is widely used in harsh environments that reveal many problems such as (1) *Conflict collision*: passing the information to the reader from multiple RFID tags simultaneously causing the reader to get incorrect data. (2) *Uniform coding*: Currently, there is no internationally uniform encoding standard for RFID tag [3]. This problem may cause other issues such as errors that occur during the reading process and authorize the reader to obtain the correct access information to the tag [3].

ii) *Malicious Sensor Commands:* Several sensors embedding in the IoT devices open away to transmit malicious commands to activate malware that might be implemented in the victim's device. The IoT sensors can be used to create communication channels between devices peripherals [10]. These channels aim to transmit malicious commands or to change the sensor parameters such as light intensity [9]. Since the light sensor can differentiate the intensity of the light source, it is easier for the attacker to transmit a bitstream via light source by turning it on and off, as the IoT devices decode the light intensity change as a bitstream [10].

iii) *Eavesdropping:* Eavesdropping refers to a type of unauthorized real-time attack where the attacker tries to steal the information that is transmitted over a network through private communications such as video conferences, phone calls, or text messages [10]. The malicious app records the audio, video, or saves texts by exploiting the audio sensors or messages sensors. In this type of attack, the attacker can save the recorded voice or listen to the conversation in real-time [9].

Transportation Layer. The transportation layer is highly sensitive to attacks, as the environment of this layer has prominent security problems, especially regarding authentication and integrity. This layer deals with issues that occur in the network layer as well. This part presents the common security issues as follows:

i) *Daniel of Service (DoS) Attack:* A DoS attack aims to prevent users from accessing the system by disabling the devices. The IoT devices can easily be affected by DoS attacks due to the constraints on time, energy consumption, and memory constraints [15]. By flooding the target with redundant requests makes the use of that target difficult or impossible for all or some users.

ii) *Man-in-the-Middle (MITM) Attack:* MITM is an attack where the attacker secretly relays, intercepts, and alters the communication between two devices. Since the attacker has access to control the communication, therefore he can change the information between the devices according to his needs [16].

iii) *Storage Attack:* The exchanged information in the communication between IoT devices usually stored in a storage environment such as storage devices or cloud, both storage environments able to be attacked by attackers. This attack is critical, especially in smart city applications, as the attacker can change the user's information to incorrect details [10].

Processing Layer. The processing or support layer is taking place between the transportation layer and the application layer. Sometimes, this layer itself is considered as a part of the transportation layer as it deals with exchanged information in the communications between two devices, as well as it deals with the storage environments. Consequently, the security issues at this level are related to security issues at transportation processing. The common security issues and attacks are as follows:

i) *Malware:* This attack base on such applications as viruses, spyware, Trojans horses, worms, and adware to collaborate with the system. It uses the executable form of scripts, contents, and codes to act against the system's requirements and steal the confidential information [19].

ii) *Exhaustion:* An attacker here uses attrition of the previous attack to disturb the processing of the IoT structure. In the IoT network, it could be a result of such attacks that impoverish the system resources.

Application Layer. The application layer is the terminal and user-centric layer of IoT architecture which performs diverse tasks for the users. Therefore, this layer has many different issues but the security issue comes as the main problem. Minutely, when the IoT is used to construct the smart home, it originates several vulnerabilities [10]. The devices used in smart homes are small and have weak resources such as low memory and computational power [11]. Common security issues in this layer are listed below:

i) *Malicious Code Attack:* This attack considers as an application security threat that cannot be discovered or controlled by the antivirus software. The attackers can attach the malicious code in any part of the software to damage the system. Furthermore, the attached code could activate by itself or could require action from the user [10].

ii) *Cross-Site Scripting:* This attack allows the attackers to inject client-side scripting in a trusted site used by other users. A cross-site attack gives full validity to the attackers to change the contents and illegally use the original policies.

Business Layer. The business layer acts as a manager for the whole system; therefore, the vulnerabilities in this layer permits the attackers to misuse the application by averting the business logic [10]. Mainly, most of the security issues at this level are weaknesses in an application that come as a result of a cracked or truant security control. The most dangerous security problem at this level is a zero-day attack [20]. The zero-day attack is an unknown security hole or problem which is exploited by an attacker to create complicated problems before the victim can detect it. This vulnerability enables the attacker to control the application without the user's knowledge and consent [20].

In addition to these security problems, the IoT system requires different communication technologies to achieve the purpose of the IoT existence. Each technology of these communication technologies has several security features and also provides security protocols, as well as these technologies that have some drawbacks which make the security more challenging in IoT [18]. Table 1 shows the different communication technologies used in IoT and illustrates the characteristics with the drawbacks for each.

Table 1. Different communication technologies used in IoT [1]

Technologies	Mechanism	Security	Applications	Characteristics	Drawbacks
ZigBee	Wireless	Encryption and Integrity	Home and Industry	Low consumption and Cheap	Fixed key
RFID	Frequency waves	Encryption (AES, DES)	Health care	Data capturing with no duplication	Lack of a uniform coding and no authorization
Bluetooth	Wireless	Encryption and Authentication	PDA, Mobiles and Laptops	Cable replacement and Low cost	Blue jacking, Bluesnarfing
Wi-Fi	Radio Signals	Authentication and Authorization	PC, Phones and Cameras	Faster, Secure and Convenient	Eavesdropping
WSN	Wireless	Key, Encryption and Authentication	Buildings and Health care	Low Cost, Power, and Resilience	DOS attack
5G Network	Wireless	Authentication and Authorization	Phone, IoT and Multimedia	Faster, Secure and Convenient	Distributed DoS

2.3 Security Challenges in the IoT

IoT security is an active research field. Various issues in different security aspects require solutions at diverse levels of security. The challenges in the security aspects of IoT could be divided into two main parts, as follows:

Security Challenges: The evolution of IoT technologies and the increasing number of connected devices to the IoT network increases the potential security threats [17]. As the IoT ameliorates the companies' productivity and improves the quality of human lives, it will increase the potential opportunities for cybercriminals and hackers. The latest studies disclose that more than 70% of the conventional used IoT devices have serious vulnerabilities [17]. The IoT will stay escalate over time; consequently, even by collecting all the security mechanisms of each layer and putting them together will not introduce reliable security for the IoT network [1]. The IoT applications are supporting several sensitive infrastructures such as health care, smart grid, and banking systems, which require a high level of security.

3 Results and Evaluation

This section aims at detailing the results obtained from the online survey, the investigation of the current technology, analyzing the used technology, and the findings from the emulation system. Furthermore, this section presents the evaluation of the entire results to propose an improved solution. This section presents aims through three main sub-sections as follows: 1) capturing stakeholders' requirements and their opinion, 2) designing and building the system, and 3) evaluations.

3.1 Capturing Stakeholders Requirements and Their Opinion

Stakeholders Identifications. The stakeholders are people who are looking to acquire this system and are actively involved in the work. Therefore, stakeholders are the user of this system and whose interests could be affected by the work, either positively or negatively [52]. The stakeholders' identification process could be done through several techniques such as consultation with organizations involved in the work, consultation with people planning to acquire such systems, and consultation with expert people working in the same field. To achieve this aim, the following potential objects have been suggested: the potential users for this technology, the available technologies to build such systems, and the system's behavior under an attack. Different potential objects and stakeholders identified within the work domain are potential users, expert people in technology, Arduino as an available technology to build the system and implement a DoS attack to analyze the system's behavior under attack.

The above stakeholders and objects can be categorized according to the method of gathering the information. The potential users and the expert people were considered as one category, where their information and requirement can be gathered via surveys or interviews. The third category's information and requirements can be extracted by studying the current researches, similar experiences, and analyzing the experts' reviews. Finally, the last object's requirements and information can be collected by implementing the real types of attacks and analyzing the findings. In order to identify the potential users' requirements and experts' reviews and their opinions, two online surveys were performed. The first survey was aimed at potential users. It focused on gathering the basic requirements that users expected from the smart locks and looks at their concerns about the security aspects. The targeted group was chosen randomly from different backgrounds and various ages, and the targeted group consisted of thirty-three participants. To gain respondents, the survey took up to three minutes to complete and gave four optional questions for who's interested in technical aspects. The structure of the survey consisted of seventeen questions, thirteen compulsory questions, and four optional questions. The questions were designed to get different requirements according to the differences of the responders' backgrounds. The first block of the survey addresses the countries, and the age ranges for the participants. Figure 3 shows the different backgrounds of the participants involved.

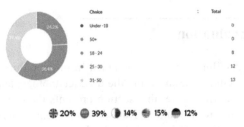

Fig. 3. Participants' backgrounds.

As can be seen from Fig. 3, the participants from different countries and their ages range from 18 to 50. A large proportion of who is interested in this technology is between the age of 25 to 50. Therefore, the people who have responsibilities or families to take care of are more interested in such systems. The next block consists of two questions that aimed to find out if the participants have already dealt with such systems. Figure 4 shows people's awareness of these technologies.

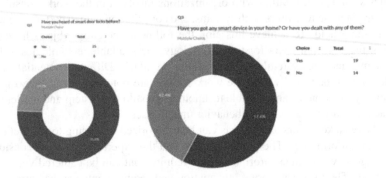

Fig. 4. Participants' awareness of smart devices.

As can be seen in Fig. 4 that 75.8% of the targeted group heard about the smart lock technology, and 57.6% of them have dealt with different IoT devices such as Apple HomePod, A/C, Smart TV, wall switches, and smart door lock. Only one participant out of 33 has dealt with the smart door lock. The next block of questions aimed to understand why the participants want to use the smart locks, what do they expect the smart lock would do for them and how much that will cost to have a smart lock. Figure 5 addresses the outcome of the participants' expectations.

From Fig. 5, it can be stated that the potential users' expected full control of the 'smart' device at a low price. In contrast, only 36% of them feel comfortable when using their phone as a key. The next set of questions show the reason why only 36% would like to use their phone as a key. Table 2 reflects that 61% of the participants are moderately

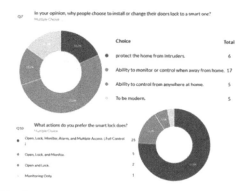

Fig. 5. The outcome of the participants' expectations.

likely to gain a smart lock. This percentage comes as a result of their satisfaction with the privacy of the internet in general. The optional questions were intended to understand the scientific background of the participants. Answered these questions, seventeen participants had technical certificates such as electronic engineering, network engineering, computer engineering, computer science, and PhD in cybersecurity. Table 3 illustrates the optional technical questions and shows that security issues are unknown to many people. Moreover, a large number of people who have a certificate in related areas are not aware of these issues. The answers to the first survey were a strong motivation to perform an additional survey. The second survey targeted four experts in Arduino to understand how well they know and able to avoid the available security issues. Table 4 illustrates the additional survey questions and the experts' answers. It reflects several aspects of the Arduino's experts. 100% of the experts do not take into consideration the security aspect while they are doing their works. Moreover, 90% of them put the security responsibility on the service provider or the remote server; as well as most of them were not aware of the most critical vulnerabilities in Arduino. However, all experts are interested to use a secure system for their future works.

Table 2. Participants' satisfaction.

Question	**Participants responds**	
Do you aware there is a general lack of security in the design of the leading IoT devices components.	65% of the participants aware that there is a general lack of security in the design of the leading IoT devices components	35% of the participants aware that there is a general lack of security in the design of the leading IoT devices components but they do not know about them in details.
How much do you aware of Memory Attacks?	29% of the participants aware about the memory attacks.	71% of participants not aware about this type of attacks.
Do you know most of IoT devices such as Arduino has Denial Of Service and Overflow Vulnerability?	15% of the participants know that Arduino devices has Denial of Service and Overflow vulnerabilities.	85% participants do not know about these vulnerabilities.

Table 3. The optional questions.

Question	Participants responds	
Do you aware there is a general lack of security in the design of the leading IoT devices components.	65% of the participants aware that there is a general lack of security in the design of the leading IoT devices components	35% of the participants aware that there is a general lack of security in the design of the leading IoT devices components but they do not know about them in details.
How much do you aware of Memory Attacks?	29% of the participants aware about the memory attacks.	71% of participants not aware about this type of attacks.
Do you know most of IoT devices such as Arduino has Denial Of Service and Overflow Vulnerability?	15% of the participants know that Arduino devices has Denial of Service and Overflow vulnerabilities.	85%participants do not know about these vulnerabilities.

Table 4. The additional survey.

Question	Expert 1	Expert 2	Expert 3	Expert 4
Developing Arduino Experience (in years)	5	6	4	6
Academic specialisation	BSc. software engineering	BSc. Electronic engineering	MSc. computer science	BSc electrical engineering
number of completed projects	78 mini projects and 7 robotics.	103 mini projects and 2 complicated projects.	50 mini projects.	97 mini projects, 6 robotics and 1 complicated project.
Do you know about security issues in Arduino?	I know that the security in Arduino is weak.	DDoS attacks issues	None.	limited resources
How do you secure your projects?	Depends on the cloud computing security only	Connecting the device to internet through remote server.	None.	Depends on the service provider
Have any of your projects been hacked?	None.	Two of them under university experiments	I never connected my projects to the internet.	no security tests have been applied to my projects
Do you take security aspects in count while you are building your projects?	No	No	No	No
Will you be interested in using a secure system in your future projects?	Yes	Yes	partly	Yes
Do you aware of Memory Attacks?	No	Yes	No	Yes
Do you know Arduino has Denial Of Service and Overflow Vulnerability?	No	I know that it has denial of service vulnerability but not overflow.	No	Yes

3.2 Designing and Building the System for Evaluation

In order to specify the requirements to propose an improved system, this section identifies the smart locks' key requirements followed by available types and then investigates the security vulnerabilities in Arduino. Furthermore, this section addresses the challenges and requirements to build a system for the evaluation. This section aims to understand and match the requirements extracted from the questionnaires and previous studies.

The Smart Door Identification and Types. In a smart home, the smart door is a door fitted with an electronic and mechanical device that allows a homeowner to control the door wirelessly. The user can wirelessly verify and unlock the door by using a smart key such as a smartphone or a key fob instead of the traditional keys. The common types of smart locks include password-based (2013), social networking site-based (2015), door phone-based (2013; 2019), and combined systems (2018).

Arduino. Arduino is an open-source programmable circuit board. This programmable board can be integrated into several complicated experiments. Arduino board contains a programmable microcontroller to sense and control objects in the physical world. Arduino's flexibility makes it a popular choice for building IoT devices. Arduino UNO, one of the most popular Arduino boards. To further study the proposed security mechanisms and its efficiency on the vulnerabilities, an emulation system was built and tested in this work. The following sections illustrate such requirements followed by the results.

The System Requirements. To know the requirements of the system, the experiment's scheme needs to be detailed. The emulated system considered different technology-based mechanisms such as cloud computing and fog computing. However, Fig. 6 addresses the scheme for the emulated system. The smart lock controller connecting to the edge device (Laptop) which acts as a gateway. To connect the IoT device to the Internet, the edge device connects to a remote server, which makes the mobile able to control the smart lock [21]. This system implements different security mechanisms such as cloud interface access and local authorization. Thereafter, we have used the Blynk application to run the experiments.

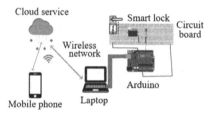

Fig. 6. Emulated system setup.

Faced Challenges. During the process of building the emulated system, the process faced critical challenges such as unknown errors while programming the board, errors while connecting the controller to the edge device, and difficulties while analyzing the security aspects. This section illustrates these challenges in two categories as follows:

Construction Stage Challenges. The first challenge appeared while uploading the code to the controller, an error message appear, and the serial port turned into disable mode. Figure 7 shows the error that occurred. This challenge was resolved by ordering a new Arduino board. The error occurred because of the damage that happened to a chip responsible for converting the USB port to a serial port. Another error was occurred to prevent the application to run the servo motor code. This challenge was resolved by replacing the library and the servo parameters.

Implementation Phase Challenges. The challenge faced here was a technical issue. The system was freezing when the sniffing command was calling Wireshark to capture packets. No error messages appeared at this stage. The challenge here has been resolved by updating the operating system.

Fig. 7. Error message and disabled port.

3.3 Evaluation: Findings and Examination Results

This section illustrates the findings which are shown through figures. Blynk application is used in the smartphone to communicate with the remote server. The Blynk sends a specific Auth code to each user in order to protect the controller from unauthorized devices. Figure 10 shows the application and its interface. The aim of this experiment is not to show how to build the smart lock but to show the security issues in the smart lock. Figure 8(a) shows the code built for this task whereas Fig. 8(b) shows the setup in working mode before implementing the DoS attack. The next stage of this experiment is to implement a DoS attack and analyze its outcome. The DoS attack was implemented on the system by using Pentmenu scripts in the Kali Linux environment.

(a) Blynk application interface and code.   (b) Smart door emulation system.

Fig. 8. Blynk application interface and experimental setup.

Figure 9(a) shows the attacking process for DoS attack as Slowloris. Slowloris is a type of denial of service attack that targets a single machine to take down another machine's web server with minimal bandwidth on unrelated services and ports. Figure 10 shows several packets that are sent to this device to perform a denial of service attack. Several attempts were made in a very short time. Different sources with different IP addresses were configured in the Linux environment to target a smart lock device (IP address 192.168.1.25) over the transmission control protocol (TCP). Each packet sent was 54 bytes in length. The application was running on source ports ranging from 9506 to 9522, whereas the destination port was fixed as 80. After flooding the network with these packets, the IoT device stop working correctly. As shown in Fig. 9(b), due to flood of the number of packets targeted to a single device in a very short time could result in disabling the device, and hence, denial of the service is performed (device does not respond). Thereafter, all the packets were also monitored using Wireshark to detect this DoS attack traffics. In this section, we demonstrated how to perform an attack over a smart lock. It also reflects that such smart devices can be hacked because they do not contain sufficient security to make the device secure against potential threats. As per these results and findings, the next section analyses all requirements to propose the improved system.

(a) Running a DoS attack.   (b) Disabled device after the attack.

Fig. 9. DoS attack successful attempts.

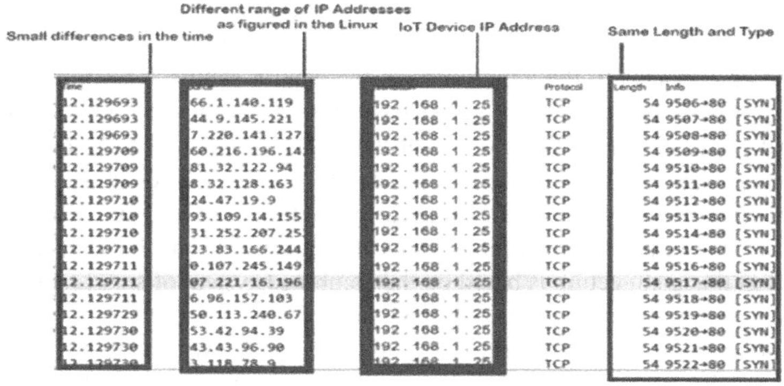

Fig. 10. DoS attack successful attack detection.

4   Analysis and Proposal for Improved System

This section aims to analyze the survey responses, the investigation of the build systems, and the experiment's results. The analyzation process aims to study the established investigation of available smart locks and the emulated experiment. Consequently, the analyzation process could be detailed as follows:

Stakeholders' and Experts' Opinions. According to the surveys, the targeted stakeholders are two different categories as follows:

Random Public: This diversity provides a general idea of the requirements and available security concerns that people have. Most of the respondents were aged between 25 to 50 that makes the answers more accurate. More than 57% of the participants dealt with IoT devices as well as more than 70% of them want a smart lock which has full control of the door. On the other hand, 61% of them not very likely to get such a smart lock system. The reasons behind lie behind two reasons: 1) 65% of them are not very confident using it and 2) lack of security in the IoT devices.

Experts: The answers to this survey show the massive gap between IoT developers and IoT security. Some of them aware of the lack of security in IoT but never considered security aspects.

The Investigation of Available Smart Locks. The investigation of the available smart locks covers most aspects of the stakeholders' requirements. Most of them are offering semi-full control of the door. On the other hand, the security aspects still weak and need some enhancements. Moreover, the most commonly used technology in smart lock shows several security vulnerabilities which make the IoT security a critical issue in the smart home. We have demonstrated one attack on such a smart lock.

Proposal for an Improved System. We proposed an improved system that combines three different mechanisms to avoid different security issues. Each IoT device in this architecture connects to the cloud through three different stages. Firstly, the IoT device connects to the edge device to enhance computation speed and protect the private information in a personal device [8]. Secondly, the edge device connects to the Internet through a local substation for authentication and authorization purposes [20]. Finally, the substation connects to the cloud through the central station. The proposed architecture keeps each specific group of IoT have their authentication and authorization station. All the devices from all different substations can communicate through the central station according to their roles [14]. Hence, this can avoid such attacks by placing authentication and access control based security controls. Furthermore, the smart lock in this architecture can provide different types of controls based on the users' needs. The smart lock in this architecture is based on the combined system of smart locks [6]. The built system used fog computing as a gateway to the Internet that offers the system more secure. Furthermore, the cloud system provides the owner with an authentication key which saved in his edge device [21]. The use of fog computing and the authentication key secure the controller from unauthorized users. However, the results of the experiment show the weakness of the authorization system used in the remote server and the edge device. The attacker did slowdown the smart lock performance without been blocked from the server. The experiment shows critical problems related to authentication and denial of service that can be avoided in the enhanced system.

5 Conclusion

IoT technologies are proliferating, and all modern countries around the world compete to convert into smart cities [12]. The work carried out highlighted the tendency for a further rise in IoT technologies, especially in smart homes and personal life. However, as the technologies spread quickly, the security issues increase as well. Therefore, this work aimed at analyzing and studying the security issues in a specific IoT device. Particularly, this work studied the security in the smart lock by following variable methods to gather the stakeholders' requirements and investigate the current smart lock by developing a setup. We demonstrated the insecurity (authentication issue and DoS attack possibility) present in a smart lock. The proposed architecture combines different security mechanisms to prevent the IoT device from several types of attacks. This work needs further studies to implement and analyze other attacks on a real IoT device. The emulated system needs to do further tests and mount attacks to explore threats and enhance using fog computing.

References

1. Bhuvaneswari, V., Porkodi, R.: The internet of things (IoT) applications and communication enabling technology standards: an overview. In: International Conference on Intelligent Computing Applications, pp. 324–329 (2014)
2. Weber, R.: Internet of Things – new security and privacy challenges. Comput. Law Secur. Rev. 26(1), 23–30 (2010)
3. Suo, H., Wan, J., Zou, C., Liu, J.: Security in the internet of things: a review.In: Intern'l Conference on Computer Science & Electronics Engineering, pp. 648–651 (2012)
4. Wan, J., Yan, H., Suo, H., Li, F.: Advances in cyber-physical systems research. KSII Trans. Internet Inf. Syst. 5(11), 1891–1908 (2011)
5. Desai, P., Sheth, A., Anantharam, P.: Semantic gateway as a service architecture for IoT interoperability. In: IEEE International Conference on Mobile Services, pp. 313–319 (2015)
6. Divya, M., Rao, M.: Centralized authentication smart locking system using RFID, fingerprint, password and GSM. Int. J. Eng. Technol. 7(3.12), p. 516 (2018)
7. Jing, Q., Vasilakos, A., Wan, J., Lu, J., Qiu, D.: Security of the internet of things: perspectives and challenges. Wireless Netw. 20(8), 2481–2501 (2014)
8. Shi, W., Cao, J., Zhang, Q., Li, Y., Xu, L.: Edge computing: vision and challenges. IEEE Internet Things J. 3(5), 637–646 (2016)
9. Kumar, A., Petracca, G., Aksu, H., Jaeger, T., Uluagac, S.: A survey on sensor-based threats to internet-of-things (IoT) Devices and Applications. arXiv, vol. 14 no. 1, pp. 2–14 (2018)
10. Burhan, M., Rehman, R., Khan, B., Kim, B.: IoT elements, layered architectures and security issues: a comprehensive survey. Sensors 18(9), 2796 (2018)
11. Khan, R., Khan, S., Zaheer, R., Khan, S.: Future internet: the internet of things architecture, possible applications and key challenges. In: 10th International Conference on Frontiers of Information Technology, Islamabad, pp. 257–260 (2012)

12. Sethi, P., Sarangi, S.: Internet of things: architectures, protocols, and applications. J. of Electr. Comput. Eng. **20**(9), 1–25 (2017)
13. Xiaohui, X.: Study on security problems and key technologies of the internet of things. In: International Conference on Computational and Information Sciences, pp. 407–410 (2013)
14. Saxena, N., Choi, B., Lu, R.: Authentication and authorization scheme for various user roles and devices in smart grid. IEEE TIFS **11**(5), 907–921 (2016)
15. Prabhakar, S.: Network security in digitalization: attacks and defence. Int. J. Res. Comput. Appl. Rob. **5**(5), 46–52 (2017)
16. Conti, M., Dragoni, N., Lesyk, V.: A survey of man in the middle attacks. IEEE Commun. Surv. Tutorials **18**(3), 2027–2051 (2016)
17. Lee, I., Lee, K.: The internet of things (IoT): applications, investments, and challenges for enterprises. Bus. Horiz. **58**(4), 431–440 (2015)
18. Al-Sarawi, S., Anbar, M., Alieyan, K., Alzubaidi, M.: Internet of Things (IoT) communication protocols: review. In: 8th International Conference on Information Technology (ICIT), pp. 685–690 (2017)
19. Canzanese, R., Kam, M., Mancoridis, S.: Toward an automatic, online behavioral malware classification system. In: IEEE International Conference on Self-Adaptive and Self-Organizing Systems, pp. 111–120 (2013)
20. Sharma, V., et al.: A consensus framework for reliability and mitigation of zero-day attacks in IoT. Secur. Commun. Netw. **17**(1), 1–24 (2017)
21. Cai, Y., Genovese, A., Piuri, V., Scotti, F., Siegel, M.: IoT-based architectures for sensing and local data processing in ambient intelligence: research and industrial trends. In: IEEE International Instrumentation and Measurement Technology Conference, pp. 1–6 (2019)

Trust-Based Adversarial Resiliency in Vehicular Cyber Physical Systems Using Reinforcement Learning

Felix O. Olowononi, Danda B. Rawat$^{(\boxtimes)}$, and Chunmei Liu

Data Science and Cybersecurity Center (DSC^2), Department of Electrical
Engineering and Computer Science, Howard University, Washington D.C 20059, USA
{felix.olowononi,danda.rawat,chuLiu}@howard.edu

Abstract. Vehicular cyber physical systems (VCPS), by leveraging on
advancements in sensing, wireless technologies and vehicular ad hoc networks (VANET) have improved driving experience and birthed systems
like cooperative adaptive cruise control, and have formed the foundation for autonomous and platooned vehicles. However, its deployment
is adversely affected by security concerns even as attackers continue to
improve their attacks methods. In recent years, machine learning has
become an invaluable tool for research, and investigations into its application in CPS security is increasingly active. Although, supervised learning techniques were used for most tasks initially, reinforcement learning
due to the excellent results obtained in peculiar cases like the environment in which vehicles operate have become popular. Trust management
systems are also very useful in identifying adversaries in a vehicular network. In this paper, a data-oriented trust-based method for improving
the resiliency of vehicles to adversarial attacks is investigated using RL.
Improving on other works that combine direct and indirect trusts and
assume that vehicles interact for a long time, this method is suited for
the dynamic environment vehicles operate in and the high mobility they
experience. Specifically, the Q-learning learning algorithm is used to learn
and adapt the weight used to estimate the trust value and therefore
reflect the real environment. The simulation results obtained show that
the proposed methodology is efficient and establishes the contributions
of the application of RL to CPS security.

Keywords: Adversarial attacks · CPS security · Reinforcement
learning

1 Introduction

The trend in technology recently reflects an increase in the levels of automation and intelligence in various systems. Rising from the vast interconnection of

This work is partly supported by the U.S. NSF under grants CNS-1650831, CNS/SaTC
2039583, CCF-0939370 and HRD-1828811, and by the DoD Center of Excellence in AI
and Machine Learning (CoE-AIML) at Howard University under Contract Number
W911NF-20-2-0277 with the U.S. Army Research Laboratory.

S. M. Thampi et al. (Eds.): SSCC 2020, CCIS 1364, pp. 139–151, 2021.
https://doi.org/10.1007/978-981-16-0422-5_10

things (IoT) that has caused a revolution in fields like entertainment, healthcare, transportation, power, warfare, home and industrial systems, cyber physical systems (CPS) have become a subject of high research interest due to the advanced functionalities they offer by seamlessly integrating a feedback control with the communication and computing capabilities of the IoT.

Vehicular cyber physical systems (VCPS) are a class of CPS that leverage on a fusion of advancements in computing, communication and control technologies to improve the intelligence or automation of vehicles [12,13]. In principle, sensors and other devices like Lidar, geographic positioning system (GPS) devices and cameras capture information regarding the state of the environment, send it over the vehicular network to computing devices that analyze the data and give a feedback in response to the instruction it receives for the utmost benefit of the driver. VCPS therefore have the potential to address challenges of vehicular congestion, environmental concerns, reduce accidents and therefore improve the overall efficiency of transportation systems, especially in cities around the world that are beginning to suffer from population explosion. The adoption of standards for vehicular communications, including the dedicated short range communications (DSRC) have contributed to the seamless exchange of information between vehicles. The infrastructure in the vehicular ad hoc network (VANET) include the on-board units in the connected vehicles, the road side infrastructure (RSU) and another central authority in some cases. The exchange of information between vehicles is done through vehicle-to-vehicle (V2V) communications, while the exchange of information between vehicles and the RSU's is done through vehicle-to-infrastructure (V2I) communications. The vehicular networks in intelligent transportation systems, by sharing road-related messages concerning road conditions and traffic congestion between vehicles have improved the driver experience, helped to address safety concerns and improve the overall efficiency. VCPS, by leveraging on advancements in sensing, wireless technologies and VANET have improved the driving experience and birthed systems like cooperative adaptive cruise control and advanced braking systems, the foundation for autonomous and platooned vehicles. However, VCPS deployment has been inhibited by security concerns that stem from an increase in the frequency of adversarial attacks and the advancements in methods used for such attacks.

Cryptography-based authentication methods have been extensively used for securing VCPS from cyber attacks. Security is achieved through a combination of software and hardware infrastructure such as certificates, signatures, public key infrastructure and trusted third parties [8,16]. However, challenges such as delay encountered in the process of carrying out the required checks before authenticating participating vehicles necessitated the quest for more efficient methods. Furthermore, cryptographic techniques, which essentially are an access control method have proven efficient in preventing unauthorized users or attackers from accessing the network. However, with the advent of other attacking methodologies like bad-mouthing and ballot-stuffing [9], it has been discovered that vehicles can be legitimate members of the network but compromise the network and other vehicles in it by acting selfish. They therefore receive messages from other members but refuse to send it to others in a bid to conserve their resources. In another case, the vehicles give false feedback to either improve or reduce the ratings of other vehicles.

Trust management systems for securing VCPS from adversarial attacks have therefore been investigated and found to be more efficient in solving the challenge of insider attackers, identification of selfish users and form effective collaboration with other nodes through the use of incentives that encourage them to forward messages [8]. Other trust-based services in VCPS include routing, clustering, data aggregation, distributed denial-of-service (DDoS), location privacy and authentication [7]. They are also distributed in nature, place little or no emphasis on external infrastructure, little delay concerns and operational in highly dynamic environments [1]. Trust establishment in vehicular networks is usually evaluated from the history of direct interactions between vehicles and the recommendation of third-party nodes in the absence of direct interactions. Furthermore, trust models in VCPS have been classified into entity-oriented, data-oriented and a hybrid of both.

Research has progressed from a focus on the behaviour of vehicles as an entity to the analysis of the messages that are sent by the vehicles [15]. Recent research in data-oriented models are presented in [5,9,18]. Also, game theory has been used to model the interactions between the attacker and other vehicles for trust evaluation at any point in time [17]. Furthermore, since machine learning (ML) has become an invaluable tool for research especially in the security of CPS, the recent direction is to use ML models to evaluate the trust of systems thereby make it dynamic. Specifically, reinforcement learning (RL) has proven to obtain more suitable results than traditional ML algorithms like Bayesian Inference and K-Nearest Neighbor.

This paper therefore focuses on the use of RL to dynamically compute trust of events exchanged in vehicular networks to make vehicles resilient to adversarial attacks from malicious nodes within the network.

The remainder of this paper is organized as follows. Section 2 presents the related works. Then, the problem is well-defined in Sect. 3. This is done by discussing in detail the system model and the adversary model considered in the research. The proposed method is detailed in Sect. 4, while Sect. 5 presents the results of simulations run to evaluate the performance of the proposed approach. Finally, the research is concluded in Sect. 6.

2   Related Works

In this section, research about trust management in vehicular networks and VCPS are first presented, and then succeeded by a summary of research endeavors directed at the application of RL in VCPS security. As already highlighted, trust evaluation has become very important in securing VCPS from attacks. Different models have been presented by researchers and various metrics have also been used to evaluate the performance of these proposed schemes. Rawat et al. [14] presented the probabilistic and deterministic methods of estimating trust among vehicles in a VANET. The probabilistic method was based on

Bayesian inference while the deterministic approach was based on distance calculation between vehicles using relevant metrics like received signal strength and the geo-location. The authors conclude that a combination of both methods is able to achieve better results. Zhao et al. [21] proposed a novel trust model to theorize the trust relationship in a dynamic environment of the VCPS. The proposed method leveraged on intransitive non-interference and cryptography technologies. However, the authors suggested that for further research, artificial intelligence can be used to enhance the proposed dynamic trust model.

Notwithstanding that various trust management models have been proposed to detect attacks in vehicular networks, a study of literature has shown that existing models need to be improved upon because they do not capture the dynamic behaviors of malicious and selfish/greedy vehicles, and also do not account for the highly volatile environment in vehicular networks. In response to this, ML models that are based on trust evaluation have been applied in the security of VCPS in recent times. In our earlier work, we developed a distributed ML algorithm to enhance the resiliency of vehicles to adversarial attacks [11]. The proposed model was also based on Bayesian inference. In [3], a trust model was combined with a Bayesian neural network to detect malicious nodes in vehicular networks. However, the authors only presented the framework and stated the actual simulation as a further work. Furthermore, Liang et al. [10] presented a trust-based recommendation scheme that leveraged on K-Nearest Neighbor (KNN) for filtering malicious/selfish nodes in VCPS.

Moreover, the need to learn trust dynamically, and the results obtained by RL in other tasks in autonomous vehicles made researchers investigate its application to the security of VCPS. Ferdowsi et al. [4] sought to improve the robustness of autonomous vehicles to adversarial attacks by formulating a non-cooperative game between the attackers and the vehicle, and proceeded to use the deep RL to solve the formulated game. However, this research does not focus on trust evaluation of the vehicle and others around it. Xing et al. [20] are one of the few authors to have investigated the security of VCPS through trust evaluation and RL. The proposed framework begins with a trust evaluation model, the presentation of a two-level intrusion detection framework and the use of RL to encourage vehicles to send their warnings about the condition of traffic and other safety related messages through the offer of incentives. However, only the framework of the proposed model was presented. Guo et al. [6] proposed a context aware trust model for VANET using RL. They compared their model with other trust models and concluded that it was more efficient. Also, unlike previous assumptions, the authors stated that their model can perform efficiently even when the malicious nodes are more than the honest nodes. This paper is therefore set to research the application of RL for the development of a dynamic trust model.

3   System Model

This section describes the system model and assumptions in its design. Furthermore, it discusses the adversary model.

3.1 Network Model

The VANET which comprises of a wireless network of heterogeneous sensors and other computing devices located in vehicles, is a major component of the VCPS. An illustration of the system model is seen in Fig. 1. In the network, the vehicles continue to monitor the state of the road and the environment and share this information and the status of the vehicles among themselves. The vehicles are assumed to be equipped with sensors, on-board units (OBU's) to communicate with other vehicles and RSU's through an open wireless channel. Various devices embedded within vehicles enable continuous monitoring of driving conditions. Vehicles are equipped with computing, communications, storage and controlling devices including cameras, sensors, radars, lidars and GPS devices. The vehicles are therefore able to gather contextual information about their environment through the sensors and cameras and exchange information about events to other vehicles. Events such as accidents and traffic congestion's are sent to other connected vehicles.

3.2 Adversary Model

The complex wireless interactions between vehicles have also increased the attack surface in VCPS. The attackers have therefore used the opportunity to launch various attacks with an intent to compromise the security and privacy of these systems. Such attacks have been widely classified into the active and the passive attacks. We have already established that access control methods like authentication can be used to stop outside attacks. However, the trust-based system

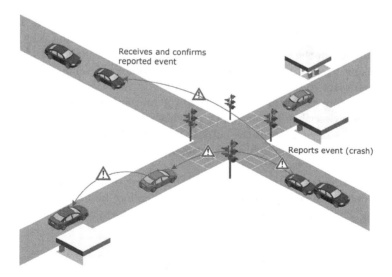

Fig. 1. System model of the vehicular cyber physical system.

proposed in this paper focuses on insider attacks. Specifically, malicious and selfish vehicles are the focus of the proposed model.

The major attack focused on in this paper is the bad mouth attack. Specifically, the attacker attempts to send messages about the occurrence of events that are contrary to the truth. We therefore consider two types of vehicles; honest and malicious vehicles. The event reports sent by the former correlate with the state of the environment while those sent by the latter contradict it.

4   Proposed Method

The proposed method comprises of a trust model for estimating the trust of messages exchanged about the occurrence of events, and the use of RL to obtain the optimal strategy. The information entropy is used to estimate the trust of messages sent.

4.1   Trust Model

Trust is a function of uncertainty and is used to quantify or describe the probability that the agent carries out an action from the perspective of the subject [19]. Furthermore, it is a measure of reliance and is therefore used in VCPS. The trust management system discussed in this section is data-centric. As already described in the system model, connected vehicles send messages about their state and events that occur that other vehicles should be aware of. These messages typically contain identity of the vehicles from which the message originated, identification of the reported event, location of the event, the time of occurrence of the reported event and the trust that is a reflection of the level of certainty of the occurrence of the event. The knowledge of such an event will help the receiving vehicle take decisions that guide its driving behavior and thus guarantee efficiency. From the adversary model, the possibility of malicious and selfish nodes refusing to send messages about the occurrence of events in the vicinity makes it necessary to introduce the concept of trust into the system. The recipient must therefore ascertain the veracity of the message. For the purpose of this research, trust describes the certainty of whether an event has occurred from the perspectives or opinion of the subject based on the contextual information available to it. The overall goal is to estimate the trust level of the occurrence of an event.

Also, referring to information theory, the entropy of a message is a measure of its certainty. The entropy of a message can therefore be used to estimate the trust value. The entropy-based trust [19] value can be expressed as:

$$T = \begin{cases} 1 - H(p), & \text{for } 0.5 \leq p \leq 1 \\ H(p) - 1, & \text{for } 0 \leq p < 0.5 \end{cases} \tag{1}$$

where $H(p) = -p \log_2(p) - (1 - p) \log_2(1 - p)$ and p is the probability that the agent will perform the action in the subject's point of view. Trust is therefore a function of p and $0 \leq p < 0.5$ represents a negative trust while $0.5 \leq p \leq 1$ represents a positive trust.

The information needed to form the trust about the occurrence of an event that has the potential of affecting the driving behaviour of a vehicle in the network is obtained from two sources. These are referred to as self-acquired data and the reported data. The analysis of the self-acquired data gathered by the sensors in the on-board unit of the focal vehicle and the reported data by other vehicles about an event are used to form the trust about the event. Similar to the study of entity-centric trust model, where the overall trust is a combination of the weights of direct trust and the indirect trust estimated from recommendations of third parties about a vehicle or node, the trust model here focuses on weighted sums of trust evaluation from direct experience and reported data about the occurrence of an event. Equation 2 below shows how the final trust is evaluated.

$$T_{event} = \Theta T_{self} + (1 - \Theta)T_{reported} \tag{2}$$

where T_{event} represents the final trust about the occurrence of the event, T_{self} represents the trust evaluation from direct experience, and $T_{reported}$ represents the reported data about the occurrence of an event and Θ is a parameter that adjusts the weight place on the contribution of $T_{reported}$ and T_{self} to T_{event}. Furthermore, it will be seen that to address the state-of-the art challenges, trust is learned in this approach using RL. The process is discussed in the next section.

4.2   Reinforcement Learning for Dynamic Weight Evaluation for Optimal Strategy

In RL, an agent operates in an unknown environment and seeks to achieve some rewards by its interactions with the environment. The agent therefore learns the environment by taking actions, with a goal to maximise the cumulative rewards. In other words, through trials in an experiment-like fashion, and the feedback received from such trials, the agent gradually adapts itself to the environment and thus arrives at a good strategy for future actions. A typical RL model has major components like states, actions, rewards, policy and value function. The agents policy directs it on the optimal action to carry out in a particular state to maximise the total rewards. The value function in a state gives a prediction of the amount of rewards obtainable in the future when the corresponding policy is applied. The focus of the whole algorithm is therefore to learn the policy and value functions.

The state space reflects the characteristics of the information available with respect to a request for trust evaluation. We have already established that because different states have different behaviors and thus strategy for trust evaluation, the state at a particular point in time reflects the condition of the road at that point and the trust-related information that are available to it. Because different states may correspond to different evaluation strategies, a state should reflect the road condition related to the request and the quality and quantity of available trust information related to the request. The entropy is therefore used to measure the quality of trust information.

The action space of the proposed model is the value range of Θ. This is because it determines the contributions of the trusts attained from the contextual information available to the system. From Eq. 2, we know that Θ ranges between 0 and 1.

Algorithm Structure. In this research, the RL algorithm used is the Q-learning. Q-learning is a model-free RL algorithm for value-based updating. It is usually used in problems that can be modeled as a Markov Decision Process (MDP), and thus works well where the transition from a state to the other are stochastic and associated with a reward. Q-learning therefore, beginning with the current state finds an optimal policy that maximizes the expected value of the total reward over the successive steps.

Algorithm 1. RL Algorithm for learning of optimal strategy

Input: The state space, action space and iterative rewards for an action on a state
Output: The optimal action-value function
1: Initialize the Q(s,a) value functions arbitrarily
2: Perceive the current state s
3: Using the described policy, select an appropriate action a for the given state s
4: Update the Q value according to (4):
   $Q(s, a) \leftarrow \alpha r_{t+1} + \gamma \max_{a \in A} Q(s_{t+1}, a_{t+1}) + (1 - \alpha) Q(s, a)$
5: Perceive the current state s
6: Go to step 3 until s state represents the terminal state

In principle, the agent first chooses an action, obtains a reward from the environment and constantly updates the Q-table. The Q-table therefore provides a reflection of the best strategy. The Q-value of a single state can be expressed as:

$$Q(s, a) = R + \gamma \cdot \max Q(s_{t+1}, a_{t+1}) \tag{3}$$

Equation 3 is the Bellman equation and typically expresses the maximum future reward as the sum of the reward the agent obtains from being in the present state s and the maximum future reward it will obtain when it transitions to state s_{t+1}, after taking an action a_{t+1}. $\gamma \in [0,1]$ represents the discount factor, a measure of the weight given to future rewards in the value function.

Furthermore, based on Eq. 3 above, the iterative updates of the Q-value over successive states can be expressed as the Q-learning equation, given by:

$$Q(s_t, a_t) \leftarrow Q(s_t, a_t) + \alpha[r_{t+1} + \gamma \max_{a \in A} Q(s_{t+1}, a_{t+1}) - Q(s_t, a_t)] \tag{4}$$

where $\alpha \in [0,1]$ represents the learning rate that controls how much the difference between previous and new Q value is considered, and $\gamma \in [0,1]$ represents the discount factor.

In a real scenario, a vehicle which receives a message about an event and seeks to evaluate the trust of the event checks with the available information available to it about the event in question. This analysis of the available trust information results in the state of the event. With the information about the state of the event, the optimal strategy is obtained with Eq. 5

$$\Theta = AS[a] \max_{a \in A} Q(s_t, a_t) \tag{5}$$

Algorithm 1 shows the principle for learning the optimal strategy.

5 Performance Evaluation

In this section, the performance of the proposed approach is evaluated. As already highlighted in the adversary model, we consider the malicious and the honest vehicles. The event reports sent by the honest vehicles correlate with the state of the environment while the event reports sent by the malicious vehicles contradict it. To evaluate the performance of our system, two metrics are used. These include the precision rate (PR) and the event detection probability (EDP).

The precision rate is based on the variant of the precision, which is commonly used to evaluate the performance of ML algorithms. Typically, the precision refers to the proportion of positive results that are correctly classified.

$$Precision = \frac{TP}{TP + FP} \tag{6}$$

where TP and FP refers to the number of true positive and false positives respectively. In similar manner, PR used for the evaluation of the performance of the proposed approach is expressed as follows:

$$PR = \frac{N_t}{N_e} \tag{7}$$

where N_t refers to the number of true decisions made and N_e refers to the number of events that are evaluated. We therefore evaluate the effects of the learning rate α and number of malicious events broadcast on the precision rate.

Considering Eqs. 2 and 3, the major parameters for this simulation are the learning rate (α), discount factor (γ) and the weighting factor (Θ). For this simulation, γ is set to zero in Algorithm 1. This implies that only the historical learning result and the current reward are considered while updating the Q-table. As earlier highlighted, Θ is learnt from the RL process, and in line with Eq. 5.

Figure 2 shows the effect of learning rate on precision rate over 200 rounds or iterations. From the figure, we see that three learning rates are considered. These include $\alpha = 0.5$. 0.8 and 1. We therefore observe that the precision rate

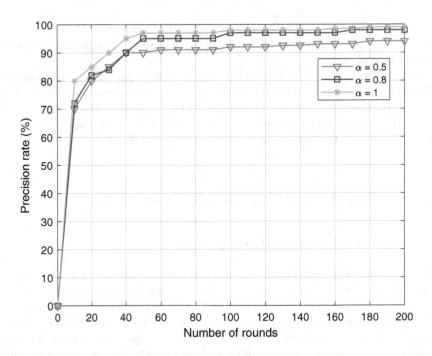

Fig. 2. The effect on learning rate on precision rate

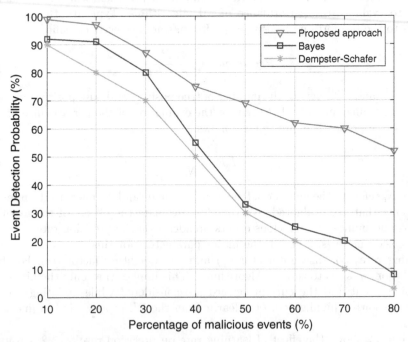

Fig. 3. Comparison of the performance of the proposed approach with other data-centric methods

rises gradually at the beginning at almost the same rate for the three cases. Due to the nature of the state, which includes the verification of events, it is noticed a fair precision rate of about 70% is already achieved after about 10 iterations. Thereafter, the plots at the learning rate of 1 is quicker to converge to a precision rate of over 90% before the others. Looking further, we see that after 100 iterations, the plot obtained when $\alpha = 0.8$ and 1 achieve a relatively steady precision rate greater than 90%. Furthermore, after 200 iterations, the plot of $\alpha = 0.5$ continues to move steadily with a precision rate of about 95%.

Furthermore, to evaluate the performance of the proposed method and compare it with existing data centric methods like Bayesian Learning and Dempster-Shaefer methods as in [15], we compare the event detection probability (EDP) of the methods when infused with varying proportions of malicious events. EDP [2] is expressed in Eq. 8 below as:

$$EDP = \frac{\sum(E_t - E_m)}{E_m} \tag{8}$$

where E_t refers to the total number of events generated and E_m refers to the number of malicious events.

In Fig. 3, the proposed approach is compared with two common data-centric methods. The metric used for comparing their performance is the EDP, in the presence of changing malicious events. The figure shows that at 10% of malicious events, the proposed scheme performs excellently well with an EDP of 99%. The other two schemes also have an EDP of above 90%. With 20% of malicious events present, the other schemes experience a significant decline in performance when compared to the proposed scheme. Furthermore, the decline steeps largely from 30% till almost 0% of EDP as the number of malicious events become higher. However, despite a decline in the performance of the proposed approach, the rate of decline in performance is not as steep as the other schemes. This therefore proves the superiority of the proposed scheme over the other schemes. With an EDP of 50% in the presence of 80% of malicious events, it has a relatively better performance. We attribute the performance of the proposed approach to the challenges with the Q-learning algorithm for RL. However, it is impractical to have above 30% of malicious events in a typical vehicular network.

6   Conclusion

This paper has focused on achieving resiliency in VCPS with the use of a trust management system and reinforcement learning. The goal is to improve on our earlier research that approached the problem of adversarial attacks in vehicles using Bayesian learning, and also the works of other researchers who designed models that used other methods like the Dempster-Shaefer evidence theory and Bayesian Learning. Moreover, it was shown that RL model is better suited to the dynamic environment vehicles travel in and does need the assumptions of a limited number of malicious users made in other works. The ability of the RL model to adapt to the environment by learning the trust values make it supersede other systems that have a fixed threshold. Our future works include the investigation of other factors like computational complexity and the effect of the proposed method on delay. We will also consider the implementation of the Deep-Q Network (DQN), a more robust Deep Reinforcement Learning (DRL) algorithm to solve the problem.

References

1. Adewuyi, A.A., Cheng, H., Shi, Q., Cao, J., MacDermott, Á., Wang, X.: Ctrust: a dynamic trust model for collaborative applications in the internet of things. IEEE Internet Things J. **6**(3), 5432–5445 (2019)
2. Ahmad, F., Adnane, A., Kurugollu, F., Hussain, R.: A comparative analysis of trust models for safety applications in IoT-enabled vehicular networks. In: 2019 Wireless Days (WD), pp. 1–8. IEEE (2019)
3. Eziama, E., Tepe, K., Balador, A., Nwizege, K.S., Jaimes, L.M.S.: Malicious node detection in vehicular ad-hoc network using machine learning and deep learning. In: 2018 IEEE Globecom Workshops (GC Wkshps), pp. 1–6 (2018)
4. Ferdowsi, A., Challita, U., Saad, W., Mandayam, N.B.: Robust deep reinforcement learning for security and safety in autonomous vehicle systems. In: 2018 21st International Conference on Intelligent Transportation Systems (ITSC), pp. 307–312. IEEE (2018)
5. Gazdar, T., Belghith, A., Abutair, H.: An enhanced distributed trust computing protocol for vanets. IEEE Access **6**, 380–392 (2017)
6. Guo, J., et al.: Trove: a context awareness trust model for vanets using reinforcement learning. IEEE Internet Things J. **7**(7), 6647–6662 (2020)
7. Hussain, R., Lee, J., Zeadally, S.: Trust in vanet: a survey of current solutions and future research opportunities. IEEE Trans. Intell. Transp. Syst. 1–19 (2020)
8. Kerrache, C.A., Calafate, C.T., Cano, J., Lagraa, N., Manzoni, P.: Trust management for vehicular networks: an adversary-oriented overview. IEEE Access **4**, 9293–9307 (2016)
9. Kerrache, C.A., Calafate, C.T., Lagraa, N., Cano, J.C., Manzoni, P.: Trust-aware opportunistic dissemination scheme for vanet safety applications. In: 2016 International IEEE Conferences on Ubiquitous Intelligence & Computing, Advanced and Trusted Computing, Scalable Computing and Communications, Cloud and Big Data Computing, Internet of People, and Smart World Congress (UIC/ATC/ScalCom/CBDCom/IoP/SmartWorld), pp. 153–160. IEEE (2016)
10. Liang, W., Long, J., Weng, T.H., Chen, X., Li, K.C., Zomaya, A.Y.: TBRS: a trust based recommendation scheme for vehicular cps network. Future Generation Comput. Syst. **92**, 383–398 (2019)
11. Olowononi, F.O., Rawat, D.B., Garuba, M., Kamhoua, C.: Security engineering with machine learning for adversarial resiliency in cyber physical systems. In: Pham, T. (ed.) Artificial Intelligence and Machine Learning for Multi-Domain Operations Applications, vol. 11006, pp. 605–611. International Society for Optics and Photonics, SPIE (2019). https://doi.org/10.1117/12.2519372
12. Rawat, D.B., Alsabet, R., Bajracharya, C., Song, M.: On the performance of cognitive internet of vehicles with unlicensed user-mobility and licensed user-activity. Comput. Netw. **137**, 98–106 (2018)
13. Rawat, D.B., Bajracharya, C.: Adaptive connectivity for vehicular cyber-physical systems. Vehicular Cyber Physical Systems, pp. 15–24. Springer, Cham (2017). https://doi.org/10.1007/978-3-319-44494-9_2

14. Rawat, D.B., Yan, G., Bista, B.B., Weigle, M.C.: Trust on the security of wireless vehicular ad-hoc networking. Ad Hoc Sensor Wireless Netw. **24**(3–4), 283–305 (2015)

15. Raya, M., Papadimitratos, P., Gligor, V.D., Hubaux, J.P.: On data-centric trust establishment in ephemeral ad hoc networks. In: IEEE INFOCOM 2008-The 27th Conference on Computer Communications, pp. 1238–1246. IEEE (2008)

16. Safavat, S., Rawat, D.B.: On the elliptic curve cryptography for privacy-aware secure ACO-AODV routing in intent-based internet of vehicles for smart cities. IEEE Trans. Intell. Transp. Syst. (2020). https://doi.org/10.1109/TITS.2020. 3008361

17. Shivshankar, S., Jamalipour, A.: An evolutionary game theory-based approach to cooperation in vanets under different network conditions. IEEE Trans. Veh. Technol. **64**(5), 2015–2022 (2014)

18. Shrestha, R., Nam, S.Y.: Trustworthy event-information dissemination in vehicular ad hoc networks. Mobile Inf. Syst. **2017**, 1–16 (2017)

19. Sun, Y.L., Yu, W., Han, Z., Liu, K.R.: Information theoretic framework of trust modeling and evaluation for ad hoc networks. IEEE J. Sel. Areas Commun. **24**(2), 305–317 (2006)

20. Xing, R., Su, Z., Zhang, N., Peng, Y., Pu, H., Luo, J.: Trust-evaluation-based intrusion detection and reinforcement learning in autonomous driving. IEEE Network **33**(5), 54–60 (2019)

21. Zhao, H., Sun, D., Yue, H., Zhao, M., Cheng, S.: Dynamic trust model for vehicular cyber-physical systems. J. Network Secur. **20**(1), 157–167 (2018)

Benchmarking Behavior-Based Intrusion Detection Systems with Bio-inspired Algorithms

Paulo Ferreira[1] and Mário Antunes[1,2,3(✉)]

[1] School of Technology and Management, Polytechnic of Leiria, Leiria, Portugal
`2180047@my.ipleiria.pt`, `mario.antunes@ipleiria.pt`
[2] CIIC, School of Technology and Management, Polytechnic of Leiria - Portugal,
Leiria, Portugal
[3] INESC-TEC, CRACS, University of Porto - Portugal,
Porto, Portugal

Abstract. Network security encompasses distinct technologies and protocols, being behaviour based network Intrusion Detection Systems (IDS) a promising application to detect and identify zero-day attacks and vulnerabilities exploits. In order to overcome the weaknesses of signature-based IDS, behaviour-based IDS applies a wide set of machine learning technologies to *learn* the normal behaviour of the network, making it possible to detect malicious and not yet seen activities. The machine learning techniques that can be applied to IDS are vast, as are the methods to generate the datasets used for testing. This paper aims to evaluate CSE-CIC-IDS2018 dataset and benchmark a set of supervised bioinspired machine learning algorithms, namely CLONALG Artificial Immune System, Learning Vector Quantization (LVQ) and Back-Propagation Multi-Layer Perceptron (MLP). The results obtained were also compared with an ensemble strategy based on a majority voting algorithm. The results obtained show the appropriateness of using the dataset to test behaviour based network intrusion detection algorithms and the efficiency of MLP algorithm to detect zero-day attacks, when comparing with CLONALG and LVQ.

1 Introduction

The security of computers networks encloses a wide set of technologies to protect the assets and the users' operation. For example, the use of *secure* protocols like HTTPS or the definition of virtual private networks, give protection to the application layer and hide user data between the client/server connection. However, new and unseen abnormal network behaviours have to be detected with more dedicated technologies, being IDS one of those approaches.

The sense of *normal* network activity is defined by recurrent patterns, easily identified by network activity features, like the number of packets exchanged, error rate and other network flows characteristics. Network intrusions usually explore software vulnerabilities and correspond to deviations to the normal network activity. These vulnerabilities may already be known and some kind of

© Springer Nature Singapore Pte Ltd. 2021
S. M. Thampi et al. (Eds.): SSCC 2020, CCIS 1364, pp. 152–164, 2021.
https://doi.org/10.1007/978-981-16-0422-5_11

signature may be already available for the IDS. In this case, a signature based IDS triggers an alert in the occurrence of a match between the pattern being analysed and the database of signatures. Vulnerabilities may also be unknown and correspond to a *zero day* attack. Signature based IDS is unable to detect such attacks, being behaviour based the promising approach to deal with such unknown and previously unseen patterns. Regarding behaviour based IDS, the process of learning and training is complex, taking into account the volume and variety of network traffic. Machine Learning (ML) tools and techniques are a helping hand on preprocessing network traffic and automating the learning and testing phases.

Among the multiplicity of existing ML algorithms, this paper evaluates a subset of bioinspired algorithms that are widely implemented by ML tools. The major contributions are the following: i) an open source framework and processing flow, based on WEKA [1], to ingest and process CSE-CIC-IDS2018 dataset; ii) an open source tool to automate the tests carried on with CLONALG [2,3], LVQ [4] and Back-MLP [5] classifiers; iii) a benchmark between the algorithms and an ensemble, using a *majority voting* strategy. This paper is organized as follows: Sect. 2 describes the key concepts for this work. The tests setup is described in Sect. 3, the results are presented in Sect. 4 and further analysed in Sect. 5. Finally, the conclusions and future work suggestions are described in Sect. 6.

2 Background

This section focus on the key topics addressed on this paper. A definition of behaviour-based Intrusion Detection System (IDS) and supervised learning is presented, following by the description of the dataset used in this work and, finally, the bioinspired algorithms used.

2.1 Behaviour-Based IDS

The emergence of IDS is intrinsically linked to the need for processing logs generated by the network equipment (e.g. computers and others active equipment), in order to detect anomalies and deviations to the normal behaviour. Generally, this anomalous activity is named *network intrusions*. Fuchsberger [6] claims that initially the intrusion detection software consisted of a program that processed and analysed the logs generated by different systems. With the emergence and expansion of computer networks, the same motivation was applied to "listen" to network traffic. IDS are one of the most popular applications to collect network traffic, analyse its content and classify it as normal or anomalous.

Taking into account the different types of analysis, a classification for IDS was proposed in [6]. IDS can be classified according to the object of analysis (host-based or network-based) and to the detection method (behaviour-based or signature-based). Regarding the latter, signature-based IDS compares the network traffic with a knowledge base (signatures), much similar to the way anti-virus software works. In relation to anomaly-based IDS, it detects deviations of the network traffic, comparing with a previously learned "normal behaviour".

The main advantage of signature-based IDS is its extreme efficiency in detecting known attacks, that is, those for which a signature is available. Behaviour-based IDS tries to overcome the limitations of signature-based, by trying to establish a model for normal network behaviour and further calculate deviations, which can be reported as possible positive examples [6]. Although being capable of reacting to unknown attacks, this type of IDS, if not properly trained, has the disadvantage of eventually generating a high rate of false positives.

2.2 Learning Strategies

Machine learning aims to develop methods and algorithms to learn from data [7]. It can be applied to countless domains, namely natural language processing, image recognition, detection and classification. Regarding detection and classification, ML can be used to train behaviour-based IDS to further infer about potential threats from network traffic analysis. The automatic learning process goes through several phases [8]: data preparation; training the algorithm and generating the model; producing forecasts and refining them.

Machine learning [8] can be classified as supervised and unsupervised. **Unsupervised** machine learning makes use of unclassified data, usually in massive quantities, trying to identify possible patterns with similar features that can be grouped. As the data is not classified, there is no possibility to assess whether the forecast is correct or not, being this a key difference when comparing with supervised learning [9]. In **supervised** machine learning, the algorithms are trained using previously classified (labeled) data. The meaning of "supervised" is due to the fact that the prediction made by the algorithm is compared with the original value, allowing to assess whether it is correct or not. That is, the algorithm can adjust the model and leads to better predictions. The generated and trained model is then be applied to unseen data during the testing phase [10].

2.3 Dataset CSE-CIC-IDS2018

The tests were performed using the CSE-CIC-IDS2018 public datasets [11]. Although the DARPA KDD-CUP 1999 dataset is well known and widely used to test and evaluate IDS [12], the level of criticism on the way it was built, has allowed researchers to adopt and evaluate other promising and more reliable ones [13].

In that sense, despite being recent, CSE-CIC-IDS2018 dataset is very well organized and is now starting to be widely used by the scientific community to benchmark IDS. It includes a huge volume of network traffic organized in a timeline, which mixes both normal and anomalous network packet flows. The traffic was dynamically generated, with the purpose of simulating a real-world corporate network. The dataset has seven different attack scenarios [11], performed by a set of 50 computers, whose target is a network with 420 computers and 30 servers. The network intrusion scenarios include brute-force attacks, Heartbleed, Botnet, Denial of Service (DoS), Distributed Denial of Service (DDoS), web attacks and data exfiltration.

Each attack scenario was performed by a set of software tools. For example, for DoS attacks the following tools were used: GoldenEye, Slowloris, SlowHTTPTest and Hulk. As expected, different tools generate distinct traffic patterns and challenge the IDS to accurately detect the attacks. Due to the diversity of network attacks and the massive amount of available data, we have chosen a subset of the entire dataset, selecting attacks that could better be used to simulate a zero day attack detection. Table 1 characterizes the attacks used in the experiments carried on in this paper.

Table 1. Characterization of the network attacks.

Date	Time		Type of attack	Software tool	# flows
	Begin	End			
15/02/2018	09:26	10:09	DoS	GoldenEye	41508
	10:59	11:40	DoS	Slowloris	10990
16/02/2018	10:12	11:08	DoS	SlowHTTPTest	139890
	13:45	14:19	DoS	Hulk	461912
21/02/2018	10:09	10:43	DDoS	LOIC-UDP	1730
	14:05	15:05	DDoS	HOIC	686012

We have processed the network traffic for 15-Feb-2018, 16-Feb-2018 and 21-Feb-2018, with 996077, 446772 and 360833 non-malicious (normal) flows respectively.

2.4 Bioinspired Algorithms

Bioinspired algorithms intend to mimic systems or mechanisms inspired in the nature or the human body. Some typical applications and analogies are the neural networks, inspired by the functioning of the human brain; the evolutionary and DNA computing, based on theories of evolution, that leads to genetic algorithms; the artificial immune systems, which take inspiration on the vertebrates' immune system, namely its adaptive part [14].

Artificial Immune Systems. The vertebrates' immune system and its functioning serve as the basis for Artificial Immune Systems (AIS), which encompasses a whole set of algorithms inspired on the human immune system [15]. The main function of the human immune system is to protect the body against the attacks carried out by external pathogens, while simultaneously not reacting to the *self* or *normal* body behaviour. The analogy with IDS is immediate, as its primary mission is also to adapt continuously to the network self behaviour and, at the same time, to detect potential threats against the computer network. From the whole plethora of immune-inspired algorithms, the one chosen for this work was CLONal selection ALGorithm (CLONALG) [2,3,16]. The choice was mainly due to its simplicity and its widely use (implementation in WEKA available at https://github.com/fracpete/wekaclassalgos).

The algorithm starts by creating a set of "artificial antibodies" (detectors) of predefined and fixed size **N**. This set is subsequently divided into two parts: one of them, named memory (**m**), corresponds to the solution of the algorithm; the other one, whose function is to introduce diversity into the system, is named remainder (**r**). In the following phase, and during **G** iterations, the algorithm exposes the system to all external patterns (antigens).

The detection phase works as follows: each detector is identified by a pattern and is exposed against patterns from the environment (e.g. network traffic patterns). Hammming distance is then calculated between both patterns and those detectors with higher affinity are selected and cloned proportionally, according to its affinity. Clones are then subjected to an affinity maturation process to refine the affinity each one has with the environment. Higher affinities give detectors a sense of *memory*, while those with lower affinities below a threshold will be replaced.

Artificial Neural Networks. Artificial Neural Networks (ANN) algorithm seeks its inspiration in the functioning of the brain, namely the neurons and the networks formed by them through synapses. ANN is a computational abstraction that attempts to simulate the functioning of the vertebrate brain and provides a set of tools, relatively simple to implement, that can be used to solve problems with varying degrees of complexity.

We have used two distinct ANN algorithms in this work, namely Back Propagation Multi-Layer Perceptron (MLP) and Learning Vector Quantization (LVQ). Back propagation MLP is a class of neural networks made up of at least three nodes. Each of these nodes, with the exception of the input node, is a neuron that uses a nonlinear activation function [5]. The nodes are distributed by layers, namely the input, the output and the hidden ones. The learning of this algorithm is carried out in two main phases, namely *feed forward* and *back propagation*. In the *feed forward* phase, each input vector is propagated through the network, causing reactions on the various perceptrons and producing an output value, which is then compared with the expected value and an error value for each node in the output layer is generated. Since each node contributed, in some way, to the error present in the output layer, the error values are transmitted to each node in the hidden layer immediately before the output layer, and so on, until each node in the network has received an error signal that attests to its contribution to the error in the output layer. This phase is called **back propagation**. Once the error value has been determined for each node, that value is then used by each node to adjust the weights for each input, until the network converges to a state that allows all input vectors to be represented. The purpose of the *back propagation* phase is to minimize the value of the error function. The set of weightings that minimize the error function are considered the solution to the problem.

LVQ is also a neural-based algorithm and its operation is based on a collection of elements called *codebook vectors*, which form a neural network. A *codebook vector* is a list of values with the same input and output attribute values as the training data. The model representation is a set of *codebook vectors* with a fixed size, which result from the training process [17]. In terms of neural networks, a *codebook vector* is the equivalent to the neuron, as each attribute of the *codebook vector* corresponds to a weight and the set of *codebook vectors* is the neural network.

The algorithm starts by building a collection of *codebook vectors* from the training data [17]. The initial attribute values set for each *codebook vector* is generated randomly. Each *codebook vector* has the same number of attributes as the input data, being the examples annotated with the output class. The algorithm then processes each instance of the training *dataset*, by selecting the *codebook* that most resembles among the available *codebook vectors*. If the output of the codebook vector is the same as that of the training instance, the *codebook vector* is moved closer to the training instance. If not, the *codebook vector* is moved further away. The amount by which the *codebook vector* is moved is controlled by a parameter named **learning rate**.

This operation is then repeated for each instance of the training *dataset*. Each iteration throughout the entire training *dataset* is called the *epoch*, which is initially defined. It should also be noted that the value of the learning rate does not remain constant throughout the iterations, decreasing after each epoch. The choice was also mainly due to its availability in WEKA tools set.

3   Tests Setup

This section describes the tests setup used in the experiments.

3.1   Test Scenarios

We have carried out two set of tests (modules A and B), of four scenarios each, as shown in Table 2.

Table 2. Modules and test scenarios

Module	Scenario	Training		Testing	
		Day	Traffic	Day	Traffic
A	1	15/02/2018	Normal+Attack1	15/02/2018	Normal+Attack2
	2	15/02/2018	Normal+Attack1	21/02/2018	Normal+Attack1
	3	15/02/2018	Normal+Attack2	21/02/2018	Normal+Attack2
	4	15/02/2018	Normal+Attacks	21/02/2018	Normal+Attacks
B	1	16/02/2018	Normal+Attack1	16/02/2018	Normal+Attack2
	2	16/02/2018	Normal+Attack1	21/02/2018	Normal+Attack1
	3	16/02/2018	Normal+Attack2	21/02/2018	Normal+Attack2
	4	16/02/2018	Normal+Attacks	21/02/2018	Normal+Attacks

The characterization of the tests is as follows:

- By using the same type of attack, the algorithms were trained with traffic generated by one tool, while trying to detect the attack generated by another tool. This is the case of scenario 1, where in module A, each algorithm was trained with data generated by the GoldenEye tool and tested with data generated by Slowloris. Although both tools produce a DoS attack, the goal is to detect a zero-day attack, as the generated traffic patterns are different for each tool.
- By training with data from one type of attack and trying to detect another type of attack. In scenarios 2, 3 and 4, the algorithms were trained with DoS traffic and then tested with DDoS traffic, as can be seen in Table 2.

As mentioned above, for the training process in module A we have used DoS attacks, with traffic patterns generated by two different tools: GoldenEye and Slowloris.

In the test phase, the attacks described in scenarios 2 through 4 are DDoS attacks, whose traffic patterns were generated by the tools LOIC and HOIC. In module B, DoS attacks were generated by tools SlowHTTPTest and Hulk, as can be seen in the Table 1. The DDoS attacks are the same as those used in the previous module.

The tests were performed on a set with a total of 200,000 network flows, being 70% (140,000 instances) used to train the model, while the remaining 30% (60,000 records) were part of the testing dataset. The training set records were selected from the training data file, and the test set records are selected from the test data file (see Table 2). To attain statistical significance, each test scenario was then run ten times, with independent data for each iteration, but the same for the three algorithms in each iteration.

The reproducibility and randomness were achieved by using the *seed* WEKA API feature, which aim is to tune the random number generator. Different seed values imply distinct random values and, consequently, different selected instances. The same seed value will ensure that the experimental conditions are identical for all the experiments.

We have run the experiments with CLONALG, Backpropagation MLP and LVQ algorithms. We have also considered an *ensemble* of the models generated by the three algorithms, in which the decision strategy is based on the criterion is based on a *majority voting* strategy.

3.2   Methodology

Figure 1 depicts the methodology used to run the experiments. Is is divided into four main phases: input data ingestion, data preprocessing, data processing and presentation of results.

The preprocessing phase deals with the following issues:

- To remove unnecessary attributes, such as `Timestamp`. As we use network packet flows instead of packets, the time arrival of each packet is not relevant;

Fig. 1. Overall architecture

- To normalize data, as some implementations of algorithms require that, for example, numeric values should range between 0 and 1;
- To reduce the number of classes to *benign* and *attack*, as the dataset is multi-class and each attack instance is labeled with the attack designation. This is done by aggregating every class not being "Normal" as malicious traffic. For example, before class reduction, the data looks like the example described in Table 3 (example for data related to day 16-Feb-2018):

Table 3. Dataset characterization - 16/02/2018

Class	Instances	%
Benign	446772	42,61%
DoS attacks-SlowHTTPTest	139890	13,34%
DoS attacks-Hulk	461912	44,05%
Total Instances	1048574	100,00%

After class reduction, the same data will look like this:

Table 4. Class reduction - 16/02/2018

Class	Instances	%
Normal	446772	42,61%
Malicious	601802	57,39%
Total Instances	1048574	100,00%

- To deal with missing values in the datasets, by replacing them with the average value of that attribute.

The preprocessing tasks were implemented in WEKA [1] and Orange [18] *open-source* applications. The preprocessed data was then submitted to the algorithms for training and testing. In addition, to have statistical significance, each test scenario was run ten times, with the final value of each metric being the arithmetic mean of the values obtained in each iteration. The training and test sets were randomly selected at the beginning of each iteration and, for a given iteration, the same training and test data are applied to each one of the algorithms. An application, available at Github https://github.com/paulo-ferreira-mcif/benchmarkids, was developed to automate the tests for any dataset that meets the requirements.

4   Results

This section aims to present the results obtained for each of the test modules. Table 5 shows the results obtained for scenario 1 in module A. For a given algorithm , the values of each metric correspond to the arithmetic mean of the values obtained for each iteration of the scenario.

Although we have performed the tests corresponding to the remaining scenarios, the results obtained were bad, and could not be used to assess the algorithms' performance.

Table 5. Results for module A - Scenario 1

Algorithm	TPR	TNR	FPR	FNR	Precision	Recall	Accuracy	F1
MLP	0,6524	1,0000	0,0000	0,3476	0,9954	0,6524	0,9962	0,7880
LVQ	0,0457	0,9997	0,0003	0,9543	0,1695	0,0457	0,9893	0,0702
CLONALG	0,0194	0,9830	0,0170	0,9806	0,0030	0,0194	0,9725	0,0028

The results obtained for module B are shown in Tables 6, 7, 8 and 9. Similarly to the results of module A, for each algorithm, the value presented for each metric corresponds to the arithmetic mean of the values obtained in each iteration of the scenario.

Table 6. Results for module B - Scenario 1

Algorithm	TPR	TNR	FPR	FNR	Precision	Recall	Accuracy	F1
CLONALG	0,0306	0,9997	0,0003	0,9694	0,9895	0,0306	0,5071	0,0593
Ensemble	0,0306	0,9997	0,0003	0,9694	0,9895	0,0306	0,5071	0,0593
LVQ	0,0306	0,9996	0,0004	0,9694	0,9889	0,0306	0,5071	0,0593
MLP	0,0001	1,0000	0,0000	0,9999	1,0000	0,0001	0,4917	0,0001

Table 7. Results for module B - Scenario 2

Algorithm	TPR	TNR	FPR	FNR	Precision	Recall	Accuracy	F1
CLONALG	0,0080	0,6537	0,3463	0,9920	0,0337	0,0080	0,6506	0,0103
Ensemble	0,0080	0,6537	0,3463	0,9920	0,0337	0,0080	0,6506	0,0103
LVQ	0,7025	0,0031	0,9969	0,2976	0,0034	0,7025	0,0065	0,0067
MLP	0,0000	0,9998	0,0003	1,0000	0,0000	0,0000	0,9950	0,0000

Table 8. Results for module B - Scenario 3

Algorithm	TPR	TNR	FPR	FNR	Precision	Recall	Accuracy	F1
MLP	1,0000	0,9998	0,0002	0,0000	0,9999	1,0000	0,9999	0,9999
Ensemble	1,0000	0,0026	0,9974	0,0000	0,6559	1,0000	0,6562	0,7922
CLONALG	1,0000	0,0026	0,9974	0,0000	0,6559	1,0000	0,6562	0,7922
LVQ	1,0000	0,0004	0,9997	0,0000	0,6554	1,0000	0,6554	0,7918

Table 9. Results for module B - Scenario 4

Algorithm	TPR	TNR	FPR	FNR	Precision	Recall	Accuracy	F1
MLP	0,8977	0,9996	0,0004	0,1023	0,9284	0,8977	0,9327	0,8987
Ensemble	0,9992	0,0033	0,9968	0,0008	0,6564	0,9992	0,6565	0,7923
LVQ	1,0000	0,0008	0,9992	0,0000	0,6560	1,0000	0,6561	0,7923
CLONALG	0,9992	0,0030	0,9970	0,0008	0,6564	0,9992	0,6564	0,7923

5 Results Analysis

In this section we delineate a set of considerations regarding the values obtained. The purpose of the tests was to simulate, as much as possible, the detection of a *zero-day* attack, by using the CSE-CIC-IDS2018 dataset. It is appropriate to mention that a network attack is essentially an anomaly to normal network traffic behaviour. It may be seen, for example, as a high traffic volume in a short period of time, so it might be important to find out some parameters for a system to detect it. Some of these parameters could be, for example, the number of packages per time interval or the time interval between each package. That is, the tests were not carried out on the network traffic packets, but on the packet flows features associated to the network flows generated. Regarding the *ensemble* classifier, one of the objectives of this work was to find out if the use of a classifier of this kind, with a *majority voting* strategy, contributed or not to improve the results presented by each classifier individually.

5.1 Results - Module A

The results of module A are not satisfactory. This can be caused by the fact that attacks do not generate enough patterns to allow the algorithms to learn their characteristics and, therefore, to be able to detect similar events in the testing phase.

When regarding scenario 1, we can see from Table 5 that the algorithm with the best result is MLP, with an F1 value of about 78%.

For the remaining scenarios, the obtained results were unsatisfactory, making it difficult to assess the performance of the algorithms. In spite of that, regarding scenarios 2, 3 and 4, algorithms were unable to identify the occurrence of a DDoS attack when they are trained with data from DoS attacks. This situation may be due to the fact that, during the testing phase, the algorithms cannot match DDoS attack patterns to those generated in the training phase using DoS.

In order to try to improve the results in the scenario with the worst results, we applied several configurations to the algorithms, by changing some of the parameters, simulating a *hill-climbing* technique. Only in LVQ algorithm, and in one particular configuration, we were able to achieve significant improvements. In this specific case, the algorithm has detected some of the malicious traffic, albeit very residual.

5.2   Results - Module B

The results obtained in this module are better than those obtained in module A, although the same algorithms, configured with the same parameters, were used. This situation may be due to the fact that the tools used in the attacks have produced patterns with greater resemblance. It would thus be possible for a behaviour-based IDS to use these algorithms to be able to identify a *zero-day* attack.

In scenarios 1 and 2, despite having a low True Positive Rate (TPR), the CLONALG algorithm has better results, together with the *ensemble*, as can be seen from the F1 values.

The MLP algorithm was unable to handle malicious traffic, being only capable of correctly identifying the overwhelming majority of normal traffic. In contrast, in scenario 2, the LVQ algorithm presented the highest TPR in the scenario, despite failing to identify normal traffic (lowest True Negative Rate (TNR) value in the scenario).

In scenarios 3 and 4, we can depict the predominance of the MLP algorithm, with high F1 values, very close to 100% in scenario 3. In scenario 3, as can be seen in the Table 8, all algorithms correctly identified all malicious traffic (TPR = 1), which may be related to the similarity of traffic patterns generated by the respective tools. With regard to normal traffic, only MLP has a good performance, with TNR very close to 100%, while the other algorithms have a very residual detection.

In scenario 4, despite the great diversity of malicious traffic both in the training and testing phases, the traffic generated by the two tools in each type of attack has no significant advantage when compared to the results obtained in scenario 3. In fact, the performance of MLP, translated by the F1 value, drops by about 10%, whereas, in the other algorithms, there is little improvement.

6   Conclusions and Future Work

In this paper we described a methodology to benchmark bioinspired machine learning algorithms, against the recent and promising CSE-CIC IDS-2018 dataset. We described the dataset and the methodology used to process the four scenarios defined in each module. To fully automate the tests we made available a tool for WEKA.

We have sought to obtain statistical significance by running the tests 10 times for each algorithm. The parameters set used in each algorithm was obtained empirically, combining the requirements of the algorithm itself and the data to be analysed.

We have tested two modules, with four scenarios each. In module A, the results were bad, with the algorithms mostly detecting normal traffic. In an attempt to identify whether the problem would lie in the parameterization of the algorithms, tests were carried out to obtain the best values for parameters of the algorithms. It was found that only in the case of the LVQ algorithm was it possible to improve the results, albeit not significantly.

The results of module B are promising. In the first two scenarios, the high-lighted algorithm is CLONALG, although the TPR is quite low; meanwhile, MLP algorithm reveals poor performance. In fact, despite correctly identifying the overwhelming majority of normal traffic, it clearly fails to identify malicious traffic. In the last two scenarios, the MLP performance is absolute and overwhelming, with F1 and TPR values above 89%.

In addition to results obtained by each algorithm individually, an *ensemble* classifier was also implemented, which, using a majority voting strategy, had no influence in the final results. The future work includes the optimization of the parameters set and the processing of others datasets with different attacks for training and testing.

References

1. Frank, E., Hall, M.A., Witten, I.H.: The WEKA Workbench, in Data Mining: Practical Machine Learning Tools and Techniques, M. Kaufmann, Ed., 4th ed. (2016). https://www.cs.waikato.ac.nz/ml/weka/Witten_et_al_2016_appendix.pdf
2. de Castro, L.N., Von Zuben, F.J.: Learning and optimization using the clonal selection principle. IEEE Trans. Evol. Comput. **6**(3), 239–251 (2002). https://doi.org/10.1109/TEVC.2002.1011539
3. de Castro, L.N., Von Zuben, F.J.: The clonal selection algorithm with engineering applications. In: editor (ed.) Proceedings of GECCO, vol. 2000, pp. 36–39 (2000)
4. Kohonen, T.: Self-Organizing Map. Springer Science & Business Media, New York (2001). https://doi.org/10.1007/978-3-642-56927-2
5. The Genius Blog. Basics of multilayer perceptron – a simple explanation of multilayer perceptron (2018). https://kindsonthegenius.com/blog/2018/01/basics-of-multilayer-perceptron-a-simple-explanation-of-multilayer-perceptron.html
6. Fuchsberger, A.: Intrusion detection systems and intrusion prevention systems. Inf. Secur. Techn. Report **10**, 134–139 (2005). https://doi.org/10.1016/j.istr.2005.08.001
7. Hurwitz, J., Kirsch, D.: Machine Learning for dummies. John Wiley & Sons Inc, New Jersey (2018)
8. IBM. What is machine learning? (2020). https://www.ibm.com/topics/machine-learning
9. Jones, M.T.: Unsupervised learning for data classification (2017). https://developer.ibm.com/articles/cc-unsupervised-learning-data-classification/
10. Jones, M.T.: Supervised learning models (2018). https://developer.ibm.com/articles/cc-supervised-learning-models/

11. Canadian Institute for Cybersecurity: Cse-cic-ids2018 on aws. A collab-orative project between the communications security establishment (cse) & the canadian institute for cybersecurity (cic), University of New Brunswick (2020). https://www.unb.ca/cic/datasets/ids-2018.html

12. Al Tobi, A.M., Duncan, I.: Kdd 1999 generation faults: A review and analysis. J. Cyber Secur. Technol. **2**(3–4), 164–200 (2018)

13. McHugh, J.: Testing intrusion detection systems: a critique of the 1998 and1999 darpa intrusion detection system evaluations as performed by lincolnlaboratory. ACM Trans. Inf. Syst. Secur. (TISSEC) **3**(4), 262–294 (2000)

14. Mahboubian, M., Hamid, N.A.W.A.: A machine learning based ais ids. Int. J. Mach. Learn. Comput. **3**(3), 259–262 (2013). https://doi.org/10.7763/IJMLC.2013.V3.315

15. Forrest, S., Hofmeyr, S.A., Somayaji, A.: Computer immunology. Commun. ACM **40**(10), 88–96 (1997)

16. Kim, J., Bentley, P.J., Aickelin, U., Greensmith, J., Tedesco, G., Twycross, J.: Immune system approaches to intrusion detection-a review. Nat. Comput. **6**(4), 413–466 (2007)

17. Brownlee, J.: Learning vector quantization for machine learning (2020). https://machinelearningmastery.com/learning-vector-quantization-for-machine-learning/

18. Demšar, J., et aL.: Orange: data mining toolbox in python. J. Mach. Learn. Res. **14**, 2349–2353 (2013). http://jmlr.org/papers/v14/demsar13a.html

Thermal Management in Large Data Centres: Security Threats and Mitigation

Betty Saridou[1](✉) ⓘ, Gueltoum Bendiab[2], Stavros N. Shiaeles[2],
and Basil K. Papadopoulos[1]

[1] Democritus University of Thrace, Xanthi, Greece
{dsaridou,papadob}@civil.duth.gr
[2] Cyber Security Research Group, University of Portsmouth, Portsmouth, UK
gueltoum.bendiab@port.ac.uk, sshiaeles@ieee.org

Abstract. Data centres are experiencing significant growth in their scale, especially, with the ever-increasing demand for cloud and IoT services. However, this rapid growth has raised numerous security issues and vulnerabilities; new types of strategic cyber-attacks are aimed at specific physical components of data centres that keep them operating. Attacks against temperature monitoring and cooling systems of data centres, also known as thermal attacks, can cause a complete meltdown and are generally considered difficult to address. In this paper, we focus on this issue by analysing the potential security threats to these systems and their impact on the overall data centre safety and performance. We also present current thermal anomaly detection methods and their limitations. Finally, we propose a hybrid method to prevent thermal attacks, that uses multi-variant anomaly detection and a fuzzy-based health factor to enhance data centre thermal awareness and security.

Keywords: Anomaly detection · Security · Data centre · Thermal sensors · Cooling system · Thermal attacks

1   Introduction

Data centres are experiencing unprecedented growth and will continue to scale operations to meet the ever-increasing service demands. A recent study by Gartner[1] estimated that about 425 million new servers might be needed by 2020 to support 30 billion connected IoT devices around the world, while the average data centre will support more than 100,000 servers [30]. The average data warehouse size usually ranges from $100\,\text{ft}^2$ to $400,000\,\text{ft}^2$ [35] and operates on a high-power consumption. A plethora of security issues has arisen due to this rapid growth, causing data centres to become vulnerable to strategic cyber-attacks on the physical infrastructure vital to maintaining the uninterrupted operation of data centres [12,13,19,38]. Power supply, cooling, temperature monitoring and even security systems can serve as entry points for attacks against data centre operators or companies using data centre services. Security experts warn

---

[1] https://www.gartner.com/en.

© Springer Nature Singapore Pte Ltd. 2021
S. M. Thampi et al. (Eds.): SSCC 2020, CCIS 1364, pp. 165–179, 2021.
https://doi.org/10.1007/978-981-16-0422-5_12

that new sophisticated malware such as Triton and Trisis [28] are very effective against power and HVAC (Heating, Ventilating, and Air Conditioning) systems, and therefore, put data centres' safety at risk. Moreover, reported cyber-incidents showed that cyber-attacks on such connected facilities can destroy thousands of servers by overheating the environmental atmosphere, or manipulating energy and temperature settings to cause a fire or an explosion incident [12,13,38].

Attacks against temperature monitoring and cooling systems, also known as thermal attacks, are considered dangerous and difficult to tackle. In this paper, we aim to address this issue by exploring the most important security threats against thermal management systems, as well as their overall impact on data centre security and performance. In this regard, we describe a number of vulnerabilities that may be exploited by attackers who aim to alter environmental conditions inside a data centre. Based on a combination of thermal hardware requirements, thermal anomaly detection is considered a relevant approach for detecting abnormal behaviour of data centre indoor temperature. In this context, several approaches have been proposed for temperature measurement analysis and abnormal behaviour definition on various environments, including smart homes, health, and data centres. In this paper, we analyse the effectiveness and limitations of these approaches with respect to the protection against thermal attacks in data centres. Additionally, we denote the importance of intelligent solutions and present initial work on a hybrid framework that uses multi-variant anomaly detection as a preventive measure. Finally, to further enhance thermal awareness and security of data centres, we introduce the idea of a fuzzy-based health factor.

The remainder of this paper is organised as follows. In Sect. 2, a high-level overview of temperature monitoring in large data centres is presented, along with their importance and benefits. Section 3 discusses the potential security threats on temperature monitoring systems and their impact on the overall data centre security and performance. In Sect. 4, we provide an overview of the existing solutions and their limitations. In Sect. 5, we present a conceptual model that combines multi-variate anomaly detection methods and fuzzy logic for protecting data centres against thermal attacks. Finally, Sect. 6 concludes this paper and outlines future work.

2   Thermal Management in Data Centers

Data centres are large infrastructures composed of a building or a group of buildings dedicated to house computer systems and their services [13]. They usually host a large number of high-density servers, which run simultaneously and generate extensive amounts of heat per second. Thus, existing data centres are equipped with multiple cooling technologies to cool down servers, including chilled water systems, cold aisle/hot aisle design, Computer Room Air Conditioner (CRAC), liquid cooling and free air cooling [12,32]. For efficient thermal management, they also use robust thermal design and temperature regulation and monitoring as heat countermeasures. In modern data centres, HVAC and

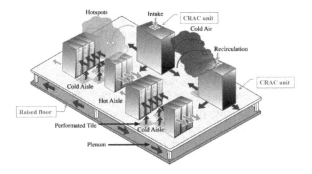

Fig. 1. Typical cooling system in data centers [11].

CRAC systems are the most widely used cooling solution for managing temperature, airflow and humidity. At the same time, continuous monitoring with Wireless Sensor Networks (WSNs) helps to create and maintain the energy-efficient cooling environment.

As shown in Fig. 1, computer rooms are arranged into hot and cold aisles; server rack fronts face each other to create cold aisles due to the front-to-back heat produced by servers [32]. CRAC units, which are usually positioned at the end of hot-aisles or around the room perimeter (see Fig. 1), push the cold air under the raised floor and through the cold aisle to absorb the heat produced by servers. The resulting hot air enters the hot aisle from the front side of the server racks and is returned to the CRAC devices to cool down by the chillers once more [12,13,32]. In order to avoid overheating, the inlet temperatures of servers are continuously monitored using a network of thermal sensors. If the inlet temperature exceeds a predefined threshold, parts of servers or even racks are forced to shut down to avoid permanent hardware damage [12].

In general, control and monitoring of heat diffusion inside a data center is a complicated process that involves rack positioning design, air flow simulations and monitoring devices distribution. The American Society of Heating, Refrigerating and Air-Conditioning Engineers (ASHRAE) supplies detailed suggestions for temperature readings and defines three models regarding placing temperature sensors: a) managing the space, b) setting up the space, and c) troubleshooting the space. More specifically, it suggests that temperature should be measured at every fourth rack position at the center of cold aisles. Additionally, temperature measurement should be taken at the center of the air intakes of the top, middle, and bottom of the equipment rack [33].

3   Security Threats and Their Impact

Data centres play an increasingly important role in modern society and digital economy. However, their security is still a challenging area with many open problems. This growing reliance on digital infrastructures to accommodate large volumes of valuable information make them prone to strategic attacks. In this context, many studies showed that most data centres and their associated building automation systems have little or no protection policies in place [8,12,13,19]. In addition, a recent report by CyrusOne[2] confirmed that its New York data centre was attacked by the REvil ransomware, also known as Sodinokibi, affecting more than six customer companies of CyrusOne [20]. Another report by Verizon found that DDoS attacks and privilege misuse were the most common attack vectors in last year's cyber attacks against data centres, mainly due to the proliferation of poorly secured connected IoT devices [21].

The temperature monitoring system, which is one of the most critical components of a data centre, is vulnerable to cyber-attacks too [12,19]. Temperature monitoring is usually guaranteed through hundreds or even thousands of temperature sensors (i.e.thermal sensors) that form a WSN, which can then be remotely controlled and configured. Thus, malicious cyber actors can easily take control of the network and manipulate the thermal conditions of a specific server or rack; for example, maintaining servers in a relatively hot environment [12,13]. To achieve their goals, attackers will run thermal-intensive workloads into victim servers or VMs (Virtual Machines) to rapidly generate large amounts of heat. This heat will consequently worsen the thermal condition of the peripheral environment, and therefore raise the inlet temperature of other servers [12,14]. What is more, these networks are vulnerable to a wide variety of attacks due to several restrictions, such as low computational capability, small memory size, limited energy resources and unreliable communication channels [31]. Overall, these insecure devices can be easily compromised in order to remotely launch attacks against the temperature monitoring system.

The adversary who launches a thermal attack can be an individual hacker, a competing provider, or a specialised organisation for committing cyber-crime. A study by [34] showed that thermal attacks can also come from insider malicious tenants, especially in the case of multi-tenant data centres. In this case, malicious tenants can inject additional thermal loads, exceeding the shared cooling system capacity, which can lead to overheating and possible system downtime. It is clear that the impact of thermal attacks is not limited to victim servers, but it can also affect surrounding environmental temperature, which, in turn, can impact thermal conditions of other servers and the entire data centre [14]. In the same context, a study by [12] found that a successful thermal attack targeting only 2% of the servers can dramatically affect the thermal conditions of the entire data centre. Similarly, affecting thermal conditions of adjacent servers and causing local hotspots would significantly raise cooling costs, or lead to a cooling breakdown.

One of the main reasons that renders data centres vulnerable to thermal attacks is the extensive use of aggressive cooling and power management policies, such as power oversubscription [12,38]. According to this phenomenon, a single data centre hosts a larger number of servers, exceeding its power capacity [12]. Implementations of power oversubscription can lead to severe security gaps;

---

[2] https://cyrusone.com/.

for instance, malicious attackers can manipulate multiple servers to create a local hotspot or generate simultaneous power peaks [38]. Another reason is that thermal attacks try to intentionally keep the outlet temperature of victim servers at a high level preventing chip-level temperature sensors from monitoring temperature at server- or data centre-level. Consequently, these sensors are unable to prevent local hotspots since they only provide information about the server's core temperature, which is different from the inlet and outlet measurements [12].

Current anomaly detection approaches in data centre temperature monitoring exhibit several weaknesses in preventing thermal attacks [12,25]. For instance, most of these approaches are not capable of distinguishing between benign and malicious thermal-intensive workloads [12]. Furthermore, a study by [13] demonstrated that existing anomaly detection approaches cannot defend against thermal attacks at data centre-level, where a large number of accounts run different workloads simultaneously.

4   Thermal Anomaly Detection in Data Centers

Anomaly detection is a relevant approach in the problem of temperature monitoring inside data centres because it allows data centre managers to identify abnormal system behaviour in a proactive manner. In general, thermal anomaly detection is based on a combination of a) thermal hardware requirements that have been applied to cooling systems, and b) historical observations that are recorded and/or streamed by environmental sensors inside the critical infrastructure.

Several researchers have suggested anomaly detection methods for temperature data in a variety of environments. In an attempt to detect possible risk events inside a household, an anomaly detection method was initially applied to smart home data by [18] through temporal data mining. For their investigation, researchers used sensors to measure temperature, humidity, light, and other environmental factors. The model looked for temporal interactions among frequent activities to learn "resident" behaviour, while events with low probability were reported as "unusual". Despite using a combination of real and synthetic data, the method proved effective but was not used to perform predictions [18].

Deviations from historical patterns were also examined on environmental data by [15]. The study presented an anomaly detection method using a data-driven uni-variate auto-regressive model and a moving window to predict the next measurement based on historical data. The method, which employed sensors reporting through telemetry, performed well without requiring previous classification of data, and proved applicable to larger data sets as well [15]. In their extensive study, [6] proposed a spatio-temporal correlation to detect anomalies from temperature, humidity and light sensor nodes in wireless sensor networks. Even though this method aimed to reduce energy and spectrum consumption, the information-gain from aggregate neighbourhood sensor data showed that it can prove critical in high-risk cases where temperature variations need to be addressed immediately.

In an attempt to ensure healthy operating conditions and reliability of High-Performance Computing systems (HPC) and data centres, researchers in [5] used autoencoders to train data collected from monitoring devices that were mounted on computing nodes. Their method used several metrics, such as core load, power consumption, room temperature, GPU usage, and cooling fans speed, and was able to catch anomalies when tested on real tier-1 HPC systems.

Despite the fact that temperature was not one of the monitoring values, research conducted by [1,16] demonstrated the use of anomaly detection in critical infrastructure. On one hand, [16] presented an analysis of multi-variate anomaly detection methods to assist in condition-based maintenance. For their application, they used real aircraft turbofan engine data, where their model was able to successfully detect anomalies and recognise failing factors. On the other hand, [1] proposed a multi-agent swarm system to detect abnormal behaviour in cloud data centres. However, neither of the approaches considered collecting data from the surrounding environment for the evaluation, but rather focused on the system's parameters only.

Following the rapid development of data warehouses around the globe, thermal anomaly detection approaches based on data centres only started to be explored during the last decade. Studies published by Marwah et al. [25–27] in 2009–10 were the first to address the issue of autonomous anomaly detection of temperature values in data centres using machine learning on sensor data sets. In their first paper on the topic, [27] underlined the importance for an autonomous system that is able to catch temperature values beyond a certain threshold. They also listed common technical reasons, as well as their symptoms, that lead to anomalies. As they stated, most of these anomalies can go undetected by traditional systems, while they demonstrated how Principal Component Analysis (PCA) can assist as the primary detection mechanism. In [25], they extended their initial hypothesis by introducing four detection mechanisms. More specifically, they compared a simple threshold method, a moving average method, an Exponentially Weighed Moving Average (EWMA) and Naive Bayes to predict thermal outliers on a three-month data set. Naive Bayes outperformed the other models and was able to predict 18% of the anomalies at an average of 12 min before occurrence. Next, in [26], they used hierarchical PCA for real-time detection, which resulted in a 98% accuracy of predicting anomalous cases. What is more, the method was applied to data coming from a part of the data centre where traditional methods would not be able to raise an alarm.

In [39], researchers introduced a sophisticated two-tier hierarchical neural network framework that detected server-level as well as data centre-level thermal anomalies. The method was able to achieve this by studying the relationships of heterogeneous sensors and consequently outperform other machine learning models. After extensive research on thermal maps for data centres, [22,23] proposed a novel anomaly detection method that compares and maximizes the accuracy of constructed and observed maps to detect Regions of Interest (RoIs). The method, which was notably based on thermal cameras and traditional temperature monitoring devices, demonstrated sufficient accuracy in anomalous cases.

Later, and responding to the growing need for fast online detection of fault cases, [3,40] introduced the use of Self-Organizing Maps and reputation systems.

In another study published in 2016, [4] presented a sophisticated four-step tool based on density estimation for anomaly detection and data exploration that was specifically designed for HPC sensors. Even though this method was tested and performed well on a real HPC environment, it was not designed for real-time detection, an approach that recent studies tend to follow. [24] focused exclusively on temperature data, when they used naive ensembles to detect anomalies in the cooling system of data centres. Nevertheless, because of its theoretical approach, their method needs to be extended to demonstrate sufficient performance on non-simulated scenarios. During the same year, another study published by [9] proposed an architecture sensing scheme. According to it, heat sensors collect server temperature data and transmit them to the cloud for further analysis. Later in 2018, [7] tested several machine learning models on server temperature data to examine cooling reliability of data centres. By constructing workload-independent cooling profiles servers, they were also able to detect both transient and lasting cooling failures of servers. Two extensive studies published by [17,41] in 2019, deployed machine learning to detect fault operations of HVAC systems. In [41], recognising the importance of air cooling systems in data centres, researchers introduced a hybrid approach for four-fault decoupling features; their study included compressor valve leakage, condenser fouling, evaporator airflow reduction, and liquid line restriction. For data manipulation, they used the random forest algorithm, which proved rather effective in fault events diagnosis. Lastly and for the same reason, in [17], researchers considered three different types of anomaly detection methodologies, namely naïve point anomalies, contextual point anomalies, and level shifts. Then, they used several machine learning methods on a real data set, achieving good precision rates.

Taking everything into consideration, there have been several approaches to analyse temperature measurements and define abnormal behaviour of the respective environments. Recent studies have started to include critical infrastructure in their analyses as well, but their approaches are mainly focused on optimal system management, energy efficiency, and reliability of services. Given the recent increase of cyber-attacks in industrial systems, we believe that real-time temperature monitoring in data centres should start to be examined by the security community as an attack mitigation measure. Moreover, temperature monitoring should not be analysed separately, but rather in conjunction with network and security monitoring measures. Additionally, there is a clear need for efficient time response in anomaly detection methods of operational processes applied to data centres; this approach can be observed across the field of financial streaming analytics [2], where having the lead in information exchange provides an advantage in transactions. Finally, we should note that the type and quality of data used in model testing is of paramount importance. In the next section, we address these issues by proposing a theoretical framework based on a combination of recent methods and tools published by [10,29,36,37].

5   Multi-variant Anomaly Detection and Fuzzy Logic

In an attempt to address the specific technical problem, we propose a hybrid method that merges the strongest elements of the methodologies found in [10, 29, 37]. A study by [10] highlighted the need for performing anomaly detection in multi-variate time sensing environments and proposed RADM, a real-time anomaly detection algorithm based on Hierarchical Temporal Memory (HTM) and Bayesian Network (BN). Their methodology outperformed anomaly detection in uni-variate sensing time-series, when tested on CPU, network and memory sensors. Additionally, [10] introduced the health factor α, which measures the overall health of the system by taking into account the individual anomaly scores calculated by HTM for each parameter (e.g. CPU). We should note that HTM is a far more accurate representation of the neural structures and mechanisms of the brain than the widely spread neural networks.

In their study, [29] demonstrated a sophisticated decentralised scheme for fault detection and classification where wireless sensor networks are prevalent. According to their methodology, neighbour sensors were grouped by conducting calculations among sensor readings. For sensor measurement, their choice of time-series model was the Auto-Regressive Moving Average model (ARMA). Fault detection was performed when reading was compared to a certain threshold and then the fault classification algorithm was initiated to determine the fault type. The fault reading was checked for the frequency and continuity, as well as the presence of an observable pattern. According to these criteria it was then classified as a) *random*, if discontinuous and appearing randomly, b) *malfunction*, if discontinuous and appearing frequently, c) *bias*, if continuous and exhibiting no pattern, d) *drift*, if continuous and following a pattern. For their investigation, they used an outdoor temperature dataset, achieving accuracy rates between 85% and 95%.

The ever-increasing need for intelligent systems in the security domain, also led to non-traditional approaches, such as Fuzzy Logic and Fuzzy Inference Systems (FIS). Researchers in [37] proposed a fuzzy-based approach to overcome complexities in Building Energy Management Systems (BEMSs). More specifically, they were able to use the nearest neighbour and fuzzy rules to extract normal building behaviour. Then, they used fuzzy linguistic descriptors for a variety of parameters, such as zone temperature, exhaust fan load, and supply fan current.

In this paper, our goal is to design an integrated anomaly detection framework that addresses the issues of existing methodologies discussed in Sects. 3 and 4. While our proposal method focuses on temperature, it considers various measured phenomena as inputs too, reflecting the highly monitored environment of data centres today. Even though our proposal is purely theoretical, it is based on well-examined methods, which were tested individually and proved effective in their respective field.

The proposed methodology combines elements from the three works described previously and splits them into four main steps. First, we perform a grouping of sensors as per the type of measured phenomenon or the spatial distribution of sensors measuring the same reading. Second, we perform fault detection on the grouped time series models individually. In the case where a faulty reading has been detected, we perform fault classification to define its type according to continuity, frequency and pattern criteria. Third, the grouped time series are inserted into the RADM framework, where the global anomaly region is defined. If once again, the system detects an anomaly on the overall system, we perform fault detection to define the type. Finally, we present a permutation of the health factor α, based on Fuzzy Logic and Fuzzy Rules. More details about each step are provided in the following subsections.

5.1 Step 1: Thermal Sensors Grouping

In this step, we acknowledge that the ambient temperature of data centres is a product of more that one factor. For instance, new or advanced cooling systems, such as rack cooling, have been employed in recent years to aid in reserving the servers' ideal state. Consequently, there is a clear need to consider more than one input when building time series models for anomaly detection. For this reason, we propose a sensor grouping technique that groups same phenomenon sensor readings, e.g. grouping of all ambient air temperature sensors in a room, fan motor speed, etc. Similarly, sensors can be also grouped spatially, for example aggregating high-mounted ambient temperature sensors of a specific aisle in a single group, low-mounted ambient temperature sensors in a different one, creating a dedicated group for high-mounted rack temperature sensors, and so on. For this method, we employ the Neighborhood Voting scheme proposed by [29]. According to them, *the system does not require a priori knowledge about the environment. Instead, it takes advantage of the redundancy in measurements of sensor readings.* By changing the notation to keep the consistency of our framework, we present the Neighbourhood Voting algorithm as it appears in their study:

1. Collect the set of readings $R = r[1 \ldots |Neighbour(Y_i)|]$ from all neighbours, excluding its own reading r_i .
2. Calculate the median of the group, $\mu = \{R\}_{\frac{1}{2}} = \bar{r}$.
3. Calculate the difference between r_i and $\bar{r}$, $D_{r_i \bar{r}} = |r_i - \bar{r}|$.
4. Compare the difference $D_{r_i \bar{r}}$ with a threshold τ, that can be adjusted.
   - If $D_{r_i \bar{r}} < \tau$ then r_i is a good reading.
   - If $D_{r_i \bar{r}} \geq \tau$ then r_i is a faulty reading. We define faulty readings as $D_{r_i \bar{r}} = \varepsilon_i$.

where Y_i is a node measuring a specific phenomenon, r_i is its reading. The set of its neighbours is denoted by $Neighbour(Y_i)$ and the number of neighbours by $|Neighbour(Y_i)|$.

5.2 Step 2: Fault Detection

In this step, we propose fault detection on the aforementioned grouped measurements. Because of the many advantages it exhibits for anomaly detection over traditional time-series, grouped readings are modelled with HTM time-series as suggested by [10], and not the ARMA model preferred in [29]. If a faulty reading is detected, the Fault Classification Algorithm proposed in [29] is initiated. The algorithm is run parallel to the HMT modelling to classify the faulty measurement as either *malfunction, random, bias*, or *drift*, according to the Fault Classification Algorithm (Algorithm 1), where T represents time intervals, $|\varepsilon_i|$ the numbers of faulty occurrences, and θ the desired threshold.

Algorithm 1: Fault Classification [29].

   Input:
    1. $R[1..T]$: vector of T sensor readings
    2. $E[1..T]$ vector of the faulty state of $R[1..T]$

   Output: C: fault type of sensor node in the interval
 1 compute the occurrences of faults $|\varepsilon_i|$ in R
 2 check the continuity
 3 **if** ε_i *is discrete* **then**
 4   Check the frequency
 5   **if** $|\varepsilon_i| \geq \theta\ i$ **then**
 6         $C = Malfunction$
 7   **else**
 8         $C = Random$

 9 **if** ε_i *is continuous* **then**
10   Check the fault function ε_i
11   **if** $\varepsilon_i = const$ **then**
12        $C = Bias$
13   **else**
14        $C = Drift$

15 **return** C

5.3   Step 3: Anomaly Region Detection

During the third step of the process, the HTM time-series of the grouped variables are combined with the Bayesian Network to detect the anomaly region. The time-series follow the RADM framework proposed by [10]. As previously discussed, we define the temperature T of the data centre as a product of factors X, Y, and Z, according to Eq. 1:

$$T(t) = (X(t), Y(t), Z(t)) \tag{1}$$

Then, the overall process, including steps 1, 2, and 3, is described in Fig. 2.

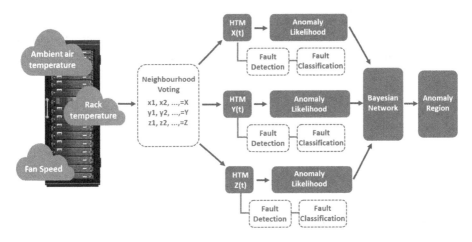

Fig. 2. Steps 1, 2, and 3 of the combined methods. Boxes in red represent methods proposed by [29], while boxes in blue comprise the RADM framework proposed by [10].

5.4 Step 4: Fuzzy Sets

In the fourth step of our methodology, we propose a permutation of the health factor α proposed by [29], in order to assess the overall well being of our framework. Our method uses linguistic descriptors to describe the concept of the system's anomaly state in an aggregated and intelligent manner. The method uses fuzzy rules similar to the analysis by [37], except the input variables consist of the anomaly scores S_i calculated by the HTM model for the grouped variables. More specifically, the input variables are represented using five fuzzy sets, namely *very low*, *low*, *medium*, *high*, and *very high*. The output variable *Health* is represented again by five fuzzy sets, that describe the state of the system as: *very bad*, *bad*, *average*, *good*, and *very good*. Input and output linguistic descriptors are shown in Fig. 3. Fuzzy rules are then constructed according to experience and describe the contribution of individual anomalies to the general state. The linguistic descriptors for the healthiest state with the three inputs used in our example would be:

IF $S_{X(t)}$ **IS** Very Low **AND** $S_{Y(t)}$ **IS** Very Low **AND** $S_{Z(t)}$ **IS** Very Low
THEN Health **IS** Very Good

By using this fuzzy-based system, the proposed methodology is able to use its own metrics -the anomaly scores- to assess the overall state of the system. FISs are able to support a large number of inputs and rules to achieve the desired accuracy. This approach offers enormous scalability for a critical environment with multiple sensors, as it is able to include many factors affecting server temperature. Finally, for a data set that could fit into a future application of this framework, we propose the DAD data set published by [36]. The DAD data set is a labelled IoT data set, which contains real-world behaviours of a data centre as seen from the network perspective. The network and environmental values were obtained from a physical data centre, combined with temperature measurements transmitted by NFC smart passive sensor technology.

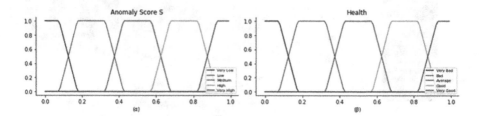

Fig. 3. Linguistic descriptors for (α) individual Anomaly Scores and (β) overall Health.

6   Conclusions and Future Work

In this paper, we examined how temperature monitoring systems can be used by attackers to manipulate heat distribution in such environments. We also presented and reviewed existing model-based anomaly detection methods that have been focused on measuring temperature deviations inside critical infrastructures. According to our findings, thermal attacks are fundamentally not addressed as potential cybersecurity attacks for data centres, and consequently, there is a serious lack of frameworks proposed to eliminate this threat. We believe that future studies on the current topic should be focused on constructing intelligent solutions. In our research, we found several approaches to tackle this issue and addressed the most important aspects for a thermal attack mitigation methodology. As part of our initial work, we have designed a multi-variate anomaly detection method for fault classification, and a fuzzy-based health factor to assess the overall state of the system. Finally, we propose a curated data set that could assist in the exploration of the aforementioned models.

In future work, we intend to extend our research by conducting experiments on large data sets from real settings to further test the effectiveness of this approach. We also intend to compare it against previous studies to evaluate its performance and further explore aspects of development.

Acknowledgement. This project has received funding from the European Union's Horizon 2020 research and innovation programme under grant agreement no. 786698. This work reflects authors' view and Agency is not responsible for any use that may be made of the information it contains.

References

1. Adhikari, A.T.B., Karunananda, A.S.: Real time anomaly detection of cloud data centers with multi agents swarm. Sri Lanka Association for Artificial Intelligence, p. 5 (2015)
2. Ahmad, S., Purdy, S.: Real-time anomaly detection for streaming analytics. arXiv preprint arXiv:1607.02480 (2016)
3. Aransay, I., Sancho, M., Garcıa, P., Fernández, J.: Self-organizing maps for detecting abnormal thermal behavior in data centers. In: Proceedings of the 8th IEEE International Conference on Cloud Computing (CLOUD), pp. 138–145 (2015)
4. Baseman, E., Blanchard, S., DeBardeleben, N., Bonnie, A., Morrow, A.: Interpretable anomaly detection for monitoring of high performance computing systems. In: Outlier Definition, Detection, and Description on Demand Workshop at ACM SIGKDD, San Francisco, Aug 2016 (2016)
5. Borghesi, A., Libri, A., Benini, L., Bartolini, A.: Online anomaly detection in HPC systems. In: 2019 IEEE International Conference on Artificial Intelligence Circuits and Systems (AICAS), pp. 229–233. IEEE (2019)
6. Bosman, H.H., Iacca, G., Tejada, A., Wörtche, H.J., Liotta, A.: Spatial anomaly detection in sensor networks using neighborhood information. Inf. Fusion **33**, 41–56 (2017)
7. Chen, C., Wang, G., Sun, J., Xu, W.: Detecting data center cooling problems using a data-driven approach. In: Proceedings of the 9th Asia-Pacific Workshop on Systems, pp. 1–8 (2018)
8. Chou, J.S., Telaga, A.S.: Real-time detection of anomalous power consumption. Renew. Sustain. Energy Rev. **33**, 400–411 (2014)
9. Das, N., Kundu, A.: Cloud based thermal management system design and its analysis. In: Satapathy, S.C., Mandal, J.K., Udgata, S.K., Bhateja, V. (eds.) Information Systems Design and Intelligent Applications. AISC, vol. 433, pp. 519–528. Springer, New Delhi (2016). https://doi.org/10.1007/978-81-322-2755-7_54
10. Ding, N., Gao, H., Bu, H., Ma, H., Si, H.: Multivariate-time-series-driven real-time anomaly detection based on bayesian network. Sensors **18**(10), 3367 (2018)
11. ENERGY.GOV: Management technology for energy efficiency in data centers and telecommunications facilities. https://www.energy.gov/eere/amo/management-technology-energy-efficiency-data-centers-and-telecommunications-facilities. Accessed 05 Aug 2020
12. Gao, X., Liu, G., Xu, Z., Wang, H., Li, L., Wang, X.: Investigating security vulnerabilities in a hot data center with reduced cooling redundancy. IEEE Trans. Dependable Secure Comput. (2020)
13. Gao, X., Xu, Z., Wang, H., Li, L., Wang, X.: Why some like it hot too: thermal attack on data centers. In: Proceedings of the 2017 ACM SIGMETRICS/International Conference on Measurement and Modeling of Computer Systems, pp. 23–24 (2017)
14. Gao, X., Xu, Z., Wang, H., Li, L., Wang, X.: Reduced cooling redundancy: a new security vulnerability in a hot data center. In: NDSS (2018)
15. Hill, D.J., Minsker, B.S.: Anomaly detection in streaming environmental sensor data: a data-driven modeling approach. Environ. Modell. Softw. **25**(9), 1014–1022 (2010)
16. Hu, X., Subbu, R., Bonissone, P., Qiu, H., Iyer, N.: Multivariate anomaly detection in real-world industrial systems. In: 2008 IEEE International Joint Conference on Neural Networks (IEEE World Congress on Computational Intelligence), pp. 2766–2771. IEEE (2008)

17. Huang, J., Chai, Z., Zhu, H.: Detecting anomalies in data center physical infrastructures using statistical approaches. J. Phys. Conf. Ser. **1176**, 022056 (2019)

18. Jakkula, V., Cook, D.J., et al.: Anomaly detection using temporal data mining in a smart home environment. Methods Inf. Med. **47**(1), 70–75 (2008)

19. Knapp, K.J., Denney, G.D., Barner, M.E.: Key issues in data center security: an investigation of government audit reports. Govern. Inf. Q. **28**(4), 533–541 (2011)

20. Korolov, M.: Cyrusone confirms ransomware attack, says six customers affected. https://www.datacenterknowledge.com/cyrusone/cyrusone-confirms-ransomware-attack-says-six-customers-affected. Accessed 04 Aug 2020

21. Korolov, M.: The four main types of cyberattack that affect data center uptime. https://www.datacenterknowledge.com/security/four-main-types-cyberattack-affect-data-center-uptime. Accessed 04 Aug 2020

22. Lee, E.K., Viswanathan, H., Pompili, D.: Model-based thermal anomaly detection in cloud datacenters. In: 2013 IEEE International Conference on Distributed Computing in Sensor Systems, pp. 191–198. IEEE (2013)

23. Lee, E.K., Viswanathan, H., Pompili, D.: Model-based thermal anomaly detection in cloud datacenters using thermal imaging. IEEE Trans. Cloud Comput. **6**(2), 330–343 (2015)

24. Li, C.: Cooling anomaly detection for servers and datacenters with naive ensemble. In: 2016 32nd Thermal Measurement, Modeling & Management Symposium (SEMI-THERM), pp. 157–162. IEEE (2016)

25. Marwah, M., Sharma, R., Bash, C.: Thermal anomaly prediction in data centers. In: 2010 12th IEEE Intersociety Conference on Thermal and Thermomechanical Phenomena in Electronic Systems, pp. 1–7. IEEE (2010)

26. Marwah, M., Sharma, R., Lugo, W., Bautista, L.: Anomalous thermal behavior detection in data centers using hierarchical PCA. In: Knowledge Discovery from Sensor Data (SensorKDD 2010), p. 78 (2010)

27. Marwah, M., Sharma, R.K., Lugo, W.: Autonomous detection of thermal anomalies in data centers. Int. Electr. Packag. Tech. Conf. Exhibition **43604**, 777–783 (2009)

28. Mehrfeld, J.: Cyber security threats and incidents in industrial control systems. In: Moallem, A. (ed.) HCII 2020. LNCS, vol. 12210, pp. 599–608. Springer, Cham (2020). https://doi.org/10.1007/978-3-030-50309-3_40

29. Nguyen, T.A., Bucur, D., Aiello, M., Tei, K.: Applying time series analysis and neighbourhood voting in a decentralised approach for fault detection and classification in WSNS. In: Proceedings of the Fourth Symposium on Information and Communication Technology, pp. 234–241 (2013)

30. RACK-SOLUTION: 400 million new servers might be needed by 2020. http://shorturl.at/cqzCY. Accessed 04 Aug 2020

31. Salehi, S.A., Razzaque, M.A., Naraei, P., Farrokhtala, A.: Security in wireless sensor networks: issues and challenges. In: 2013 IEEE International Conference on Space Science and Communication (IconSpace), pp. 356–360. IEEE (2013)

32. Schmidt, R.R., Cruz, E.E., Iyengar, M.: Challenges of data center thermal management. IBM Journal of Research and Development 49(4.5), 709–723 (2005)

33. Seaton, I.: Temperature Sensor Location - Data Center Efficiency — Upsite, October 2018. https://www.upsite.com/blog/data-center-temperature-sensor-location/, library Catalog: www.upsite.com Section: Blog

34. Shao, Z., Islam, M.A., Ren, S.: A first look at thermal attacks in multi-tenant data centers. ACM SIGMETRICS Perform. Eval. Rev. **46**(2), 93–94 (2019)

35. Shehabi, A., et al.: United states data center energy usage report. Technical report, Lawrence Berkeley National Lab. (LBNL), Berkeley, CA (United States) (2016)

36. Vigoya, L., Fernandez, D., Carneiro, V., Cacheda, F.: Annotated dataset for anomaly detection in a data center with IoT sensors. Sensors **20**(13), 3745 (2020)
37. Wijayasekara, D., Linda, O., Manic, M., Rieger, C.: Mining building energy management system data using fuzzy anomaly detection and linguistic descriptions. IEEE Trans. Ind. Informat. **10**(3), 1829–1840 (2014)
38. Xu, Z., Wang, H., Xu, Z., Wang, X.: Power attack: an increasing threat to data centers. In: NDSS (2014)
39. Yuan, Y., Lee, E.K., Pompili, D., Liao, J.: Thermal anomaly detection in datacenters. Proc. Inst. Mech. Eng. Part C J. Mech. Eng. Sci. **226**(8), 2104–2117 (2012)
40. Zapater, M., Fraga, D., Malagón, P., Banković, Z., Moya, J.M.: Self-organizing maps versus growing neural gas in detecting anomalies in data centres. Logic J. IGPL **23**(3), 495–505 (2015)
41. Zhu, X., Du, Z., Jin, X., Chen, Z.: Fault diagnosis based operation risk evaluation for air conditioning systems in data centers. Build. Environ. **163**, 106319 (2019)

Anomaly Detection in CAN-BUS Using Pattern Matching Algorithm

Ilia Odeski[✉] and Michael Segal

School of Elecrical and Computer Engineering,
Ben-Gurion University of the Negev, Beer Sheva, Israel
eliao@post.bgu.ac.il, segal@bgu.ac.il

Abstract. With recent advances of the automotive industry, advanced systems have been integrated at in-vehicle communication. However, with the change of perception to data sharing instead of standalone systems, the susceptibility to systemic vulnerability increases. The automotive intra-communication is based on the CAN (Connected Area Network) network protocol. Many types of research have analyzed the protocol's vulnerability to various types of cyber-attacks, and its implications on vehicle systems, with emphasis on safety systems. Research has found that the communication system is not immune to various types of attacks, thus providing access to crucial functions of the vehicle. This paper explores the design and implementation of intrusion detection method in intra-vehicle communication, which aims to identify malicious CAN messages. Based on the historical traffic rate, the algorithm uses a KMP approximate string-matching. Through theoretical analysis and experiments carried out on a real CAN dataset with different attack scenarios, we received very high performance during high and medium intensity attacks. To the best of our knowledge, this work is the first study that applies the KMP approximate pattern matching to IDS for the in-vehicle network security.

Keywords: Pattern matching · CAN bus · Anomaly detection

1 Introduction

In the world of transportation, there is a technological buildup that includes the integration of an increasing inclusion of safety systems, passengers' comfort systems, etc. Accordingly, there has been an increase in the need for fast and secure interconnection between the various systems in the vehicle. As a result of interconnection between the various systems and interfacing with external communications (such as Wi-Fi, cellular, and Bluetooth), the in-vehicle network becomes exposed to malicious interventions that can primarily affect travel safety.

The main in-vehicle communication system is based on CAN protocol. The CAN protocol is based on message-oriented communication. Accordingly, there is no information about the message's source and destination, which makes it difficult to validate the message or its sender, implement encryption or other identification processes.

S. M. Thampi et al. (Eds.): SSCC 2020, CCIS 1364, pp. 180–196, 2021.
https://doi.org/10.1007/978-981-16-0422-5_13

Several works, like in [1, 16], have demonstrated different ways of interfacing to in-vehicle communication via the diagnostic port or wireless communication. In [6], the authors showed examples of the effects of hacking into the in-vehicle network, like the ability to control a wide range of automotive functions.

This paper investigates an anomaly detection algorithm based on an approximate string-matching technique [14], and applies it to CAN bus traffic on the in-vehicle network. The general principle of our solution is identifying similar recurring instances and predicting the network's traffic behavior based on the historical data.

The remainder of this paper is organized as follows: Sect. 2 includes description of related works. Section 3 describes the proposed IDS technique and shows its theoretic analysis. Section 4 presents the experimental evaluation and comparison of the results versus theory. Discussion and conclusions are given in Sect. 5.

2 Related Work

2.1 Statistical Techniques

In [14, 23], the entropy of data has been used as a diagnosis of normal and abnormal behavior. The main idea is based on entropy characteristics of CAN network, which is associated with low entropy, comparing to a scenario of attacks where entropy increases. In [3], the authors proposed partitioning the CAN traffic data into four categories (Engine, Fuel, Gear, and Wheel) and used a one-way Analysis of Variance (ANOVA) test to identify anomalies by clustering the data. In [9], Hyunsung et al. presented an intrusion detection method that is based on the analysis of the offset ratio and time interval between request and response messages in the CAN network.

2.2 Sequential Techniques

In [12], Marchetti and Stabili proposed to find the "normal" value sets for each message ID and try to identify abnormal behavior by analyzing repetition sequences of the messages in the network. The use of hierarchical temporal memory (HTM) to predict the sequential flow of data in real-time is suggested in [22]. Kuwahara et al. [5] applied a counting of the number of messages per sequence and vector of the appearance as features for IDS that is based on nearest neighbored algorithm. In [10], the authors presented an IDS that identifies anomalous events using an additional regression model, by using a dynamic threshold (log likelihood function) as input to the HMM model. In [13], the authors suggested an algorithm that is based on message sequence modeling, which use N-grams distributions and calculation of the frequency of each sequence to calculate the probabilities of the anomaly that are based on historical data at windows of size W.

2.3 Frequency Based Techniques

In [18], the authors suggested light-weight IDS based on the analysis of time intervals of CAN messages. The IDS analyzes the arrival interval of each message ID and classifies it according to the time gap obtained. In [2], Cho and Shin proposed an anomaly detector called Clock-based IDS, which relies on the fact that most of the CAN messages are periodic and suggests to analyze time intervals of messages. This method is useful only for valid periodic messages, but when an attacker inserts messages periodically, the IDS may not detect it. In [7], the authors suggested a lightweight system to detect malicious messages injected into CAN bus, by analyzing the quantized intervals and the absolute difference in payloads, used for periodic and non-periodic messages. In [24], Han, Kwak and Kim used a survival model to classify the network behavior. This method is based on counting the number of appearances of each ID in a period. In [19], an algorithm that measures inter-packet timing over a sliding window, where the mean time compares to the historical mean, was presented.

2.4 Machine Learning Techniques

In [4], J. Kang and Je-Won proposed a technique that reduces high-dimensional CAN data to figure out the underlying statistical properties of normal and attack packets and extracts the corresponding features to identify the attack in the CAN network. In [20], Taylor, Leblanc and Japkowicz proposed using a Long Short-Term Memory (LSTM) Recurrent Neural Network (RNN) for CAN bus anomaly detection. The detector works by learning to predict the next data originating from each sender (message ID) on the bus. In case of a large deviation between the prediction value and message's data, the message is classified as an anomaly, where in [15] the authors used separate LSTM for each message ID. In [21] the authors presented IDS that consists of two stages: The first stage is a robust rule-based system (ID's validation, time interval) where the second stage uses Deep Neural Network (DNN) and features of the number of messages per second, entropy, message ID, and relative distance for anomaly detection. In [8], Song, Woo and Kim proposed a Deep Convolutional Neural Network (DCNN), that learns the sequential network patterns and detects malicious traffic without hand-designed features. In [17], Gan based IDS (GIDS) technique using a deep-learning model, which encodes a large number of CAN IDs with simple one-hot-vector and analyzes them with image processing tools. In [11], the authors used deep learning and a set of an experience knowledge structure (SOEKS) to improve the versatility of intrusion detection for different types of vehicle networks. They use entropy and probability of appearance of ID to classify the sequences.

3 Proposed Detection Technique

3.1 General Approach

We used the KMP approximate pattern matching that was proposed by Mateless and Segal in [14]. Our algorithm is based on approximate string matching of patterns in the historical traffic rate of the CAN network. It examines the repetition of network's behavior by estimating expected behavior and comparing it to actual behavior. This is based on the assumption that the message appears periodically in most cases.

We are considering the historical traffic rate measurements as R, P as the last verified pattern of traffic rate measurements and the currently measured traffic that we want to verify as vector V. The idea is to find patterns of non-overlapping approximate appearances of P in R. Then, we create an estimated network behavior vector E which is based on all of the appearances matches of approximate string-matching algorithm, and examine it with the currently measured traffic (vector V), Fig. 1 shows an example.

Two parameters are being used to control the approximate appearance of P in R. The instant error parameter which defines the upper bound of the degree of similarity between each measurement in P versus corresponding measurement in R, and cumulative error parameter which defines the upper bound on the total difference between all measurements in P versus potential matching in R. The output of the pattern matching is a vector of start indexes of all non-overlapping matching that is defined as S. We build estimated vector E by calculating the mean value for each corresponding measurement between the next pattern of all matches of P in R. The matching test is based on using a calculation of the mean square error (MSE) on V and E. Another possible scenario is that no match is found. This scenario is covered by comparing the statistical parameters of the currently measured traffic (vector V) to cold start statistical parameters.

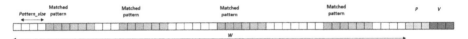

Fig. 1. Pattern matching, Yellow color describes P pattern, Blue color describes vector V and Orange color describes the matched patterns. (Color figure online)

3.2 Anomaly Detection Algorithm

The novelty of this research is the analysis and implementation of an anomaly detection algorithm, which bases on a prediction of the message's traffic behavior in the CAN network by using the estimated pattern matching algorithm. The main benefit of this approach is its complete independence from the content of CAN messages, which is a proprietary data.

The algorithm is divided into three modules: pre-processing, KMP algorithm for approximate pattern matching and estimation of pattern classification. Figure 2 shows the algorithm's flowchart.

3.3 Pre-processing

The purpose of the pre-processing is to convert the raw data of CAN bus to a traffic rate measurement to be used by the following modules. The input to the pre-processing module is a raw data from the CAN bus. According to the *ID_rate* parameter which defines the length of a time step, the data is converted to traffic rate measurements vector. Let R be traffic rate measurements vector that defined in (1), where r_k is traffic rate measurement of pattern k and t_i is the time tag of message i that described in (2).

$$R = \{r_k\}_{k=1}^{\infty} \qquad (1)$$

$$r_k = \left\{ \sum_i 1 | i \cdot ID\_rate \le t_i < (i+1) \cdot ID\_rate \right\} (messages/timestep) \qquad (2)$$

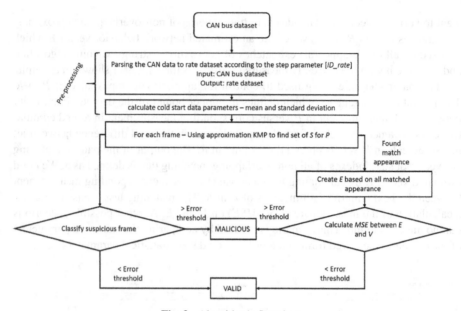

Fig. 2. Algorithm's flowchart.

3.4 Cold Start

Our approach is based on unsupervised learning. As part of the initial process, the algorithm needs an input of valid network behavior. Let R_{cs} be vector initial segment of traffic rate measurements, as defined in (3); our work assumption is that R_{cs} does not include attacks and includes steady-state behavior of the CAN network, where N is a value representing the size of R_{cs}.

$$R_{cs} = \{r_1, \cdots, r_N\} \tag{3}$$

The algorithm computes statistical characteristics of R_{cs}, the mean ($\mu_{coldstart}$) and standard deviation ($\sigma_{coldstart}$), as defined in (4) and (5), where r_k is traffic rate measurement of time duration k, μ is the expected traffic rate value.

$$\mu_{coldstart} = \frac{1}{N} \sum_{k=1}^{N} r_k \tag{4}$$

$$\sigma_{coldstart} = \sqrt{\frac{1}{N} \sum_{k=1}^{N} (r_k - \mu)^2} \tag{5}$$

Equation (6) shows as N increases, the standard error of the mean (SEM) decreases, σ is the expected standard deviation of the traffic rate measurements. We aim to increase the N value to decrease the difference between the measured mean and the expected mean, but as N gets bigger, the learning time increases. Our working assumption is to allow minimal learning time while minimizing the damage to the accuracy of the statistical variables.

$$SEM = \frac{\sigma}{\sqrt{N}} \tag{6}$$

We examined the effect of N on SEM according to (6) and also examined the effect on the calculated mean for our dataset. In accordance with our work assumption and the results we decided to set N to be 2000.

3.5 Data Mining - Analyzing CAN Bus Valid Data

As part of our research, we analyzed the raw data of CAN network, message types and message's traffic dynamics, frequency of each message, traffic behavior (which is dependent on *ID_Rate* parameter), CDF, and we set assumptions about the statistical characteristics of the CAN bus.

The traffic dynamics and *ID_rate* parameter influence on the frequency of traffic rate. As part of the research, we examined the distribution of the valid network's traffic (based on the dataset of [17]). We found that over half of the messages have a very high frequency that is larger in more than two orders of magnitude from other messages. Therefore, we chose to examine the impact of parameter *ID_rate* in the range of values where the minimum value is at least the maximum value of message's ratio.

Let μ_R be the measured mean rate that defined in (7) and σ_R be the measured standard deviation that defined in (8), Δ be maximum delta of r_k from μ_R that defined in (9), and Δ_σ maximum delta of r_k from the μ_R as function of σ that defined in (10).

$$\mu_R = \frac{1}{N} \sum_{k=1}^{\infty} r_k \tag{7}$$

$$\sigma_R = \sqrt{\frac{1}{N} \sum_{k=1}^{\infty} (r_k - \mu_R)^2} \tag{8}$$

$$\Delta = \max(r_k - \mu_R) \tag{9}$$

$$\Delta_\sigma = \frac{\max(r_k - \mu_R)}{\sigma} \tag{10}$$

Table 1 contains statistical data of the traffic rate measurements as a function of the *ID_rate* parameter

Table 1. Statistical data of traffic rate measurements for different *ID_rate* values.

ID_rate value (msec)	μ_R	σ_R	Δ	Δ_σ
25	50.28	4.34	12.71	2.92
50	98.44	2.15	6.54	3.04
100	196.05	1.33	5.05	3.79
200	391.35	1.44	7.64	5.3

To strengthen insights of data analysis, testing was performed with another dataset (taken from [15]) having length of more than 6 h. Results were obtained with statistics similar to those for our dataset.

After analyzing the traffic rate measurements distribution of the two datasets, it is reasonable to assume that for valid data the traffic rate distribution is close to normal distribution. From another point of view, by using the central limit theorem, we can assume that the data distribution becomes normally distributed when the number of observations is sufficiently large, as in our case. Accordingly, we chose to continue the analysis under the assumption that the traffic rate has normal distribution (also assumed in [5]). Therefore, R has a normal distribution, as defined in (11), where μ is the traffic expected rate, and σ is the standard deviation of traffic rate.

$$R \sim N\left(\mu, \sigma^2\right) \tag{11}$$

3.6 Pattern Matching Algorithm

The approximate pattern matching is based on KMP algorithm and modified prefix function that proposed in [14]. It used to detect patterns in historical traffic data on the CAN network. The input arguments to the algorithm are R, W, P, α, β. Vector R represents the last historical traffic rate measurements with length size W, P is the last verified pattern of the traffic rate measurements, that is described in (12), α is the instant error parameter which defines the upper bound of similarity between each measurement in P versus corresponding measurement in R, and β is the cumulative error parameter which defines the upper bound on the total difference between all measurements in P versus potential matching in R, where p_j is the j_{th} traffic rate measurement of pattern P.

$$P = \left\{p_1, \cdots, p_{pattern\_size}\right\} \tag{12}$$

The output of the pattern matching algorithm is a vector of start indexes of all the non-overlapping matching, defined as S and recalculated with each iteration of a new pattern matching test. S is defined in (13), where M is the number of approximate matchings of P in R, and s_l is the start index in R of the matching result l.

$$S = \begin{cases} \{s_l\}_{l=1}^M, & \text{for matching case} \\ \phi, & \text{for unmatching case} \end{cases} \tag{13}$$

Method of Selecting the Error Parameter's Values (α, β)
The traffic rate behavior in CAN bus can be changed due to different reasons, like different network architecture of vehicles, vehicle systems, changes in driving situations. Therefore, the parameters of the approximate matching algorithm need to be adapted to network's behavior. Therefore, we define the parameters to be relative to the standard deviation of network's behavior so instant error threshold (α) and cumulative error threshold (β) values will be calculated according to the relative parameters $(\alpha_{rel}\beta_{rel})$, $\sigma_{coldstart}$ and $pattern\_size$ parameter.

Instant Error Parameter (A)

The instant error threshold parameter is defined in (14), where α_{rel} is the relative parameter that is defined by the user and $\sigma_{coldstart}$ is the standard deviation of the cold start traffic rate measurements. This parameter has a large effect on the sensitivity of the anomaly detection algorithm.

$$\alpha = \sigma_{coldstart} \cdot \alpha_{rel} \tag{14}$$

We want to examine the probability of a scenario in which the examined pattern (P) will be rejected by the instant error test when checked with pattern in the historical traffic rate measurements (R). The strict case for the instant error test is for a condition where the traffic rate measurement r_k and the traffic rate measurement p_j are in distance of z from the mean value but in the opposite direction. Therefore, based only on the instant error test, the maximum probability of rejecting a valid pattern is described in (15).

$$P_{rejection-by-instant-test} = 1 - 2 \cdot erf\left(\frac{z}{\sigma}\right) \tag{15}$$

We choose that the rejection will be less than 0.03 as a working assumption. Therefore, under the assumption of normal distribution and $P_{rejection-by-instant-test} \leq 0.03$ we choose z to be 3σ. Accordingly the α parameter needs to be at least 6σ, as described in (16). Selecting a much greater value from the lower bound can lead to impaired attack detection performance, so the rationale is to select the relative parameter values that are close to the lower bound. For value lower than the maximum distance, we increase the probability of rejecting and receiving false alerts.

$$\alpha \geq 2 \cdot z = 2 \cdot 3\sigma = 6\sigma \tag{16}$$

Cumulative Error Parameter (B)

Using this test allows examining the behavior of the entire pattern compared with historical traffic rate.

The cumulative error threshold is defined in (17), where β_{rel} is the relative parameter that is defined by the user, $\sigma_{coldstart}$ is the standard deviation of the cold start traffic rate measurements and *pattern_size* is the pattern length.

$$\beta = \sigma_{coldstart} \cdot \beta_{rel} \cdot pattern\_size \tag{17}$$

The calculated cumulative error defined in (18), where k is an index in R, and j is an index in P.

$$cum_{error} = \sum_{pattern_{size}} |r_k - p_j| \tag{18}$$

We assume that for valid pattern the maximum rejection of valid pattern by the cumulative test is less than 0.03%. Therefore, like in the instant error analysis, β needs to have a maximum value of $6\sigma \cdot pattern\_size$ as described in (19). In most cases, the calculated instant error will be less than the bound. We chose the cumulative error threshold to be within 50–70% of α. Equation (20) is describes the 50% case.

$$\beta = 6\sigma \cdot pattern\_size \tag{19}$$

$$\beta = 0.5 \cdot \alpha \cdot pattern\_size = 3\sigma \cdot pattern\_size \tag{20}$$

3.7 Pattern Classification

There are two options for the KMP's algorithm output: matching an approximate behavior in history, and the un-matched case. Based on the KMP result, the anomaly detection algorithm classifies the examined pattern.

Matched Case of P in R

The pattern classification process is based on predicting the traffic rate behavior of the network. After the vector of start indexes of all the non-overlapping matching (vector S) created, the algorithm creates a prediction vector E as described in (21), where e_i is the mean of measurements in index i in the next pattern of all matched patterns in R for pattern P and s_l is the start index in R of the matching result l.

$$E = \left\{ e_1, \cdots, e_{pattern\_size} \middle| e_i = \frac{1}{|S|} \cdot \sum_j^{|S|} r_{s_l + pattern\_size + i} \right\} \tag{21}$$

The currently measured traffic rate pattern that we want to verify is vector V, that is defined in (22), where v_i is the traffic rate measurement in index i.

$$V = \left\{ v_1, \cdots, v_{pattern\_size} \right\} \tag{22}$$

Classification of the network behavior is based on the comparison between the matched error threshold parameter and the result of the mean squared error (MSE) of E and V, as described in (23).

$$MSE(E - V) = \frac{1}{pattern\_size} \cdot \sum_{pattern_{size}} (e_i - v_i)^2 = Var(E - V) + Bias^2(E - V) \tag{23}$$

For valid pattern case, vectors E, V has normal distribution $\sim N(\mu, \sigma^2)$, and they are i.i.d. Therefore, the value of MSE for valid behavior is as described in (24).

$$MSE_{valid}(E - V) = 2\sigma^2 \tag{24}$$

We define the matched error threshold as ε, as described in (25), where ε_{rel} is the relative matched parameter that is set by the user.

$$\varepsilon = \varepsilon_{rel} \cdot \sigma_{coldstart}^2 \tag{25}$$

The classification is according to the following test ((26) and (27)).

$$Result = \varepsilon - MSE(E - V) \tag{26}$$

$$\text{classification of vector } V \ = \ \begin{cases} VALID, & result \geq 0 \\ MALICIOUS, & else \end{cases} \tag{27}$$

In order to prevent false alerts, the threshold value of ε is required to be as defined in the (28).

$$\varepsilon \geq MSE_{valid}(E - V) = 2\sigma^2 \tag{28}$$

Equation (29) describes the expected MSE for attack scenario, and (30) shows the difference between the expected MSE for attack scenario and expected MSE for valid pattern, where $\Delta\sigma_a^2$ is the variance of the traffic rate attack and $\Delta\mu_a$ is the mean of the traffic rate of attack (per time step).

$$MSE(E - V) = \left(2\sigma^2 + \Delta\sigma_a^2\right) + (\Delta\mu_a)^2 \tag{29}$$

$$\Delta MSE_{from-valid}(E - V) = \Delta\sigma_a^2 + \Delta\mu_a^2 \tag{30}$$

Any injection attack that will meet the requirements of (31) will classified as valid, where ΔR_a be the mean of the traffic attack rate per sec, as described in (32).

$$\varepsilon - 2\sigma^2 \geq (\Delta\sigma_a)^2 + (\Delta R_a \cdot ID_{rate})^2 \tag{31}$$

$$\Delta R_a = \frac{\Delta\mu_a}{ID\_rate}(m\backslash s) \tag{32}$$

Un-matched Case
If no matches were found by KMP algorithm, the classification of the examined pattern (vector V) is done with two tests by comparing the mean and the standard deviation of the pattern to network characteristics, which are defined in cold start module. If V complies the tests, it will be defined as valid pattern else it will be defined as an attack. The purpose of using two tests is to handle different types of attacks.

Mean Test – Test (a)
99.7% of sampled mean observation is distributed in range of $3 \cdot SEM$ from the expected mean and, therefore, we define the mean comparison test as described in (33), where μ_V is the mean of vector V, $\gamma_{1\,rel}$ is the relative mean error parameter for the unmatched case test, γ_1 is the mean error parameter for unmatched case that is described in (34). Equation (35) describes the maximum difference of μ_V from the expected mean (μ) that will pass this test. Increasing parameter γ_1 will increase the acceptable mean difference, and accordingly, attacks with low attack rate can pass the test and be classified as valid. Decreasing the parameter value below the threshold of 1 can lead to increase of false alarms.

$$Mean_{error} = |\Delta\mu_V| - \frac{6\sigma \cdot \gamma_1}{\sqrt{pattern\_size}} \leq 0 \tag{33}$$

$$\gamma_1 = \frac{100 + \gamma_{1\,rel}}{100} \tag{34}$$

$$|\Delta \mu_V| \leq \gamma_1 \frac{6\sigma}{\sqrt{pattern\_size}} \tag{35}$$

Standard Deviation Test – Test (B)

We define the standard deviation comparison test as described in (36), where σ_V is the standard deviation of measurements in V, $\gamma_{2_{rel}}$ is the relative deviation threshold parameter for unmatched case, γ_2 is the deviation threshold parameter for unmatched case that is defined in (37), and $\Delta \sigma_V$ is the maximum difference of standard deviation that will pass this test that described in (38). Increasing parameter γ_2 will increase the acceptable standard deviation difference, and accordingly, an attack with low variance can pass. Decreasing the parameter value below the threshold of 1 can lead to increase of false alarms.

$$STD_{error} = (1 - \gamma_2)\sigma_{coldstart} + \Delta \sigma_V \leq 0 \tag{36}$$

$$\gamma_2 = \frac{100 + \gamma_{2rel}}{100} \tag{37}$$

$$\Delta \sigma_V \leq (\gamma_2 - 1)\sigma_{coldstart} \tag{38}$$

$$classification\ of\ vector\ V = \begin{cases} VALID, & STD_{error} \leq 0\ and\ Mean_{error} \leq 0 \\ MALICIOUS, & else \end{cases} \tag{39}$$

Any injection attack that will meet the requirements of (35), (38) will classified as valid. For attack with constant rate the threshold is defined in (40), where ΔR_{a-um} is the mean of attack traffic rate per second.

$$\Delta R_{a-um} \leq \frac{|\Delta \mu_V|}{ID_{rate}} = \gamma_1 \frac{6\sigma}{ID_{rate} \cdot \sqrt{pattern_{size}}}(m/s) \tag{40}$$

4 Evaluation and Results

4.1 Data Set

Our dataset is based on the dataset of [17]. Hyundai's YF Sonata used as a testing vehicle. The original dataset includes four types of attacks (DoS, Fuzzy, RMP and Gear) on the CAN bus. The attacks injected in real time to the CAN bus and are not included in the post-processing of the dataset. Our dataset is a combination of all the four attacks with variable duration and variable attack rate with a total duration of 3:32 h. As seen in Table 2, different types of attacks have different behavior and impact.

Table 2. Statistical data of different attack scenarios.

Attack type	Attack rate	μ_R	σ_R	Δ	Δ_σ
DoS	3333	115.33	69.44	281	4
RPM	600	234.63	4.92	23.63	4.8

4.2 Evaluation Parameters

We evaluate the algorithm performance with the *ROC* graph for evaluation of parameters. Our working assumption is to reduce the amount of non-detection of attacks. Therefore, we performed optimization on the parameter values to obtain a maximum *TPR*, while maintaining a minimum *FPR*.

Algorithm performance analysis was carried out by checking the effect of each parameter on the algorithm performance. We compared the performance with the combined dataset, which contains different attack scenarios. The influence of the dominant parameters on algorithm performance is shown in Fig. 3.

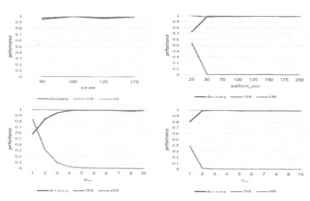

Fig. 3. Influence of the dominant parameters on algorithm performance, Blue color describes accuracy, Orange color describes *TPR* and Gray color describes *FPR*. (Color figure online)

The Central Insight of the Algorithm's Performance

The ID_rate parameter affects the percentage of false alarms. The parameter *W* (Historical window size) has no effect on the performance; it is relevant to the stability frequency of messages on the network. For the unmatched tests, we have concluded that only very high values of the two-test parameters will lead to a significant performance degradation. For the other parameters, very low values (different thresholds for each parameter) significantly affect the percentage of false alerts. The analysis shows that there is no significant effect of the parameters on the detection of attacks performance (*TPR*), but mainly on increasing the percentage of false alerts (*FPR*).

4.3 Algorithm Performance

We compared the final set of parameters with different datasets that contains a variety of attack durations with a constant attack rate (per dataset). We received high performance for high and middle attack rates, and good performance for small attack rate, the results are summarized in Table 3.

Table 3. Algorithm performance for different attack scenarios.

#	Dataset	Data description	*TPR*	*FPR*	Accuracy
1	Combined	10–3333 attack messages per second	0.995	0.004	0.99
2	High-rate	100–1000 attack messages per second	1	0.002	0.999
3	Middle-rate	10–100 attack messages per second	0.988	0.012	0.988
4	Small-rate	1–10 attack messages of per second	0.811	0.016	0.895

4.4 Comparison the Results with Theoretical Analyzes

We examined the algorithm's actual performance versus the theoretical analysis. As shown in Table 4, the simulation results validate the theoretical analysis.

Table 4. Algorithm performance for different attack scenarios.

Attack rate	Test scenario (matched\un-matched)	Expected threshold (m\s)	Real attack rate (m\s)	Obtained performance (*TP*)
High	Un-matched	6	100–1000	100%
Mid	Matched	18	10–100	99.8%
Small	Matched	18	1–10	81.1%

4.5 Comparison with Previous Works

It is important to note that most of the works in this area are based on proprietary databases, which, due to their sensitivity, are not published. Accordingly, there is difficulty in comparing the algorithm's performance with the databases of other algorithms (Table 5).

In comparing the performance with different algorithms based on the same dataset, with the exception of examining our algorithm performance, the rest was tested as part of research in [8]. The performance was very close to that of Reduced Inception-ResNet algorithm that was proposed in [8], where in most of the tests, our algorithm performed better than the others.

Table 5. Comparison of different algorithms based on the same dataset

Dataset	Algorithm	FNR (%)	ER (%)	Precision	Recall (TPR)
DOS	Ours	0.07	0.03	0.93	1
	Reduced Inception-ResNet [8]	0.1	0.03	1	0.9989
	LSTM (256 hidden units)	0.22	0.07	1	0.9978
	ANN (2 hidden layers)	0.18	0.07	0.9995	0.9982
	Support Vector Machine	0.56	0.17	1	0.9944
	k-nearest neighbors (k = 5)	0.7	0.22	0.9998	0.9929
	Naïve Bayes	1.18	0.35	1	0.9882
	Decision Trees	1.18	1.34	0.9762	0.8681
Gear spoofing	Ours	0.1	0.05	0.9	1
	Reduced Inception-ResNet [8]	0.11	0.05	0.9999	0.9989
	LSTM (256 hidden units)	0.32	0.24	0.9975	0.9968
	ANN (2 hidden layers)	0.16	0.11	0.9989	0.9984
	Support Vector Machine	0.35	0.15	1	0.9965
	k-nearest neighbors (k = 5)	1.58	0.67	1	0.9842
	Naïve Bayes	0.84	0.36	1	0.9916
	Decision Trees	2.19	1.72	0.9815	0.9781
RPM spoofing	Ours	0.08	0.04	0.93	1
	Reduced Inception-ResNet 8]	0.05	0.03	0.9999	0.9994
	LSTM (256 hidden units)	0.3	0.13	1	0.9971
	ANN (2 hidden layers)	0.11	0.09	0.999	0.9989
	Support Vector Machine	0.23	0.11	1	0.9977
	k-nearest neighbors (k = 5)	0.8	0.36	0.9999	0.992
	Naïve Bayes	0.51	0.23	1	0.9949

(*continued*)

Table 5. (*continued*)

Dataset	Algorithm	FNR (%)	ER (%)	Precision	Recall (TPR)
	Decision Trees	2.18	1.68	0.9842	0.9782
Fuzzy	Ours	0.09	0.05	0.92	1
	Reduced Inception-ResNet [8]	0.35	0.18	0.9995	0.9965
	LSTM (256 hidden units)	0.84	0.65	0.9936	0.9916
	ANN (2 hidden layers)	1.97	1.37	0.9886	0.9803
	Support Vector Machine	4.45	2.26	0.9928	0.9555
	k-nearest neighbors (k = 5)	93.42	41.18	1	0.0658
	Naïve Bayes	9.03	4.25	0.9933	0.9098
	Decision Trees	10.26	7.23	0.9359	0.8974

5 Discussion and Conclusions

This paper explored the analysis and implementation of IDS methods in intra-vehicle communication, which aims to identify malicious CAN messages that are part of different cyber-attacks. Our unsupervised algorithm is based on approximate string matching of patterns in historical traffic rate data on the CAN bus. It examines the repetition of network behavior by estimating expected behavior and comparing it to actual behavior. The algorithm's detection performance was demonstrated through experiments carried out on real CAN traffic gathered from an unmodified licensed vehicle. As far as we know, this work is the first study to apply the KMP approximate pattern matching to IDS for the in-vehicle network security.

As part of the paper, we investigated the related work on IDS in CAN bus, anomaly detection using pattern matching, analyzed the CAN data, its statistical characteristic. We examined KMP approximate algorithm performance for valid data and attacks, developed and implemented the anomaly detection algorithm. We also examined the effect of the algorithm's parameters accordingly to the research methodology, optimized the performance with different attack scenarios, compared the results with theoretical analysis and with previous works performance. Our algorithm's performance yields very good results, with *TPR* of 0.995 and *FPR* 0.004 for the combined dataset. Based on [16, 20], which mentioned that in order to override the legitimate sender, the attack messages must be transmitted in a high rate, the algorithm's performance is high. The limitations of the algorithm are the incapability to detect IDs of attack messages and to detect attacks that had been performed by changing the message content without changing the rate of the network.

References

1. Checkoway, S., et al.: Comprehensive experimental analyses of automotive attack surfaces. USENIX Security Symposium **4**, 447–462 (2011)
2. Kyong-Tak, C., Kang, G.S.: Fingerprinting electronic control units for vehicle intrusion detection. In: 25th USENIX Security Symposium, pp. 911–927 (2016)
3. Han, M.L., Lee, J., Kang, A.R., Kang, S., Park, J.K., Kim, H.K.: A statistical-based anomaly detection method for connected cars in internet of things environment. In: International Conference on Internet of Vehicles, pp. 89–97 (2015)
4. Kang, M.J., Kang, J.W.: Intrusion detection system using deep neural network for in-vehicle network security, PloS One, vol. 11, no. 6 (2016)
5. Kuwahara, T., et al.: Supervised and unsupervised intrusion detection based on can message frequencies for in-vehicle network. J. Inf. Process. **26**, 306–313 (2018)
6. Koscher, K., et al.: Experimental security analysis of a modern automobile, In: IEE SSP, pp. 447–462 (2010)
7. Koyama, T., Shibahara, T., Hasegawa, K., Okano, Y., Tanaka, M., Oshima, Y.: Anomaly detection for mixed transmission can messages using quantized intervals and absolute difference of payloads. In: Workshop on Automotive Cybersecurity, pp. 19–24 (2019)
8. Song, H.M., Woo, J., Kim, H.K.: In-vehicle network intrusion detection using deep convolutional neural network. Vehicular Commun. **21**, 100–198 (2020)
9. Lee, H., Jeong, S.H., Kim, H.K.: OTIDS: a novel intrusion detection system for in-vehicle network by using remote frame, In: PST, p. 5709 (2017)
10. Levi, M., Allouche, Y., Kontorovich, A.: Advanced analytics for connected car cybersecurity, In: IEEE 87th Vehicular Technology Conference (VTC Spring), pp. 1–7 (2018)
11. Gao, L., Li, F., Xu, X., Liu, Y.: Intrusion detection system using SOEKS and deep learning for in-vehicle security. Cluster Comput. **22**(6), 14721–14729 (2018). https://doi.org/10.1007/s10586-018-2385-7
12. Marchetti, M., Stabili, D.: Anomaly detection of CAN bus messages through analysis of ID sequences. In: IEEE Intelligent Vehicles Symposium (IV), pp. 1577–1583 (2017)
13. Tomlinson, A., Bryans, J., Shaikh, S.A., Kalutarage, H.K.: Detection of automotive CAN cyber-attacks by identifying packet timing anomalies in time windows. In: 48th Annual IEEE/IFIP DSN-W, pp. 231–238 (2018)
14. Mateless, R., Segal, M.: Approximate string matching for DNS anomaly detection, In: SPACS, pp. 490–504 (2019)
15. Hanselmann, M., Strauss, T., Dormann, K., Ulmer, H.: CANet: An Unsupervised Intrusion Detection System for High Dimensional CAN Bus Data. IEEE Access **8**, 58194–58205 (2020)
16. Miller, C., Valasek, C.: A survey of remote automotive attack surfaces. Black Hat USA, p. 94 (2014)
17. Seo, E., Song, H.M., Kim, H.K.: GIDS: GAN based intrusion detection system for in-vehicle network, In: PST, pp. 1–6 (2018)
18. Song, H.M., Kim, H.R., Kim, H.K.: Intrusion detection system based on the analysis of time intervals of CAN messages for in-vehicle network, In: ICOIN, pp. 63–68 (2016)
19. Taylor, A., Japkowicz, N., Leblanc, S.: Frequency-based anomaly detection for the automotive CAN bus, In: WCICSS, pp. 45–49 (2015)
20. Taylor, A., Leblanc, S., Japkowicz, N.: Anomaly detection in automobile control network data with long short-term memory networks, In: IEEE DSAA, pp. 130–139 (2016)
21. Zhang, L., Shi, L., Kaja, N., Ma, D.: A two-stage deep learning approach for can intrusion detection. In: Proceedings Ground Vehicle System Engineering Technology Symposium (GVSETS), p. 11 (2018)

22. Wang, C., Zhao, Z., Gong, L., Zhu, L., Liu, Z., Cheng, X.: A distributed anomaly detection system for in-vehicle network using HTM. IEEE Access **6**, 9091–9098 (2018)
23. Wang, Q., Lu, Z., Qu, G.: An entropy analysis based intrusion detection system for controller area network in vehicles, In: 31st IEEE SOCC, pp. 90–95 (2018)
24. Han, M.L., Kwak, B.I., Kim, H.K.: Anomaly intrusion detection method for vehicular networks based on survival analysis. Vehicular commun. **14**, 52–63 (2018)

Conjunctive Keyword Forward Secure Ranked Dynamic Searchable Encryption Over Outsourced Encrypted Data

Md Asrar Ahmed[1]([⊠]), S. Ramachandram[1], and Khaleel Ur Rahman Khan[2]

[1] CSE Department, University College of Engineering, Osmania University, Hyderabad, India
asrar7.ahmed@gmail.com, ramachandrams@gmail.com
[2] CSE Department, ACE Engineering College, Rangareddy, India
khaleelrkhan@gmail.com

Abstract. Cloud Computing enables individuals and organizations with extensive computing capabilities along with scalable storage services. However the security of outsourced data brings about privacy concerns when confidential data is outsourced to third party service providers. The Searchable Symmetric Encryption (SSE) is a solution towards enabling data owners to securely outsource and later retrieve the matching documents based on encrypted queries. Majority of existing SSE schemes lack support for relevance based retrieval of matching documents to queried keywords, expressive queries, and privacy of query terms and documents. In this paper we present a novel dynamic SSE scheme which retrieves documents ranked based on their relevance to the queries, and ensures forward and backward privacy definitions given by R Bost et al. Our scheme is lightweight as it allows the server to compute document-query relevance in a secure manner without affecting the entire outsourced index, especially during update operations, which is normally the case in existing state of the art. We employ an indexing mechanism which is alternate to the most frequently used Inverted Index structure but overcomes drawbacks of such an index. Experimental analysis of our scheme on RFC dataset demonstrated a sub-linear search time and efficient update operations. The proposed scheme also ensures forward and backward security during search and update operations.

Keywords: Dynamic searchable symmetric encryption (DSSE) · Forward privacy · Backward privacy · Ranked SSE · TF-IDF based relevance ranking

1 Introduction

With the widespread acceptability of Cloud Computing framework in business and IT industry, cloud storage has also become an inevitable solution for data storage needs of clients. It offers benefits such as high availability, scalability, ease of access, and efficient remote data storage service. However, these guarantees come at an expense of security vulnerabilities such as loss of control over confidential data, threat to data privacy and integrity. One default solution to this is to encrypt the data before it is being outsourced.

© Springer Nature Singapore Pte Ltd. 2021
S. M. Thampi et al. (Eds.): SSCC 2020, CCIS 1364, pp. 197–212, 2021.
https://doi.org/10.1007/978-981-16-0422-5_14

This ensures the end to end data privacy but incurs a heavy cost on functionality to retrieve the data from cloud [1]. To address this problem, Searchable Symmetric Encryption (SSE) was first introduced in [2], which enables a client to encrypt the data so that it can be queried later using encrypted search token to servers. All of the existing SSE schemes have been targeted to achieve Security, Efficiency and Functionality. Major research focus has been to ensure functionality such as single keyword, multi-keyword, phrase, and fuzzy keyword searches, etc. In addition, researchers have also focused on achieving efficient SSE schemes with help of various index structures. And most of the schemes while addressing functionality and efficiency, consider a security threat model which guarantees security notions such as IND-CKA and IND-CKA2 (defined in [3]). As mentioned in [4], single and multi-keyword Boolean searches are unrealistic as they incur heavy network bandwidth and client side processing in filtering out relevant documents. Therefore to address these issues, Ranked SSE schemes were proposed in [4–10] aimed at more practical schemes in a pay as you go model of cloud.

But most of these schemes lack practicality in following means: dynamic update operations on outsourced collection, privacy of outsourced index and queries in the event of potential File Injection Attacks [11], leakage of significant information to adversary during setup, search and update operations. It is also noted that in existing Ranked Dynamic SSE schemes, the update operations necessitates changes to significant portion of outsourced index and thus incur heavy leakage and computing efforts. Motivated by these shortcomings, we propose a scheme that enables a client to carry out multi-keyword ranked search with minimal changes to the index in the event of update operations and ensures forward and backward privacy. Our scheme incurs very less overhead in index building by outsourcing the relevance score calculation to the server in a secure and randomized manner. Whereas the existing schemes such as [4, 6, 7, 10] require client to fully build a tree based index or inverted index populated with relevance scores for each keyword-document pairs. **Our contributions**: in this work we propose a DSSE scheme which is:

1. **Ranked:** retrieves matching documents based on relevance score calculated partially by server for conjunctive queried keywords.
2. **Dynamic:** supports update operations such as insert and delete of documents to the outsourced collection with minimal leakage.
3. **Forward and Backward Secure:** ensures that future insert operations do not compromise query privacy and future delete operations are not carried out on deleted documents (and index entries thereof).
4. **Sublinear Search and Update Complexity:** the index structure ensures searches and updates to be carried out efficiently.

2 Related Work

Searchable Encryption (SE) has been under consistent research since it was first introduced by Song et al., in [1] due to the ubiquitous storage services offered by cloud
service providers to the resource constrained clients. Searchable Encryption techniques
have been proposed in literature using both public key cryptography and symmetric key
encryption schemes. The initial work on Symmetric Searchable Encryption schemes
(SSE) can be found in [2, 3, 12, 13]. First explicit consideration for SSE was given by
Song et al., in [2] where the authors proposed a non-interactive SE scheme whose search
time was linear to the length of all documents in the collection. The prominent works
which lead to stronger security definitions of SSE schemes and index data structures
were carried out in [3, 12, 13]. In [12], authors defined a secure index for the first time
to perform search operation in O(1) time.

The limitation of these schemes was that they considered document collection to be
static. The initial work on dynamic schemes was proposed by Leisdonk et al., in [14],
with logarithmic search time. The subsequent works in this direction were proposed in
[15], which was IND-CKA2 secure and first usage of inverted index for dynamic data
collection. Despite being dynamic and efficient, these schemes lack expressive query
support. The works in [16–19] designed schemes with support for multi-keyword queries
and similarity searches. But the Boolean search turns out to be of little utility at client
side as it will return documents with mere occurrence of search terms. This has a severe
impact on network latency, communication costs and client side processing. Thus to
make it more practical, ranked multi-keyword SSE schemes were proposed in [4–10].
In [4], authors used a Random Traversal Algorithm on a hierarchical index structure,
and designed a random grouping of documents to facilitate random traversal. Sun et al.
[5], gave a hierarchical index structure using TF-IDF relevance score between query
and document. Cao et al. [6] designed a multi-keyword ranked scheme based on Vector
Space Model based index. Z. Xia et al. [7], proposed a special tree based index and a
greedy depth first search algorithm to perform ranked search. In [8, 9], authors proposed
an inverted index based structure with relevance scores encrypted using homomorphic
encryption technique stored in posting lists. The drawback is that though they support
dynamic SSE but the update operations cause relevance score changes in the entire index
structure thus suffers leakage and incurs heavy computations. In [10], authors used an
inverted index to store randomized relevance score information but it does not support
dynamic operations. A comparison of the existing strategies and our proposed work is
presented in below Table 1.

Table 1. Comparison framework

Scheme	Search complexity	DSSE	Update complexity	Index type	Forward privacy	Multi keyword
[5]	$O(\theta m \log n)$	No	NA	Tree based	No	Yes
[6]	$O\left(m^2\right)$	No	NA	Forward index	No	Yes
[7]	$O(\theta m \log n)$	Yes	$O\left(m^2 \log n\right)$	Tree based $O\left(mn^2\right)$	No	Yes
[9]	$O(R \log M)$	No	NA	Inverted index $O(mn)$	No	Yes
[4]	$O\left(e^2 m\right)$	No	NA	Tree based $O\left(\theta mbe^2\right)$	No	Yes
[10]	$O(m.m')$	No	NA	Inverted index $O(m + mn)$	No	Yes
Proposed	$O(a_w)$	Yes	$O(|d_j|)$	Dual index $O(mn + mn)$	Yes	Yes

Notations: θ: # of leaf nodes, m: # of keywords, n: # of documents, $O(R \log M)$: complexity of OPM algorithm, e: vector length, b: # of groups, a_w: # of keyword-document pairs in dictionary for keyword w, m': # of keywords in query.

3   The Proposed CFR DSSE Scheme

In this section we describe and define our proposed **C**onjunctive keywords **F**orward Secure **R**anked Dynamic SSE scheme (CFR-DSSE) with respect to notations, data structures and algorithms. We consider the most frequently assumed threat model of honest-but-curious server which is most widely used mode [1, 2, 20].

3.1   Preliminaries and Model

Let $G : \{1,0\}^{\lambda} X \{1,0\}^{l} \rightarrow \{0,1\}^{l}$ be a pseudorandom function (PRF) family. Let $\{P_K : \{0,1\}^n \rightarrow \{0,1\}^n | K \in \{0,1\}^{\lambda}\}$ be a pseudorandom permutations family with the property that it is easy to compute $P_K(x)$ and satisfies indistinguishability. Let $H : M X K \rightarrow C$, be a collision resistant hash function for all PPT adversaries A, there exists a negligible function negl(.) such that $Pr\left[k \leftarrow K; (x, x') \leftarrow A(H, k) : (x \neq x') \wedge \left(H(k, x) = H(k, x')\right)\right] \leq negl(\lambda)$. H_2 is also a keyed has function. The keys generated by the hash functions are assumed to be linear in size of N, which is number of keyword-document pairs in the outsourced data.

Let $D = \{d_1, d_2, \ldots, d_n\}$ be document collection the client outsources by encrypting it using a symmetric key encryption scheme like AES, along with an encrypted index using a dictionary/map data structure ($WMap, DMap$) which support $O(1)$ update operations. As a preprocessing step, client extracts unique keywords from documents with stemming and stop word removal, $W = \{w_1, w_2, \ldots, w_m\}$. Our proposed scheme supports conjunctive keyword queries, that is, $F_{w_1 \wedge w_2 \wedge \ldots \wedge w_q} = \{d_j : d_j \in D \wedge (w_1 \in d_j \wedge w_2 \in d_j \wedge \ldots \wedge w_q \in d_j)\}$. And these documents are retrieved based on their relevance to the queried keywords using a standard relevance score formula given in [Sect. 4 of [24]]:

$$Score(d_j, Q) = \sum\nolimits_{w_t \in Q} \frac{1}{|d_j|} \cdot (1 + \ln f_{d_j,t}) \cdot \ln\left(1 + \frac{n}{f_{w_t}}\right) \tag{1}$$

Existing schemes like [4, 6–8, 10] require the client to compute the Eq. 1 and encrypt it using some homomorphic encryption scheme like Paillier Cryptosystem and post it in outsourced index. In our proposed scheme we compute this relevance score partially at client and server as some of the values of Eq. 1 are already known to the server during index building. The term frequency of a keyword w_t in a document d_j denoted as $f_{d_j,t}$ is however known only to the client and to improve the security against possible statistical analysis attacks based on this value, we randomize this value using a random integer R_1. Whereas the server already knows n, # of documents outsourced and f_{w_t}, number of documents containing the keyword w_t. But this information is known to server only for those keywords which were/are searched by client. Therefore our proposed scheme incurs less computational overhead at client and it does not involve decryption of relevance scores at client side after the search process returns documents ranked based on encrypted relevance scores.

3.2 Definitions

A **C**onjunctive **K**eywords **F**orward **S**ecure **R**anked **D**ynamic **SSE** scheme (**CFR-DSSE**) consist of following probabilistic polynomial time algorithms defined as below.

1. $K \leftarrow KeyGen(1^\lambda)$: this algorithm takes as input a security parameter λ and outputs following secret keys: K_1, K_2, K_3, used during probabilistic symmetric encryption of document collection, P, and G respectively.
2. $c_j \leftarrow Enc_{K_1}(d_j)$: it takes as input a secret key K_1, and a file d_j from document collection and returns encrypted file to be outsourced as c_j.
3. $d_j \leftarrow Dec_{K_1}(c_j)$: it takes as input a secret key K_1 and an encrypted file c_j and does a deterministic decryption of it to obtain plaintext file d_j.
4. $T_w, WMap, DMap \leftarrow BuildIndex(W, D, I)$: this algorithm is first run at client side followed by server side. It takes as input D, W, and an indexing of keywords in W. It returns client side state as a table T_w consisting of following format: $\langle P_{k_2}(i), x_i, f_{w_i}\rangle$. x_i is a keyword specific random integer. The server side indexes are returned as label-value maps: $WMap$ and $DMap$.

5. $\left\{ F_{w_1 \wedge w_2 \wedge ... \wedge w_q} \right\} \leftarrow Search(T_w, nK, K, F, WMap, DMap)$: takes as input client side state table T_w, set of new keys, existing keyword-specific keys, file count for each queried keyword and server side data structures. It returns to client a set of ranked file identifiers $F_{w_1 \wedge w_2 \wedge ... \wedge w_q}$. It also removes the retrieved entries during search and re-inserts them using new keyword-specific keys supplied by client.

6. $T_w', WMap', DMap' \leftarrow Update(d_k, op)$: this algorithm performs update operation on a specified document d_k, with respect to type of operation given as op: insert/delete

Security Definitions: in a Dynamic SSE setup, the subsequent search and update operations (in any order), cause leakage to server. In [11], authors have shown that attacker can inject new files to adaptively carryout a devastating attack revealing contents of a query by inserting as few as 10 files. These attacks are termed as File Injection Attacks. The schemes which use either inverted index or hierarchical index maintaining explicitly keyword-document relation are subject to these attacks. Hence we employ an innovative solution proposed in [20], and extend it to support efficient ranked retrieval of documents with improved security guarantees. A DSSE scheme leaks information to server in two ways, (a) adding a file f to database reveal that f contains keywords that were searched before and (b) searching for a keyword w might reveal which files from past contained w, [21]. Schemes that avoid leakage of type a are called Forward Private and which avoid type b are called as Backward Private. We use the definition of forward and backward privacy as given in [21] and ensure that our proposed scheme satisfies these definitions.

3.3   CFR – DSSE Scheme: Detailed Working and Algorithms

Key Generation: In our proposed scheme, we require three secret keys: $K_1, K_2, and K_3$. The first key is used to carry out the probabilistic symmetric encryption using AES algorithm for the document collection. The second key is used to randomize the keyword index from the set I, and the third key is used during generation of a keyword and document specific key, i.e., k_w or k_j with help of a PRF G by supplying inputs as keyword and document identifier along with some randomness.

Index Setup: In our proposed scheme, the index structure is based on tuples of the form (label, value) where *label* is an index in a map and its corresponding entry contains the *value*. This structure of outsourced index is of size $N = m * n$, where $m = |W|$ and $n = |D|$. Our proposed index structure is based on work proposed by [20] with significant improvements towards security guarantees. The data structures used are fully defined in the algorithm 1 given below. Client maintains a table T_w of the form $P_{k_2}(i), x_i, f_{w_i}$, where $P_{k_2}(i)$ is the randomized index of keyword w_i in set I, x_i corresponds to a random number initially zero and changes with every search to randomize the search process, and f_{w_i}. is initially zero and reflects number of files containing keyword w_i after every update operation. The work in [20], uses monotonically increasing search counter for every keyword, which can be easily subject to guessing attack. Hence we employ a random number during every search operation to improve indistinguishability of search token. The client computes the term frequency of each keyword as it is processed for each of the files d_j using formula: $tf_{ij} = \frac{1}{|d_j|} \cdot (1 + \ln f_{d_j,i})$, as given in Eq. 1. This component helps the server in computing relevance of queried keyword to a document. In order to protect the fields like size of document and keyword frequency in a document from server, we randomize this value before outsourcing it to the server as part of the index entries. The client now prepares the entries of two maps: *WMap* and *DMap*, in such a way that when outsourced to the server, the server will not be able to infer based on an entry of either of the maps, whether an entry corresponds to a specific document. Therefore privacy of distribution of keywords to the documents in index is fully preserved, as an immediate improvement over existing Inverted Index based schemes such as [8–10].

Algorithm 1: *BuildIndex*

Input: $W, D, I, K_2, K_3, PRF\ F\ and\ G$: {W – set of unique keywords, D – set of documents, I – an index for keywords in W}

Client Steps:

1. Let $I = \{(i, w_i) \mid w_i \in W\}$, be an index of all unique keywords in set W.
2. Initialize a table $T_w = <P_{k_2}(i), x_i, f_{w_i}>$, initially $x_i=0\ \forall\ w_i \in W$, of size $|W|$. f_{w_i} is initially zero and is count of number of files containing w_i.
3. Extract the term frequency of each $w_i \in d_j, \forall 1 \leq i \leq m\ and\ \forall 1 \leq j \leq n$ as follows: $tf_{ij} = \frac{1}{|d_j|} \cdot (1 + \ln f_{d_j,i})$
4. *for all* $d_j \in D$:
    a. *generate a key for* d_j: $K_j = G(K_3, id(d_j)||R_2)$, where R_2 is a random number.
    b. *for all* $w_i \in d_j$: //1 $\leq i \leq |d_j|$
        i. $dlabel_i = H_2(K_j, i)$
        ii. *if* $T_w[P_{k_2}(i)].x_i = 0\ then\ x_i = randInd()$
        iii. $T_w[P_{k_2}(i)].f_{w_i} = T_w[P_{k_2}(i)].f_{w_i} + 1$
        iv. $K_{w_i} = G(K_3, w_i||x_i)$
        v. $label_i = H(K_{w_i}, T_w[P_{k_2}(i)].f_{w_i}||0)$
        vi. $dval_i = \langle label_i \rangle$
        vii. $val_i =$
            $(\langle id_j, tf_{ij} * R_1 \rangle \oplus H(K_{w_i}, T_w[P_{k_2}(i)].f_{w_i}||1), dlabel_i)$
        viii. $AllPairsD = \{dlable_i, dval_i\} \cup AllPairsD$
        ix. $AllPairsW = \{(label_i, val_i)\} \cup AllPairsW$
    c. Encrypt d_j using probabilistic encryption algorithm: $c_j \leftarrow Enc_{K_1}(d_j)$
5. $C = \{c_1, c_2, ..., c_n\}$, $AllPairsW$, and $AllPairsD$ is sent to Server ($|AllPairsW| = |AllPairsD| = N = m * n$.)

Server Steps:

6. Creates two empty Maps $WMap$ and $DMap$ to store values from sets $AllPairsW$ and $AllPairsD$ respectively.

Search: The algorithm for search operation is presented below. For a client to search a group of q keywords $Q = \{w_1, w_2, \ldots, w_q\}$, the client generates following input: the existing keyword specific keys each of w_q, the new keyword specific keys for each of w_q, file count of each of queried keywords, i.e. $T_w[w_q].f_{w_q}$. These inputs are described in the algorithm at step 1. The server on receiving conjunctive keywords query in the form of token $\langle K, nK, F \rangle$, parses it to retrieve existing keyword-specific keys and also new keys to be used to re-insert already retrieved entries from *WMap* and *DMap* in order to ensure the Forward and Backward Privacy. The forward privacy is ensured by generating keyword-specific keys during every search and update operation, so that the adversary (server) will not be able to re-run an old query onto a newly inserted document to carry out the File Injection Attacks. Unlike the schemes in [20–22], which maintain the entries of deleted keywords also in the index leading to increased occupancy in the hash table, we ensure that *WMap* stores only entries of currently available keywords in documents. This mechanism ensures that the server will not be able to retrieve files by running previously executed queries. This setup of keyword-document pairs in hash table ensures the freshness of entries and every search/update operation disables reuse of past query tokens.

The server retrieves the entries from hash table pertaining to keywords being searched, and reads from them following information: file identifier, randomized term frequency value, and corresponding label in *DMap* which will be used during re-hashing. The contents of each entry in *WMap* is: $(\langle id_j, tf_{ij} * R_1 \rangle \oplus H(K_{w_i}, T_w[P_{k_2}(i)].f_{w_i}||1), dlabel_i)$ as mentioned above. The server runs the search algorithm for every queried keyword as described in step 4 of algorithm 2. The rank of a document with respect to searched/queried keyword is computed using randomized term frequency value contained in above format of entry as tf_{ij}, n, and f_{w_i} using the Eq. (1). The sum of scores of each document for all queried keywords are calculated and finally those documents which contain all queried keywords are sorted in ascending order based on their ranking score and these documents are then sent in response to user query.

CFR DSSE is non-interactive as the client sends newly generated keyword-specific keys to the server to carry out subsequent removal and re-hashing of entries into *WMap* to ensure forward and backward security guarantees. The details of re-hashing are described in the Search Algorithm at step 4 (instructions at v-viii). The advantage of using a second map is that update operations can be carried out as efficiently as in the inverted-cum-forward (hybrid) index based approaches and yet preserving privacy of keyword-document pairings from server. However our scheme has an overhead of maintaining two separate label-value maps to ensure effect of a hybrid index.

Algorithm 2: *Search*

Client Input: Old and New Keyword-specific keys $K = \{K_{w_1}, K_{w_2}, \dots, K_{w_q}\}$, $nK = \{K_{w_1}, K_{w_2}, \dots, K_{w_q}\}$, word-file counts $F = \{f_{w_1}, f_{w_2}, \dots, f_{w_q}\}$ from the T_w table.

Server Input: $WMap, DMap$, and n

Client Steps:

1. Generates a conjunctive keyword query of q distinct keywords: $Q = \{w_1, w_2, \dots, w_q\}$, and their corresponding new keys for re-hashing as follows:

    a.   *for all* $w_q \in Q$

        i.   Generate random integer for w_q as x_q and update $T_w[w_i]$ index.

        ii. $K_{w_q} = G(K_3, w_q||x_q)$

        iii. $nK = nK \cup \{K_{w_q}\}$

        iv. $F = F \cup \{T_w[P_{K_2}(q)].f_{w_q}\}$

    b.   Send $\langle K, nK, F\rangle$ as a conjunctive keywords query to server.

Server Step:

2. Parse the token $\langle K, nK, F\rangle$ as $F = \{f_{w_1}, f_{w_2}, \dots, f_{w_q}\}$ and $K = \{K_{w_1}, K_{w_2}, \dots, K_{w_q}\}$ and $nK = \{K_{w_1}, K_{w_2}, \dots, K_{w_q}\}$,

3. Initialize a $ResultSet = \emptyset$ and $Res_i = \emptyset \ \forall 1 \le i \le q$.

4. *for* $i = 1$ to $|F|$

    a.   *for* $j = 1$ to f_{w_i}

        i. $label_j = H(K_{w_i}, j||0)$ //existing keyword-specific keys used.

        ii. $val_j = WMap[lable_j] \oplus H(K_{w_i}, j||1)$

        iii. *parse* val_j *as* $(\langle id_j, tf_{ij}\rangle, dlabel_j)$

        iv. *add* id_j *to set* Res_i

        v. *delete* $WMap[label_j]$ *and re − insert*

        vi. $nlabel_j = H(K_{w_i}, j||0)$ //new keyword-specific keys used

        vii. $nval_j = (\langle id_j, tf_{ij}\rangle \oplus H(K_{w_i}, f_{w_i}||1), dlabel_i)$

        viii. Add $(nlabel_j, nval_j)$ pair to $WMap$ and update $DMap[dlabel_i] = nlabel_j$

        ix. *compute Rank of* id_j: $score_{ij} = tf_{ij} * n/f_{w_i}$ and store in local arrays

5. Compute $ResultSet = \cap_{i=1}^{|F|} Res_i$, and compute sum of $score_{ij}$ for each of resultant file identifier in $ResultSet$

6. Sort $ResultSet$ based on scores of each document & send encrypted files to client.

The second map in our proposed scheme, the *DMap*, is used only during update operations to efficiently carry out the insert and delete operations without affecting other entries pertaining to any of the other documents. In case of insert operation, both *WMap* and *DMap* have new entries added to them, whereas a delete operation helps the server in locating entries belonging to document to be deleted in *WMap*. This task of locating entries belonging to document to be deleted is otherwise easier in a dual index employing a two-dimensional data structure. Hence the *DMap* does exactly the same here in just $O(|d_j|)$ amount of time, where $|d_j|$ is the size of jth file in document collection. The insert and delete operations are discussed next.

Algorithm 3: *Update*

Client Input: $c_k \leftarrow Enc_{K_1}(d_k)$, $\langle nlabel_i, nval_i \rangle$ pairs for $\forall 1 \le i \le |d_k|$, and T_w, Op: insert/delete.

Server Input: $WMap, DMap$

Client Steps:

(*if op == insert*)

    1. Extract distinct keywords from d_k as $W_k = \{w_1, w_2, ..., w_t\}$, $|d_k| = t$.

    2. Obtain encryption of file d_k to be outsourced as: $c_k \leftarrow Enc_{K_1}(d_k)$

    3. *for i = 1 to t*:

        a. Create $\langle nlabel_i, nval_i \rangle$ pairs as in *BuildIndex* algorithm.

        b. Update the T_w table with respect to newly added file: $\langle P_{k_2}(k), x_i, f_{ik} * R, \rangle$ for each of w_i.

        c. Send $\langle AllPairsW, AllPairsD, c_k, op \rangle$ to Server.

(*if op == delete*)

    4. Generate document specific key: $K_k = G(K_3, id_k || R_2)$

    5. Sends the delete token to Server: $\langle K_k, |d_k|, op \rangle$

Server Step:

    6. *if (op == insert)*

        a. Server adds the received pairs of label-value to appropriate maps.

        b. Add $\langle AllPairsW \rangle$ to $WMap$.

        c. Add $\langle AllPairsD \rangle$ to $DMap$.

    7. *if (op == delete)*

        a. *for i = 1 to $|d_k|$*:

            i. $dlabel_i = H_2(K_k, i)$

            ii. *delete* $WMap[DMap[dlabel_i]]$

            iii. *delete* $DMap[dlabel_i]$

        b. Update the encrypted document collection as: $C' = C - \{c_k\}$

Update Operation: The update operation is carried out for either inserting a new document into the outsourced collection or deleting an existing document from it. The inverted index based schemes leak significant information about overall statistics of document-keywords pairing to the server, to carryout statistical analysis attacks. In our proposed scheme, we have designed the outsourced index to be such that it does not leak any such information as it uses a label-value map rather than a two-dimensional structure like arrays.

In order to insert a new document d_k consisting of t distinct keywords, the client first generates keyword-specific keys for each of keywords in d_k and accordingly updates the field in its state table T_w. The fields in T_w to be updated are of two types: keywords already existing in older documents and keywords newly being added to document collection. In case of former keywords, client just increases the f_{w_i}, $\forall i, 1 \le i \le t$, the count of number of files containing keyword w_i. Whereas for latter keywords, it creates new entries in T_w, i.e., $\langle P_{k_2}(k), x_i, f_{w_i} \rangle$ $\forall w_i$, $such that w_i \notin W$. The client then prepares the pairs of label-value for both $WMap$ and $DMap$ and sends it to server.

In case of deleting a file from document collection outsourced to server, the client does a very simple step unlike the case of insert operation. It just creates the document specific key as follows: $K_k = G(K_3, id_k||R_2)$, and sends it to server along with total number of distinct keywords in file d_k to be deleted. On receiving such a key and count, the server generates label values pertaining to keyword entries to be deleted from both *DMap* and *WMap*. This deletion with help of *DMap* map entries is depicted in Update algorithm at step 7a. Therefore the insert and delete operations are carried out in time proportionate to number of distinct keywords in files to be added or removed respectively, i.e. $O(|d_k|)$. Though a dual index utilizing a two-dimensional structure requires similar time complexity but it has two severe drawbacks: fixed structure of table and addition of new keywords impact unrelated documents.

4 Security and Performance Analysis

In this section we first analyze the security of our proposed CFR DSSE scheme followed by experimental setup and performance analysis with respect to building index, trapdoor generation, search operation, update operation and relevance based retrieval of documents.

4.1 Security Analysis

In our proposed CFR DSSE scheme, the security guarantees are achieved in presence of an adversary who adaptively chooses keywords from previous queries but the design of index and search operations ensure that we achieve *Keyword-Trapdoor Indistinguishability* defined in [10]. We achieve this indistinguishability between keyword and trapdoor or encrypted query as the queries are generated each time using a unique random integer as a seed and also re-hashing of retrieved entries take place after every search operation. Consider a search for keyword w_1, at time t_1, the client generates the trapdoor as follows (step 1a and 1b of search algorithm): $newKey = K_{w_1} = G(K_3, w_1||x_{t_1})$, the client sends as trapdoor to server: $\langle oldKey, newKey, f_{w_1} \rangle$. The server retrieves value available at label computed using *oldKey* and removes this entry from hash table, and then re-inserts it using a new label being generated by *newKey*. Now at time t_2, after having searched polynomial number of queries, the adversary again adaptively searches for the same keyword w_1. The *newKey* being generated this time is entirely different from key at time t_1 as it uses a fresh random seed (integer). The probability that K_{w_1} being generated at time t_2 is same as the key generated at time t_1 is bounded by a negligible function in security parameter. Hence we achieve the *Keyword-Trapdoor Indistinguishability*. It is also observed that the two successive queries for keyword w_1 reveal to the server $\langle oldKey, newKey, f_{w_1} \rangle$ at times t_1 and t_2. In case of existing schemes such as [20–22], the server has the higher probability of predicting the keyword as the key generation involves a search counter as randomness. So two successive queries differ in their input to the hash function generating key in terms of only monotonically increasing search counter. If the search counter at time t_1 was w_1^{cnt} then at time t_2 it is certainly $w_1^{cnt} + 1$. Hence the server's possibility of predicting random seed used in our scheme is bounded by a negligible function which is the probability of predicting an integer from a set of integers given the size of largest integer is significantly large.

The CFR DSSE scheme achieves forward privacy as the queries being sent to server can no longer be reused in subsequent searches after a careful insertion of a chosen file by adversary into document collection. As demonstrated above, the queries being generated at two different times for a single keyword successively result in randomized queries, the File Injection Attacks will be unsuccessful in our scheme. We provide only a theoretical sketch of achieving forward privacy as it is inherent from our index structure that we always ensure trapdoor unlinkability. As far as backward privacy is concerned, we achieve it using a simple approach as follows: since every update (delete) operation on document collection causes encrypted file and its corresponding entries from *WMap* and *DMap* to be permanently removed, any future search request on keywords contained in deleted files, does not return this removed file identifier in result set.

With respect to update (delete) operation, the existing ranked schemes such as [4, 6, 9] require explicit changes in index tree structure as well as require changes in calculation of relevance scores stored at nodes which lie on paths from nodes to be deleted to the root node. This has significant impact on security of outsourced index as it reveals statistical information at not just nodes to be deleted but also other nodes on such paths. Whereas in our proposed scheme, we compute the relevance score partly at client during index setup time and partly at server during search without revealing the confidential information about number of files containing a queried keyword. This results in a lightweight and secure relevance score calculation process which is independent of other entries in the index. This is a major improvement on security and efficiency in our proposed scheme.

4.2 Performance Analysis

In this section we present our experimentation results and analysis of proposed CFR DSSE scheme through its implementation in Python on a Windows 10 machine using a client server architecture. We use the RFC dataset [25] to conduct experimental study of our proposed scheme. This dataset has around 8,785 files consisting of approximately 5,14,245 unique keywords. During experiments we incurred sub-linear search and update time as we use maps to store the index which hides keyword-document distribution. It outperforms the schemes like [4, 6, 10] as it employs an efficient relevance based indexing mechanism to carryout search. The advantage of our proposed scheme is that it performs search and update operations with minimum computations at server side, leading to improved operation efficiency, which is pivotal for practicality of scheme. A novel feature of our scheme is that it is non-interactive, requires just one roundtrip of communication for both search and update operations. A detailed comparison of our proposed scheme with existing works is given in Table 1. The complexity of our proposed search and update operations is $O(a_w)$, where a_w is the number of keyword-document pairs for keyword w. However search for each queried keyword in case of multi-keyword queries, require a_w entries to be retrieved from dictionary for each w.

We performed experimental analysis of the scheme with respect to following parameters. Figure 1 shows the amount of time taken to build the index at client and server side, which is much lower when compared to time it takes for [4, 9, 10]. These schemes considered keyword collection of 12000 to 120,000 keywords, whereas we have taken nearly 5 lakh keywords in all our experiments (includes technical keywords from RFC). This reduction in amount of time in building database is due to the reason that we use a data structure which is independent of other entries in index, unlike the data structures used in [4, 8–10], where either a two dimensional matrix inverted index or hierarchical index like trees, require updates to substantial parts of index in case of search and update operations. This not only results in increase in search time but also leaks significant amount of information about document-keyword relationship to the server.

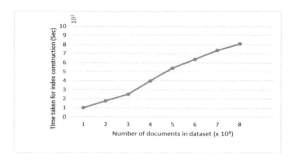

Fig. 1. Time taken for Index building with varying size of dataset.

Figure 2 shows the time taken for search operation in response to a multi-keyword conjunctive query of same size (in terms of number of keywords in it). Here we do not consider the time taken for re-hashing post search query, as it can be carried out in parallel to the operation which sends search results to client. We also note that the amount of time taken to retrieve top-k documents matching the queries keywords, does not incur additional overhead as value of k increases unlike in the [8]. In [8, 9], as the value of k increases, the server has to carry out order preserving mapping based comparison of relevance scores to sort matching documents in ascending order. In our case, we simply use a uniformly randomized term frequency in calculation of Eq. 1, and hence the ranking can be done effortlessly. Figure 3 shows the search time for queries of varying size with fixed dataset consisting of 2000 documents, it shows that search time is independent of number of keywords in query. Figure 2 and 3 show that search time is dominated by number of documents in dataset while the number of keywords in query has very little impact on it. Therefore we achieve a sub-linear search time and a scheme which scales gracefully with increasing dataset size. The update operations such as insertion or deletion of document is done in a non-interactive manner with single roundtrip of communication. It is observed during experiments that update operation requires sub-linear time complexity in terms of size of document to be added or removed.

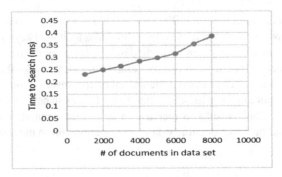

Fig. 2. Time to search for same keywords with varying size of dataset.

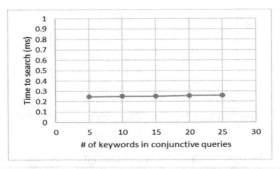

Fig. 3. Time to search for varying # of keywords with a fixed dataset of size n = 2000

5   Conclusion and Future Work

In this paper, we have proposed a forward and backward secure conjunctive keyword ranked searchable symmetric encryption scheme for encrypted data outsourced in cloud. We achieve forward privacy and backward privacy by building the index in such a way that randomized (key used to generate trapdoor is changed every time) queries fetch the matching documents without revealing either the keyword contained in the query or the keyword-document relationship in future update operations. The backward privacy is achieved by ensuring that a delete operation completely removes entries pertaining to deleted document from outsourced index, hence the future search queries do not return deleted file. Our proposed scheme returns the matching documents sorted in ascending order with respect to their relevance to the searched keywords. This enhances the practicality of our scheme as it returns documents which are relevant based on the TF-IDF model from literature. This relevance score of each document to queried keyword calculated partially at client and server in a way such that resulting relevance score is randomized uniformly so that adversary at cannot learn any statistical information about outsourced data. The novel feature of our scheme is that future update operations do not affect the entire index as it is the case in existing hierarchical index based schemes. This results in improved update efficiency and better security of outsourced index. Our scheme achieves search operation with sub-linear search time using a hash based index.

Future work will be to extend this work in the setting of multi-user scenario with fine-gained access control. And also, to extend it to support more expressive search such as semantic based searches to make this scheme more usable.

Acknowledgement. This work was supported by Ministry of Electronics and Information Technology, Government of India, under the Visvesvaraya PhD Scheme (Electronics and IT), with unique awardee number MEITY-PDH-1597. (Visvesvaraya PhD scheme: File Number PhD-MLA-4(63)/2015-16.

References

1. Kamara, S., Papamanthou, C.: Parallel and dynamic searchable symmetric encryption. In: Sadeghi, A.-R. (ed.) FC 2013. LNCS, vol. 7859, pp. 258–274. Springer, Heidelberg (2013). https://doi.org/10.1007/978-3-642-39884-1_22
2. Song, D.X., Wagner, D., Perrig, A.: Practical techniques for searches on encrypted data. In: Proceeding 2000 IEEE Symposium on Security and Privacy. S&P 2000. IEEE (2000)
3. Curtmola, R., et al.: Searchable symmetric encryption: improved definitions and efficient constructions. J. Comput. Secur. **19**(5), 895–934 (2011)
4. Ding, X., Liu, P., Jin, H.: Privacy-preserving multi-keyword top-k similarity search over encrypted data. IEEE Trans. Dependable Secure Comput. **16**(2), 344–357 (2017)
5. Sun, W., et al.: Privacy-preserving multi-keyword text search in the cloud supporting similarity-based ranking. Proceedings of the 8th ACM SIGSAC Symposium on Information, Computer and Communications Security (2013)
6. Cao, N., et al.: Privacy-preserving multi-keyword ranked search over encrypted cloud data. IEEE Trans. Parallel Distrib. Syst. **25**(1), 222–233 (2013)
7. Xia, Z., et al.: A secure and dynamic multi-keyword ranked search scheme over encrypted cloud data. IEEE Trans. Parallel Distrib. Syst. **27**(2), 340–352 (2015)
8. Wang, C., et al.: Secure ranked keyword search over encrypted cloud data. In: 2010 IEEE 30th International Conference on Distributed Computing Systems. IEEE (2010)
9. Wang, C., et al.: Enabling secure and efficient ranked keyword search over outsourced cloud data. IEEE Trans. Parallel Distrib. Syst. **23**(8), 1467–1479 (2011)
10. Tahir, S., et al.: A new secure and lightweight searchable encryption scheme over encrypted cloud data. IEEE Trans. Emerg. Top. Comput. (2017)
11. Zhang, Y., Katz, J., Papamanthou, C.: All your queries are belong to us: The power of file-injection attacks on searchable encryption. In: 25th {USENIX} Security Symposium ({USENIX} Security 2016) (2016)
12. Goh, E.-J.: Secure indexes. IACR Cryptol. ePrint Arch. **2003**, 216 (2003)
13. Chang, Y.-C., Mitzenmacher, M.: Privacy preserving keyword searches on remote encrypted data. In: Ioannidis, J., Keromytis, A., Yung, M. (eds.) ACNS 2005. LNCS, vol. 3531, pp. 442–455. Springer, Heidelberg (2005). https://doi.org/10.1007/11496137_30
14. van Liesdonk, P., Sedghi, S., Doumen, J., Hartel, P., Jonker, W.: Computationally efficient searchable symmetric encryption. In: Jonker, W., Petković, M. (eds.) SDM 2010. LNCS, vol. 6358, pp. 87–100. Springer, Heidelberg (2010). https://doi.org/10.1007/978-3-642-155 46-8_7
15. Kamara, S., et al.: Dynamic searchable symmetric encryption. In: Proceedings of the 2012 ACM Conference on Computer and Communications Security. 2012
16. Wang, C., et al.: Achieving usable and privacy-assured similarity search over outsourced cloud data. 2012 Proceedings IEEE INFOCOM. IEEE (2012)

17. Wang, B., et al.: Privacy-preserving multi-keyword fuzzy search over encrypted data in the cloud. IEEE INFOCOM 2014-IEEE Conference on Computer Communications. IEEE (2014)

18. Kuzu, M., et al.: Efficient similarity search over encrypted data. In: 2012 IEEE 28th International Conference on Data Engineering. IEEE (2012)

19. Ahmed, MD.A., Ramachandram, S., Khan, K.U.R.: Privacy preserving dynamically indexed multi-phrase search over encrypted data. In: 2018 International Conference on Advances in Computing, Communications and Informatics (ICACCI). IEEE (2018)

20. Etemad, M., et al.: Efficient dynamic searchable encryption with forward privacy. Proc. Privacy Enhancing Technol. **1**, 5–20 (2018)

21. Ghareh Chamani, J., et al.: New constructions for forward and backward private symmetric searchable encryption. In: Proceedings of the 2018 ACM SIGSAC Conference on Computer and Communications Security (2018)

22. Kim, K.S., et al.: Forward secure dynamic searchable symmetric encryption with efficient updates. In: Proceedings of the 2017 ACM SIGSAC Conference on Computer and Communications Security (2017)

23. Yavuz, A.A., Guajardo, J.: Dynamic searchable symmetric encryption with minimal leakage and efficient updates on commodity hardware. In: Dunkelman, O., Keliher, L. (eds.) SAC 2015. LNCS, vol. 9566, pp. 241–259. Springer, Cham (2016). https://doi.org/10.1007/978-3-319-31301-6_15

24. Witten, I.H., et al.: Managing Gigabytes: Compressing and Indexing Documents and Images. Morgan Kaufmann, Burlington (1999)

25. Request for comments. http://www.rfc-editor.org/index.html

Performance Study of Multi-target Tracking Using Kalman Filter and Hungarian Algorithm

N. P. Arun Kumar$^{(\boxtimes)}$, Renganathan Laxmanan, S. Ram Kumar, Vobbilisetty Srinidh, and R. Ramanathan

Department of Electronics and Communication Engineering, Amrita School of Engineering, Amrita Vishwa Vidyapeetham, Coimbatore 641112, India
arunkumar.n.p31@gmail.com, r_ramanathan@cb.amrita.edu

Abstract. We present the method for multi-target tracking using the combination of Kalman filter and Hungarian algorithm and test the efficiency of this method with two different data sets. In Data set – I, no target leave or enter the frame and in Data set – II, targets leave and enter the frame at regular intervals. This tracking method deals with the data association problem that arises with multiple targets in a single frame and also the dimensionality problem that arises due to repeated changes in the size of state-space associated with multiple targets. We use 2 important methods to achieve this. The first is the Kalman filter which is an extension of Bayesian filter. It uses a probabilistic approach to deal with the estimation of data. The second one is the Hungarian algorithm, used to overcome the data association problem and data association comes into the picture only when there are multiple targets.

Keywords: Multi-target · Kalman filter · Data association · State-space · Hungarian

1 Introduction

The multiple objects detection and tracking is a problem in many areas. Examples include video surveillance, anomaly detection, navigation of robots and aircrafts, virtual reality and most importantly, autonomous vehicle navigation. Bayesian recursive filter is the cornerstone for target tracking as it forms the core principle for many other filters used for tracking. It uses a probabilistic approach and it helps in the modeling of erroneous models like sensor error, ambient noise, etc. It is driven by the Bayes theorem which includes Prior probability, Posterior probability and Likelihood probability. Here, the posterior probability is being updated with the help of prior and likelihood probabilities. In a recursive point of view, the posterior probability after each iteration is considered as the prior probability for the following iteration and the posterior probability keeps on updating for every iteration that passes. This is the core principle in the Bayesian recursive filter. In the case of tracking multiple objects in a real world context, the Bayesian recursive estimation cannot be used as it is hindered by two major obstacles. Since, most of the measurement processes in real-world situations are non-Gaussian and

© Springer Nature Singapore Pte Ltd. 2021
S. M. Thampi et al. (Eds.): SSCC 2020, CCIS 1364, pp. 213–227, 2021.
https://doi.org/10.1007/978-981-16-0422-5_15

nonlinear no closed-form analytic equations are feasible. Closed-form equations for the likelihood models are applicable only when the models are Gaussian and linear.

Data association happens to be the second problem which is due to the unlabeled data from sensors. Assigning all these data to the targets when occlusion of targets takes place and in the presence of clutter is a difficult task. There are many strategies for tracking multiple objects; we are only using a combination of two methods to obtain an algorithm to track these objects. All these models have been developed from single object tracking which is linear and Gaussian. So, in the case of non-Gaussian and nonlinear models, approximations derived from single object tracking can be used. To overcome the problems faced by Bayesian recursive filters, we use the Kalman filter. Since Kalman is modeled using a limited set of unknown variables it is easy for the filter to account for the dynamic dimensions involved in tracking. The Multiple object tracking method involves two steps-target detection, target tracking – which has to be done separately. Target detection involves image processing techniques to filter the image using different image filters and Kalman filter for target tracking.

2   Existing Techniques

There are a plethora of techniques being used to detect and track images in a frame. Now that surveillance has become a key objective, there has been a steady increase in the methods used for tracking the objects. The objects being a person, vehicles etc. [1–3].

2.1   Statistical Method

In most of the tracking cases, uncertainties like measurement noise and random object motion are present and are unavoidable. This method estimates the position of the object after taking all these uncertainties into account. This method is considered to be robust but very complex than the deterministic model. This method completely depends upon the object movement probabilities. This is the most commonly used method for tracking purposes. Bayesian recursive filter, Kalman filter, and Extended Kalman filter are some of the filters that use a statistical approach to track the targets [4].

2.2   Template Method

This method is relatively simple because this method makes use of the color, texture and image intensity of an object while tracking. An object template from the frame at an instant t − 1 is matched with another frame at an instant t and thereby the position of the object is calculated. In this method, the single object and multi-object tracking are treated differently.

2.3   Multi-view Based Method

In the previous methods, a given object's particular unique outlook only is considered and the computations are done based on it. If the object changes its shape or motion rapidly from one frame to another, a single view of the object alone won't be enough to match the object between frames. One way to overcome this is a subspace-based approach, where eigenspace is used to model the transformation obtained from object's image and image reconstruction with the help of eigenvectors [5].

2.4 Clustering Method

This method, when compared to others, is a bit different. This method focuses on finding a common relationship between the targets and using that it helps in keep track of the target across frames. The targets with similar attributes are grouped together to form a cluster. There are different cluster methods – Graph cluster, Centroid cluster, Fuzzy cluster, Hierarchical cluster. The cluster methods produce accurate results in real-life situations when compared to Multi-view based method [6].

All the tracking techniques mentioned above can be associated either with online or offline methods based on how they utilize the data obtained from detecting the objects. Usually, Offline strategies make use of all possible object detections from the entire image series and perform tracking while associating separate tracks to these detections as a global optimization problem. This makes these methods not suitable for real-time applications, where you don't have access to the entire image sequence beforehand. The method explained in this paper, is an online method, which makes use of the object detections only till the current frame and it helps in predicting the future positions of the objects in the upcoming frame with minimum error. This attribute of the method makes it the more suitable for real-life tracking than the other offline methods mentioned above. Since, the object detection data is limited, the main challenge in this method is incorporating the changes in number of objects at a particular time instant. Since different objects leave and enter the frame at different intervals, it becomes more complex to alter the matrix dimensions of the kalman filter and assign new tracks to the new objects and scrape the tracks of the objects that has left the frame.

3 Algorithm Overview

Figures 1, 2, 3, 4, 5, 6, in the chronological order – 1, 2, 3, 4, 5, 6, – represents the code-flowchart model of target tracking. To start with, we take a video that has the data sets and we start by sampling out the frames from the video to make the processing easier. First background elimination is done on every frame to remove the static part in the frames and let only the moving objects in the frame. This method helps in segregating the target from the background.

Next is smoothening the frames to minimize the noise using the Gaussian filter. It reduces the noise by smoothening out the lines, interferences, black spots, etc. This helps in providing a uniform background and this makes the detection process easier. Next, the Laplacian Gaussian filter is used to determine the boundaries of the targets clearly. Now we have blob-like objects on a uniform background. Now, the whole frame can be visualized as a uniform value matrix with some peak values in some indices. The peak values represent the targets. With the help of pre-defined Matlab functions, the coordinates of the peak values (local maxima) can be found. Hence the targets can be detected.

Now the detected coordinate values and the velocity values are fed to the Kalman filter Measurement prediction matrix. The Kalman filter is modeled in such a way that the inputs of the filter are the position coordinates (X_P, Y_P) and velocity coordinates (X_V, Y_V) of the target. With the help of prior measurements, the Kalman filter predicts the next probable position of the target. It also takes into account, the acceleration noise of the targets and measurement noise (sensor error).

Next, each target is assigned tracks and is followed throughout the frame and when the target leaves the frame its tracks are destroyed. Also, the Hungarian algorithm helps in matching the data to the respective targets in the frame.

Note: We have only included minimal code inside the boxes in Figs. 1, 2, 3, 4, 5, 6.

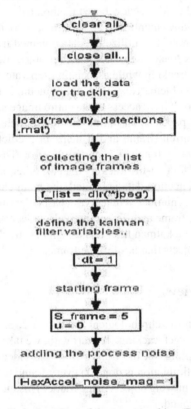

Fig. 1. Code-flowchart of the target tracking (Part – I)

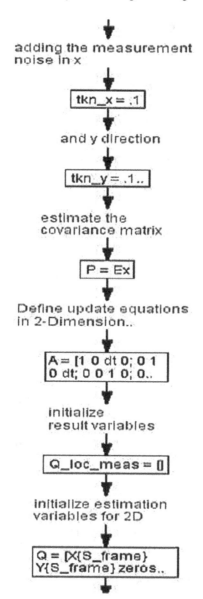

Fig. 2. Code-flowchart of target tracking (Part – II)

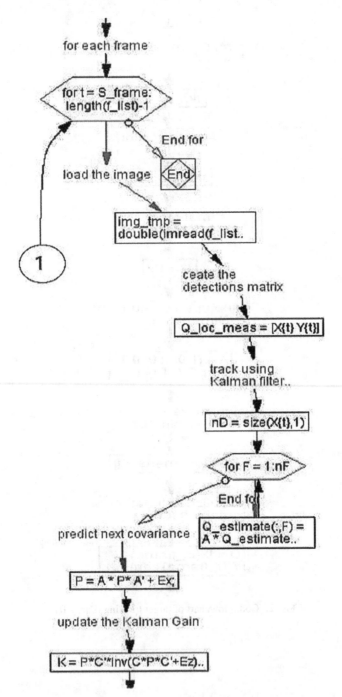

Fig. 3. Code-flowchart of target tracking (Part – III)

Note: The connecter (1) included in Fig. 3 ends in Fig. 6.

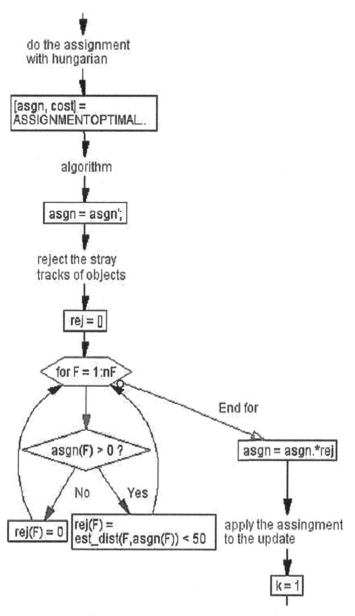

Fig. 4. Code-Flowchart of target tracking (Part – IV)

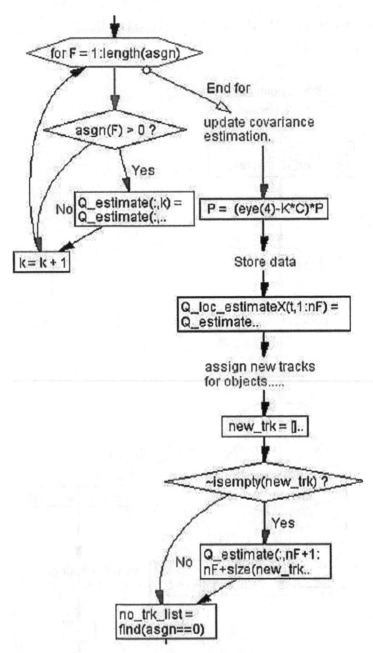

Fig. 5. Code-Flowchart of target tracking (Part – V)

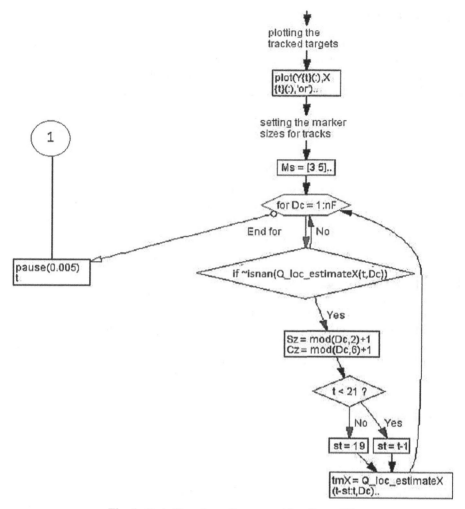

Fig. 6. Code-Flowchart of target tracking (Part – VI)

4 Object Detection

First, the video is sampled into individual frames. Then background elimination is done on all the frames and Gaussian filters are used [7, 8].

4.1 Background Elimination

This is a method that is used predominantly in surveillance systems. This method can be used when the background is stationary for a certain number of frames. This would yield the foreground objects that are in motion in all the frames separately. Here the background pixel values are considered as '0' and the foreground pixel value is considered as '1' [9].

4.2 Gaussian Filter

This filter is utilized to minimize the noise in a particular frame. It smoothens out the image and makes the surface uniform so that other image processing operation can be done in the frame. This filter also helps in the edge and boundaries detection of an object present in the frame. This filter's impulse response is given by the gaussian function,

$$F(x) = \frac{1}{\sqrt{2\pi\sigma^2}} e^{-\frac{x^2}{2\sigma^2}} \tag{1}$$

For 2 dimensions, the impulse response is given by,

$$F(x, y) = \frac{1}{\sqrt{2\pi\sigma^2}} e^{-\frac{(x^2+y^2)}{2\sigma^2}} \tag{2}$$

Where, σ is the standard deviation of both the distributions [10].

5 Object Tracking

In the tracking part, we make use of Kalman filter for tracking the targets and to overcome data association problem we use Hungarian algorithm. Kalman filter is utilized to anticipate the succeeding probable position of the targets and on the other hand Hungarian algorithm is applied to allocate the measurement data to respective targets in the case of multiple targets.

5.1 Kalman Filter

The Kalman filter gives the probability of the hypothesis at any time t, given the prior information, the action variable, and the data. The data, in this case, can be any sensor information like GPS. Kalman filters are modeled using the laws of motion in our case. A target's position coordinates and velocity coordinates are the inputs to the filter and this will help in finding the state prediction and the measurement prediction. Based on the constant K (Kalman gain), the next position of the target is updated through each iteration [11].

State update matrix, Measurement update matrix are the two important matrices in this model. The modeling of state matrix is done by the following two equations.

$$P_t = P_{t-1} + V_{t-1}t + \frac{1}{2}at^2 \tag{3}$$

$$V_t = V_{t-1} + at \tag{4}$$

In Eqs. (3) and (4) Pt and P_{t-1} are target's position at a given instant t and t − 1 respectively. V_t and V_{t-1} are the target's velocity at any instant t and t − 1 respectively.

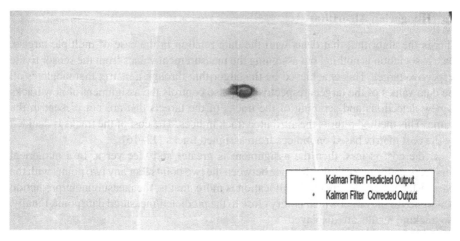

Fig. 7. Kalman output when acceleration error of the target is low

5.2 2-D Kalman Filter Matlab Implementation

In Fig. 7, a single bug (target) is being tracked using the Kalman filter. Here, the acceleration magnitude of the bug is very slow and hence the acceleration error is low. Therefore the predicted outcome of Kalman filter overlaps with the Kalman filters corrected output. The predicted output is corrected using the appropriate Kalman gain over every single iteration.

In Fig. 8 a single bug (target) is being tracked and the acceleration magnitude of the bug is high and hence a high acceleration error. The initial Kalman predicted value is erroneous and it loses track of the bug while the corrected Kalman output in the next iteration provides much more accurate tracking. As the iteration progresses the accuracy increases despite the increase in acceleration of the target [12].

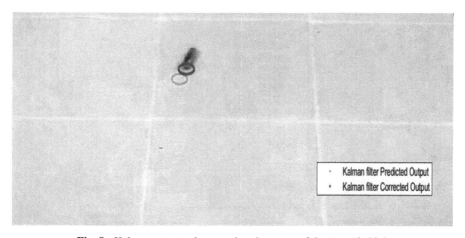

Fig. 8. Kalman output when acceleration error of the target is high

5.3 Hungarian Algorithm

This is the algorithm that deals with the data relation in the case of multiple targets. Data association is nothing but assigning the measurement values from the sensor to the respective target. This is achieved by this algorithm through a matrix that tabulates all the data values of the targets respectively. It also controls the assignment of new tracks to new detections and scraping of the tracks of the targets that are not present in the frame. This method returns the attributed track indices. The cost of the tracks is decided by the cost matrix based on indices from assigned tracks [13–16].

If the cost is less, then the assignment is greater and vice versa. In a numerical perspective, the metric is the distance between the two points. For any two points with the least distance between them, the allocation is more, that is, the measurement/prediction is assigned to the target which is very close to the predicted/measured data point. Finally, the tracking results are displayed.

6 Simulation Results

We used a series of images with dimensions 596×336 pixels and horizontal and vertical resolution 96 dpi and obtained from https://www.shutterstock.com/. Figure 9 (Data Set – I) and Fig. 10 (Data Set – II) show the result we obtained by using the same algorithm for 2 different datasets. In Data set – I the number of targets (bugs) is fixed. So the tracking is very efficient with minimum RMSE and the Hungarian algorithm performs efficiently. For Data set – II, the number of targets at any given time is not fixed. The targets leave the frame and new targets enter the frame. In this case, the tracking efficiency is not as good as the data set – I and this could be seen from the RMSE results in Fig. 11 and Fig. 12.

Fig. 9. Data Set – I Kalman filter tracking (Multi-target)

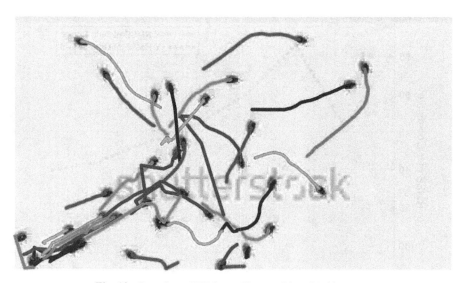

Fig. 10. Data Set – II Kalman filter tracking (Multi-target)

6.1 Root Mean Square Error (RMSE) Results

In Fig. 11 and Fig. 12, we can see the X and Y coordinate RMSE values for both, Data set – I and Data Set – II. The RMSE values of both data sets decrease over every iteration. The RMSE values for every iteration is computed by obtaining the difference between the true position coordinates of the targets (obtained by image processing algorithms) and the Kalman filter predicted coordinates of same targets.

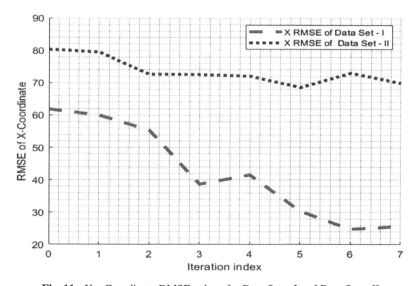

Fig. 11. X – Coordinate RMSE values for Data Set – I and Data Set – II

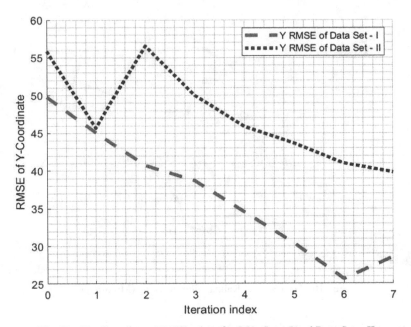

Fig. 12. Y – Coordinate RMSE values for Data Set – I and Data Set – II

7 Conclusion

We have proposed an algorithm for tracking multiple objects and tested the efficacy of the algorithm using two different data sets with different properties.

The Kalman filter performs efficiently for the data set – I as the targets are fixed and no targets leave or enter the frame. Therefore the data association problem is well managed. There is no need for adding new tracks or removing the stray tracks. It detects and tracks the targets with an error rate of 4.16%. As the iterations progress the error rate is decreasing to a minimal extent.

In the case of Data set – II the targets keep leaving and entering the frame at regular intervals. This means that new targets entering the frame has to be assigned with new detections and tracks and leaving targets' detection and tracks have to be scrapped. As the number of targets keeps on increasing, the Hungarian matrix dimensions increase and this leads to an increase in computational complexities. In some cases, two tracks are assigned to a single target (can be seen in Fig. 10) and at times the targets don't get assigned with tracks. On the whole, as the targets count increase, the data association algorithm fails to function as efficiently as it did for the first data set in which the number of targets is less and predetermined.

Also, the RMSE value for Data set – II has always been higher than the RMSE value for Data set – I, even though it is decreasing with every iteration as a whole.

References

1. Loncaric, S.: A survey of shape analysis techniques. Pattern Recogn. **31**(8), 983–1001 (1998)
2. Magee, D.R.: Tracking multiple vehicles using foreground, background and motion models. In: Proceedings of Statistical Methods in Video Processing Workshop, pp. 7–12, June 2002
3. Lipton, J., Fujiyoshi, H., Patil, R.S.: Moving target classification and tracking from real-time video. In: Proceedings of Workshop Applications of Computer Vision, pp. 129–136 (1998)
4. Ramanathan, R., Nair, A.S., Thaneshwaran, L., Ponmathavan, S., Valliappan, N., Soman, K.P.: Robust feature extraction technique for optical character recognition. In: ACT 2009 - International Conference on Advances in Computing, Control and Telecommunication Technologies, Trivandrum, Kerala (2009)
5. Anuj, L., Krishna, M.T.G.: Multiple camera based multiple object tracking under occlusion: a survey. In: 2017 International Conference on Innovative Mechanisms for Industry Applications (ICIMIA), Bangalore, pp. 432–437 (2017)
6. Henschel, R., Leal-Taixé, L., Cremers, D., Rosenhahn, B.: Fusion of head and full-body detectors for multi-object tracking. In: 2018 IEEE/CVF Conference on Computer Vision and Pattern Recognition Workshops (CVPRW), Salt Lake City, UT, p. 150909 (2018)
7. Nandashri, D., Smitha, P.: An efficient tracking of multi object visual motion using Hungarian method. Int. J. Eng. Res. Technol. (IJERT) **04**(04) (2015)
8. Anand, R., Veni, S., Aravinth, J.: An application of image processing techniques for detection of diseases on brinjal leaves using K-means clustering method (2016). In: Fifth International Conference on Recent Trends in Information Technology 2016 (ICRTIT 2016). Anna University, Chennai campus (2016)
9. Kim, I., Awan, T.W., Soh, Y.: Background subtraction-based multiple object tracking using particle filter. In: IWSSIP Proceedings, Dubrovnik, pp. 71–74 (2014)
10. Jaward, M., Mihaylova, L., Canagarajah, N., Bull, D.: Multiple object tracking using particle filters. In: IEEE Aerospace Conference, Big Sky, MT, p. 8 (2006)
11. Vermaak, J., Godsill, S.J., Perez, P.: Monte Carlo filtering for multi target tracking and data association. IEEE Trans. Aerosp. Electron. Syst. **41**, 309–332 (2005)
12. Seth, R., Kumar Swain, M.S., Kumar Mishra, D.S.: Single object tracking using estimation algorithms. In: 2nd International Conference on Power, Energy and Environment: Towards Smart Technology (ICEPE), Shillong, India, pp. 1–6 (2018)
13. Yu, Y.: Distributed target tracking in wireless sensor networks with data association uncertainty. IEEE Commun. Lett. **21**(6), 1281–1284 (2017)
14. Bar-Shalom, Y., Daum, F., Huang, J.: The probabilistic data association filter. IEEE Control Syst. Mag. **29**(6), 82–100 (2009)
15. Attari, M., Habibi, S., Gadsden, S.A.: Target tracking formulation of the SVSF with data association techniques. IEEE Trans. Aerosp. Electron. Syst. **53**(1), 12–25 (2017)
16. Karunasekera, H., Wang, H., Zhang, H.: Multiple object tracking with attention to appearance, structure, motion and size. IEEE Access **7**, 104423–104434 (2019)

SaaS - Microservices-Based Scalable Smart Contract Architecture

Eranga Bandara[1]($\boxtimes$), Xueping Liang[2], Peter Foytik[1], Sachin Shetty[1], Nalin Ranasinghe[3], Kasun De Zoysa[3], and Wee Keong Ng[4]

[1] Old Dominion University, Norfolk, VA, USA
{cmedawer,pfoytik,sshetty}@odu.edu
[2] University of North Carolina at Greensboro, Greensboro, NC, USA
x_liang@uncg.edu
[3] University of Colombo School of Computing, Colombo, Sri Lanka
{dnr,kasun}@ucsc.cmb.ac.lk
[4] School of Computer Science and Engineering, Nanyang Technological University,
Jurong West, Singapore
awkng@ntu.edu.sg

Abstract. Existing blockchain smart contract platforms are designed as monolithic architectures. Even though there are multiple smart contracts with fully independent business logic, they run on a single monolithic container. This dependence on a monolithic container can be a performance bottleneck during the processing of a large number of transactions. To address this challenge, microservice-based architecture is adopted in the blockchain smart contracts by introducing a novel architecture to run independently on separate microservices. The new smart contract architecture is built on top of Mystiko blockchain, a functional programming and actor-based "Aplos" concurrent smart contract platform. Aplos is identified as a "Smart Actor" platform since it is built using Actor-based concurrency handling. Based on the philosophy of microservices, the Aplos Smart Actor platform on Mystiko blockchain is redesigned. This architecture is introduced as "SaaS - Smart actors as a service". With SaaS, different Aplos smart actors in the blockchain are deployed as separate independent services (e.g. docker containers) instead of a single monolith service. This ensures different smart actors can execute transactions independently. An additional benefits to SaaS is that the architecture increases the scalability by guaranteeing concurrent execution of transactions, producing high transaction throughput on the blockchain.

Keywords: Blockchain · Microservices · Actors · Smart contract · Functional programming

1 Introduction

Most blockchain platforms introduce the function of "smart contracts" to interact with the blockchain ledger through scripting and programming. Blockchain

© Springer Nature Singapore Pte Ltd. 2021
S. M. Thampi et al. (Eds.): SSCC 2020, CCIS 1364, pp. 228–243, 2021.
https://doi.org/10.1007/978-981-16-0422-5_16

software programs and platforms are written with these smart contracts in a way that users can interact with them. Most of the existing blockchain smart contracts platforms are designed as a Monolithic architecture [34]. Though there are multiple smart contracts with fully independent business logic, they run on a single monolithic container. Because of this design architecture, it's not possible to run different smart contracts independently even though smart contracts have no dependency between them. This produces less transaction throughput on blockchain and scalability suffers. To address this concern we have adapted a microservices philosophy into the smart contract design.

Microservice [34] is a new architecture that is widely used to design highly scalable distributed software systems. Instead of building systems as single monolithic systems, microservices builds them as multiple small services which are introduced as microservices. These services, built based on Unix Philosophy, are built to achieve one task perfectly. To work on different tasks, the microservices communicate with other services. Communication between services is managed using message brokers like Kafka [23], AMQP or REST [16] APIs based on a reactive programming philosophy. Existing blockchain system architectures are built as monolithic systems where consensus handling, block creating, and sharing happens as a single monolithic service. This monolithic architecture produces considerable challenges when the blockchain system is scaled up. To address this concern Mystiko blockchain platform is restructured with a microservices architecture designed in its blockchain platform. The consensus handling, storage, block generation and smart contracts functions are handled on different small microservices within Mystiko. It leads to a higher scalable blockchain based system producing more throughput and allowing more transactions to occur.

In this research, we have adapted a microservices philosophy into blockchain smart contracts and built scalable smart contract architecture for real-time applications that demand high throughput transactions. Instead of building software systems as single monolithic systems, microservices are built as multiple small services. These services are built based on Unix Philosophy, "Do only one thing well". Microservices communicate with other collectively to perform complex operations. To communicate between the services, message brokers like Kafka, AMQP or REST APIs based on reactive programming philosophy are used. Based on the microservice philosophy Aplos smart actors platform on Mystiko blockchain is redesigned. Instead of having a single monolithic service to run smart actors, independent smart actors run on separate services as docker containers. This architecture, "SaaS - Smart actors as a service", allows different smart actors to execute transactions independently increasing the scalability and transaction throughput on the blockchain.

1.1   Outline

The structure of the paper has been organized in the following. Section 2 discusses the design of the Mystiko blockchain architecture. A detailed description of SaaS architecture is presented in Sect. 3. Section 4 performance evaluation. Section 5 Related works. Section 6 conclusion and future works.

2   Mystiko Blockchain

2.1   Mystiko Overview

Mystiko is an enterprise blockchain platform which targeted for highly scalable, concurrent applications such as big data, IoT, smart cities etc. It designed with using Apache Kafka-based [23] federated consensus [25]. Mystiko uses Apache Cassandra [26] as it's asset storage and facilitate the full-text search on Blockchain data with using Lucene index [9] based API [17]. The federated learning services in the Mystiko blockchain capable of performing data analytics and machine learning functions with the blockchain data in a privacy-preserving manner. Three main performance bottlenecks on existing Blockchain platforms are investigated and addressed, namely order-execute architecture, full node data replication, and imperative style smart contracts.

To address the issues in the "Order-Execute" architecture and support real-time transactions, "Validate-Execute-Group" blockchain architecture is proposed. This architecture supported to validate and execute transactions concurrently when clients submit them to the network [7]. The new architecture provides high transaction throughput, high scalability and lightweight consensus [25] in the Mystiko blockchain. This architecture first validates and check the double spend [29] when clients submit transactions to the blockchain. Then execute the transaction with the smart contract and replicate state updates on the ledger. Finally, create blocks based on the executed transactions. To achieve real-time transactions in this model, it required strong consistent storage with linearizable consistency [35]. Mystiko used eventually consistent distributed storage and built a linearizable consistency model on it [3,24].

To address the issues with existing imperative style smart contracts and support concurrent transactions, Mystiko introduces functional programming [22] and actor [20] based Aplos smart contract platform(which introduced as Aplos smart actor platform). Blockchain programs(smart contracts) is written using actors. Different actors may interact with one another via message passing. This smart actor platform supports concurrent execution of transactions; this yields high transaction throughput and scalability. Scalable and concurrent applications always deal with back-pressure operations [14]. Mystiko uses reactive-streaming [2,13,23] based approach to handle the back-pressure operations. Clients can submit the transactions to the blockchain as streams. Smart contract actors in the blockchain will stream these transactions and execute them. Mystiko blockchain used an eventual consistency distributed storage as the underlying storage platform [26]. Every peer in the network will have its own storage node. These storage nodes are connected as a ring cluster. All the transaction, blocks, assets will be stored in this storage. After a node executes a transaction with smart contracts, the state updates will be replicated to other nodes via sharding [36].

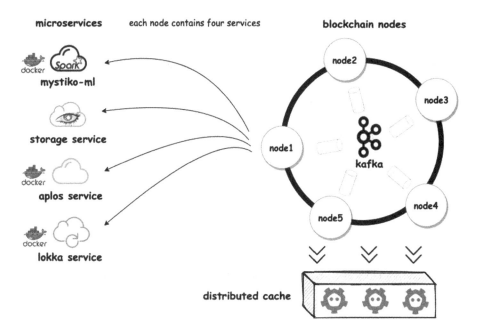

Fig. 1. Mystiko blockchain microservices-based architecture. Each blockchain node contains four services - Mystiko-ML service, Storage service, Aplos service and Lokka service.

2.2   Mystiko Architecture

Mystiko blockchain designed with using Microservices-based [5,34] architecture. The consensus handling, smart contracts, asset storage and block generation functions implemented in independent microservices services in the Mystiko blockchain. All these microservices are dockerized [28] and available for deployment using Kubernetes [10]. The architecture of the Mystiko blockchain described in Fig. 1. Following are the main services/components of Mystiko blockchain:

1. Aplos service - Smart contract service.
2. Storage service - Blockchain asset storage.
3. Lokka service - Block generation service.
4. Apache Kafka - Consensus and message broker service.
5. Mystiko-Ml - Federated machine learning service.

2.3   Aplos Smart Actors

Mystiko blockchain introduced Scala functional programming language [4,22,31] and Akka actor [1,18] based Aplos smart contract platform [8]. Aplos introduced as a Smart Actor platform since it built using Actor-based concurrency handling [20,21]. It enables concurrent transaction execution on Mystiko blockchain

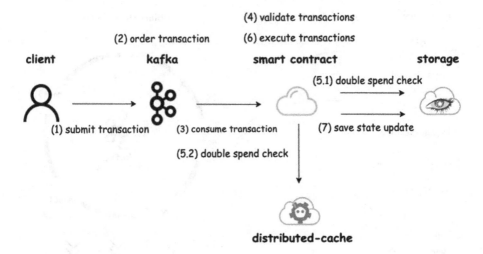

Fig. 2. Mystiko blockchain transaction flow. Two step transaction validation happens with asset storage and distributed cache.

and produces high transaction throughput [8]. The transaction flow of the Mystiko blockchain with Aplos smart actors is described in Fig. 2. All blockchain-based software programs and the messages that pass between them are written as Akka actors [1,18] and saved in the Aplos service. Each blockchain node in the cluster has Aplos service. Theses services consume transactions from Kafka message broker. Each Aplos service is connected to separate Kafka topic and consume transactions parallelly. Clients publish transactions to these Kafka topics. A transaction message contains a JSON encoded object with smart actor name and transaction parameters. Aplos service streams these transaction messages from Kafka and delegates them to corresponding smart actors based on the actor name in the message. Once a transaction message receives, smart actor validates and executes the transaction and generates the asset update. Finally, the asset update saved in the storage service and replicated with other blockchain nodes in the network as shown in Fig. 2.

3   SaaS

3.1   Overview

SaaS "Smart actors as a service" is a new architecture that we are proposing to run smart contracts on top of the blockchain network. In a blockchain environment, there will be multiple smart contracts. Traditionally, all of these smart contracts run on a single monolithic service even though there is no interconnection between them. We have been identified that this would lead to major performance bottleneck on the blockchain architecture. With SaaS architecture, instead of having a single monolithic smart contract service, independent smart contracts run on separate services(microservices) as actors. The SaaS smart contract architecture built on top of Mystiko blockchain Aplos smart actor platform. With SaaS, microservices architecture is introduced into Aplos smart actors on Mystiko. In this way, different smart actors can execute transactions independently. It will increase the scalability and produce high transaction throughput on the blockchain.

3.2 SaaS Scenario

As a use case of SaaS, we have built a document approving application on top of Mystiko blockchain using SaaS architecture. This application can be used to automate the document approval process on an organization(or cross-organization). Current document approval in an organization happens as a manual process. When multiple persons(e.g. multiple managers) need to sign a document, an employee of the company takes the document from one manager to another by hand and gets the document approved(e.g. signatures). We automate this process by using the Lekana platform. An administrator can upload documents and define the signatories of the document. It can define signing flow, assume A, B, C managers need to sign and the flow would be first A, second B, and third C. Once this document is uploaded to the Lekana, it will be notified to the first manager that needs to be signed via Lekana mobile application. When the notification is received, the manager pulls the document to the mobile application and approves or rejects it. When the document is approved, it digitally signs the document as well as adds the physical signature to the document by using PDF annotations. Once the first manager signs, the second manager will be notified. All document creating, notifying, user management functions are handled by smart actors on Mystiko blockchain.

3.3 Smart Contract Services

In Aplos, the business logic of the blockchain applications is written using Akka actors. Actors consume transaction messages and execute business logic based on the message parameters. `AccountActor`, `DocumentActor`, and `DeviceActor` are the three smart actors on Lekana platform. The user account related functions(account creation, activation) handles with the `AccountActor`. The push notification related functions handle with `DeviceActor`. The `DocumentActor` handles document creation, update, approval functions. With SaaS architecture, all these actors run as separate services(microservice) on Mystiko blockchain. These actors consume messages via Apache Kafka with Akka streams. Each actor service has its Kafka topic, Fig. 3. Clients submit messages to these actor services via Kafka as transaction messages. For an example when creating a document client summit transaction message shown in Fig. 5. When approving a document client submits the transaction message shown in Fig. 4. These messages first go to Gateway service in the Mystiko. Gateway service identifies the

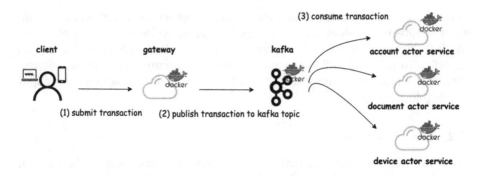

Fig. 3. Smart actor services in Lekana application. Different smart actors run independently on top of Docker containers.

```
{
    "id": "<transaction id>",
    "execer": "<transaction executing user>",
    "messageType": "sign",
    "documentId": "<document id>",
    "documentSigner": "<document signing user>",
    "documentSignature": "<document digital signature>",
    "documentBlob": "<base64 encoded document payload>",
    "documentStatus": "<approve/reject status>",
    "digsig": "<digital signature of transaction>"
}
```

Fig. 4. Document approve message in Lekana application

message type based on the `messageType` field and routes the message to corresponding smart contract service via Kafka. Then smart contract consumes the transaction, executes it and returns the response to the client side for execution.

3.4   Smart Contract Service Communication

In some scenarios, one smart contract needs to communicate with another smart contract. For example, when document approves `DocumentActor`(resides in document service) needs to communicate with the smart actor on `DeviceActor`(resides in devices service) to send push notifications. In this case, `DocumentActor` in document service creates notification messages, shown in Fig. 6 and publishes Kafka topic on device service. Then device service picks it up and sends the push notification to the given client.

3.5   Concurrent Transaction Execution

When executing transactions, traditional blockchain use order-execute architecture. They execute transactions sequentially(one after one). In Mystiko with validate-execute-group architecture, it can execute transactions concurrently. For

```
{
    "id": "<transaction id>",
    "execer": "<transaction executing user>",
    "messageType": "create",
    "documentId": "<document id>",
    "documentCreator": "<document creating user>",
    "documentName": "<document name>",
    "documentCompany": "<document own company>",
    "documentType": "<document type>",
    "documentBlob": "<base64 encoded document payload>",
    "documentSigners": "<signinig user details>",
    "digsig": "<digital signature of transaction>"
}
```

Fig. 5. Document create message in Lekana application

```
{
    "id": "<transaction id>",
    "execer": "<transaction executing user>",
    "messageType": "notify",
    "notifyDevice": "<notifying device>",
    "notifyMessage": "<notification message>",
    "digsig": "<digital signature of transaction>"
}
```

Fig. 6. Notify message in Lekana application

example, consider a scenario where concurrent transactions come to create an account(transaction A) and create a document(transaction B). These contracts are not interrelated. In the transitional blockchain, these transactions will be executed with the order they created, for example 'transaction A' after 'transaction B'. All these transactions will be executed in a single smart contract service. With Aplos SaaS architecture, these transactions will be executed concurrently in different smart contract services. 'transaction A' will be on account service and 'transaction B' will be on document service. Unlike other blockchains, Mystiko blockchain executes transactions only one time. After executing the transaction, the asset will be updated and the result will be shared on other nodes based on the process of sharding.

3.6   Scalability and Load Balancing

With SaaS, multiple replicas of smart actor services can be run in the cluster. For example, we can run multiple replicas of document actor service on the cluster as shown in Fig. 7. Since Mystiko blockchain executes transactions only one-time, multiple replicas can be run parallelly. These replicas connected on a Kafka consumer group, via partitioned Kafka topic. Then Kafka handles the message partitioning and message broadcasting between the smart contract services(load balancing), guaranteeing total order(provide total order by sending a message only to one consumer by topic partitioning 8. Mystiko blockchain supports the

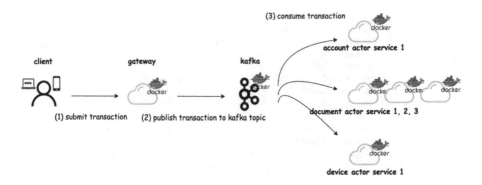

Fig. 7. Multiple replicas of Document smart actor service run parallelly in Lekana application.

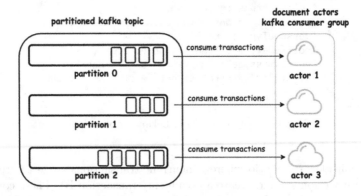

Fig. 8. Document actor connected as Kafka consumer group. Kafka will handle message broadcasting between multiple Document actor services with guaranteeing total order.

deployment of its services via Kubernetes. We can have dynamic load balancing with smart actors services via Kubernetes as well. For example, depending on the load of the system, we can dynamically increase the instance of the document service via Kubernetes. Then Routing will be handled with Kubernetes. With this approach, we have added enterprise distributed systems features into the blockchain.

4   Performance Evaluation

The evaluation of the proposed smart contract architecture has been done in the following five areas.

1. Performance of Invoke(write) transactions
2. Performance of Query(read) transactions

3. Scalability performance
4. Transaction latency
5. Transaction execution rate

These results have been obtained from the Lekana document approving application. To get the statistics, we have built two versions of the Lekana application with different smart contract architectures on Mystiko blockchain. The first version builds with default monolithic architecture which all smart contracts run on single services. The second version built with SaaS architecture where smart contracts run on different services. The performance results obtained on both these Lekana versions and evaluated.

4.1 Performance of Invoke Transactions

Invoke transactions write state update to the ledger. In this evaluation, we have executed concurrent Invoke transactions in different blockchain peers and recorded all the completed transactions in each second. As shown in Fig. 9 we compared the Invoke transaction on both monolithic smart contract platform and SaaS-based platform. The SaaS-based platform provides high invoke transaction throughout. In SaaS, different smart contracts can run independently/parallelly, so it increased the transaction throughput.

4.2 Performance of Query Transactions

Query transactions just read the state from the ledger. In this evaluation, we have executed concurrent Query transactions in different blockchain peers and recorded the completed transactions(per second), Fig. 10. As same as Invoke transactions, Query transactions throughput is high on SaaS-based implementation since it can run smart contracts parallelly. Query transactions do not update the ledger status while invoke transactions update the ledger state. Due to this reason, the throughput is higher than Invoke transaction throughput.

4.3 Scalability Performance

The scalability performance obtained against the number of executed invoke transactions in second and the total number of peers in the network. The scalability results have been recorded up to 7 blockchain peers. As shown in Fig. 11 we have compared the scalability of monolithic smart contract architecture with SaaS architecture. Both architectures increase transaction throughput when increasing the number of peers in the network. But due to concurrent transaction execution on SaaS, it produces high scalability when compared with the monolithic system.

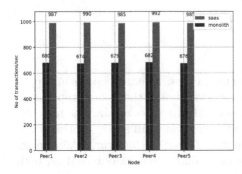

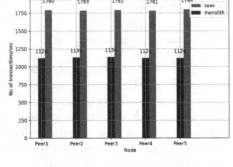

Fig. 9. Invoke transaction throughput of monolith smart contract service and SaaS based service.

Fig. 10. Query transaction throughput of monolith smart contract service and SaaS based service.

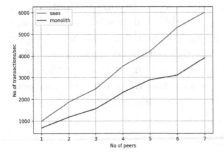

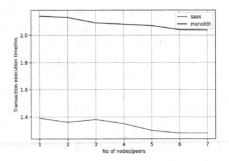

Fig. 11. Transaction scalability of monolith smart contract service and SaaS based service.

Fig. 12. Transaction latency of monolith smart contract service and SaaS based service.

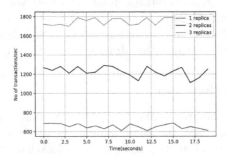

Fig. 13. Transaction execution rate comparison with number of smart contract service replicas.

4.4   Transaction Latency

The latency results obtained with the invoke transaction latency(in milliseconds) and the number of blockchain peers in the network. Concurrency invoke transactions have been executed in different blockchain peers and calculated the average transaction latency. As shown in Fig. 12 we have compared the latency results of monolithic smart contract services with SaaS-based smart contract service. The SaaS-based system produces less latency due to high transaction throughput on it.

4.5 Transaction Execution Rate

Finally, we evaluate the transaction execution rate with the number of smart contract service replicas. We run multiple smart contract service replicas of Document Actor service in Lekana platform and record the total number of executed transactions when recording the time. Figure 13 shows how transaction execution rate varies when having a different number of smart contract replicas. When the number of replicas increases, the rate of executed transactions is increased relatively. There is a back-pressure operation [14] between the rates of submitted transactions and executed transactions. We have used a reactive streaming-based approach with Apache Kafka to handle these back-pressure operations.

5 Related Work

Recent effort has been taken to address the issues and improve the performance of existing Smart contract platforms [6,19]. A large portion of the current smart contracts are using the imperative style programming which has side effects. In this manner, concurrent transactions are not upheld in the blockchain. Simplicity [30], Scilla [33] and Pact [32] smart contracts are constructed dependent on functional programming semantics. Their fundamental objective is to have side-effects less blockchain functions by utilizing a functional programming based methodology. Simplicity is a composed, combinator-based, smart contract language. It is intended to function as Turing complete without the existence of loops and recursion, to be utilized for cryptographic forms of money and blockchain applications. By doing so, it intends to enhance existing cryptocurrency dialects such as the Script in Bitcoin. It keeps away from the shared global state, where the transaction doesn't have to access any data not related to the transaction. It additionally doesn't uphold communication contracts, that implies contracts don't talk with one another. Scilla [33] is a smart contract language for verified contracts which are designed mainly considering smart contract security. Scilla oversees the read and write operations to the shared address space and is intended for the implementation of the account-based model, in which smart contracts exchange messages with one another. Scilla isn't completely implemented as a functional language since the transactions could affect the outer state. Basically, Scilla utilizes recursive functions, which can be demonstrated statically. Pact [32] is another smart contract programming language which is essentially focused for private blockchain. Pact adopts the Turing incomplete semantic and the recursion causes a quick termination at each module load. But supports looping via map and fold. An advantage of this limitation is that Pact doesn't have to utilize any sort of cost model such as the Ethereum's "gas" [27] to restrict calculation. The functional programming configuration and module definitions are adopted, as well as the atomic transaction executions. The Pack smart contracts are stored in the blockchain ledger itself as an unmodified human-readable form.

Rholang [15] is an alternate kind of smart contract platform which is mostly intended for concurrent applications. It is intended to implement smart contracts on top of general-purpose blockchain platforms. The Rho virtual machine (RhoVM) used to execute the compiled Rholang smart contract programs. It concedes unbounded recursion, which is a behaviorally typed and Turing complete programming language. Rholang smart contract language is designed to handle concurrent transactions with using message-passing through channels. This concurrent design modelled based on pi-calculus [11]-based semantic.

Solidity [12] and Chaincode [7] are two general-purpose smart contract platforms. Solidity is the most mainstream smart contract platform currently available. It is Turing complete and looks similar to Javascript, which underpins Turing schematic and the complex business logic can be actualized in smart contracts, simultaneously faced with several weaknesses. To forestall infinite loops and address the halting problem, execution is restricted by "gas", which is paid for in Ether, to the miner. At the point when the gas is run out, the exchange is invalidated however the gas is as yet paid in order to guarantee they are made up for the calculation endeavours. Solidity utilizes shared status and doesn't uphold concurrent transaction execution. Hyperledger Chaincode characterizes resources on the blockchain and the capacities to create, update, get resources from the blockchain record are actualized as contract functions, following the imperative style programming and Turing complete smart contracts. Hyperledger isn't proposed to be public blockchain, it is a private blockchain. Smart contracts won't be transferred to the blockchain by any single participant. To forestall possible weaknesses, engineers and inner groups should completely test smart contracts before use.

Table 1 compares the features of these smart contracts platforms with Aplos/SaaS smart contract platform. It discusses Turing completeness of the smart contract language, loop/recursion support of the smart contract language, functional/imperative style of the smart contract language, concurrent transac-

Table 1. Comparison of existing smart contract platforms with the Aplos/SaaS smart actor platform.

Platform	Blockchain	Public/Private	Turing complete	Loops	Functional	Concurrent transactions	Shared state	Communication contracts	Implemented language
Aplos/SaaS	Mystiko	Private	Yes	Yes	Yes	Yes	No	Yes	Scala
Solidity [12]	Etherium	Both	Yes	Yes	No	No	Yes	Yes	C++/Solidity
Chaincode [7]	Hyperledger	Private	Yes	Yes	No	No	Yes	Yes	Golang
Simplicity [30]	Bitcoin	Public	No	No	Yes	No	Yes	No	Tcl/Haskell
Scilla [33]	Zilliqa	Public	No	Recursion	No	No	Yes	Yes	OCaml
Pact [32]	Kadena	Both	No	No	Yes	No	Yes	Yes	Haskell
Rholang [15]	Rchain	Both	Yes	Yes	Yes	Yes	No	Yes	Java

tion execution support, communication contract support and smart contract implemented language details.

6   Conclusions and Future Work

SaaS introduced microservices-based highly scalable smart actor architecture for blockchain. Instead of having a single monolithic smart contract service, SaaS can run independent smart contracts on separate services as actors. These smart contracts which are introduced as smart actors can execute transactions independently. It will increase the scalability and produce high transaction throughput on the blockchain.

The evaluation has proven the scalability and transaction throughput of SaaS smart contract architecture. We have integrated SaaS-based smart contracts into production-grade blockchain applications(e.g. Lekana). This deployment is a vote of confidence for SaaS as an ideal smart contract architecture to build scalable blockchain applications. Currently, we have integrated SaaS architecture into Mystiko blockchain. We are planning to incorporate secure multiparty computation [37] of Aplos framework in a future release.

References

1. Akka documentation. https://doc.akka.io/docs/akka/2.5/actors.html
2. Akka streams documentation. https://doc.akka.io/docs/akka/2.5/stream/
3. How do i accomplish lightweight transactions with linearizable consistency? https://docs.datastax.com/en/cassandra/3.0/cassandra/dml/dmlLtwtTransactions.html
4. The scala programming language. https://www.scala-lang.org/
5. Aderaldo, C.M., Mendonça, N.C., Pahl, C., Jamshidi, P.: Benchmark requirements for microservices architecture research. In: 2017 IEEE/ACM 1st International Workshop on Establishing the Community-Wide Infrastructure for Architecture-Based Software Engineering (ECASE), pp. 8–13. IEEE (2017)
6. Adrian, O.R.: The blockchain, today and tomorrow. In: 2018 20th International Symposium on Symbolic and Numeric Algorithms for Scientific Computing (SYNASC), pp. 458–462. IEEE (2018)
7. Androulaki, E., et al.: Hyperledger fabric: a distributed operating system for permissioned blockchains. In: Proceedings of the Thirteenth EuroSys Conference, p. 30. ACM (2018)
8. Bandara, E., Ng, W.K., Ranasinghe, N., De Zoysa, K.: Aplos: smart contracts made smart. In: Zheng, Z., Dai, H.-N., Tang, M., Chen, X. (eds.) BlockSys 2019. CCIS, vol. 1156, pp. 431–445. Springer, Singapore (2020). https://doi.org/10.1007/978-981-15-2777-7_35
9. Białecki, A., Muir, R., Ingersoll, G., Imagination, L.: Apache lucene 4. In: SIGIR 2012 Workshop on Open Source Information Retrieval, p. 17 (2012)
10. Burns, B., Grant, B., Oppenheimer, D., Brewer, E., Wilkes, J.: Borg, omega, and kubernetes. Queue 14(1), 70–93 (2016)
11. Cristescu, I.D., Krivine, J., Varacca, D.: Rigid families for CCS and the π-calculus. In: Leucker, M., Rueda, C., Valencia, F.D. (eds.) ICTAC 2015. LNCS, vol. 9399, pp. 223–240. Springer, Cham (2015). https://doi.org/10.1007/978-3-319-25150-9_14

12. Dannen, C.: Introducing Ethereum and Solidity. Apress, Berkeley, CA (2017). https://doi.org/10.1007/978-1-4842-2535-6
13. Davis, A.L.: Akka streams. In: Reactive Streams in Java, pp. 57–70. Springer, Berlin (2019)
14. Destounis, A., Paschos, G.S., Koutsopoulos, I.: Streaming big data meets back-pressure in distributed network computation. In: IEEE INFOCOM 2016-The 35th Annual IEEE International Conference on Computer Communications, pp. 1–9. IEEE (2016)
15. Eykholt, E., Meredith, L.G., Denman, J.: Rchain architecture documentation. Retrieve. Jan. **19**, 2019 (2017)
16. Fernandes, J.L., Lopes, I.C., Rodrigues, J.J., Ullah, S.: Performance evaluation of restful web services and amqp protocol. In: 2013 Fifth International Conference on Ubiquitous and Future Networks (ICUFN), pp. 810–815. IEEE (2013)
17. Gormley, C., Tong, Z.: Elasticsearch: the definitive guide: a distributed real-time search and analytics engine. O'Reilly Media, Inc. (2015)
18. Gupta, M.: Akka essentials. Packt Publishing Ltd, Birmingham (2012)
19. Harz, D., Knottenbelt, W.: Towards safer smart contracts: A survey of languages and verification methods (2018)
20. Hewitt, C.: Actor model of computation: scalable robust information systems. arXiv preprint arXiv:1008.1459 (2010)
21. Hoare, C.A.R.: Communicating sequential processes. Commun. ACM **21**(8), 666–677 (1978)
22. Hughes, J.: Why functional programming matters. Comput. J. **32**(2), 98–107 (1989)
23. Kreps, J., Narkhede, N., Rao, J., et al.: Kafka: a distributed messaging system for log processing. In: Proceedings of the NetDB. pp. 1–7 (2011)
24. Kurath, A.: Analyzing Serializability of Cassandra Applications. Ph.D. thesis, Master's thesis. ETH Zürich (2017)
25. Kwon, J.: Tendermint: Consensus without mining. Draft v. 0.6, fall 1, 11 (2014)
26. Lakshman, A., Malik, P.: Cassandra: a decentralized structured storage system. ACM SIGOPS Oper. Syst. Revi. **44**(2), 35–40 (2010)
27. Marescotti, M., Blicha, M., Hyvärinen, A.E.J., Asadi, S., Sharygina, N.: Computing exact worst-case gas consumption for smart contracts. In: Margaria, T., Steffen, B. (eds.) ISoLA 2018. LNCS, vol. 11247, pp. 450–465. Springer, Cham (2018). https://doi.org/10.1007/978-3-030-03427-6_33
28. Merkel, D.: Docker: lightweight linux containers for consistent development and deployment. Linux J. **2014**(239), 2 (2014)
29. Nakamoto, S.: Bitcoin: A peer-to-peer electronic cash system (2008)
30. O'Connor, R.: Simplicity: A new language for blockchains. In: Proceedings of the 2017 Workshop on Programming Languages and Analysis for Security. pp. 107–120. ACM (2017)
31. Odersky, M., et al.: An overview of the scala programming language. Technical Report (2004)
32. Popejoy, S.: The pact smart contract language 2017 (2016)
33. Sergey, I., Kumar, A., Hobor, A.: Scilla: a smart contract intermediate-level language (2018)
34. Thönes, J.: Microservices. IEEE Softw. **32**(1), 116–116 (2015)

35. Traiger, I.L., Gray, J., Galtieri, C.A., Lindsay, B.G.: Transactions and consistency in distributed database systems. ACM Trans. Database Syst. (TODS) **7**(3), 323–342 (1982)
36. Zamani, M., Movahedi, M., Raykova, M.: Rapidchain: a fast blockchain protocol via full sharding. IACR Cryptol. ePrint Arch. **2018**, 460 (2018)
37. Zyskind, G., Nathan, O., Pentland, A.: Enigma: decentralized computation platform with guaranteed privacy. arXiv preprint arXiv:1506.03471 (2015)

GIDS: Anomaly Detection Using Generative Adversarial Networks

Rinoy Macwan[1], Sankha Das[2], and Manik Lal Das[1(✉)]

[1] DA-IICT, Gandhinagar, India
rinoymacwan@gmail.com, maniklal@gmail.com
[2] BITS Pilani, Rajasthan, Rajasthan, India
umasankhadas@gmail.com

Abstract. Cyber security in modern digital age has become a major challenge before an individual/organization to protect assets from malicious entities. Machine learning technique has been used in advanced intrusion detection system (IDS) which detects new attacks by analyzing existing attacks' metrics with the help of rich collection of datasets. Generative Adversarial Networks (GAN) has found lots of attentions in recent times, in particular, for forgery detection in image data. GAN also shows its potential that can be used in text-based traffic inspection to check whether the traffic contains any suspicious strings. In this paper, we present an intrusion detection system using GAN, termed as GIDS, that detects anomalies in input strings with a reasonable accuracy. GIDS minimizes the mapping error without using an external encoder. The analysis and experimental results show that GIDS detects anomalies with an accuracy of 83.66%, while keeping false positive rate low.

Keywords: Network security · Intrusion detection · Generative adversarial network · Anomaly detection

1 Introduction

In modern digital age, Information and Communication Technology enables household objects to reach out to powerful cloud server and vice-versa. With this Internet of Things scenario, security of data as well as communicating entities is of prime concern. At the same time, the intellectual game between application developer and attacker has also been evolved in multi-fold defense-attack layers. Intrusion Detection Systems (IDS) [1] have been widely deployed by organizations to protect their valuable assets as well as perimeter from the defense-attack game.

An intrusion is defined as an activity that poses a threat to system and network resources. Intrusion detection is the process of monitoring and identifying an attempt that may bypass or break systems' defenses. Based on the nature of monitoring, IDS is classified into two types - Host Intrusion Detection System (HIDS) and Network Intrusion Detection System (NIDS). HIDS analyzes an

S. M. Thampi et al. (Eds.): SSCC 2020, CCIS 1364, pp. 244–251, 2021.
https://doi.org/10.1007/978-981-16-0422-5_17

individual system by inspecting networks and logging events. Typically, HIDS monitors the events on a system and checks the systems' logs and/or the events' logs for suspicious/malicious activity. NIDS analyzes network traffic that consists of network tap or port mirroring. A network tap is a device which captures the network traffic passing through it. Port Mirroring, on the other hand, makes a copy of the network traffic and sends it to another port for analysis. Generally, NIDS are placed at strategic points in the network to analyze network traffic where any plausible attack may happen in near term.

Broadly, an IDS works by the principle of signature/pattern-based behaviour detection or by anomaly-based detection. Signature-based IDS monitors the network traffic and match the packet characteristics against a database of known attack signatures. The drawback of using this approach is that if there is large list of signatures in the database, the matching time would be impractical for stopping an attack. Another drawback of signature-based IDS is the inability to detect new attacks, as the signature/pattern for such upcoming attack does not exist in the database. To overcome these limitations on signature-based IDS, anomaly-based IDS is commonly preferred, which can observe any abnormal behavior that deviates from the normal behavior. Anomaly-based IDS uses the network traffic to determine normal or benign traffic and then compares the incoming traffic with the baseline observation. If any anomaly or deviation from the normal behaviour exceeds a predefined threshold, the IDS raises an alarm, which not only stops the known attacks but also detects any new attacks. However, one main drawback of anomaly-based IDS is that the system hits a higher number of False Positives (FP).

In recent times, Generative Adversarial Networks [2] has shown significant potentials for discriminating anomalies from normal behaviour. Although GAN is mostly employed in image-based characteristics [3,13], the model has shown potential in other input samples. In [3], an encoder-based adversarial training is proposed, which samples data into Gaussian distribution space and then a discriminator checks whether the input comes from normal latent space or it is an anomaly.

In this paper, we present a GAN-based intrusion detection system, termed as GIDS, which trains textual data on the normal training samples and identifies anomalies with a reasonable accuracy. The proposed GIDS minimizes the mapping error without using an external encoder. In our analysis and experiment, GIDS is trained with NSL-KDD dataset [8] to prevent the system from any bias and the results show that GIDS detects anomalies with an accuracy of 83.66%, while keeping false positive rate substantially low.

The paper is organized as follows: Sect. 2 discusses the related work. Section 3 presents the proposed intrusion detection system using GAN. Section 4 provides the analysis and experimental results of the proposed GIDS. We conclude the paper with Sect. 5.

2   Related Work

Network security has been studied extensively by numerous researchers in past decades. We put our focus primarily on machine learning based IDS. Sangkat-sanee et al. [4] proposed a real-time IDS using decision trees, where several existing machine learning algorithms have been studied using decision tree, rip-per rule and neural networks. The study in [4] showed that IDS powered decision tree outperforms in terms of detection accuracy. Principle component analysis is quite successful for dimensionality reduction, where the training phase reduces time because of decrease in the number of features. Heba et al. [5] used Support Vector Machine to create an IDS using principle component analysis. Garcia-Teodoro et al. [6] and the work in [14] have discussed multiple approaches useful for anomaly detection in networks. Schlegl et al. [3] proposed a system using GAN to detect disease markers using anomaly detection. In their work [3], a deep convolutional GAN is used to train the system on benign images.

In [11], the authors proposed anomaly detection for medical images using GAN. Ganomaly was proposed in [12], which uses the original idea of AnoGAN [3] by adding an additional encoder.

3   Background and the Proposed System

3.1   Generative Adversarial Networks

Generative Adversarial Networks (GAN) [2] is generative in nature as opposed to discriminative algorithm. Discriminative algorithms classify the input data, that is, the features of the input data instance, into a category of output to which the data may belong. For example, a discriminative algorithm could predict whether a packet is an attack from the details it can gather from the packet. A discriminative algorithm gives a probability of the data instance belonging to an output class. Therefore, discriminative algorithm maps features to labels. Generative models on the other hand perform the opposite of classification. Generative algorithm gives the probability of the features given that the data instance belongs to a specific class. Using the network analogy, it can be noted that the generative algorithm tries to answer the question that how likely are these features given that a string/packet is an attack, and provides a probability for the same. In general, discriminative model learns the boundary between output classes and generative model learns the data distribution of the classes. A generative adversarial network consists of two neural networks: a generator and a discriminator. The generator generates new data instances, whereas, the discriminator tries to tell apart the real data from the generated data. One can think of the generator as a counterfeiter and the discriminator as the cop, where the counterfeiter tries to produce real samples and fool the cop and the cop's job is to identify which samples are from real data and which are the counterfeits.

3.2   Anomaly Score

Once the model using GAN has learned the real data distribution, samples are generated which can fool the discriminator. After the adversarial training is done, the model can map noise to a realistic data instance. The anomaly score of a query x tells how likely it is to be an anomaly, and based on a threshold one can classify whether it as an anomaly. To find an anomaly score for data x, one has to find the point z in the latent space that corresponds to $G(z)$, such that x and $G(z)$ are similar. The extent of similarity depends on how close x is to the data that was used to train the network. Schlegl et al. [3] proposed AnoGAN, which uses a GAN to detect anomalies on image samples. The summary of the AnoGAN is captured below, as the posed GIDS goes by the similar principles. In AnoGAN, two loses - residual and discriminator - play important roles. The residual loss measures the dissimilarity between the query data and the generated data $G(x)$, defined as:

$$L_R(z_y) = \Sigma |x - G(z_y)| \tag{1}$$

Discriminator loss is the difference in the discriminators output when the query data and the generated data $G(z)$ are passed through the discriminator. However, instead of using the scalar output of the discriminator, a new loss function was proposed which uses an intermediate feature of the discriminator.

$$L_D(z_y) = \Sigma |f(x) - f(G(z_y))| \tag{2}$$

Here, $f(.)$ is the output of an intermediate layer of the discriminator. Instead of using only the decision of the discriminator, whether or not the generated image fits the learned distribution, this new loss takes the information of the feature representation which is learned by the discriminator during the adversarial training. The overall loss as weighted sum of both components is defined as:

$$L(z_y) = (1 - \lambda).L_R(z_y) + \lambda.L_D(z_y) \tag{3}$$

Using the above equations the corresponding latent variable z is obtained by minimizing $L(z)$. The minimization is done by iterative methods. After a fixed number of iterations the anomaly score of the query data is computed.

In our proposed GIDS, we have used the similar principles of AnoGAN with the objective of anomalies detection on textual data. To detect anomalies, KDD CUP 99 dataset [7] is used, which consists of around 48,98,431 data instances each of which is a single connection [9]. In the proposed GIDS, NSL KDD dataset [8] is used. KDD'99 dataset contains 34 continuous features and 7 categorical features for a total of 41 features. Before using the 7 categorical features, they have to be one-hot encoded. What one hot encoding does is that it creates columns for all possible values for a feature and assigns '1' to the column that the particular instance belongs to and '0' to all other columns. Using this one-hot encoding technique, GIDS ends up with 126 features. The data is then normalized to between -1 and 1, so that they are at a comparable range. GIDS uses the following architectures for the generator and the discriminator for experimentation. The generator contains 4 dense layers. A dense layer is a fully connected neural network layer. The first, second, third and the fourth dense layers contain 256, 512, 1024 and 126 neurons, respectively. The relatively higher number of neurons in the generator help the generator learn more features about the dataset. Batch normalization is also used. Similar to the normalization done before providing input to the networks, the batch normalization normalizes the data, and is usually placed before the activation layers. Batch normalization reduces the amount by which the hidden unit values shift. Multiple dropout layers were also used, where the dropout method prevents over fitting. Dropout method drops out some random neurons while training which helps prevent over fitting. A dropout rate is a value between 0 and 1, which decides what percentage of neurons have to dropped out on random.

An activation function is used in GIDS that introduces non-linearity to the network. For example, ReLu (Rectified Linear Unit) [10] is one of the most widely used activation functions in neural networks. In such model, the discriminator contains 3 dense layers. The first, second and third layer contain 126, 512 and 126 neurons, respectively. In addition, there is one more dense layer which is the output of the discriminator that contains just one neuron, which uses the sigmoid activation function and essentially outputs the probability of the data originating from the real dataset. One important aspect of training a GAN is the stopping point. There is no fixed formula to calculate it; however, a good point to stop GAN training is when both the generator and the discriminator have gotten extremely good at their tasks, especially the generator. When a generator creates data which is similar to the training data and when the discriminator has a hard time telling apart real and generated data, the GAN is said to be trained. However, it is difficult to tell, if a generated sample resembles a somewhat similar sample from the real dataset. To mitigate this, one can use the outputs of the discriminator. When the losses of both the generator and the discriminator have converged sufficiently, a few samples are generated from the generator and pass them through the discriminator. The discriminator outputs how confident the discriminator is in labelling the data real or generated. If we get a value of the range 0.4 to 0.6, we can assume that the discriminator is having a hard time placing a binary label on the data sample, this it, is a good indication that the generated sample has a close resemblance to the training data. Following parameters are considered in the training and testing phases:

batch size $= 128$

epochs $= 7500$

dim z $= 100$

lr $= 0.0002$

slope of LeakyRelu $= 0.2$

dropout rate for G $= 0.5$

dropout rate for D $= 0.3$

The batch size of training was set to 128 for 7500 epochs. The input noise dimension dim_z was set to 100. The learning rate of the GIDS was set to 0.0002. The dropout rate was set to 0.5 and 0.3 for the generator and the discriminator, respectively.

4   Analysis and Experimental Results

Figure 1 depicts various losses of the GIDS during the training phase, where 'd_loss_real' is the loss of the discriminator while being trained on real data samples from the dataset, 'd_loss_fake' is the loss of the discriminator while being trained on the generated data samples created by the generator, and 'g_loss' s the loss of the proposed GIDS. The generated samples are passed on as being real data and by using the output of the discriminator the generator updates its weights accordingly. As there is no specific stopping criteria for GAN, a good point to end training is when the network is in equilibrium, that is, when the discriminator is not able to distinguish efficiently between real data and generated data. We have experimented the proposed GIDS on an Intel i7 CPU with 6 cores and 12 threads with 16 GB of RAM. The training of the GIDS took 8 min. Anomaly score was calculated for all the entries. Anomaly score for benign data was calculated with a mean of 10.36 and anomaly score for attack data was calculated with mean of 23.18. Attack data generates a higher anomaly score than benign data.

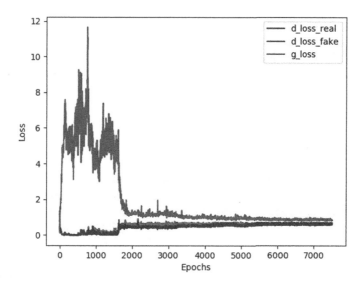

Fig. 1. Loss graph

Table 1. Confusion matrix

	Actual attack	Actual benign
Predicted attack	83.66	16.34
Predicted benign	7.67	92.33

Table 2. Comparisons of the models

	Normal	DoS attack	Probe
GAN based model	92.33	85.64	79.56
Decision Tree based model	99.43	99.17	98.73
Neural Network based model	98.60	96.37	95.72

A confusion matrix is a common way to represent the results of a classification model. There are two possible classes: attack and benign. Actual class of the data, that is, whether it actually is an attack or not. It is noted from the confusion matrix Table 1 that the GIDS model is able to detect 83.66% of all attacks. GIDS is able to classify 92.33% of the benign data correctly. As GIDS is anomaly-based, false positives observe 16.34% and false negatives stood at 7.67%. The following confusion matrix is obtained:

Setting a threshold to detect anomalies depends on the level of defenses one wants to getting away. In our experiment, a threshold value 18 is used. Table 2 provides the performance of the proposed GIDS. The table shows the classification rates of different attack types like DoS and Probe using different methods. Sangkatsanee et al. [4] shows an accuracy of 99.6%; however, they used only 10% of the KDD dataset. The proposed GIDS provides an accuracy of 96.7%, which uses the whole KDD dataset, which is more practical with reasonable accuracy than having tested the model with 10% data in the case of [4].

5   Conclusion

We discussed GAN-based intrusion detection for anomalies in perimeter defense. We proposed an adversarial generative training architecture, termed as GIDS, for an network intrusion detection system that minimizes the mapping error without the use of an external encoder. We have shown with experiments that GIDS successfully detects network intrusions for anomalies with an accuracy of 83.66%. Although GAN is commonly used for image dataset for identifying the correctness of images, we show that GAN can also be used with textual data for identifying anomalies with a reasonable accuracy.

References

1. Crothers, T.: Implementing intrusion detection systems: a hands-on guide for securing the network. Wiley (2020)
2. Goodfellow, I.J., et al.: Generative adversarial networks. Commun. ACM **63**(11), 139–144 (2014)
3. Schlegl, T., Seeböck, P., Waldstein, S.M., Schmidt-Erfurth, U., Langs, G.: Unsupervised anomaly detection with generative adversarial networks to guide marker discovery. In: Niethammer, M., et al. (eds.) IPMI 2017. LNCS, vol. 10265, pp. 146–157. Springer, Cham (2017). https://doi.org/10.1007/978-3-319-59050-9_12
4. Sangkatsanee, P., Wattanapongsakorn, N., Charnsripinyo, C.: Practical real-time intrusion detection using machine learning approaches. Comput. Commun. **34**(18), 2227–2235 (2011)
5. Heba, F.E., Darwish, A., Hassanien, A.E., Abraham, A.: Principle components analysis and support vector machine based intrusion detection system. In: Proceedings of International Conference on Intelligent Systems Design and Applications, pp. 363–367 (2010)
6. Garcia-Teodoroa, P., Diaz-Verdejoa, J., Macia-Fernandeza, G., Vazquezb, E.: Anomaly-based network intrusion detection: techniques, systems and challenges. Comput. Secur. **28**(1–2), 18–28 (2009)
7. KDD cup 1999 data. http://kdd.ics.uci.edu/databases/kddcup99/kddcup99.html
8. NSL KDD dataset. https://www.unb.ca/cic/datasets/nsl.html
9. Tavallaee, M., Bagheri, E., Lu, W., Ghorbani, A.A.: A detailed analysis of the KDD cup 99 data set. In: Proceedings of IEEE Symposium on Computational Intelligence for Security and Defense Applications, pp. 1–6 (2009)
10. Chintala, S.: How to train a GAN? tips and tricks to make GANs work (2016). https://github.com/soumith/ganhacks
11. Schlegl, T., Seebock, P., Waldstein, S.M., Langs, G., Erfurth, U.S.: f-AnoGAN: fast unsupervised anomaly detection with generative adversarial networks. Med. Image Anal. **54**, 30–44 (2019)
12. Akcay, S., Atapour-Abarghouei, A., Breckon, T.P.: GANomaly: semi-supervised anomaly detection via adversarial training. In: Jawahar, C.V., Li, H., Mori, G., Schindler, K. (eds.) ACCV 2018. LNCS, vol. 11363, pp. 622–637. Springer, Cham (2019). https://doi.org/10.1007/978-3-030-20893-6_39
13. Yi, X., Walia, E., Babyn, P.: Generative adversarial network in medical imaging: a review. Med. Image Anal. **58**, 101552 (2019)
14. Radford, A., Metz, L., Chintala, S.: Unsupervised representation learning with deep convolutional generative adversarial networks. arXiv preprint arXiv:1511.06434 (2015)

Audio Steganography Using Multi LSB and IGS Techniques

Chinmay D. Kuchinad, N. Chiranjeevi, Kartik Vishnu Hegde, and Shikha Tripathi(✉)

Department of Electronics and Communication Engineering, PES University, Bengaluru, India
shikha.eee@gmail.com

Abstract. With advances in communication technologies and the flow of enormous amount of data, the need for providing a secure pathway for the same has become a necessity. In this paper, different methodologies are explored to find an efficient steganographic method for embedding one form of data into another, with the aim of enhancing data security. The proposed approach involves embedding an image into an audio signal. Image encryption methods are also explored with the intention of adding an extra layer of security to the system. The proposed system shows improvement in capacity and SNR. Various attacks are carried out on the stego signal to check the robustness of the resulting steganographic system.

Keywords: Audio steganography · Data hiding · Least Significant Bit · IGS quantization

1 Introduction

Steganography is the practice of concealing a file, message, image or video within another file, message, image or video [1]. The word steganography derives its origin from the Latin word *steganographia* which in turn is the combination of the Greek words *steganos* and *graphia* meaning "covered or concealed" and "writing" respectively. Multimedia data hiding techniques have developed a strong basis for steganography with a wide range of applications in various fields like covert communications, data management and managing digital rights. In an ideal steganographic system, visual cues about the presence of secret data within the cover medium should be minimum or absent. This basically implies that upon visual inspection, the cover and secret data should be indistinguishable.

The performance of a steganographic system is measured based on its robustness, imperceptibility, capacity and accurate extraction of the secret data at the receiver end. While encryption techniques have been long in use for the purpose of data security, they may arouse suspicion no matter how unbreakable they are resulting in data being obtained by third parties. Meanwhile, in steganography, the changes are so subtle that someone not specifically looking for data is

S. M. Thampi et al. (Eds.): SSCC 2020, CCIS 1364, pp. 252–261, 2021.
https://doi.org/10.1007/978-981-16-0422-5_18

unlikely to find it. Steganography is broadly classified into image steganography, audio steganography, text steganography and video steganography based on the host used.

This work deals with audio steganography where an audio file is selected as the host medium and secret image data is embedded into it. Different genres and durations of audio files have been used for the same. For the ease of implementation, the audio files are first converted into their image equivalents and then the embedding is carried out. A discrete wavelet transform based algorithm is used to achieve the same. There are many methods for embedding secret data into an image, the most common being Least Significant Bit (LSB) and Discrete Wavelet Transform (DWT) based techniques. The LSB method is used in this work and for further enhancing the embedding capacity, multiple LSB approaches coupled with Improved Grayscale Quantization(IGS) is employed.

Rest of the paper is structured as follows. Section 2 describes the literature review. Section 3 elaborates the proposed methodology and Sect. 4 highlights the results and observations. Section 5 concludes the paper.

2   Literature Review

With the increased flow of data due to the advancements in internet technologies, the development of secure data transmission systems has become the need of the hour. Extensive studies have been carried out in the steganographic domain too which are aimed at improving the robustness and capacity.

The effectiveness of any steganographic system is estimated mainly based on its imperceptibility, capacity and robustness. Keeping these in mind, in this work, it was decided that audio would be chosen as the host medium since it offers high capacity, i.e. more data could be hidden in it. Even though Human Auditory System (HAS) is more sensitive than Human visual system (HVS) [2], there will always be some distortions that occur so frequently in any audio that the Human Auditory System tends to ignore them. These are exploited in audio steganography.

An efficient steganographic system should satisfy the following requirements: (1) Imperceptibility - The stego signal embedded with the secret message should be indistinguishable from the original one, which can guarantee that it does not become suspicious about the existence of the secret message within the cover signal. (2) High capacity: the maximum size of the secret message that can be embedded should be as long as possible [3]. Other performance metrics include Signal-to-Noise Ratio(SNR), Peak Signal-to-Noise Ratio(PSNR), Structural Similarity Index (SSIM).

In this paper, an audio steganographic scheme based on wavelet-based audio-to-image transform is proposed [4,5]. The original audio signal is first transformed using wavelet transform and then the coefficients of the wavelet transform are sampled and rearranged to attain an image form of the audio signal. Through this method, the audio steganographic problem will be converted into an image steganographic one which has been extensively studied and successfully resolved [6]. The secret data is then embedded into the cover medium using Least Significant Bit(LSB) method at the transmitter end. Subsequent extraction process at the receiver end uses the same LSB based approach. The conventional Least Significant Bit modification technique is vulnerable to steganalysis [7]. In order to ensure that the resulting system is efficient (i.e., it performs well with respect to the performance parameters chosen) and to enhance the capacity of the existing system, a modified approach involving Multiple LSB method [8] coupled with Improved Grayscale Quantization (IGS) is used. An additional layer of security is added by means of an XOR cipher that provides a key-based encryption method before steganography is performed.

3   Proposed Methodology

In this work, the audio medium is selected as the host to embed the secret data. The audio files are first converted into their image equivalents using a DWT based algorithm [9] followed by multi LSB embedding and extraction [10]. Following is the workflow adopted in detail (Fig. 1).

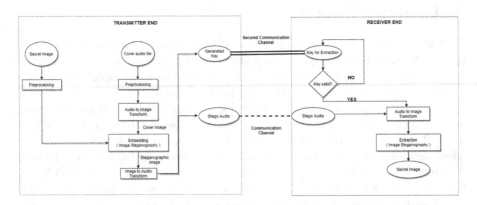

Fig. 1. Block diagram of proposed methodology

3.1   Transmitter End

Pre-processing. The Image: the input secret image can either be grayscale or colour. So to maintain a common format and to embed higher dimension images, the secret image is converted into grayscale.

$$Grayscale = 0.299 * R + 0.587 * G + 0.114 * B \tag{1}$$

Where, Grayscale is the output and R, G, B are the Red, Green and Blue channels of the input colour image respectively.

The Audio: the input host audio can have 2 channels (stereo) or only one channel (mono). To maintain a general format, the audio is converted to mono audio format.

Audio to Image Transform. The ultimate result of the proposed stegano-graphic model is to conceal an image file within a cover audio file. But internally this is converted into an image in image steganographic system to make the operations easier. The first step towards doing this is to have an image representation of the cover audio. Discrete Wavelet Transform(DWT) is applied on the pre-processed host audio to obtain first level approximate and detailed DWT coefficients. Subsequently DWT is applied on the first level approximate coefficients to obtain second level coefficients. The required second level detailed coefficients are chosen, their dimensions are determined . The level of the detailed coefficient 'cdx' is considered as a parameter for analyzing the output and then it will be set to the level which gives the better result. Since the detailed coefficients are one dimensional, it has to be converted to 2-Dimensional to give it image like structure, this 2-Dimensional matrix can called as the cover image for image steganographic method. The dimensions obtained are used to reshape the coefficients by row-major ordering to obtain 'Ih' and subsequently normalized (for the range 0 to 1).

$$Normalized = (Ih - minIh)/(maxIh - minIh)$$

Where, Ih is the Host Image/Cover Image 2D matrix, minIh and maxIh are the minimum and maximum values of the matrix Ih.

The 'maxIh' and the 'minIh' values are noted down (upto 8 places after decimal point) and shared with the intended receiver because these values are considered as the 'keys' for the LSB embedding technique for increasing the security. The array is then scaled and converted to uint8 format. The image equivalent of the cover audio is thus obtained.

Embedding. The 2-Dimensional image obtained from the preceding stage is converted into 1-Dimensional by Row major ordering or Column major ordering. The pixel intensity values of the cover image are converted into 8 bit binary format representation. If the parameter 'igs' is set to 1, then IGS quantization is used with the secret image, it is converted to binary representation with quantization level specified by the parameter 'qLevel'. The bits required to represent a secret image will be reduced with some loss of quality. If the parameter 'igs' is set to 0, then convert all the pixel intensity values of the secret image into 8 bit binary format representation. The bits of secret image are arranged in a column wise fashion and the bits of the cover image pixels are replaced, starting from the 1st LSB of each intensity of the cover image pixel, until all the bits of 'nth' LSB specified by the parameter 'numberOfLSB' is reached or total number of bits of secret image is reached, whichever is earlier, with that of the bits of the column wise arranged secret image binary value. The 8 bit ASCII format is converted back into 8 bit unsigned integer format representation. The result obtained is rearranged into 2-Dimensional form by Row or Column major ordering which has to be done in the opposite manner to what was done earlier. The resultant image is the Steganographic Image.

Image to Audio Transform. Image to audio transform is applied to convert the encrypted steganographic image to detailed coefficients and then to the steganographic audio. The steganographic image will be of 8 bit unsigned integer format. Denormalization is done to get back the coefficients in the original range.

$$denormalization = (stegoImg/255) * (maxIh - minIh) + minIh$$

Where stegoImg is the steganographic image obtained, minIh and maxIh are the minimum and maximum values of the Host or Cover Image.

After the denormalization, the obtained values are considered as reconstructed detailed coefficients. These coefficients alongwith detailed and approximate coefficients of the wavelet transform of Cover Audio file, the Steganographic Audio is constructed with the help of 'Inverse Wavelet Transform'. The obtained coefficients are the representation of the steganographic audio file, and then using 'audiowrite' function in MATLAB, the coefficients are written as audio file with the '.wav' extension with specified sampling frequency. This completes the steps involved at the transmitter end.

Improved Grayscale Quantization. The Improved Grayscale Quantization or IGS is a type of image coding or lossy compression technique where data is coded by taking 'psycho-visual redundancy' into consideration. The term psycho-visual redundancy is called so because the Human Visual System(HVS) does not respond to all the intensity information with equal sensitivity. The advantage of IGS is that it reduces the false contouring which is very common if normal quantization is used for compression. But quantization is a lossy compression technique, the data cannot be perfectly reconstructed. With the higher IGS quantization level, i.e the number of bits of IGS code, which approximately represent original intensity value, the loss of information is reduced. The balanced trade off between quality of secret image and capacity is what is achieved with the use of IGS quantization.

3.2   Receiver End

Audio to Image Transform. The stego audio generated at the transmitter end is sent over the channel and at the receiver end it is decomposed into 3 levels using wavelet transform using 'haar' or 'db5' wavelet, whichever is set at the transmitter end. The level of detailed coefficient is set same as the level chosen at the transmitter end. The discrete wavelet transform with the appropriate wavelet (which has to be same as the parameter set at the transmitter side) to get all the approximate and detailed coefficients. The one dimensional vector thus obtained is converted into two dimensional image representation which is then normalised and converted into 8 bit representation form. This 8 bit unsigned integer represented matrix is the extracted steganographic image which will be fed as input to the extraction algorithm.

Extraction. The number of rows and columns of the secret image that has to be extracted is based on the aspect ratio and total number of pixels of the cover image extracted. The number of rows or columns of the secret image embedded is given to the receiver as the key for extraction. If any of these exceeds the capacity of embedding, then resizing is done at the pre-processing stage. The extracted steganographic image is converted to 8 bit binary format. Select the first Least Significant Bit of every pixel of the steganographic image and arrange in a column form. Proceed to the next LSB and repeat the procedure until all the bits have been extracted. These bits are grouped based on the quantisation level chosen. The grouped bits are converted into decimal representation. Multiply The decimal representation of grouped bits at 'qLevel' (Quantisation level chosen) at a time with 2 raised to the power (8-qLevel), thus obtaining the IGS decoded value. The resulting column vector is converted to 8 bit unsigned integer format and rearranged into 2-Dimensional format with the appropriate rows and columns. The matrix thus obtained is the extracted secret image.

4   Results and Observations

In 'Audio Steganography', the main purpose is hiding secret information in the cover audio file, without letting the unauthorised person know the presence of secret data in the steganographic audio.

The algorithm implemented is tested with Haar and Daubechies 5 (db5) wavelet and with audios of 5 different genres namely, classical, jazz, metal, pop and rock. The testing is done with hiding the data up to Least Significant Bit 6 and with IGS quantization of levels 4,5 and 6. The horizontal axis of the chart below indicates the input combination of test data.

The conclusions drawn from Fig. 2, Fig. 3 is that, with the increase in the number of LSB embedding, the quality of steganographic audio decreases. Use of 'db5' wavelet is better than 'haar' in terms of quality of audio of steganographic audio. The audios of classical and jazz genre give far better results both in terms of PSNR of stego audio and SSIM of the extracted image with the original. Since the music genre of pop, metal and rock contains high frequencies, the loss of information is high while normalization. Figure 4 indicates embedding capacity only depends on the level of Least Significant Bits available for embedding. It doesn't depend on the wavelet, audio genre used. The capacity of embedding doubles with every increase in the level of LSB used. The higher level of LSBs used for embedding, the higher is the embedding capacity. The input image is quantized using IGS quantization method has a direct effect on the capacity of embedding. Figure 5 indicates the effect of quantization level on the embedding capacity when different levels of LSBs used for data hiding. Figure 6 indicates as the capacity of embedding increases the PSNR between stego audio and original audio decreases. Table 1 shows the comparison of the performance of the different audio steganographic method with that of the proposed method.

Considering the cover audio of 50 s long, sampled at 44.1 kHz and quantized at 16 bits per sample, using the steganographic method used in [6], a maximum

Audio PSNR ('haar' v/s. 'db5')

without IGS quantization

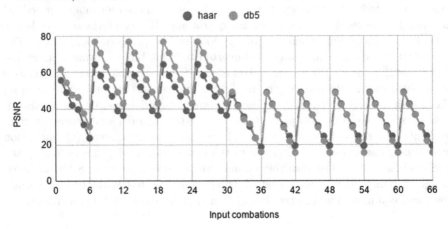

Fig. 2. Comparison of PSNR of steganographic audio with haar v/s db5 with embedding up to 6 least significant bit

SSIM ('haar' v/s. 'db5')

without IGS quantization

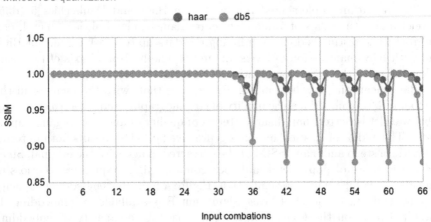

Fig. 3. Comparison of structural similarity of the extracted image with haar v/s db5 with embedding up to 6 least significant bit

of 28000 bits can be embedded (or equivalent to 560 bps). Using the cover audio of the same type mentioned in [6], we have achieved a maximum embedding capacity of 6610800 bits (or equivalent to 132216 bps) in the cover audio, using Multiple Least significant bit data hiding technique using LSBs up to 6. The previously mentioned result is with the audio quality of steganographic audio

Capacity (bps)

without IGS quantization

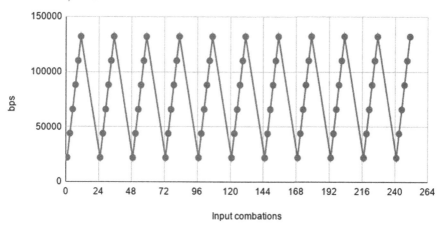

Fig. 4. Comparison of hiding capacity of the secret image with up to 6 least significant bit embedding without IGS quantization

Table 1. Comparison of performance of different audio steganographic methods.

	Secret data Type	Hiding capacity (max)	Stego SNR (max)
Proposed Method (Multi LSB embedding with IGS Quantization)	Image	264275	52.64
W. Sun, R. Shen, F. Yu and Z. Lu [6]	Text	560	48.18
S. Shirali-Shahreza and M. T. Manzuri-Shalmani [11]	Data	230000	35
Ali, Ahmed Hussain, Mohd Rosmadi Mokhtar and Loay E. George [8]	Data	176400	73.9

around 52, but with all 8 LSB used to hide data, the maximum embedding capacity will be 176273 bps with quality of steganographic audio reduced to 45. The method in this paper uses Multiple LSB embedding technique and IGS quantization which balances the trade-off between embedding capacity, quality of steganographic audio and perceptual quality of secret image for extraction. In [11], as embedding capacity increases, quality of audio decreases which might lead to suspicion of secret data embedded by unauthorised persons. With the same quality of steganographic audio, the proposed method achieves higher capacity using IGS quantization technique. The method proposed in this paper yields better result compared to the previous steganographic systems, and also this one has more capacity, better security and better perceptual quality of the extracted image.

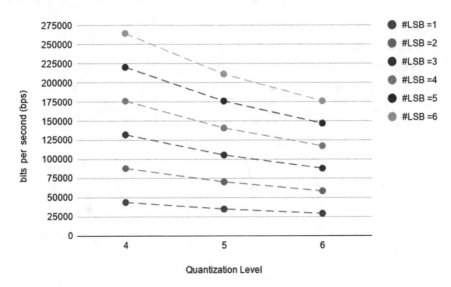

Fig. 5. Maximum Embedding Capacity v/s. quantization level 4,5 and 6 with Level of LSBs used for data hiding 1 to 6

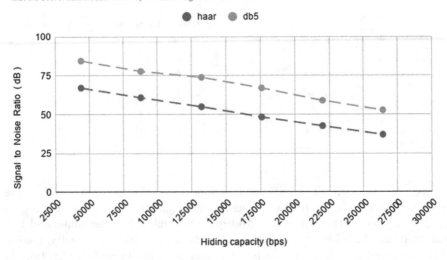

Fig. 6. Maximum Embedding Capacity v/s. SNR (dB) with haar and db5 with secret image quantization level 4

5   Conclusion and Future Work

This paper discusses an efficient audio steganographic system where the capacity of data that can be hidden and transmitted has been enhanced while also making sure that there is minimal or no data corruption during extraction at the receiver end. Multiple LSB method helps in enhancing the capacity of the system significantly while Improved Gray Scale Quantization helps in ensuring the Structural Similarity Index of the extracted data to the original data that was transmitted data is within desired levels. The cryptographic method used provides an additional layer of security making the system highly secure. This work can be further improved upon by looking at ways to increase the embedding capacity while maintaining the good steganographic audio quality with the LSB technique. Techniques can be formulated to show robustness even with lossy compression attacks such as mp3 compression. The executable file for the developed method for real-world applications can be developed.

References

1. Provos, N., Honeyman, P.: Hide and seek: an introduction to steganography. IEEE Secur. Priv. **1**(3), 32–44 (2003). https://doi.org/10.1109/MSECP.2003.1203220
2. Gopalan, K.: Audio steganography using bit modification. In: International Conference on Multimedia and Expo., Baltimore, MD, USA, pp. I–629 (2003). https://doi.org/10.1109/ICME.2003.1220996
3. Tan, D., Lu, Y., Yan, X., Wang, X.: A simple review of audio steganography. In: 3rd Information Technology, Networking, Electronic and Automation Control Conference (ITNEC), Chengdu, pp. 1409–1413(2019). https://doi.org/10.1109/ITNEC.2019.8729476
4. Santosa, R.A., Bao, P.: Audio-to-image wavelet transform based audio steganography. In: 47th International Symposium ELMAR., Zadar, pp. 209–212 (2005). https://doi.org/10.1109/ELMAR.2005.193679
5. Shahreza, S., Shalmani, M.T.: High capacity error free wavelet domain speech steganography. In: 2008 IEEE International Conference on Acoustics, Speech and Signal Processing, Las Vegas, NV, pp. 1729–1732 (2008). https://doi.org/10.1109/ICASSP.2008.4517963
6. Sun, W., Shen, R., Yu, F., Lu, Z.: Data hiding in audio based on audio-to-image wavelet transform and vector quantization. In: 2012 Eighth International Conference on Intelligent Information Hiding and Multimedia Signal Processing, Piraeus, pp. 313–316 (2012). https://doi.org/10.1109/IIH-MSP.2012.82
7. Asad, M., Gilani, J., Khalid, A.: An enhanced least significant bit modification technique for audio steganography. In: International Conference on Computer Networks and Information Technology., Abbottabad, pp. 143–147 (2011). https://doi.org/10.1109/ICCNIT.2011.6020921
8. Cvejic, N., Seppanen, T.: Increasing the capacity of LSB-based audio steganography. In: IEEE Workshop on Multimedia Signal Processing, St.Thomas, VI, USA, pp. 336–338 (2002). https://doi.org/10.1109/MMSP.2002.1203314
9. Kaul, N., Bajaj, N.: Audio in image steganography using wavelet transform. Int. J. Comput. Appl. **79**, 7–10 (2013). https://doi.org/10.5120/13719-1502
10. Thangadurai, K., Sudha Devi, G.: An analysis of LSB based image steganography techniques. In: 2014 International Conference on Computer Communication and Informatics, Coimbatore, pp. 1–4 (2014). https://doi.org/10.1109/ICCCI.2014.6921751
11. Shirali-Shahreza, S., Manzuri-Shalmani, M.T.: Adaptive wavelet domain audio steganography with high capacity and low error rate. In: International Conference on Information and Emerging Technologies, Karachi, pp. 1–5 (2007). https://doi.org/10.1109/ICIET.2007.4381305

A Forensic Analysis on the Availability of MQTT Network Traffic

Naga Venkata Hrushikesh Chunduri[✉] and Ashok Kumar Mohan[✉]

TIFAC-CORE in Cyber Security, Amrita School of Engineering, Coimbatore,
Amrita Viswa Vidyapeetham, Coimbatore, India
cb.en.p2cys19004@cb.students.amrita.edu, m_ashokkumar@cb.amrita.edu

Abstract. IoT is a diversified technology which have large scalability integrating hardware and software components. IoT comprises of protocols that are light weight, sensors which are attached to field components and finally software that integrates all the above. These light weight protocols are prone to have many security issues which among one is MQTT protocol that operates with client/server architecture. Our work focuses on showcasing the poor impact of security measures on the protocol by attacking MQTT brokers which act like servers. We have performed intrusion and denial of service attack on publicly available MQTT test brokers to obtain sensitive information and validate it's security implications. We also have mentioned our observations in machine learning built random forest algorithm to detect the attack logs and the reasons to shift for a forensic approach.

Keywords: MQTT · MQTT Malaria · DoS · Challanges in IoT forensics

1 Introduction

1.1 Overview of MQTT

MQTT is the most prevalent protocol used for IoT devices to communicate. It stands for Message Queuing Telemetry Transport, and was developed in the late 1990s. As it abbreviates for carrying small telemetry messages, its usage was mainly for industrial automation with low bandwidth, low power usage and high latency data links. The protocol doesn't confine for a predefined format for carrying a payload and it operates through subscriber/publisher architecture. MQTT working can be briefed as: A broker that acts as a medium for all the communicating devices that are connected to it ie., with any appropriate name titled as topic, any client can publish their information to the broker and any client who knows the topic name can subscribe to it [13]. Before the advent of MQTT protocol almost 80% of the information regarding the devices at remote location cannot be accessible which paved a strong requirement for this protocol

© Springer Nature Singapore Pte Ltd. 2021
S. M. Thampi et al. (Eds.): SSCC 2020, CCIS 1364, pp. 262–274, 2021.
https://doi.org/10.1007/978-981-16-0422-5_19

usage. This protocol serves as great advantage for scalability of low computational devices for fast broadcasting the messages and it was implicitly included in IoT environment.

Components of MQTT:

1. **Topic:**A label that is directing the MQTT clients to share and identify appropriate information
2. **Message:**Data that clients share through the broker
3. **Broker:**A medium by which all clients share information through publishing and subscribing.
4. **Publish & subscribe**: Sending and retrieving data to/from the broker respectively.

1.2   Vulnerabilities, Attacks and Reasons

MQTT protocol is a subset of WSN (Wireless Sensor Neworks) which is becoming an appealing technology emerging in IoT. In 2019, Ismail et al. [1] explained lack of proper implementation in infrastructure and vital importance of CIA triad. They [1] highlighted the scalability of the attacks and their taxonomies which are classified into active and passive. Most of the attack possibilities mentioned by them are possible by the sensitive information we revealed in Sects. 3.2 and 3.3. Securing our information plays a vital role and the communication protocols in IoT devices will not offer a comprehensive security mechanism. The packet format, useful commands for communication and the functioning of each command has been widely discussed. We will not cover protocol format as there are many articles that can be much useful for a better understanding and diving deep into the packet inspection [2,23]. As MQTT is said to be a light weight protocol, we need to understand the word "light weight". Protocol offers security measures like SSL/TLS, authorisation and encryption as an "option", which is not advisable because of the alarming statistics by SHODAN which says about 112,950 (28-may-2020) MQTT brokers are using port 1883, default port reserved for mqtt over TCP/IP. Few other points were described by Andy et al. [3] which says the reasons

1. Resource Constrained Device (limited computational performance)
2. Vast Number of Devices (more connected, more security)
3. Lack of Awareness

IoT devices have limited computational capabilities, in terms of RAM, ROM and limited memory. They [3] also have added the packet analysis of MQTT logs which lack the CIA triad and mentioned about the botnet attacks over MQTT through bot master which resulted in launching of DDoS attack on MQTT Clients. Another vulnerability is usage of wildcards # and +. The reason it is coined as a 'vulnerability' is because, there are publicly available 'test brokers' which don't require any of security implementations (optional). We can connect to them and can obtain all the messages regardless of the topic through

#, this is be termed as an intrusion into a broker. In second section of analysis Sect. 3.2 we have shown the information obtained by intruding. Aim of this paper is to showcase and analyse poor implementations in the protocol by two different attacking scenarios. The next section is divided into 3 categories of mitigation strategies and details about the existing approaches in addressing the security issues in MQTT. Among the 3, forensics analysis was less exploited so, in Sect. 3.1 we have mentioned our observations on the challenges in IoT Forensics.

2   Related Works

2.1   Additional Layer of Security and Suggestion Frameworks

In 2018, Rahman et al. [4] introduced a framework called S-MQTT which provides multi-tier authentication mechanism for the protocol. They [4] also compared RSA and ECC cryptographic algorithms with various parameters like time taken for key generation, data/code memory where ECC offered a better light weight communication. Cruz-Piris et al. [5], in 2018, proposed a easy and secure scheme a for data in sensors and actuators. They have chosen an UMA, (OAuth) 2.0 for users to have protected resources. In 2019, Palmieri et al. [6] came up with a tool that assist the implementation of safe MQTT brokers - MQTTSA. This architecture will determine the flaws and give a detailed overview report of vulnerabilities, their severity and offer proper mitigations to be done via snippets of safe code and hints. In 2019, a better confidentiality and integrity than symmetric encryption algorithms have been achieved by Dinculeană et al. [7] with a Value-to-Keyed-Hash Message Authentication Code (Value-to-HMAC) mapping by implementing a Keyed-Hash Message Authentication Code generation algorithm.

2.2   IDS and Machine Learning

IoT systems are time critical, So, by adding a layer of security in some way or the other, generating a session key and distributing through SSL/TLS reduces the performance of MQTT. A lot of attacks are possible where, DoS is very rampant for MQTT. So, at network level to defend against the attacks on the devices few IDS mechanisms were introduced which among one is in 2013, Raza et al. [8] came up with a novel IDS framework called SVELTE for 6LoWPAN networks which can be personalised for WSNs also. They have focused IDS to detect and alert from data altering, spoofing and sinkhole attacks. In 2019, Haripriya et al. [9] came up with a fuzzy approach at network level for MQTT brokers which is a lightweight IDS unlike snort, that is able to stop and alert us based on the rules that are dynamically updated using Fuzzy interpolation. Their [9] framework proposes two ratios: CMR and CAMR. The fuzzy rule engine selects the rule and decides whether the request is a legitimate or not by those 2 ratios. Defuzzification converts the complex inputs into a simple output. In 2019 yet again, Alaiz-Moreton et al. [10] came up with a machine learning approach, mainly ensemble models to classify DoS attack. They further classified intrusion and MiTM attacks. Their model [10] got an accuracy of 99.337 for random forest and 99.373 for boosting gradient. There are numerous other approaches in machine learning that are effectively detecting DoS attacks. But, we have observed some limitations with regard to the features and as a proof of concept, We will analyse the provided data set by [10] and draw some conclusions further in Sect. 3.4.

2.3   Forensic Approach

At device level, Shah et al. [11] have done a memory forensic analysis on Brokers and clients by simulating them. They have mentioned 5 sensitive parameters that MQTT brokers reveal, which are:

1. IP address of broker and client
2. Topic name
3. Message sent by the subscriber
4. Location of broker
5. Client ID.

This memory dump analysis done with 5 different brokers where every broker almost revealed all the above mentioned information. The same analysis is done on 3 different MQTT clients which in addition exposed the username and password. Anthraper, et al. [12] done a comprehensive analysis on CIA triad along with authentication, authorisation, sensitive information and the security issues in MQTT. Both these works are confined for brokers that are privately configured in their systems. Now, our work highlights on testing the efficacy of publicly available MQTT (test) brokers by exploiting them, collect the logs in wire shark through which a hex dump analysis on random samples have uncovered sensitive data.

3   Analysis

3.1   Challenges in IoT Forensics

IoT forensics is an evolving and challenging domain that have a wide range of issues because the device configurations. Extraction of data from devices in a privacy preserving manner becomes a hurdle. As IoT is not limited to devices, its forensics investigation can have a culmination of cloud, network and device forensics. We have observed a wide range of challenges that are listed below. To add few solutions for the challenges, there is DFaaS (Digital-Forensics-as-a-service) where cloud service provides are ought to provide forensic data of the IoT ecosystem that it is connected with. A cross-layer forensic investigation is carried for IIoT devices by correlating with the OSI layers so as to get effective information from the networking attacks. Figure 1 is inspired from the work done by Rondeau et al. [14] which gives a insight of availability of information at different layers. Our work is concentrated on an application layer protocol by analysing its hex dump of the attack payloads (Table 1).

Table 1. Challenges in IoT forensics

Less memory space	Data can be easily altered
Difficult to replicate because of size	More hardware/software configurations
Limited temporal information and metadata	Limited available tools
Ambiguity in laws and compliance rules	Cloud security issues

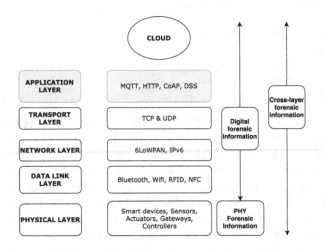

Fig. 1. Availability of forensic information for IoT layer protocols

3.2 Intrusion into MQTT Broker

The publish subscribe architecture with possible attack scenario is shown in Fig. 2. Clients for a typical MQTT broker can mostly be a sensor/smart devices, mobile and a computer/laptop. Majority of the clients would be sensors and smart devices that continuously send data to the broker. Our main purpose is to exploit the sensitive data from these sensors. Intrusion attack can be done with a simple wildcard # in the subscribe option (mqtt.fx as client) is shown in Fig. 3, which is connected to a test broker (mqtt.eclipse.org). Surprisingly we got over 14,756 messages irrespective of topics with QOS 0 in just 5 seconds. We have collected over 18,619 samples by intruding into the test broker and analysed random samples to find vulnerable and sensitive information. The statistics of evidence files are shown in Table 2 and the repository link is given here.

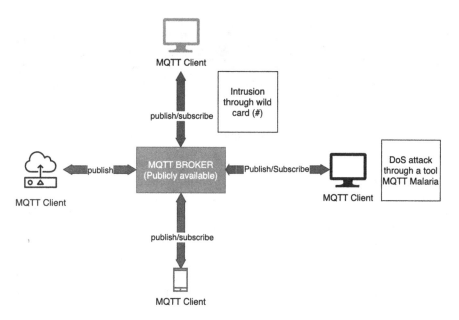

Fig. 2. An architecture of MQTT broker and clients with attack scenario.

Fig. 3. An instance of MQTT.fx client for the subscribe message #.

Table 2. Statistics of evidence files provided

Name of the File	MD5 of the File	Samples collected
DoS.csv	**55486abc7f58cadae6e0af08399a1dfa**	94,626
#eclipse.pcapng	**6db27117222e3598b7a53735bf2018fe**	18,619
hivedos.pcapng	**522ba13a50ca8d93199982a5ffd778f6**	39,078
modifiedDoS.csv	**a2a0fadabf7759c61c3f6cb1c38bac7f**	94,626
myDoS.csv	**a84fde2ee8ee60479917f238e0f2d92e**	57,698

2278	334.778166	137.135.83.217	172.20.10.2	MQTT	1214	Publish Message [wled/mesa/v], Publish Message [Codesysr
2279	334.778247	137.135.83.217	172.20.10.2	MQTT	1214	Publish Message [CodesysMqtt1284284166/MQTTWill/Codesys
2280	334.778365	137.135.83.217	172.20.10.2	MQTT	1214	Publish Message [grow/wi/room1/sensors/moisture/2/min],
2281	334.778367	137.135.83.217	172.20.10.2	MQTT	1214	Publish Message [grow/wi/room1/sensors/moisture/1/defau
2282	334.797491	137.135.83.217	172.20.10.2	MQTT	1214	Publish Message [grow/wi/room1/sensors/temphumid/1/temp
2283	334.797494	137.135.83.217	172.20.10.2	MQTT	1214	Publish Message [grow/wi/room1/sensors/light/1/percent]
2284	334.797494	137.135.83.217	172.20.10.2	MQTT	1214	Publish Message [grow/wi/room1/sensors/water/1/enable],
2285	334.797495	137.135.83.217	172.20.10.2	MQTT	1214	Publish Message [grow/wi/room1/sensors/pump/3/value], P
2286	334.801203	137.135.83.217	172.20.10.2	MQTT	1214	Publish Message [grow/wi/room1/sensors/tank/2/value], P
2287	334.834193	137.135.83.217	172.20.10.2	MQTT	1214	Publish Message [grow/wi/room1/sensors/tank/value], Pub
2288	334.834196	137.135.83.217	172.20.10.2	MQTT	1214	Publish Message [grow/mi/room1/sensors/moisture/1/water
2289	334.838192	137.135.83.217	172.20.10.2	MQTT	1214	Publish Message [grow/mi/room1/sensors/water/1/value],
2290	334.874248	137.135.83.217	172.20.10.2	MQTT	1214	Publish Message [sadsnknxjvxc], Publish Message [cc3200,

Fig. 4. Wireshark snippet highlighting sensors

All the information mentioned in Fig. 5 and 6 are from the file (#eclipse. pcapng) and based on log files collected from wireshark we can see the topic names highlighted for different sensors in random which is shown in Fig. 4. From Fig. 5a we can get the BSSID which is the MAC address of WAP and its IP address. We can know the sensor's manufacturer, version, its schema, device configurations and its MAC address which is shown in Fig. 5b. Figure 6a, 6b gives information about the ip addresses of sensors that are attached to a pump and tank. These data about sensors pave a high risk security threat to the IoT devices by leading to attacks such as IP spoofing, Eavesdropping and tampering for sensors/smart devices as MQTT clients. As many of the major decisions for IoT smart devices are based on sensor values, altering or turning off them will make a big difference in functionality for Industrial IoT systems in particular. A large section of cyber attacks are possible if IP addresses are known for PC/Laptops behaving as MQTT clients.

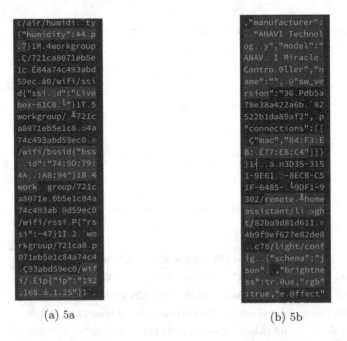

(a) 5a   (b) 5b

Fig. 5. Evidences for intrusion attack

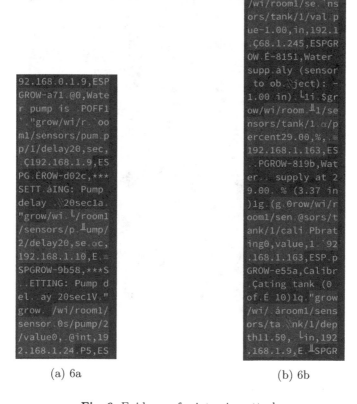

(a) 6a   (b) 6b

Fig. 6. Evidences for intrusion attack

3.3   DoS Attack on MQTT Broker

The previous works haven't done an Hex analysis of DoS attack logs. There are many publicly available test brokers. Lack of awareness is leading to disclosure of sensitive information. Many IoT practitioners, who are using MQTT for divergent purpose, are not configuring their own local host Brokers, instead they rely on these test brokers. So, we have chosen a publicly available MQTT broker (broker.hivemq.com) and performed DoS attack with a tool called MQTT Malaria that is widely used for testing the scalability and load behaviour of MQTT environments. We can also customise the payload and processes to be sent for the attack and collected logs through wire shark and observed a pattern for PUBLISH messages in DoS attack which is obvious, showing a ratio of messages that are successful to the messages that are fixed as a payload. We can also see the string "malaria-beem-lodr" in client ID which cannot be modified and static. All the snippets are combined and shown in Fig. 7 and from the file (hivedos.pcapng) mentioned in Table 2.

Fig. 7. Client ID and pattern showing success to fixed payload ratio

3.4   Observations on Machine Learning Approach

Few of the existing approaches that are detecting DoS attack are using scenario specific features ie., there is a less chance of probability for these models to classify dynamic data other than the data set that is considered. Also, the importance for the features must be equally distributed among the attributes so as to construct a optimal classifier. This analysis is done on an existing data set that has been published by Alaiz-Moreton et al. [10]. We took the same data set for DoS attack and applied the same ensemble approach - random forest. The reason to perform this is importance for the attributes are not optimally distributed. We have plotted a variable importance graph shown in Fig. 8, for the data set which have 43 features and the rest are eliminated as random forest cannot handle categorical predictors more than 53. We got slightly more accuracy which is 99.82. MeanDecreaseGini can be interpreted as higher value indicates higher variable importance. From Fig. 8, this model is constructed based on 9–13 features which are given more priority. We further extracted those particular 13 best features (modifiedDos.csv) and build a model to observe for an accuracy drop. But, as the graph suggested, we got an accuracy of 99.8. To cross verify our result, we have taken our own samples (myDoS.csv) with the same features (9) and got the accuracy 99.8. Variable importance graphs for both are given in Fig. 9a, 9b. Importance for the features may vary with data being different. The reason for having same accuracy is because all these models are built and dependent on few features which are static. From these observations we can say that, those 9 best features are sufficient to train our model, which saves a lot of computational complexity for the classifier to train. On the other hand, this can also be understood as there is a need to pass more dynamic data for evaluating the performance of our models which can be done by generative adversarial model (GAN). This is also a reason to switch for a forensic outlook, having limitations with machine learning approach (Table 3).

Table 3. Performance comparision

Classifier	9 best features	43 features
Random forest	99.82	99.337

mqtt.fit.rf

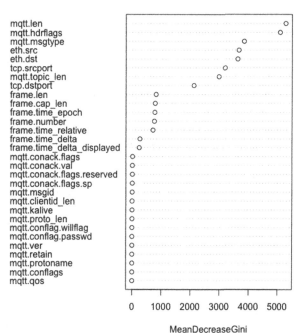

Fig. 8. Variable importance graph

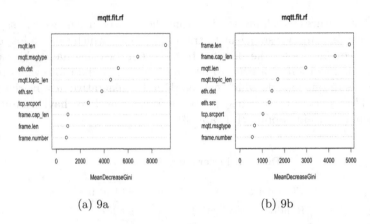

(a) 9a   (b) 9b

Fig. 9. VarImp graphs for (9a) modified and (9b) new datasets

4   Conclusion and Future Work

In this paper, we have showcased the vast usage of primary version in the protocol and exploited by intruding into a test broker to grab a random IP/MAC addresses of sensors, version, configuration etc. that puts our sensitive information at stake. This can be understood as a poor impact of security on MQTT protocol. Inspite of many frameworks and the patches that MQTT protocol undergone in Sect. 2.1 which are comparatively way better than a basic MQTT implementation, lack of awareness among the users and our deduction from Sects. 3.2 and 3.3 proved conversely because security is offered as an option. We can overcome this mostly by creating awareness about the severity of risk involved in using the test brokers, mandating and upgrading to newer versions where the older cannot be downgraded. Our future work focuses on two aspects, first is by testing the performance of machine learning models built by generating synthetic data through GAN and automating the hex dump into to a file rather than a manual analysis. Second is to propose multi class classification techniques on the malware network traffic in IoT devices.

References

1. Butun, I., Österberg, P., Song, H.: Security of the internet of things: vulnerabilities, attacks, and countermeasures. IEEE Commun. Surv. Tutor. **22**(1), 616–644 (2019)
2. Yassein, M.B., et al.: Internet of things: survey and open issues of MQTT protocol. In: 2017 International Conference on Engineering & MIS (ICEMIS). IEEE (2017)
3. Andy, S., Rahardjo, B., Hanindhito, B.: Attack scenarios and security analysis of MQTT communication protocol in IoT system. In: 2017 4th International Conference on Electrical Engineering, Computer Science and Informatics (EECSI). IEEE (2017)

4. Rahman, A., et al.: A lightweight multi-tier S-MQTT framework to secure communication between low-end IoT nodes. In: 2018 5th International Conference on Networking, Systems and Security (NSysS). IEEE (2018)
5. Cruz-Piris, L., et al.: Access control mechanism for IoT environments based on modelling communication procedures as resources. Sensors **18**(3), 917 (2018)
6. Palmieri, A., et al.: MQTTSA: a tool for automatically assisting the secure deployments of MQTT brokers. In: 2019 IEEE World Congress on Services (SERVICES), vol. 2642. IEEE (2019)
7. Dinculeană, D., Cheng, X.: Vulnerabilities and limitations of MQTT protocol used between IoT devices. Appl. Sci. **9**(5), 848 (2019)
8. Raza, S., Wallgren, L., Voigt, T.: SVELTE: real-time intrusion detection in the internet of things. Ad Hoc Netw. **11**(8), 2661–2674 (2013)
9. Haripriya, A.P., Kulothungan, K.: Secure-MQTT: an efficient fuzzy logic-based approach to detect DoS attack in MQTT protocol for internet of things. EURASIP J. Wirel. Commun. Netw. **2019**(1), 1–15 (2019). https://doi.org/10.1186/s13638-019-1402-8
10. Alaiz-Moreton, H., et al.: Multiclass classification procedure for detecting attacks on MQTT-IoT protocol. Complexity (2019)
11. Shah, A., Rajdev, P., Kotak, J.: Memory Forensic Analysis of MQTT Devices. arXiv preprint arXiv:1908.07835 (2019)
12. Anthraper, J.J., Kotak, J.: Security, privacy and forensic concern of MQTT protocol. In: Proceedings of International Conference on Sustainable Computing in Science, Technology and Management (SUSCOM), Amity University Rajasthan, Jaipur-India (2019)
13. Avast Blog. https://blog.avast.com/mqtt-vulnerabilities-hacking-smart-home
14. Rondeau, C.M., Temple, M.A., Lopez, J.: Industrial IoT cross-layer forensic investigation. Wiley Interdisc. Rev. Forensic Sci. **1**(1), e1322 (2019)
15. Meidan, Y., et al.: ProfilIoT: a machine learning approach for IoT device identification based on network traffic analysis. In: Proceedings of the Symposium on Applied Computing (2017)
16. Understanding Random Forest. https://towardsdatascience.com/understanding-random-forest-58381e0602d2
17. Perrone, G., et al.: The day after mirai: a survey on MQTT security solutions after the largest cyber-attack carried out through an army of IoT devices. In: IoTBDS (2017)
18. Available MQTT Brokers. https://github.com/mqtt/mqtt.github.io/wiki/public_brokers
19. Bali, R.S., Jaafar, F., Zavarasky, P.: Lightweight authentication for MQTT to improve the security of IoT communication. In: Proceedings of the 3rd International Conference on Cryptography, Security and Privacy (2019)
20. Paul, S., Sarath, T.V.: End to end IoT based hazard monitoring system. In: 2018 International Conference on Inventive Research in Computing Applications (ICIRCA). IEEE (2018)
21. Sharad, S., Sivakumar, P.B., Narayanan, V.A.: The smart bus for a smart city–a real-time implementation. In: 2016 IEEE International Conference on Advanced Networks and Telecommunications Systems (ANTS). IEEE (2016)
22. MQTT.FX. https://mqttfx.jensd.de/index.php/download
23. [mqtt-v5.0]. https://docs.oasis-open.org/mqtt/mqtt/v5.0/mqtt-v5.0.html
24. Servida, F., Casey, E.: IoT forensic challenges and opportunities for digital traces. Digit. Investig. **28**, S22–S29 (2019)

25. Halabi, T., Bellaiche, M.: How to evaluate the defense against dos and DDoS attacks in cloud computing: a survey and taxonomy. Int. J. Comput. Sci. Inf. Secur. **14**(12), 1 (2016)
26. Testing the scalability and load behaviour of MQTT environments. https://github.com/etactica/mqtt-malaria

The Concerns of Personal Data Privacy, on Calling and Messaging, Networking Applications

Angeliki Kalapodi and Nicolas Sklavos[✉]

SCYTALE Group, Computer Engineering and Informatics Department, University of Patras, Patras, Hellas
nsklavos@ieee.org

Abstract. The General Data Protection Regulation (GDPR) was adopted in 2018 and had as main objective the establishment of the protection of personal data as a right of European citizens. However, the information, being the most valuable asset of our time, is a necessary element for the professional activity of most websites and applications. Secure design is fundamental for ensuring and maintaining trust between devices and user. IoT devices are the future of technology and communication. Given the multi-device interface technology, we must consider the ability to protect the user from leaks to other devices, applications and websites. Encryption is an important tool that can help us, ensure users trust in the devices they use. Privacy of personal data must therefore be ensured, especially since they are now a protected right of users. In this work, we examine the most commonly used calling and messaging, networking applications, of everyday life: Ayoba, Facebook Messenger, Line, Signal, Skype, Slack, Telegram, Whatsapp, and Viber. Especially, the permissions they ask from the user, the protection and the guarantees they provide under the General Data Protection Regulation, is explored. The additional permissions requested, or the shared data, are figured out. The results of our research, have proven the leakage of personal data and information, from the smart hand held devices, of the users, to third-party websites. Finally, the intersection of the third-party websites and, consequently, the sharing of the users information to other parties, without their immediate permission, are reported.

Keywords: Privacy · Personal data · General Data Protection Regulation (GDPR) · Calling and messaging applications · Handheld devices · Internet of Things (IoT)

1 Introduction

Information and data, are the most valuable "products" of our times. Internet has enabled the user, to provide personal information and make themselves a part of a global database. Many enterprises and organizations need this information for commercial and other purposes. However, is the provision of the personal information always voluntary?

© Springer Nature Singapore Pte Ltd. 2021
S. M. Thampi et al. (Eds.): SSCC 2020, CCIS 1364, pp. 275–289, 2021.
https://doi.org/10.1007/978-981-16-0422-5_20

Calling and messaging, networking applications, has led users to display parts of their privacy, business and views. All these information and data, in addition to being shown to friends or followers of users, is made available to organizations that can use them for their business. Several commercial companies introduce their products online, others collect statistics e.g. to predict election results, etc. Other services, have been aided in many cases by users' personal data, being shared online. Personal data collection can be useful in some cases, but in other cases it may be harmful to the user.

As of May 25, 2018, all EU countries have started implementing the General Data Protection Regulation (GDPR), [1, 2]. This legislation aims to protect and regulate the data privacy and applies to any organization that maintains or processes data for EU citizens, regardless of where it resides. As a result, compliance with the GDPR is essential for all companies dealing with user data. Nowadays, the trademark for the data collection is the mobile devices and more specifically, Internet of Things (IoT) devices [3, 4].

As part of the users' protection, from internet platforms and applications, that extract users' personal information against their will, the European Union, has been led to establish the European General Data Protection Regulation (EU-GDPR), [1, 2]. This regulation sets out the protection of personal data as a fundamental right of users. Particularly, for the users' data to be available on each internet platform and application, their approval must first be requested. Although, if they are not accepted, the users may be led to a lengthy text, that will try to persuade them to accept them, or worse, not even be able to open the internet platform or application.

All the mentioned above lead us to the following question: have all organizations complied with the European Personal Data Protection Regulation?

The purpose of this work, is to examine the most commonly used calling and messaging, networking applications, of everyday life: Ayoba, Facebook Messenger, Line, Signal, Skype, Slack, Telegram, Whatsapp, and Viber. The record of the optimal preset privacy settings that must be displayed by the various online applications, in order to meet the legal requirement for data protection by default. This legal requirement is set by the latest GDPR, and the level of harmonization of these applications with this requirement is investigated. Initially, the licenses requested by the user and the security of their implementation are analyzed. Real-time portable devices are used, in which experimental recording of information provided by the user is performed, for a long period of time. More specifically, the information that is transmitted through the applications of this category is "recorded", and the cases of their "leakage" are highlighted. Then, the specific data is analyzed, that proves whether the online communication providers are complying with the terms of user privacy, or not.

2 Legal Framework

Every company established within the European Union, or located outside the European Union and handling personal data relating to people within the European Union, is required to comply fully with the requirements of the new General Data Protection Regulation (GDPR), which came into force on May 25, 2018 [1, 2]. Data protection reform is a legislative commitment to update and modernize existing data protection rules.

Enhancing the transparency of the processing of personal data, setting specific obligations to those who process personal data, while strengthening the rights of individuals is the main goal of the GDPR. Appropriate practices and technologies must be adopted by those who process personal data in order to ensure compliance with the requirements of legality - and, consequently, respect for this fundamental individual right [2]. With the introduction of the GDPR, new technological challenges were automatically raised, which in turn create new research questions. Considering the above, this study focuses on the following aspects:

- Have personal data controllers complied with the data protection requirement in accordance with the European Directive?
- Can we determine the objective indicators of conformity assessment?

2.1 Personal Data

Personal data is any information that refers to a person, such as: name and profession, marital status, age, place of residence, racial origin, political views, religion believes, philosophical views, trade union action, health, love life and any criminal prosecutions and convictions.

The distinction of personal data is very important, as each type of data is handled differently and is also subject to different legal frameworks in the event of a breach. So, we have that personal data is divided into [5–8]:

- Common data: non sensitive personal data and in order to collect and process them, the consent of the subject is sufficient.
- Sensitive data: they result from the privacy of the individual and a ban on collection and processing has generally been established, unless there is a relevant authorization from the competent Personal Data Protection Authority.
- Public data: information related to the public, i.e. it is the data produced by public or private bodies.
- Government data: data and information generated or commissioned, by governments or by government-supervised entities.
- Open Data: data freely used, reused and redistributed by anyone - provided that the authors are referred to and made available under the same conditions.
- Open government data: data and information generated, or outsourced by governments or government-supervised entities.

So, what is personal data and what is sensitive personal data? "Personal data", may mean any information relating to a specific person. They are divided, into simple and sensitive. The legislature provides extended protection to sensitive personal data, setting stricter conditions for access to it and the keeping of records containing it.

2.2 The Terms of Security and Data Privacy

The security and privacy requirements of data utilized in information systems arising from the need to protect them include the following [6, 9, 10]:

- Confidentiality: which refers to the protection against possible disclosure of data to unauthorized entities.
- Integrity: which refers to protection against unauthorized entry, modification or deletion of data.
- Availability: which concerns the protection against non-availability of data.
- Authenticity: which involves securing the identity of all the entities involved.
- Non-Repudiation: which refers to protection against an entity refusing to perform a particular activity.

In order to transform the concept of privacy from a general concept, a technical requirement defines individual privacy requirements, which are presented below [6, 8, 11]:

- Authentication: it refers to the process by which the identity of an entity is verified. It is primarily a security requirement rather than the privacy of an information system, but it also makes a significant contribution to privacy requirements.
- Authorization: it refers to the process by which an entity acquires rights/access to one or a set of services of an information system.
- Identification: which refers to the process by which authentication is required and then authorization or not to access the service or data.
- Data Protection: it refers to the process by which the principles required by the new General Data Protection Regulation (GDPR) are secured.

Other useful terms found in data protection environments that describe privacy enhancement techniques or technologies are:

- Anonymity.
- Pseudonymity.
- Unlinkability.
- Unobservability.

2.3 The Need for Personal Data Protection

The development of technology has increased the risks to our privacy. Within, only few seconds, it is efficient to draw various data about the personal, financial or social status of a person. Most importantly, all this data may be combined with other sources of information, so as to lead to a comprehensive record of the user's personality, i.e. the composition of his individual "Profile".

In just a few years, it is estimated that, rapid technological developments (internet, mobile telephony, big data, etc.) have led to an increase in the scope and intensity of the collection, exchange and processing of personal data by private companies and public authorities with geometric progress. Both personal and non-personal data have acquired a strong commercial dimension, creating a new global market for the smooth operation, of which required their free movement. Finally, the way individuals themselves manipulate their data has changed, making personal information more and more public, and therefore easier to make available (for example, social media).

The results of the Eurobarometer survey on personal data protection, clearly show that there is a need for horizontal management of the issue, and room for improvement, in the trust between data subjects and data processors [12].

2.4   General Regulation on Personal Data Protection (GDPR)

The General Data Protection Regulation (GDPR), radically changes the way companies and organizations collect, process and manage personal data of any kind. The main changes that will take place are:

- *Protection of children's rights.*
- *Right to oblivion.*
- *Right to information and access to data.*
- *Right to correction.*
- *Right to object to the processing.*

A new requirement of the regulation from the respective controller is the protection of personal data, by default and by design. It is definitely necessary, in order to harmonize from the beginning of data collection/processing, and always in a way, aimed at protecting the personal data of the subjects. In Fig. 1, the representation of the requirements, based on GDPR, that a company must follow, is illustrated.

Fig. 1. GDPR: 12 Steps to take now.

2.5   Privacy Enhancing Technologies: Categories and Tools

Privacy Enhancing Technologies (PETs), are technologies that incorporate fundamental data protection principles, minimizing the use of personal data, maximizing data security, and empowering individuals [13, 14]. PET tools include the following:

1. Nickname.
2. Dark reference: refers to the many practices of adding snippets or misleading data to a log or profile, which can be particularly useful for falsifying accurate data after data has already been lost or disclosed.
3. Differential privacy: A limitation on the algorithms used to publish aggregate information about a statistical database in order to limit the privacy impact of individuals whose information is contained in the database. A differential private algorithm ensures that the output cannot state whether a particular person's information was used in the calculation.

2.6 Social Engineering Attacks

Social engineering is "the management of human beings according to their place and function in society". Here are some of the most well-known social engineering attacks used in our daily lives, [9]:

1. *Phishing.*
2. *Baiting.*
3. *Shoulder Surfing.*
4. *Reverse Social Machine Attack.*
5. *Dumpster Diving.*
6. *Pretexting.*
7. *Cross Site Request Forgery (CSRF).*
8. *Malware.*
9. *Search Engine Poisoning (SEP).*
10. *Tailgating.*

One of the most detailed classifications of social machine attacks, analyzes them, in three stages: orchestration, exploitation and execution [15]. The scientists who developed this classification did so in order to help deal with the attacks. Training and raising awareness of users is particularly important in dealing with social engineering attacks. "Malware" is a major problem for information systems security [16]. The software is characterized as malicious when according to the intentions of the developer the resulting software has the necessary commands in order to damage a computer system. Malware can be divided into two categories. One that needs a "host" program and one that does not need a "host" and can run on its own like any other program.

3 Data Privacy: By Design and By Default

With the proliferation of calling and messaging, networking applications, the volume and the variety of personal data is exposed daily, to a wide range of recipients. It ends up being available for use and exploitation is increasing exponentially. Thus, technology has evolved into a "self-denying good of socialization", as it has "greatly enhanced the need to separate our presence from other users, and minimize our natural interaction with friends/acquaintances/partners". At the same time, overexposure to data has led to breaches, leading to the development of problematic ways of integrating technology, data protection practices, and in particular the need to invent methods that would facilitate lawful processing without requiring data subjects to take additional action. This principle is called privacy by default and is to ensure privacy as a basic and normally integrated choice of a system, application or process [17]. The aim is to protect the hitherto proven to be little to not at all informed user, about the risks of disclosing their data. Strategic planning for privacy and data protection is defined and divided by the General Regulation into eight steps, which are:

- *Minimize.*
- *Hide.*
- *Separate.*
- *Aggregate/Abstract.*
- *Inform.*
- *Control.*
- *Enforce.*
- *Demonstrate.*

Therefore, taking and adhering to design protection measures is an indication of compliance, but does not guarantee compliance. It is the responsibility of the Commission, the competent national protection authorities, as well as the European Data Protection Council, to issue relevant detailed guidelines, specifying and describing the appropriate technical measures [15].

4 Research Work and Contribution

In this section, our research work and contribution, is analyzed in detail, in the following sections.

4.1 Experimental and Monitoring Environment

Our experimental and monitoring environment, was based on a modern *last year, smart phone device, with MIUI Global 11.0.3 and Android 9.0 Pie*, operating system. The handheld device was used, in order to install and control, the examined calling and messaging, networking applications.

A great number of widely used and modern, messaging and calling applications, nine in total, where examined, which are listed, with their version number, in the following Table 1, in alphabetical order. The study and recording of the preset privacy settings, of the messaging and calling applications, selected set during their installation, account creation and first use, was carried out, for a period, of six months. It is important to note that our research is based, on real time data, with normal, daily use of the smart phone, and not with forced communication, or fictitious users.

Lumen Privacy Monitor, Version 2.2.2, was selected for the purposes of our research work [18]. At this point, it is significant to highlight that Lumen Privacy Monitor, is not an open source, software application. However, it was chosen and trusted, since it has been created by the academic community, for research purposes, and is used by several remarkable research groups, in scientific literature.

Table 1. Messaging and calling applications.

Application	Version
Ayoba	0.30.2
Facebook messenger	259.0.0.18.120
Line	10.5.2
Signal	4.58.5
Skype	8.58.0.93
Slack	20.03.30.0
Telegram	6.0.1
Viber	12.7.5.1
Whatsapp	2.20.108

4.2 Processing Transparency

Based on the results of our study, Fig. 2, illustrates the list of detected leaks, and the list of applications with blocked traffic, based on Lumen Privacy Monitor tool, for the examined cases.

Fig. 2. List of detected leaks, list of applications with blocked traffic.

The following Fig. 3, shows in detail, links and traffic detected by the Lumen Privacy Monitor tool, between the applications authorized by the user and third-part websites that access those applications.

Thus, the users realize that they authorized an application to have access to their files, contacts and information. This application is connected to other domains and links. However, those domains and links have not been authorized to have access to their "smart" handheld device, right?

Fig. 3. Links/traffic to domain from the investigated applications.

4.3   Research Results

The links appearing in the previous Fig. 3, can be checked and evaluated further, by "whotracks.me". This tool checks the websites/trackers, contains statistics of the various domains, and informs us about the type and tracking methods, used by this domain. It also contains information of the holder in the cases of trackers.

Figure 4 incorporates the check of some websites, tracked by the Lumen Privacy Monitor tool, during our observation.

The work that was carried out, showed that most of the websites and trackers, are in advertising and monitoring user activity business. Some of those domains have been recognized by the Lumen Privacy Monitor tool, and others should be checked by "whotracks.me", as performed above. As it is carried out from our research results, domains and trackers connected to the applications authorized by the user, have access to their information. All this information can be used by the detected domains, without user's direct authorization.

Thus, we used the whotracks.me tool, which informs us about the type and tracking of domains, that are inserted while using the applications. In this case, we checked two websites and two trackers. Referring to rakuten.com for example that appears in the Viber Flows, we notice that tracking is observed during 70% of the loads of this page. And the trackers are sorted to the left in the corresponding pie, with the redundant advertising trackers and the other categories, as shown in the picture. As for trackers, we chose to check for example Google User Content. Whotracks.me Tool, informs us that this is a tracker, that implements tracking, via cookies.

Table 2 incorporates the total traffic, the trackers detected, the overhead, the permissions requested and the leaks detected by Lumen Privacy Monitor tool, per application.

Fig. 4. Website and tracker domains: operation, methods of use, evaluation statistics, owner, etc.

Table 2. Analysis of lumen privacy monitor tool, results per application.

	Applications	Traffic (MB)	Trackers	Overhead	Permissions requested	Leaks
1	Ayoba	100	2	4,70%	47	0
2	Facebook messenger	1000	0	0,00%	62	0
3	Line	400	1	12,40%	43	1
4	Signal	2850	0	0,00%	65	0
5	Skype	680	0	0,00%	53	0
6	Slack	810	1	14,90%	19	0
7	Telegram	700	0	0,00%	54	0
8	Viber	2300	8	40,90%	68	3
9	Whatsapp	1000	0	0,00%	59	0
	Sum	9050	12	0,729	470	4

The graphs below, illustrates all the data shown in the above Table 2. The total traffic monitored is ~10.000 MB. Figure 5, illustrates the traffic per application.

The total trackers detected per application are shown in Fig. 6. As shown below, trackers were detected only at four, of the nine investigated applications. Viber has displayed the most.

It is important to note that each domain contains multiple trackers related to advertising, entertainment and web analytics services (statistics, etc.). Moreover, it is significant to highlight the trackers per application, with the most numerous application Viber, compared to others (e.g. Signal, Telegram, etc.), that have resulted to zero value, Fig. 7.

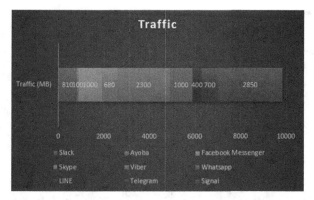

Fig. 5. Graphic illustration of the total traffic monitored.

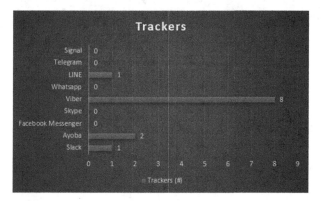

Fig. 6. Graphic illustration of the total traffic monitored.

Additionally, several applications have shown an overhead percentage of total communication, caused by ads, monitoring and analytics links, and data leaks from applications (Fig. 8). It is speculated that the Lumen Privacy Monitor application, may not have been able to collect the full charge, due to the encryption used in the communication channel, on several of the connections.

As mentioned above, the Lumen Privacy Monitor tool, separates licenses into high, medium and low risk. The following Fig. 9, shows the results recorded by the Lumen Privacy Monitor tool. And then, we observe the level of risk of the respective permissions requested by the user. Whereas, we must note that the license to access the camera is a lot more dangerous compared to the license to operate the application in full screen mode.

Last but not least, the leaks detected by the Lumen Privacy Monitor. As shown in Fig. 10, only two of the nine applications investigated, displayed leaks: Viber and Line.

The statistics results, reported above, can lead us to the conclusion, that many applications are associated with third-party domains, that in many cases are identical

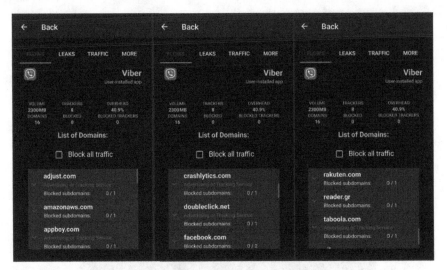

Fig. 7. Website and tracker domains: operation, methods of use, evaluation statistics, owner, etc.

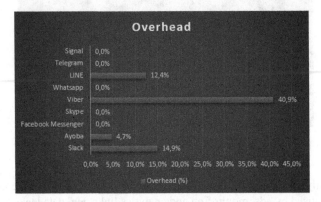

Fig. 8. Graphic illustration of the overhead monitored.

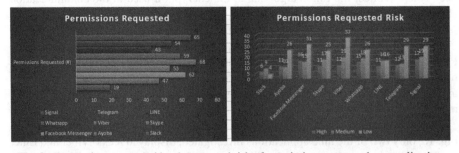

Fig. 9. Permissions requested by the user and risk of permissions requested per application.

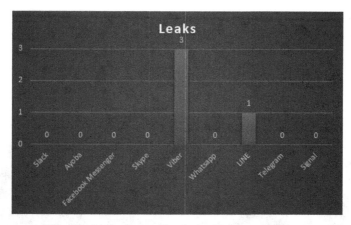

Fig. 10. Leaks detected by the lumen privacy monitor.

between different applications. In addition, the required permissions between different applications give the third-party domains multiple information.

It is very important to mention that in many cases the third-party domains that intersect, concern social networks, whose connection has not been required from the user to browse the application. This fact raises suspicions about the interceptions that have taken place in integrated personal databases, as they have been shaped by social media. It is reasonable, therefore, to consider that modern social networks exchange information in order to create the full profile of each user [18].

Another important concept, that we have to remark, is that the third-party domains "inherit" the access permissions, that the user has given to the respective application, that they use. These applications have been recognized by the Lumen Privacy Monitor tool, as monitoring/advertising services and can collect information from the user and then delineate their social/consumer profile etc. This fact makes them malicious internet users, as long as they have obtained information about the user against their will and (in many cases) their permission.

ICSI Haystack Panopticon [19], is based on data collected by Lumen Privacy Monitor tool and is an interactive map of the intersections between all the monitoring/advertising domains observed per application, (Fig. 11).

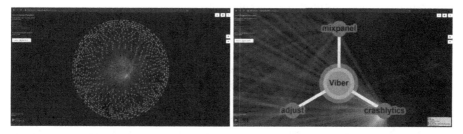

Fig. 11. The intersections of viber.

Getting navigated to the ICSI Haystack Panopticon, we can search for the application of our interest. For example, Viber has been searched. The research led us to an intersection with mixpanel, adjust and crashlytics. Choosing for example the crashlytics link, we get led to another intersection with numerous other domains that have gained access to our personal data and information (Figs. 11 and 12).

Fig. 12. The intersections of crashlytics.

5 Conclusions and Future Work

In this work, we analyzed a great number of internet communication applications, the permissions they request from the user, the protection and the guarantees they provide, from the point of General Data Protection Regulation (GDPR). Using the Lumen Privacy Monitoring tool, the additional permissions asked, or the data shared with other applications were examined. The results of our research work, on monitoring and recording of the applications, prove the leakage of personal data and information from the "smart" handheld device, of the user to third-party websites. Then, we presented the intersection of the third-party websites and, consequently, the sharing of the user information to other organizations, without his immediate permission.

All the mentioned above emphasize the need to protect the user's personal data by design and by default. Therefore, design is fundamental for ensuring and maintaining trust between devices and the user [20]. It is important to consider ways of privacy practices' integration. This raises the need to invent methods that facilitate lawful processing without requiring users to perform additional actions.

This is where future work on personal data protection should be focused. The users should be able to choose their new devices based on the protection they provide, in addition to the technical features, price and appearance. This will add more value to the user's preferences towards the respective provider and make them feel more secure against malicious internet users.

References

1. Regulation (EU) 2016/679 of the European Parliament and of the Council, Official Journal of the European Union, April 2016
2. Vollmer, N.: Article 25 EU General Data Protection Regulation, EU-GDPR, September 2018
3. Sklavos, N., Zaharakis, I.D.: Cryptography and security in Internet of Things (IoT): models, schemes, and implementations. In: Proceedings of 8th IFIP International Conference on New Technologies, Mobility and Security (NTMS 2016), Larnaca, Cyprus, 21–23 November 2016 (2016)
4. Hu, F.: Security and Privacy in Internet of Things: Models, Algorithms and Implementations. CRC Press (2016). ISBN: 9781498723183
5. Warren, S.D., Brandeis, L.D.: The right to privacy. Harvard Law Rev. Assoc. **4**(5), 193–220 (1890)
6. Stallings, W.: Cryptography and Network Security, 6th edn. Pearson, Upper Saddle River (2014). ISBN: 0133354695
7. Barker, K., et al.: A data privacy taxonomy. In: Sexton, Alan P. (ed.) BNCOD 2009. LNCS, vol. 5588, pp. 42–54. Springer, Heidelberg (2009). https://doi.org/10.1007/978-3-642-028 43-4_7
8. Limniotis, K.: Anonymization and pseudonymization of personal data. In: 7th International Conference on e-Democracy - Workshop on Technologies and Procedures as Tools for Compliance with the General Data Protection Regulation (GDPR), Athens, 14 December 2017 (2017)
9. Krombholz, K., Hobel, H., Huber, M., Weippl, E.: Advanced social engineering attacks. J. Inf. Secur. Appl. **22**(C), 113–122 (2015)
10. Mitnick, K.D., Simon, W.L.: The Art of Deception: Controlling the Human Element of Security. Wiley Publishing, Indianapolis (2003)
11. Clarke, R.: Introduction to Dataveillance and Information Privacy and Definitions of Terms, Computer Science (1997)
12. Eurobarometer, "Personal data protection", Survey 431, European Parliament, Figures 2015 (2015)
13. de la Torre, L.F.: What are privacy-enhancing technologies (PETs)? A medium corporation. Am. Bee J. March 2019
14. European Union Agency for Network and Information Security (ENISA), A tool on Privacy Enhancing Technologies (PETs) knowledge management and maturity assessment—ENISA, February 2019
15. Heartfield, R., Loukas, G.: Mechanisms for semantic social engineering attacks, a taxonomy of attacks and a survey of defense. ACM Comput. Surv. December 2015
16. Milosevic, J., Sklavos, N., Koutsikou, K.: Malware in IoT software and hardware. In: Proceedings of Workshop on Trustworthy Manufacturing and Utilization of Secure Devices (TRUDEVICE 2016), Barcelona, Spain, 14–16 November 2016
17. Solove, D.J.: A taxonomy of privacy. Univ. Pennsylvania Law Rev. **154**(3), 477 (2006). GWU Law School Public Law Research Paper No. 129
18. Lumen Privacy Monitor, Version 2.2.2 (2020)
19. Website. www.icsi.berkeley.edu/icsi/projects/networking/haystack
20. ICSI Haystack Panopticon. www.haystack.mobi/panopticon (2020)
21. Sklavos, N., Zaharakis, I.D., Kameas, A., Kalapodi, A.: Security & trusted devices in the context of Internet of Things (IoT). In: 20th EUROMICRO Conference on Digital System Design, Architectures, Methods, Tools (DSD 2017), Vienna, Austria, 30 August–1 September 2017 (2017)

Analysis of Orthogonal Time Frequency Space Transceiver in Baseband Environment

Vangara Saiprudhvi[✉] and R. Ramanathan

Department of Electronics and Communication Engineering Amrita School of Engineering, Coimbatore, Amrita Vishwa Vidyapeetham, Coimbatore 641112, India
saiprudhvi000@gmail.com, r_ramanathan@cb.amrita.edu

Abstract. In this letter, we investigate Orthogonal Time Frequency Space (OTFS) modulation, a newly proposed modulation scheme for emerging wireless communication applications in time-frequency selective channels, from symbol detection perspective. The studies identify the advantages of OTFS performance over OFDM in many aspects, such as data rate increase in high mobility. Another advantage is the sparsity of the channel produced by OTFS that allows using low-complexity algorithms for the detection of the data. We provide the analysis on the baseband OTFS system and then analyze the Message Passing algorithm for OTFS symbol detection. We analyze the effects of damping factor and channel taps on the performance of the system. Simulation results show the error performance of the OTFS system under various channel conditions.

Keywords: Orthogonal Time Frequency Space · Doubly-dispersive channel · Message passing · Symbol detection · Receiver design

1 Introduction

Emerging wireless networks need to design in such a way that it must support various use cases such as ultra-reliable communications (e.g. e-health services), high mobility (e.g. aircraft, vehicular communication, high-speed trains). Developing such technology is a challenging task because it must overcome the drawbacks of current multicarrier technologies such as OFDM. The major challenge is to address high Doppler shifts, which degrading performance in current multicarrier schemes, The current multicarrier scheme is known to achieve good performance for time-invariant channels but it suffers performance loss with time-varying channels, where Doppler shifts are high. To overcome this a novel modulation scheme called OTFS is proposed. Orthogonal Time Frequency Space (OTFS) is a 2D modulation schemes designed in delay-Doppler domain, which converts modulation symbols in delay-Doppler domain to symbols in time-frequency domain. The OTFS holds three properties namely invariability, separability and bi-orthogonality. It is proven that OTFS can extract full

© Springer Nature Singapore Pte Ltd. 2021
S. M. Thampi et al. (Eds.): SSCC 2020, CCIS 1364, pp. 290–303, 2021.
https://doi.org/10.1007/978-981-16-0422-5_21

channel diversity because it hold separable property. It is shown in literature that OTFS can be designed by using current multicarrier techniques by just including pre-coding block and post processing block. Each and every symbol will experience the same channel. OTFS is shown to perform better than OFDM under similar conditions. Various detection algorithms used for OTFS symbol detection is given in [4–9]. Design, features and parameters used in design for OTFS, spectral efficiency of OTFS and mathematical model describing OTFS principle is given in [1–3]. Linear equalization (MMSE and ZF equalizers), pilots embedded in data frame, impulses as pilots used as channel estimation techniques for OTFS symbol estimation is given in [10,11,13]. A simple two-stage equalizer for OTFS symbol estimation is given in [12]. Peak-to-Average-Power-Ratio (PAPR) analysis for OTFS signal is given in [15]. Diversity analysis on OTFS channel matrix is given in [13,14]. MIMO-OTFS formulation and analysis is given in [18]. Multiple access techniques used for OTFS is given in [17,19]. We know that Doppler shifts and phase noise is high in mmWave communication in [16] it is shown how OTFS is used in mmWave communication. In this letter, we investigate Orthogonal Time Frequency Space (OTFS) modulation, a newly proposed modulation scheme for emerging wireless communication applications in time-frequency selective channels, from symbol detection perspective. The studies identify the advantages of OTFS performance over OFDM in many aspects, such as data rate increase in high mobility. Another advantage is the sparsity of the channel produced by OTFS that allows using low-complexity algorithms for the detection of the data. We provide the analysis on the baseband OTFS system and then analyze the Message Passing algorithm for OTFS symbol detection. We analyze the effects of damping factor (Δ) and channel taps on the performance of the system. Simulation results show the error performance of the OTFS system under various channel conditions.

2   Related Work

In [1] a novel two-dimensional modulation scheme is presented for future wireless communications and it is termed as Orthogonal Time Frequency Space (OTFS) modulation. The key features in this modulation scheme are: It is represented in delay-Doppler domain, an hypothesis about channel diversity is given, and finally one of the key feature is it transforms fading time-varying channel into non-fading time-invariant channel. This paper explains the principle of OTFS modulation using mathematical model. In [2] it is shown that OTFS modulation scheme can be designed using conventional modulation techniques such as OFDM by just using pre-coder transform at the transmitter and post-processing transform at the receiver. Mathematical model representing this type of design is presented. By this arrangement, it is shown that the design complexity and computational complexity is greatly reduced. In [3] OTFS system is investigated in terms of spectral efficiency and proposed a spectral efficient OTFS system. This system uses windowing cyclic prefix and post-fix (WCPP) technology as reduction technique to minimize Out-of-Bound power level. Simulation results confirmed that the proposed system minimizes power level in AWGN environment and in multipath environment ISI is mitigated by employing FFT window sliding technique. In [4] a joint interference cancellation and iterative detection algorithm is proposed. The detailed relation between input and output of OTFS system is described by using mathematical model. Next analyzes the system using different types of waveforms like ideal pulse-shaping, rectangular, Gaussian etc., with bi-orthogonality condition and observations are given. Analysis on various types of interference is performed and suggested mitigating techniques. Simulation results shows that the proposed uncoded OTFS system performs better than traditional multicarrier schemes such as OFDM over time-varying channels. In [5] by using mathematical model, the detailed relation between input and output of OTFS system is described with random number of paths and specified delay and Doppler taps. A message passing detection algorithm is proposed for exhaustive OTFS system by using built-in channel sparsity. Interference plus noise terms are approximated as Gaussian to further reduce the complexity. Simulation results shows that the effect is combated by adapting the proposed algorithm. In [6], by assuming perfect channel knowledge, a Markov Chain Mote Carlo (MCMC) sampling detection algorithm is proposed for OTFS system and by relaxing this assumption a channel estimation algorithm is proposed, which uses pseudo-random noise as pilots in channel. In this well-known MCMC technique called Gibbs sampling is presented for OTFS system and the drawbacks of using this technique is addressed by simply modifying the distribution and randomizing the update rule. In [7] to further reduce the complexity of message passing algorithm an improved stopping criteria is presented. Pre-processing Doppler compensation block is equipped at receiver and generated result is then given to the algorithm. In addition, an approximate message passing (AMP) is proposed, which applies covariance processing to it. Simulations result confirmed that the approach performs better than the conventional MP detection algorithm. In [8] to reduce complexity of receiver a Variational Bayes (VB) approach is proposed, which approximates the joint a posteriori distribution family to maximizie the Evidence Lower Bound. The Evidence Lower Bound is strictly minimized to guarantees the convergence. Simulation results confirmed that in practical multipath environment the proposed approach quickly gets converged and it is shown that the approach performs better than MP detection algorithm. In [9] using maximal ratio combining procedure, a low complexity iterative rake detection algorithm is proposed. In this the author reformulates the relation between input and output of OTFS system in vector form, by placing some null symbols in the delay-Doppler plane. Thus, made use of block circulant nature of the channel matrix in the proposed algorithm. Simulation results confirmed that the proposed algorithm gives similar BER performance but with lower complexity compared to MP algorithm. In [10] a channel estimation technique for OTFS system is proposed. The information on channel impulse response is necessary to detect the symbols at the receiver. Pilot symbols are included into the chunk to estimate the channel. First threshold based method is used to estimate information on channel and for that estimated information message passing algorithm is presented in this paper. Simulation results show OTFS with non-ideal channel estimate better when compared with OFDM with ideal channel estimate. In [11] the low-complexity ZF and MMSE equalizers for OTFS are proposed by exploiting the arrangement of time-varying channel matrix of OTFS modulation. To reduce complexity at the receiver, the proposed algorithm uses the block circulant property of the OTFS time-varying channel matrix. Simulation results justify that OTFS equalizers outperform the other conventional equalizers in BER performance. In [12] an equivalent delay-Doppler channel matrix for OTFS is derived and by using this a simple two-stage equalizer is designed for OTFS modulation. The first stage is equalization of received signal using OFDM single-tap equalizer in frequency do-main, by which the multipath effected gets removed. Next, low-complexity delay-Doppler equalizer is designed, by which the interference caused by Doppler spread can be mitigated. Simulation results validated the performance enhancement of pro-posed scheme when compared with conventional single-tap equalizer and MMSE equalizer of OFDM system. In OTFS literature, an hypothesis on achieving full channel diversity is given, where full diversity refers to fulfilling separable property. In [13], it is analyzed and shows that this property holds by OTFS system. Simulation results give the diversity order for SISO-OTFS and the analysis on diversity is extended to MIMO-OTFS. In [14] the concept of Effective Diversity is proposed to address the issue of high Doppler shifts in OFDM transmission. The proposed concept is derived for OTFS by considering rectangular waveforms. Simulation results shows the analysis on the diversity of OTFS over two-path channels. Difference between standard diversity and effective diversity is studied and showed effective diversity is the remarkable parameter while expressing error performance. Peak-to-Average Power Ratio (PAPR) is the most important parameter in analysis on any communication signal. In [15] the effect of PAPR for OTFS system is given and obtain an upper limit for it. For different pulse shapes, Complementary Cumulative Distribution Function (CCDF) of the PAPR for OTFS system is simulated and compared with other similar multicarrier modulation schemes such as OFDM AND GFDM. In [16] it is shown that the OTFS system can be used in milli-meter wave communication. First vectorized version of input-output relation for OTFS modulation in delay-Doppler domain is mathematically described. By using message passing detection algorithm, it is shown that OTFS outperforms OFDM when oscillator phase noise is introduced in the channel. In [17] it is shown how OTFS system can be used for multi-user communication on uplink and it is titled as OTFS based Multiple Access (OTFS-MA). In this multiple access system, consumers are multiplexed on delay-Doppler plane and each bin is allocated to each user. Different allocation schemes are discussed and simulation results suggests better BER performance of proposed scheme when compared with other multiple access systems. In [18] MIMO-OTFS system is presented and input-output relation is formulated for this system. By assuming perfect channel knowledge, message passing detection algorithm is employed to detect symbols and simulation results show that it achieves good performance. Now, by relaxing perfect channel assumption a channel estimation scheme is proposed, in which impulses are used as pilots for channel estimation and show better performance over the performance with perfect knowledge. In [19] the author examines a multiuser uplink scenario using OTFS modulation and presented a scheme called, interleaved time-frequency multiple access (ITFMA). This scheme reduces complexity by enabling interference-free reception for multiple users in time-frequency plane. Simulation results show the comparison of bit error performance among the pro-posed and other OTFS based multiple access schemes. PAPR is computed for proposed scheme and analytically characterizes its CCDF.

3   OTFS System Model

The basic theory of Orthogonal Time Frequency Space modulation is the use of delay – Doppler domain to spread the information symbols on it. OTFS modulation is the composition of two 2D OTFS transforms at both the transmitter and the receiver. First, the information QAM symbols are given as input to the OTFS modulator. In OTFS modulator, the 2D sequence of information QAM symbols $x[k, l]$ in the delay-Doppler domain are mapped to a 2D sequence of symbols $X[n, m]$ in the time-frequency domain using 2D OTFS transform (ISFFT) and then the resulted sequence is applied to Heisenberg transform, which results in the time domain signal $s(t)$ for transmission over the time-varying channel. In OTFS demodulator, the received signal $r(t)$ is applied to Wigner transform, which results in the time-frequency domain sequence $Y[n, m]$ and then the resulted sequence is given to inverse 2D OTFS transform (SFFT) block to get back the estimate of transmitted symbol $y[k, l]$ for symbol detection. Figure 1 pictorially represents the Orthogonal Time Frequency Space system.

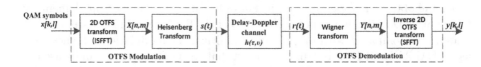

Fig. 1. Orthogonal time frequency space system

4   Message Passing Algorithm for OTFS Symbol Detection

Message passing (MP) detection algorithm is proposed by exploiting the relation between input and output of OTFS modulation/demodulation. The received signal $s(t)$ in vector notation is given by

$$\hat{q} = Hq + e$$

where $\hat{q} \in \mathbb{C}^{NM*1}$, $H \in \mathbb{C}^{NM*NM}$ and $q \in \mathbb{Q}^{NMx1}$.

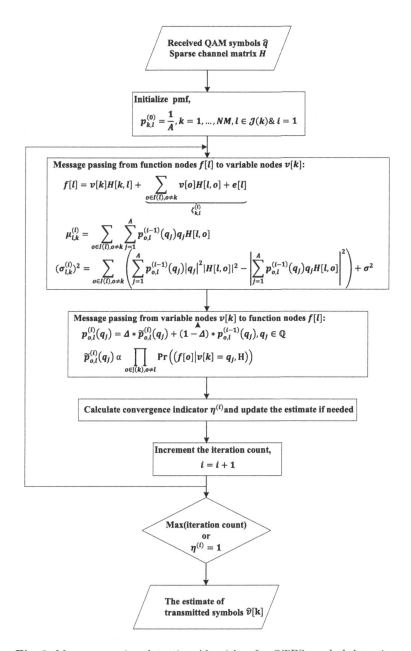

Fig. 2. Message passing detection Algorithm for OTFS symbol detection

The detailed procedure of Message Passing algorithm is given in flowchart and Fig. 2 represents it. In Message passing, mean and variance of interference plus noise terms $\zeta_{l,k}^{(i)}$ are operated as messages from function nodes $f[l]$ to variable nodes $v[k], k = 1, \ldots, NM$. The messages from function node $v[k]$ to observation node $f[l], l \in \mathfrak{I}(k)$ are updated by computing the probability mass function (pmf) of the modulation alphabet $p_{k,l} = \{p_{k,l}(q_j) \mid q_j \in \mathbb{Q}\}$. The pmf is initialized to $1/\mathbb{Q}$. The convergence rate is controlled by using damping factor $(\Delta \in (0, 1]$, which in turn enhances the performance. Convergence indicator $\eta^{(i)}$ is computed and the result obtained is updated only when the present iteration gives better approximation than the previous iteration. The MP detection algorithm stops only when one of the two conditions are met.

5   Numerical Results

Table 1 gives all relevant parameters used to simulate baseband OTFS system. The results given below are generated using MATLAB (Figs. 3, 4, 5, 6, 7, 8, 9, 10 and 11).

Table 1. Simulation parameters

Parameters	Value
Number of OTFS symbols (N)	8
Number of subcarriers (M)	8
Constellation	4-QAM 16-QAM 64-QAM
Number of frames	10000
Delay taps	4,6&8-taps
Doppler taps	4,6&8-taps
Damping factor (Δ)	0.6 (4&16-QAM) 0.7 (64-QAM)

The graph shows the Bit Error Rate performance of OTFS for 4-QAM signalling. The above simulation parameters are used to obtain the result, four delay and Doppler taps are used to generate the time-varying channel and MP detection algorithm is used for data detection with damping factor is equal to 0.6.

The graph shows the Bit Error Rate performance of OTFS for 16-QAM signalling. The above simulation parameters are used to obtain the result, four delay and Doppler taps are used to generate the time-varying channel and MP detection algorithm is used for data detection with damping factor is set to 0.6.

The graph shows the Bit Error Rate performance of OTFS for 64-QAM signaling. The above simulation parameters are used to obtain the result, four

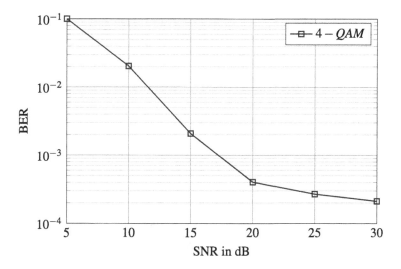

Fig. 3. BER performance of 4-QAM OTFS system

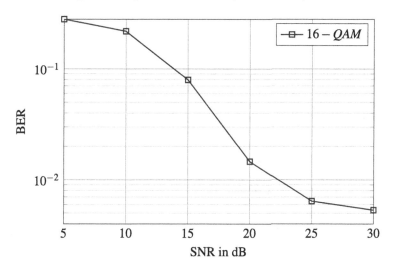

Fig. 4. BER performance of 16-QAM OTFS system

delay and Doppler taps are used to generate the time-varying channel and MP detection algorithm is used for data detection with damping factor is set to 0.7.

The graph shows the Bit Error Rate performance of OTFS for 4,16 and 64-QAM signaling. The simulation is carried out by generating a 4-tap delay-Doppler channel and the above-listed parameters. Message Passing detection algorithm is used for data detection with the damping factor (Δ) is set to 0.6. 4-QAM signaling performs better than the other two constellations at higher SNRs.

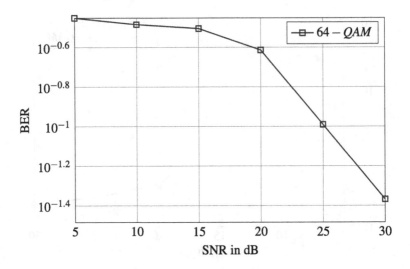

Fig. 5. BER performance of 64-QAM OTFS system

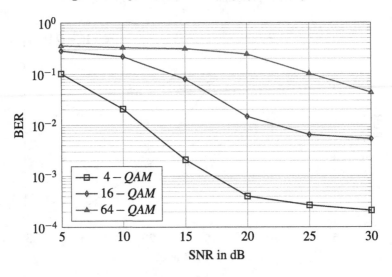

Fig. 6. BER performance of 4-tap 4, 16, & 64-QAM OTFS system

The graph shows the Bit Error Rate performance of OTFS for 4,16 and 64-QAM signaling. The simulation is carried out by generating a 6-tap delay-Doppler channel and the above-listed parameters. MP detection algorithm is used for data detection with the convergence factor is set to 0.6. 4-QAM signaling performs better than the other two constellations at higher SNRs but its performance is degraded when compared to 4-taps 4-QAM signaling. For 16 and 64-QAM constellation the performance remains almost the same.

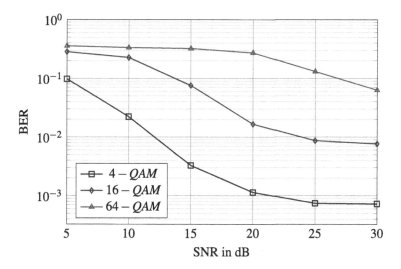

Fig. 7. BER performance of 6-tap 4, 16, & 64-QAM OTFS system

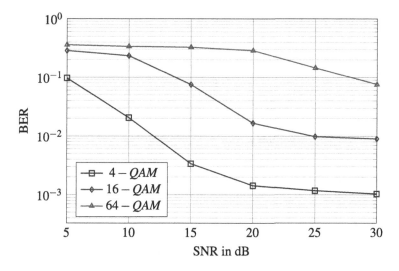

Fig. 8. BER performance of 8-tap 4, 16, & 64-QAM OTFS system

The graph shows the Bit Error Rate performance of OTFS for 4,16 and 64-QAM signaling. The simulation is carried out by generating an 8-tap delay-Doppler channel and the above-listed parameters. MP detection algorithm is used for data detection with the convergence factor is set to 0.6. 4-QAM signaling performs better than the other two constellations at higher SNRs but its performance is degraded when compared with 4-taps and 6-taps 4-QAM signaling. For 16 and 64-QAM constellation, the performance remains almost the same.

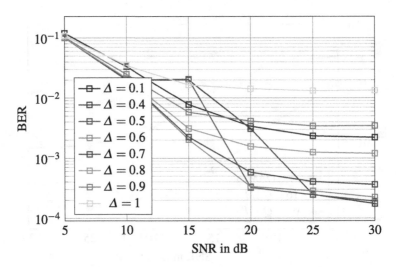

Fig. 9. Damping factor variations on BER performance of 4-tap, 4 – QAM OTFS system

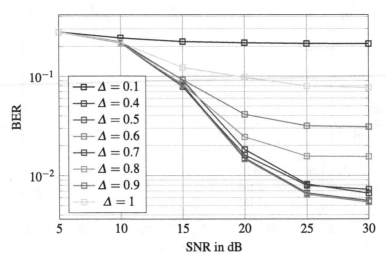

Fig. 10. Damping factor variations on BER performance of 4-tap, 16 – QAM OTFS system

The graph shows the effect of damping factor (Δ) on the performance of the MP algorithm. The simulation is carried out by generating a 4-tap delay-Doppler channel and the above-listed parameters. The graph demonstrates that the algorithm performs better when Δ is 0.6, 0.7 & 0.8 for 4-QAM OTFS signaling. So, an optimal value of 0.6 is chosen for 4-QAM OTFS simulations.

The graph shows the effect of damping factor (Δ) on the performance of the MP algorithm. The simulation is carried out by generating a 4-tap delay-

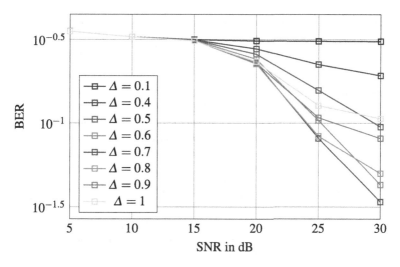

Fig. 11. Damping factor variations on BER performance of 4-tap, 64 – QAM OTFS system

Doppler channel and the above-listed parameters. The graph demonstrates that the algorithm performs better when Δ is 0.5, 0.6 & 0.7 for 16-QAM OTFS signaling. So, an optimal value of 0.6 is chosen for 16-QAM OTFS simulations.

The graph shows the effect of damping factor (Δ) on the performance of the MP algorithm. The simulation is carried out by generating a 4-tap delay-Doppler channel and the above-listed parameters. The graph demonstrates that the algorithm performs better when Δ is 0.7 at higher SNRs and $\Delta \in (0.5, 0.7]$ at lower SNRs for 64-QAM OTFS signaling. So, an optimal value of 0.7 is chosen for 64-QAM OTFS simulations.

6   Conclusion

In this letter, we described the relation between input and output of OTFS modulation/demodulation over time-frequency selective channels. We have studied and evaluated the low-complexity Message Passing algorithm for symbol detection over time-frequency selective channels in terms of BER performance. We then analyzed the effects of various parameters on the performance of the system. As future works, we will study applications of channel estimation techniques in OTFS.

References

1. Hadani, R., et al.: Orthogonal time frequency space modulation. In: IEEE Wireless Communications and Networking Conference (WCNC), pp. 1–6. San Francisco, CA (2017). https://doi.org/10.1109/WCNC.2017.7925924

2. Farhang, A., RezazadehReyhani, A., Doyle, L.E., Farhang-Boroujeny, B.: Low complexity modem structure for ofdm-based orthogonal time frequency space modulation. IEEE Wirel. Commun. Lett. **7**(3), 344–347 (2018). https://doi.org/10.1109/LWC.2017.2776942

3. An, C., Ryu, H.: Design and performance evaluation of spectral efficient orthogonal time frequency space system. In: IEEE 2nd 5G World Forum (5GWF), pp. 249–252. Dresden, Germany (2019). https://doi.org/10.1109/5GWF.2019.8911663

4. Raviteja, P., Phan, K.T., Hong, Y., Viterbo, E.: Interference cancellation and iterative detection for orthogonal time frequency space modulation. IEEE Trans. Wirel. Commun. **17**(10), 6501–6515 (2018). https://doi.org/10.1109/TWC.2018.2860011

5. Raviteja, P., Phan, K.T., Jin, Q., Hong, Y., Viterbo, E.: Low-complexity iterative detection for orthogonal time frequency space modulation. In: IEEE Wireless Communications and Networking Conference (WCNC), pp. 1–6. Barcelona (2018). https://doi.org/10.1109/WCNC.2018.8377159

6. Murali, K.R., Chockalingam, A.: On OTFS modulation for high-doppler fading channels. In: Information Theory and Applications Workshop (ITA), pp. 1–10. San Diego, CA (2018). https://doi.org/10.1109/ITA.2018.8503182

7. Li, L., Liang, Y., Fan, P., Guan, Y.: Low complexity detection algorithms for OTFS under rapidly time-varying channel. In: IEEE 89th Vehicular Technology Conference (VTC2019-Spring), pp.1–5. Kuala Lumpur, Malaysia (2019)

8. Yuan, W., Wei, Z., Yuan, J., Ng, D.W.K.: A simple variational bayes detector for orthogonal time frequency space (OTFS) modulation. In: IEEE Transactions on Vehicular Technology (2020). https://doi.org/10.1109/TVT.2020.2991443

9. Tharaj, T., Emanuele, V.: Low complexity iterative rake detector for orthogonal time frequency space modulation. IEEE Trans. Wirel. Commun. (2020). https://arxiv.org/abs/2001.10703

10. Raviteja, P., Phan, K.T., Hong, Y., Viterbo, E.: Embedded delay-doppler channel estimation for orthogonal time frequency space modulation. In: IEEE 88th Vehicular Technology Conference (VTC-Fall), pp. 1–5. Chicago, IL, USA (2018). https://doi.org/10.1109/VTCFall.2018.8690836

11. Surabhi, G.D., Chockalingam, A.: Low-complexity linear equalization for OTFS modulation. IEEE Commun. Lett. **24**(2), 330–334 (2020). https://doi.org/10.1109/LCOMM.2019.2956709

12. Li, L.A., et al.: A simple two-stage equalizer with simplified orthogonal time frequency space modulation over rapidly time-varying channels. arXiv preprint arXiv:1709.02505 (2017)

13. Surabhi, G.D., Augustine, R.M., Chockalingam, A.: On the diversity of uncoded otfs modulation in doubly-dispersive channels. IEEE Trans. Wirel. Commun. **18**(6), 3049–3063 (2019). https://doi.org/10.1109/TWC.2019.2909205

14. Raviteja, P., Hong, Y., Viterbo, E., Biglieri, E.: Effective diversity of OTFS modulation. IEEE Wirel. Commun. Lett. **9**(2), 249–253 (2020)

15. Surabhi, G.D., Augustine, R.M., Chockalingam, A.: Peak-to-average power ratio of OTFS modulation. IEEE Commun. Lett. **23**(6), 999–1002 (2019). https://doi.org/10.1109/LCOMM.2019.2914042

16. Surabhi, G.D., Ramachandran, M.K., Chockalingam, A.: OTFS modulation with phase noise in mmwave communications. In: IEEE 89th Vehicular Technology Conference (VTC2019-Spring), pp. 1–5. Kuala Lumpur, Malaysia (2019). https://doi.org/10.1109/VTCSpring.2019.8746382

17. Augustine, R.M., Surabhi, G.D., Chockalingam, A.: Multiple access in the delay-doppler domain using OTFS modulation (2019). https://arxiv.org/pdf/1902.03415

18. Kollengode Ramachandran, M., Chockalingam, A.: MIMO-OTFS in high-doppler fading channels: signal detection and channel estimation. In: IEEE Global Communications Conference (GLOBECOM), pp. 206–212. Abu Dhabi, United Arab Emirates (2018). https://doi.org/10.1109/GLOCOM.2018.8647394
19. Augustine, R.M., Chockalingam, A.: Interleaved time-frequency multiple access using OTFS modulation. In: IEEE 90th Vehicular Technology Conference (VTC2019-Fall), pp. 1–5. Honolulu, HI, USA (2019). https://doi.org/10.1109/VTCFall.2019.8891404
20. Ramanathan, R., Jayakumar, M.: A support vector regression approach to detection in large-MIMO systems. Telecommun. Syst. **64**, 709–717 (2017). https://doi.org/10.1007/s11235-016-0202-2
21. Sarayu, S., Radhakrishnan, J., Kirthiga, S.: Superimposed pilot based channel estimation for MIMO systems. In: Dash, S.S., Vijayakumar, K., Panigrahi, B.K., Das, S. (eds.) Artificial Intelligence and Evolutionary Computations in Engineering Systems. AISC, vol. 517, pp. 115–126. Springer, Singapore (2017). https://doi.org/10.1007/978-981-10-3174-8_11

Author Index

Printed in the United States
By Bookmasters